D0815141

A Threat from Within
A Century of Jewish Opposition to Zionism

Yakov M. Rabkin

Translation from French by Fred A. Reed with Yakov M. Rabkin.

*To Milton Viorst
with admiration.*

Montreal, April '08

Fernwood Publishing • Zed Books

reprinted October 2006

Editing: Brenda Conroy
Cover design: Charaf Elghernati
Printed and bound in Canada by Hignell Book Printing

Published in Canada by Fernwood Publishing
Site 2A, Box 5, 32 Oceanvista Lane
Black Point, Nova Scotia, B0J 1B0
and 324 Clare Avenue, Winnipeg, Manitoba, R3L 1S3
info@fernpub.ca • www.fernwoodpublishing.ca

Published in the rest of the world by Zed Books Ltd.
7 Cynthia Street, London NI 9JF, UK
and Room 400, 175 Fifth Avenue, New York, 10010, USA
Distributed in the USA exclusively by Palgrave Macmillan,
a division of St. Martins Press, LLC, 175 Fifth Ave., New York, 10010, USA.

Zed Books Pb: ISBN 13: 978-1-84277-699-5 ISBN 10: 1-84277-699-1
Hb: ISBN 13: 978-1-84277-698-8 ISBN 10: 1-84277-698-3

British CIP available from the British Library. American CIP has been applied for.

The translation of this book has benefited from a grant from Canada Council.

Fernwood Publishing Company Limited gratefully acknowledges the financial support
of the Government of Canada through the Book Publishing Industry Development
Program (BPDIP), the Canada Council for the Arts and the Nova Scotia
Department of Tourism and Culture for our publishing program.

Library and Archives Canada Cataloguing in Publication

Rabkin, Yakov M.
A threat from within: a century of Jewish opposition
to Zionism / Yakov M. Rabkin.

Includes index.
ISBN 10: 1-55266-171-7 ISBN 13: 978-1-55266-171-0

1. Zionism. 2. Ultra-Orthodox Jews--Israel.
3. Zionism and Judaism. I. Title.

DS149.R245 2005   320.54'095694   C2005-904238-9

Contents

About the Author

Yakov M Rabkin is Professor of History at the University of Montreal. After completing his university education, he studied Judaism with rabbis in Montreal, Paris and Jerusalem. Author of several books and hundreds of articles, he specializes in the history of science and contemporary Jewish history. His analyses of Jewish, Israeli and inter-faith issues have appeared in electronic and print media, including Jerusalem Post, Jewish Chronicle (London), La Presse (Montreal), Midstream (New York), El Milenio (Mexico City), Tikkun (Berkeley) and Süddeutsche Zeitung (Munich).

Foreword

Quite a few people in nineteenth-century Europe practiced both secularism and religion. Others practiced secularism in lieu of religion. This is how nationalism became a secular religion, turning the state into a monster that caused the worst catastrophes of the twentieth century.

This work is bound to stimulate debate on nationalism in my country, Israel. The author raises questions about the myth that Israel protects the Jews around the world and constitutes their natural homeland. This book rightly shows that this myth is anti-Jewish. Most Israelis mistake this myth for Zionism and argue that we can only reach independence once all the Diaspora Jews gather here. The Jews must therefore decide whether the interests of the State of Israel coincide or conflict with their own interests. However this question is taboo in the context of today's Zionist ideology. Moreover, this ideology deems anti-Semitism unavoidable and Israel the only place where a Jew can be safe. This view is essentially anti-democratic: it denies *a priori* any value of the emancipation of Jews in the modern world.

On the other hand, this myth gave birth to an ideology that expects the Jews to support Israel, often at the expense of the national interests of the countries in which they live. Most Diaspora leaders have nothing better to offer than the rotten motto, "My country, right or wrong." Israeli governments behave as if they were community leaders still within the ghetto walls. They disregard the interests of Israel's non-Jews, which contributes to the perpetual state of war, since a ghetto equipped with a strong army constitutes a grave danger.

This book shows why it is so important to get rid of this myth, which prevents many people, including many Israeli Jews, from acknowledging the authenticity of Judaic anti-Zionism, in particular, its loyalty to the Jewish tradition. Recognizing the legitimacy of religious anti-Zionism is crucial for an honest debate about Israel and Zionism — which remains stifled since the Zionists, both Jewish and Christian, deny all legitimacy to anti-Zionism.

It is all too evident that Torah-based opposition to Zionism needs to be well known; otherwise, the cult of the sacred cow of Zionism is reinforced. This cult includes the concept of the centrality of Israel in Jewish life and the right of the Israeli government to speak on behalf of world Jewry. This cult also makes illegitimate any criticism of Israel on the part of Diaspora Jews, whatever the Israeli policy may be. Currently, the Zionists declare that all opposition to Zionism is anti-Semitic, and this declaration has grievous consequences for Jews all over the world, including Jews of Israel. It is scandalous to deny legitimacy to criticism of official Israeli positions, and this book makes this point very clear.

It is intellectually important to think clearly, to distinguish between concepts. Its practical importance may be less evident. This is where this book becomes particularly useful. It mobilizes little known historical data in order to make distinctions between the following concepts: Zionism and Judaism; Israel as a state, as a country, as a territory and as the Holy Land; Jews (Israelis and others), Israelis (Jews and non-Jews), Zionists (Jews and Christians) and anti-Zionists (again Jews and Christians). For example, when one calls Israel "the Jewish state" this creates a real and dangerous confusion between faith and nationality.

One need not be religious in order to protest the exploitation by Israel of religious concepts. I am not religious and am not part of the current fad to find fault with Zionism and its history. But as an Israeli patriot and a philosopher, I find it imperative to make Judaic anti-Zionism a part of the badly needed debate about Israel's past, present and future.

Joseph Agassi,
Professor of Philosophy,
Tel Aviv University,
Fellow of the Royal Society of Canada

Prologue

> Do not utterly take the truth away from my mouth, for I have put my hope in Your rules. (Psalms 119:43)

Jewish schools in France and Belgium are torched, synagogues in Turkey and Tunisia are bombed. These are only among the most recent consequences of the festering, century-long Israeli-Palestinian conflict. But why have these attacks been aimed at targets in the Jewish Diaspora? How can the Hasidic children of Antwerp or Cagny be held responsible for the actions of Israeli soldiers in Jenin or Ramallah?

But what, on the other hand, could be more normal than to associate Jews with the State of Israel? Are not the Jews of the Diaspora often seen as aliens, outsiders or perhaps even Israeli citizens taking a long holiday far from "home"? Such insinuations have always been dear to anti-Semites, for whom a world Jewish conspiracy is an incontrovertible fact. But the linkage of Jews with the State of Israel is also a theme popular with the Zionists, who, ever since the creation of their political movement more than a century ago, have claimed to be the vanguard of the entire Jewish people. Some of them even assert that any threat to the survival of the State of Israel is a threat to the survival of Jews throughout the world. For them, Israel has become not only the guarantor but also the standard-bearer of Judaism.

Reality, in the event, is far more complex.

The scene is downtown Montreal; the occasion, a massive demonstration in commemoration of Israeli Independence Day. On one side of the square, a compact group of *Haredim*[1] in frock-coats and wide-brimmed black hats brandish placards that proclaim: "Stop Zionism's Bloody Adventure!" "The Zionist Dream has Become a Nightmare," "Zionism is the Opposite of Judaism." The leaflets they distribute read:

> Worse than the toll of suffering, exploitation, death, and desecration of the Torah, has been the inner rot that Zionism has injected into the Jewish soul. It has dug deep into the essence of being a Jew. It has offered a secular formulation of Jewish identity, as a replacement for the unanimous belief of our people in Torah from Heaven. It has caused Jews to view *golus* [exile] as a result of military weakness. Thus, it has destroyed the Torah view of exile as a punishment for sin. It has wreaked havoc among Jews both in Israel and America, by casting us in the role of Goliath-like oppressors. It has made cruelty and corruption the norm for its followers.
>
> Thus, this, the fifth day of the Jewish month of Iyar, is a day of extraordinary sadness for the Jewish people, and for all men. It will

be marked in many Orthodox circles with fasting and mourning and the donning of sackcloth, as a sign of mourning. May we all merit to see the peaceful dismantling of the state and the ushering in of peace, between Muslims and Jews around the world. (Neturei Karta 2001)

The pro-Israel demonstrators accuse them of treason, of not being "real Jews." Still others attempt to rip the signs from their hands. The riot squad is called in to separate the two Jewish contingents. Similar scenes take place simultaneously in New York, London and Jerusalem.

Such events may be local, but they throw light on a widely spread phenomenon: the rejection of Zionism in the name of the Torah, in the name of Jewish tradition. Such rejection is all the more significant in that it can in no way be described as anti-Semitic, recent attempts to conflate any expression of anti-Zionism with anti-Semitism notwithstanding.

At first glance this seems to be a paradox. After all, the public almost automatically associates Jews and Israel. The press continues to refer to "the Jewish State." Israeli politicians often speak "in the name of the Jewish people." Yet the Zionist movement and the creation of the State of Israel have caused one of the greatest schisms in Jewish history. An overwhelming majority of those who defend and interpret the traditions of Judaism have, from the beginning, opposed what was to become a vision for a new society, a new concept of being Jewish, a program of massive immigration to the Holy Land and the use of force to establish political hegemony there.

Curiously perhaps, both Zionist intellectuals and the Orthodox rabbis who often oppose them agree that Zionism represents a negation of Jewish tradition. Yosef Salmon, an Israeli authority on the history of Zionism, writes:

> It was the Zionist threat that offered the gravest danger, for it sought to rob the traditional community of its very birthright, both in the Diaspora and in Eretz Israel, the object of its messianic hopes. Zionism challenged all the aspects of traditional Judaism: in its proposal of a modern, national Jewish identity; in the subordination of traditional society to new life-styles; and in its attitude to the religious concepts of Diaspora and redemption. The Zionist threat reached every Jewish community. It was unrelenting and comprehensive, and therefore it met with uncompromising opposition. (Salmon 1998, 25)

This book presents readers with a history of the resistance to the "unrelenting and comprehensive" threat of Zionism, resistance whose conceptual bases, as we shall see, have changed little in the last 120 years. It throws light on a vigorous, persistent attitude, which the adherents of Zionism see, in turn, as a sacrilege. The detractors of Zionism whom we will meet in these pages are not all Jews in black frock coats. Their number includes all who base their opposition on arguments of a Judaic nature: *Hasidim* and *Mitnagdim*, Reform and Modern Orthodox Jews, Israelis and Diaspora Jews, even some National Religious Jews who have begun to question their own Zionist convictions. This work also explains how a commitment to the Torah forms the common denominator for religious opposition to Zionism. Most of the critics are rabbis who judge all aspects of Zionism according to Judaic criteria they consider eternal. What distinguishes those whose views are represented in this book from all other opponents of Zionism (Shatz) is the centrality of Torah commandments and values in their assessment of Zionism and Israel.

This book draws extensively on the rich tradition of rabbinical thought. In Jewish life, the title of rabbi need not be a position or an occupation but is a sign of Judaic scholarship. The wealth and variety of views and interpretations that have come to typify Judaism over the last two centuries, as well as its much older institutional decentralization, make it imperative to present this very diversity, even at the risk of an occasional repetition.

Jewish tradition holds that the only way to influence someone else's behavior is through love and respect. However, the rejection of Zionism is often interpreted as an act of treachery toward the Jewish people. The rabbis of the Liberal Jewish Synagogue (2001a), in London, clearly formulate the dilemma: "We seem to have to choose between loyalty to our people and loyalty to God. Did not the Prophets love their people? Yet they castigated its leadership. Did anybody ever love the Jewish people more passionately than Jeremiah? Yet he condemned their sins — and for that very reason — all the more passionately." Indeed, the detractors of Zionism are often passionate; some go as far as to diabolize both Zionism and the state that emerged from it.

The pious Jews who publicly criticize Zionism believe that they are obliged to do so for two imperious reasons spelled out in Jewish tradition. The first of these is to prevent desecration of the name of God. And since the State of Israel often claims to be acting on behalf of all the world's Jews, and even in the name of Judaism, these Jews feel they must explain to the public, and primarily to non-Jews, the falsehood of this pretension. The second commandment is to preserve human life. By exposing the Judaic rejection of Zionism, they hope to protect Jews from the outrage they believe the State of Israel has generated among the nations of the world. They work to prevent turning the world's Jews into hostages of Israeli policies and their consequences. They insist that the State of Israel be known as the "Zionist State" and not the "Jewish State."

This attempt to dissociate the destiny of the Jewish people from the fate of the State of Israel belongs to a much broader set of issues that extends well beyond the limits of Jewish history. Defining identity as distinct from state institutions is a constant concern of millions of human beings. The Jews have demonstrated that a people can preserve its identity over the course of more than two millennia without a state of its own and in conditions often threatening its very physical survival. Has the emergence of Zionism and the State of Israel so transformed the Jewish people as to bring its unique history to an end? Could it be that Israel, in the light of Jewish tradition, is not at all Jewish?

After sketching out a brief history of Zionism (Chapter 1) and the way in which it has transformed the Jewish identity (Chapter 2), we compare how Jewish tradition and Zionist ideology view messianism and the Land of Israel (Chapter 3). The Judaic legitimacy of the use of force is compared with the ideas and the reality of the Zionist enterprise in the Land of Israel for more than a century (Chapter 4). The political and economic hegemony established by the Zionists during the first half of the twentieth century and the proclamation of the State of Israel in 1948 created new challenges for practicing Jews. Is it licit for them to collaborate with Zionist organizations? Are they permitted to recognize the state and to contribute to maintaining the new political entity? Chapter 5 offers a broad overview and analysis of the different positions articulated around the question of collaboration.

The State of Israel was proclaimed in the long shadow of the Shoah,[2] which continues to be part of Israeli collective consciousness and political life. Chapter 6 compares the place of the Shoah in Zionist ideology with the lessons several eminent rabbis draw from the Shoah and its connections with Zionism. Chapter 7 presents several critical views of Israel's place in Jewish continuity, in the project of messianic redemption and in the emergence of a "new anti-Semitism."

The diversity of opinions and positions characteristic of Jewish life over the last two centuries — and which this book aspires to lay before readers — should help the reader distinguish between Judaism and Zionism, and thus undermine the myths and beliefs on which anti-Semitism continues to thrive.

Notes

1. For terms shown in italics (first usage), please consult the glossary.
2. A Hebrew term meaning "total annihilation," Shoah is more appropriate than the biblical term "holocaust," which has a positive connotation as a burnt offering to God.

Chapter 1

Orientations

I will set a king over me, as do all the nations about me. (Deuteronomy 17:14)

Zionism may be one of the last surviving collective movements that set out to transform society in the twentieth century. Zionists and their opponents agree that Zionism and the State of Israel constitute a revolution in Jewish history, a revolution that began with the emancipation and the secularization of the Jews of Europe in the nineteenth and twentieth centuries. Among the many tendencies within Zionism, the one that has triumphed set out to reach four principal objectives: 1) to transform the transnational Jewish identity centered on the Torah into a national identity, like ones then common in Europe; 2) to develop a new national vernacular based on biblical and rabbinical Hebrew; 3) to transfer the Jews from their countries of origin to Palestine; and 4) to establish political and economic control over the "new old land," if need be by force. While other nationalists needed only to wrest control of their countries from imperial powers to become "masters in their own houses," Zionists faced a far greater challenge in trying to achieve their first three objectives simultaneously.

Zionism was a bold attempt at forced modernization; its vision was to bring modernity to a country it considered backward and longing for redemption by European settlers. The State of Israel still stands as the challenge of Western modernization in a region that seems hostile to the idea. As we shall see, this hostility comes not only from Arabs, who see themselves as victims of this scheme, but also from Jews who reject the secular national identity that lies at the heart of the Zionist enterprise. Today, both groups are experiencing the most rapid demographic growth in the Holy Land.

A remark found in a popular history of the Jews provides a useful background for this book: "Judaism has always been greater than the sum of its adherents. Judaism created the Jews and not the other way around.... Judaism comes first. It is not a product but a programme and the Jews are the instruments of its fulfilment" (Johnson, 582).

In order to grasp the complexity pervading any discussion of the Jews during the nineteenth and twentieth centuries, it is necessary to understand secularization, that is, the full-scale liberation from the "yoke of the Torah and of its commandments" that continues to drive a wedge between "Jewishness" and "Judaism." To speak of the Jews before the nineteenth century is to refer to a normative concept: a Jew is someone whose behavior must by definition embody a certain number of principles of Judaism, the common denominator for all Jews. Such a Jew may transgress the Torah but does not reject its validity. "You shall be unto Me a kingdom of priests and a holy nation" (Exodus 19:6) remained a commandment, a vocation and an aspiration. A German-American rabbi has summed up the concrete effect of this approach to Jewish life:

> The Jewish people on every continent lived its own life, devoted to its Divine culture, set apart from the political history of the world around it, which had bestowed on it alternatively grudging love and boundless hatred.... There was within Judaism only one interpretation of Jewish purpose, history and future that was considered authentic. Loyalty to the Law of God was life's ultimate purpose for every individual. It was also basic for the ethnic existence, the national unity of Israel which survived the collapse of all Jewish political independence.... And then was the yearning for the Messiah of God who would rally a united mankind about the sanctuary of God, a fervent hope, an all consuming yearning for a still veiled future. (Schwab, 10–11)

Secularism revolutionized Jewish identity, turning a once normative concept, Jewishness, into a purely descriptive one. Traditional Jews can be distinguished by what they do or should do; the new Jews by what they are. This split of identity, which has continued for almost two centuries, obliges us today to use the adjective "Jewish" to denote a relationship to Jewry in general, and the adjective "Judaic" to denote phenomena or actions connected to Jewish tradition and thus endowed with a normative meaning. The established term "Jewish tradition" transcends the contemporary period and preserves the meaning of the word "Jew" as someone loyal to the Torah.

Zionism has changed Jewish life and shifted the meaning of the word "Israel." According to Rabbi Jacob Neusner, an American academic and one of the most prolific interpreters of Judaism:

> The word "Israel" today generally refers to the overseas political nation, the State of Israel. When people say, "I am going to Israel," they mean a trip to Tel Aviv or Jerusalem.... But the word "Israel" in Scripture and in the canonical writings of the religion, Judaism, speaks of the holy community that God has called forth through Abraham and Sarah, to which God has given the Torah ("teaching") at Mount Sinai.... The Psalmists and the Prophets, the sages of Judaism in all ages, the prayers that Judaism teaches, all use the word "Israel" to mean "the holy community." Among most Judaisms, to be "Israel" means to model life in the image, after

the likeness, of God, who is made manifest in the Torah. Today "Israel" in synagogue worship speaks of that holy community, but "Israel" in Jewish community affairs means "the State of Israel." (Neusner, 3–4)

When Neusner concludes that "the state has become more important than the Jews," he draws a clear line of distinction between Jews and Judaism and underscores the identity shift that the Jews have experienced over the last century, as they moved from being a *community of faith* toward forming a *community of fate*:

> If the Jews as a group grow few in numbers, the life of the religion, Judaism, may yet flourish among those that practice it. And if the Jews as a group grow numerous and influential, but do not practice the religion, Judaism (or any other religion), or practice a religion other than Judaism, then the religion, Judaism, will lose its voice, even while the Jews as a group flourish. The upshot is simple. A book (that is, a set of religious ideas, divorced from a social entity) is not Judaism, but the opinions on any given subject of every individual Jew also do not add up to Judaism. (Neusner, 3)

Secularization and Assimilation

Zionism arose in the last years of the nineteenth century among the assimilated Jews of Central Europe. After their formal emancipation, a small number of Jews aspiring to high society continued to feel excluded and rejected. They, and often their parents, no longer obeyed the commandments of the Torah and knew little or nothing of the normative aspects of Judaism. They had embarked, in fact, upon the same broad movement of secularization that was then sweeping Europe and felt frustrated at being unable to enjoy universal acceptance. It was a peculiar frustration, of a kind that a non-Jewish, secularized German or French citizen could never have experienced. It was primarily psychological, entailing few economic and even fewer physical consequences. According to Shlomo Avineri, author of a major intellectual history of Zionism, prominent political scientist and former director general of the Israeli foreign ministry, the nineteenth century laid before Jews prospects and possibilities theretofore unprecedented in the history of exile (Avineri 1981, 8). However, their attempts at assimilation had failed to produce the anticipated social and psychological benefits, and particularly to gain them the satisfaction of total acceptance, which, in any case, remains highly subjective if not outright illusory. In other words, "Zionism was an invention of intellectuals and assimilated Jews... who turned their back on the rabbis and aspired to modernity, seeking desperately for a remedy for their existential anxiety" (Barnavi, 218).

Zionism held out the hope of rejecting this flawed individual assimilation in favor of a broad collective assimilation, of the "normalization" of the Jewish people. Almost none of these assimilated Jews called into question the idea of assimilation itself, which for them remained an irrefutable sign of progress. For these Jews, many of whom belonged to the first generation to break away from loyalty to the Torah, the option of a return to traditional Judaism was no option at all. Some were to convert to Christianity either individually or collectively; none would advocate a return to the practice of their ancestral religion.

Even overt Nazi discrimination did not inspire a return to traditional practices. In 1934, Rabbi Simon Schwab (1908–1994), a leader of German Orthodoxy, called in vain for his fellow Jews to "come home to Judaism." The exclusion of the Jews from virtually all of German public and cultural life led to an upsurge of Jewish communal life, but it rarely took the form of a return to religion. "They have set up athletic associations and even an honest-to-goodness 'cultural league,' so that, God forbid, we should not 'get back into the ghetto again.'... True, we are depressed, but we are not contrite. We are downcast but not humbled, least of all in our relationship with God.... If this is so, is it still the people of God?" (Schwab, 15–16).

But individual frustrations alone, no matter how powerful, were not enough to give birth to a mass movement. Such a movement could only have gathered sufficient strength where social and political conditions were far less favorable to the Jews. The true cradle of practical Zionism was in Eastern Europe, particularly the Russian Empire. The spread of Zionist ideas mirrored a deep shift in the collective consciousness of the Jews. The Zionists had resorted to mass propaganda to bring it about. The Zionist idea, while simple and natural enough, appeared as something entirely new, a break with millennia of Jewish tradition — which explains the reticence of most Jews at the time to accept it. On the other hand, the *Haskalah* and secularization paved the way for the creation of the new Jewish consciousness. Zionism could only succeed by adding an ethnic component to the otherwise universal phenomenon of secularization.

The tsarist regime maintained most Jews in the Pale of Settlement, at a distance from the centers of Russian culture and their undeniable attraction. This is why secularization did not bring about widespread assimilation of Russia's Jews. While giving up their loyalty to the Torah, these secular[1] Jews developed a "proto-national character and a national outlook" (Leibowitz, 132). The Jews of Russia possessed at least two of the attributes of a "normal" nation: a common territory (the Pale of Settlement) and a common language (Yiddish). Several other national movements — e.g., Polish, Lithuanian and Finnish — came into being as the wave of secularization swept over the Jews of Russia at the end of the nineteenth century. Zionism, one of these movements of national rebirth, gained dominance only as a reaction to the murderous anti-Semitism that afflicted Europe during the first half of the twentieth century.

Even though only one percent of turn-of-the-century Russian Jewish emigrants were eventually to make their way to Palestine (the majority chose North America), Russian nationals formed the hard core of Zionist activism. David Ben-Gurion (1886–1973), the true founder of the State of Israel, was an admirer of Lenin and the Communist takeover in Russia, "the great revolution, the primordial upheaval that would uproot present-day reality, shaking this rotten, decadent society to its very depths" (Barnavi, 219).

Secular Jewish culture dominated the entire Zionist enterprise. Despite their determination to expunge the past, Zionist elites consciously replicated European cultural and political models in Palestine. This cultural domination would in turn provoke several sources of resistance, first from the pious Jews already residing in the Holy Land and later from Jewish immigrants from Muslim countries, who could not identify with the national structures the founders of Zionism had bequeathed to the new state.

Zionism in Russia drew its impetus from among the *Maskilim*, followers of the Haskalah, Jews educated in the *yeshivas* who had acquired some notions of European culture, usually without formal education. They adopted a new identity, that of the secular Jew (see Chapter 2 for a more detailed account). Some of the Maskilim mastered Hebrew and looked down upon the Yiddish, which was nonetheless the mother tongue of most of them. As distinct from Western Hebrew-speakers, they took up social issues, denounced economic injustice and bitterly criticized the Jewish communities of the day. The Russian Maskilim also stood apart from their Western counterparts in the weakness of their identification with their country of residence, as most of them were critical of the Russian Empire's political regime. Zionism, among other movements of social transformation, gave them a positive form of self-expression, a voice of radical idealism that would become the trademark of Zionism during its first decades (Reinharz; Avineri 1998). The pogroms of the late nineteenth century drove them further still into the embrace of secular nationalism.

Beyond the dilemma of the trade-off between utopian perfection and historical realization, Zionism also raised the issue of the legitimacy of secular nationalism and of all political and military activism. The pretension of Theodor Herzl (1860–1904), the founder of political Zionism who was born in the Austro-Hungarian Empire, to represent the entire Jewish people irritated both rabbinical authorities and community notables. But his ambitions were thoroughly in tune with the spirit of the times. The Bolsheviks, a tiny group of intellectuals, claimed to represent the entire "working class." Europe was replete with revolutionary vanguards that claimed to grasp the "laws of history" and thus to represent "the masses," who were often indifferent and even opposed to such activism on their behalf.

Several Israeli historians have decried the massive "Zionization" of the historical record produced in Israel. This reading of history emphasizes the persecutions and expulsions suffered by the Jews through the centuries. But, stripped bare of the Judaic interpretation of suffering, the new perception of Jewish history has created a sense of impasse, of despair that only a collective liberation could possibly mitigate. Zionist historiography postulates as inevitable the establishment of the State of Israel:

> With access to the hearts and minds of many, and with willingness to participate in the act of nation building, this group of historians seems to have played a critical role in shaping the consciousness of activists. Indeed, an examination of their writings immediately points to the origins of the equation Jew=Zionist.... "Jewish history itself," they asserted, "is the story of the Israeli nation, which has never expired, nor has its significance waned at any point in time." (Grodzinsky, 229)

This teleological version of history, by excluding any other option, has contributed to the education of patriotic, highly motivated soldiers. But now it is facing increasing challenges both inside and outside Israel:

> Rejecting the determinism of their elders, the new historians, specializing in Jewish history, carried out a double revision: the rehabilitation of the Diaspora on the one hand, and on the other, the re-evaluation — downward — of the nationalist trend in the evolution of Jewish history, which is now perceived as more polyphonic, more polycentric and above all, more open to surrounding society, be it Christian or Muslim. (Abitbol 1998, 20)

A few Israeli scholars, among them Aviezer Ravitzky and Menahem Friedman, have taken an interest in Judaic opposition to Zionism, which has turned out to be more tenacious than many had anticipated when the state was founded. The new historiographical climate, which has weakened the founding myths of Israel, touched off accusations of "self destruction and collective suicide" from nationalist circles. The romantic secular nationalism of the early decades of Zionism, which emphasized Jews' relation to the Land of Israel, has waned. But the National Religious movement, which selectively draws on Judaism for its legitimacy, has been expanding: it has successfully imposed its policy of settlement in the territories occupied since 1967 on the Israeli Jews, the majority of whom shared neither its political outlook nor its beliefs. As shown by the settlers' evacuation from Gaza in August 2005, its immediate ideological impact does not extend beyond those educated in National Religious schools. However, it does affect newly arrived immigrants, particularly those from the former USSR, who, as they struggle to integrate into Israeli society, find consolation in the image of the virile Zionist settler, the incarnation of the "muscular Jew" dreamt about by many a founding father of political Zionism.

History as Battlefield

The radical shift in Jewish life since the emancipation of the nineteenth and twentieth centuries stimulated an interest in history in the European sense of the term, particularly among Jews eager to move away from tradition. According to the Israeli historian Moshe Zimmermann:

> Man, both as an individual and as a member of a group, seeks to discover his place in society, not only the society in which he lives, but also in that society's temporal dimension. To achieve this goal, he turns to history, whether it presents itself as data or information, or as the work of those who write it. (Leibowitz, 47)

History is indeed present in Jewish tradition, but its presence is of a different kind, reflecting the commandment of the Torah: "Remember the days of old, consider the years of ages past" (Deuteronomy 32:7). In Jewish tradition, history provides a backdrop, a worldview, rather than a source of precise, operational information:

> Nor is the invocation of memory actuated by the normal and praiseworthy desire to preserve heroic national deeds from oblivion. Ironically, many of the biblical narratives seem almost calculated to deflate national pride. For the real danger is not so much that what happened in the past will be forgotten, as the more crucial aspect of *how* it happened. (Yerushalmi, 11)

Yosef Hayim Yerushalmi, a professor at Columbia University, affirms that the Torah presents an account of divine intervention in history, not historical deeds. Its objective is to prevent the people from succumbing to the temptation of replacing God and to attribute to itself the role of historical actor. Jewish tradition emphasizes not a historical process but moral conclusions:

> The comings and going of Roman procurators, the dynastic affairs of Roman emperors, the wars and conquests of Parthians and Sassanians, seemed to yield no new or useful insights beyond what was already known. Even the convolutions of the Hasmonean dynasty or the intrigues of Herodians — Jewish history after all — revealed nothing relevant and were largely ignored. (Yerushalmi, 24)

The oral Torah is laconic on the details of the military activities that accompanied the Roman siege of Jerusalem in the first century. But it clearly emphasizes the principal lesson: the Temple was destroyed because of the sins of the Jews and primarily because of gratuitous hatred among the Jews themselves (BT Yoma, 9b).[2] The Talmud recalls how a petty squabble over honor among prideful Jewish notables ended in this national, some say universal, tragedy (BT Gittin, 55b). The teaching drawn by Jewish tradition is clear: one must remain circumspect and prudent in one's actions, the long-term conclusions of which are impossible to foresee. More pertinent to the theme of this book, is the teaching that the Jews themselves bear final responsibility for the destruction of the Temple and their expulsion from the Land of Israel.

History in Jewish tradition must instruct. Its instructive function is laid down in the Torah, both written and oral: "Ironically, the very absence of historical writing among the rabbis may itself have been due in good measure to their total and unqualified absorption of the biblical interpretation of history…. No fundamentally new conception of history had to be forged in order to accommodate Rome, nor, for that matter, any of the other world empires that would arise subsequently" (Yerushalmi, 22).

In this interpretation, the fate of the Jews reflects the consequences of the Covenant between God and His people. The tragedies suffered by the Jews, including the exile from the promised land, can thus be seen as punishment meant to expiate their sins. To bring about relief the Jew must repent, rather than rely on military or political action, which would only defy divine providence. This interpretation recurs in Jewish historiography. Only with the advent of modernization did Jews come to examine their own history through other people's eyes, which in turn has discredited the traditional outlook in the eyes of a substantial number of Jews.

> The modern effort to reconstruct the Jewish past begins at a time that witnesses a sharp break in the continuity of Jewish living and hence also an ever-growing decay of Jewish group memory. In this sense, if for no other, history becomes what it had never been before — the faith of fallen Jews. For the first time history, not a sacred text, becomes the arbiter of Judaism. Virtually all nineteenth-century Jewish ideologies, from Reform to Zionism, would feel a need to appeal to history for validation. Predictably, "history" yielded the most varied conclusions to the appellants. (Yerushalmi, 86)

In an age when "history" had come to mean political history, i.e., the history of states, it was concluded that "Israel's history 'was brought to an end' with the collapse of the Jewish state" in the first century. In the view of British historian Lionel Kochan, Jewish intellectuals of the nineteenth century associated the Jews with other "non-historic nations," the Ukrainians, Romanians and Latvians, who, as distinct from "historic" nations like the Hungarians, Germans and Italians, did not possess a national state (Kochan, 3). Other historians drew lessons from Jewish history and, inspired by Marx, concluded that it was necessary not only to understand history, but also to change it: to create a state and "return to history." However, this opinion, categorically rejected by the rabbis at the beginning of the twentieth century, also failed to establish consensus among modernized Jewish intellectuals. Franz Rosenzweig (1886–1929) and Simon Dubnow (1860–1941), to name two, held nothing but contempt for Zionism and insisted that organic connections with exile constituted an essential precondition for the survival of the Jews through the centuries:

> Because Jewish history from the beginning moves from exile to exile, and because therefore the spirit of exile, the alienation from the land [*Erdfremdheit*], the struggle for the higher life against decline into the limitations of soil and time, is implanted in this history from its beginning. (Kochan, 105)

Religious Jews likewise reject the contention that the loss of the state has removed them from history. But while secular opponents have a place in the historiography of Zionism and of the State of Israel, religious opponents are, for all intents and purposes, missing from it. Historiography is quite deficient in this respect, but the deficiency is eloquent in and of itself. Even though Israelis are familiar with the Judaic opposition to Zionism, this opposition is rarely mentioned in histories of Zionism. Zionism is both a break in Jewish continuity and a break in the historiography of the Jews. Two popular histories of Zionism barely mention Judaic opposition to Zionism, briefly referring to Haredim in a rather sarcastic manner (Laqueur; Sachar). Aside from a handful of monographs and collections of essays devoted specifically to the history of relations between Zionism and Judaism (Almog; Ravitzky 1996; Luz 1988; Salmon 2002), the majority of national histories written in Israel and elsewhere ignore the rabbinical resistance. Even the New Historians, who have paid serious, even sympathetic attention to Arab opposition to the Zionist enterprise, tend to ignore the opposition of the Haredim, their political initiatives and the violence used against them by the Zionist establishment. Reform Jews who oppose Zionism are even less visible in the historiography of Zionism and of the State of Israel. In contrast, two histories of the Jews of Germany (Breuer; Lowenstein), as well as a history of Reform Jewish attitudes toward Zionism (Greenstein), contain a wealth of useful information on the opposition to Zionism. While there exists abundant polemical and overtly partisan literature that has spread Judaic anti-Zionist ideas (Rosenberg), it is still largely ignored in the historiography of Zionism or of Israel. This literature includes books, as well as chapters of larger works, both in Hebrew and in other languages, and constitutes, along with interviews with the leading figures of Judaic opposition to Zionism, the principal basis of this book.

While the Zionists maintain that, by and large, non-Jews have made the history of the Jews in the Diaspora, many critics of Zionism insist that, on the contrary, the Jews have always played an active role in their own history. This difference of opinion should not be surprising, for one of the objectives of Zionism is to "return the Jews to history" by making them, "for the first time in two thousand years," makers of their own fate. The Judaic critics, on the other hand, refuse to see Jews as passive, powerless victims. Instead, they locate a sense of responsibility in the relationship with God, whose attributes — justice, compassion and mercy — determine the fate of the Jews as individuals and as a group. The mechanisms of this relationship remain beyond human ken, and Jewish philosophy has provided richly varying interpretations of the effects of human behavior on the history of the Jews, and of the world. For the traditional Jewish worldview, at variance with the modern Jewish self-image, all that happens to the Jews is brought about by the actions of the Jews themselves.

In its attempt to "normalize the Jewish people," nationalism must challenge the historical continuity expressed in the dichotomy of reward and punishment, of exile and redemption. In order to combat the Jewish tradition that encourages introspection rather than outward activism, the Zionists have had no choice but to resort to history to attain their goals. In Israel, public school pupils, both secular and National Religious, are taught the founding myths of the new state; they read the biographies of the great Zionists, presented as intrepid makers of Jewish history. In the enthusiasm for reconciliation of the 1990s, young Israelis were also exposed to the founding myths of the Palestinian movement, which repudiate the exclusive Jewish claim to the Land of Israel. But above all, they are taught the values of valor, courage and heroism (Bettelheim; Peled) — those very qualities that are said to have vanished from Jewish life as a result of exile. Haredi schools, on the other hand, teach that these selfsame qualities, portrayed as pride and intransigence, are those that led to exile. The two viewpoints remain to this day deeply opposed and exert a direct influence on the lessons that each group draws from Jewish history.

The demystification of Zionist history that is underway on Israeli campuses has had echoes among those Jews who hesitate to accept Zionism. The conclusions of the New Historians and the observations of practicing anti-Zionist Jews often converge in deploring the pervasive militarism of the Zionist movement, the indifference if not the complicity of several Zionist leaders with regard to the Shoah and the "cultural genocide" inflicted upon immigrants to the State of Israel. In other words, "it is the totality of the components of the Israeli national consciousness, as 'invented' by a century of Zionism that is now called into question.... We are now indeed far removed from the day when the country spoke with a single voice" (Abitbol 1998, 21–22). In truth, the country never spoke with one voice, but dissident voices, especially those of the Judaic opponents of Zionism, were barely audible, since their language, traditional vocabulary and conceptual framework effectively excluded them from the debate.

Indeed, the Zionist experience raises serious questions for those Jews who practice Judaism and identify with Jewish tradition: How is one to interpret the return of the Jews to the Land of Israel before the coming of the Messiah? Has this return annulled the unique nature of Jewish history and its metaphysical dimension? Does political passivity constitute a pragmatic accommodation to exile or a religious principle developed by the founders of rabbinical Judaism? Finally, according to Ravitzky, those who do not accept Zionism must answer the question: what are the Zionists' real aims? Is their political rebellion directed only against Jewish political passivity, or do they intend to eradicate Judaism entirely, that is, to uproot the religious tradition that they accuse of having led to submission and political inaction?

Judaic criticism of Zionism reflects deep-seated theological convictions. Zionism strikes at the heart of messianic redemption. What is at stake is not simply the continued practice or rejection of Judaism, but the entire theological interpretation of Jewish history, in other words, what it means to be a Jew.

The historians of Judaism agree that fear of hastening final redemption is not an anti-Zionist invention (Ravitzky 1996, 18). It has not been devised to serve the cause but forms an integral part of Jewish continuity. It has deep roots in the classic Jewish literature. For generations, well before the rise of Zionism, the sages of Israel advised the Jewish people to accept the yoke of exile.

Broad as the scope of images of redemption may be, messianism lies at its vital core. This emphasis is not the particularity of any one school or intellectual trend, but reflects a constant in Jewish tradition. That it has been used for polemical purposes in the criticism of Zionism and the State of Israel takes nothing away from its central position. The rapid growth of Zionism in the nineteenth and twentieth centuries multiplied references to the characteristics of salvation. But warnings against messianic adventurism have been constant. Their intensity has grown as the feasibility of settlement in the Land of Israel increases and as messianic fervor grips the masses.

Anti-Zionists and Non-Zionists

The number of opponents to Zionism has remained relatively small, perhaps no more than a few hundred thousands (Ravitzky 1996, 60). But, argue Ravitzky and other Israeli experts, their influence has spread among the pious to an extent far exceeding their numbers. At the funeral services for Rabbi Yoel Teitelbaum (c. 1887–1979), the author of *Va-Yoel Moshe*, the fundamental text of Judaic anti-Zionism (Teitelbaum 1985), many leading rabbis, even those who opposed him during his lifetime, declared that the path of the departed was the only true one.

Anti-Zionists consider Zionist ideology and practices as contrary to the fundamentals of Judaism. Non-Zionists see Zionism as a concept foreign to Jewish tradition but tolerate it, viewing the State of Israel as they would any other temporal political structure. Both anti-Zionists and non-Zionists reject Jewish nationalism and, more strongly, any positive correlation between the rise of nationalism and divine redemption.

In today's Diaspora, Zionist organizations, far and away stronger than the handful of opposition groups, often exercise moral, economic and even physical pressure against their critics. Threats of reprisal are commonplace for those who refuse to display their solidarity with the State of Israel. Arguments that call into question either Zionism or the State of Israel touch off hostile reactions. The example of Hannah Arendt (1907–1995), a German Jewish intellectual and former Zionist activist, is instructive. No sooner had she begun to criticize the movement than she and her writings were placed off limits. Zionist detractors of Arendt's work never once debated her arguments but directed their anger against her character; they did not like "her tone": "What wounds me about your anti-Zionist statements, more than their content which we can always argue over, is the tone of the discussion" (Leibovici, 365–67), wrote Gershom Scholem (1887–1982), a German Jewish intellectual established in Jerusalem since 1924. Indeed, it appears impossible to set up a loyal opposition to Zionism: "You are either with us or against us."

Anti-Zionists are often seen as collaborators and are treated with deep contempt. They struggle to deflect accusations that their anti-Zionism "plunges a dagger into the back of the Jews." Moreover, many anti-Zionists, particularly those belonging to Hasidic circles, have difficulty in communicating the true content of their anti-Zionism to the public, which in turn finds it paradoxical that a group so desirous of maintaining its cultural independence is opposed to all forms of political independence (Rubin, 175–76).

In the wake of an anti-Zionist demonstration in Montreal, several of the city's Hasidic communities saw financial support for their schools and Talmudic study centers decline sharply. More than a few donors were offended by the public expression of anti-Zionist opinion. Financial pressure even forced one such center to close its doors. Because its director, a rabbi, had taken part in the demonstration, donors refused to finance his group. In this case, commitment to Zionism won out over the overriding value of Torah study in Jewish tradition. In another incident, a Hasidic Jew residing in a primarily Jewish town close to New York saw his request to photocopy several back issues of an anti-Zionist publication rejected. Anti-Zionists often feel they must conceal their possession of anti-Zionist literature.

Since the end of the nineteenth century, accusations have been made that Jewish media have come under Zionist control (Salmon 1998, 33). These accusations are not exaggerated. For several decades many rabbis have found it difficult if not impossible to oppose Zionism publicly for the simple reason that in the early days, the Jewish periodicals employed primarily Maskilim. A century later, when several Haredi periodicals exist, the Judaic critique of Zionism remains largely unknown, published mostly in Yiddish and Hebrew. At the same time, Zionist pressure groups such as Campus Watch, which target academics critical of Zionism and of Israel, have become much more active (McNeil).

For many religious Jews, the State of Israel has no connection with redemption. For them, the Land of Israel cannot be an absolute value independent of the Torah. From their point of view the settlement of Jews, whether in Israel or anywhere else, must be judged by the traditional criteria: does it bring the Jews closer to the Torah and its commandments or does it drive them away from Judaism?

Seen in this light, the opposition to secular settlement in Palestine was so principled that it preceded the first Zionist congress, held in Basel, Switzerland, in 1897. Three years previously, Rabbi Alexander Moshe Lapidos (1819–1906), a Russian rabbinical authority, gave voice to his displeasure at the pattern of early attempts by the Russian Zionist movement, Hovevei Tzion, to establish Jewish colonies in Palestine beginning in 1881:

> We thought that this sacred sapling would be a sapling true to the Lord and to His people, and that it would restore our souls.... But O weariness! While still in its infancy it sent forth weeds and its evil odor is wafted afar.... Indeed, it is useless to cry over spilt milk, and wherever there is profanation of the Lord, His Torah and the Holy Land, far be it for us to stand on our honor, but we say, "Indeed, we have committed a grievous error."... If they [the Zionists] repudiate this advice of ours, we withdraw our support and shall stand aside and oppose them to the best of our ability, for we muster our forces in the name of the Lord. (Salmon 1998, 25)

The establishment of the State of Israel created a new situation: opposition to Zionism as an ideology was easier to maintain than opposition to a state, which makes its presence felt in many spheres of daily life. As we shall see further on, collaboration with the state does not mean accepting it as either desirable or legitimate. Several Jewish groups, both inside and outside Israel, share this pragmatic approach. They come from varying geographical, ideological and cultural backgrounds. The most recent Haredi group to have taken shape is the *Shas* movement. Originating in the Arab countries, these Jews encountered stronger cultural pressure in Israel than did the European Ashkenazi Jews. The new *yishuv* (Zionist settlements) and the State of Israel were, as we have seen, an incarnation of European concepts derived from the realities faced by Jews in the Russian Empire. Most Jews who came to Israel from the lands of Islam found these concepts and realities alien to them. Their relations with their Muslim neighbors were more harmonious, more cordial; they spoke the local languages (Arabic,

Farsi, Pashto) with greater fluency; and their history was far less marked by violence and persecution than that of the Jews of Christian Europe. Shas is both a movement that seeks to promote Sephardic pride and a political party that boasts a network of educational institutions and social services (Shas website). The Jewish immigrants from the Arab countries "thought they would make their way into modernity through Zionism and the state-religious educational system, but it didn't work (Rotem). Shas is non-Zionist, but its leaders can occasionally be heard to utter sharp criticisms of Zionism, all the while continuing to sit in the Knesset (*Kol ha-neshama*). While the party draws its political support primarily from former citizens of Moroccan and other Arab countries, many of whom consider themselves Zionist, serve in the army and sing the national anthem, it is strongly influenced by the so-called "Lithuanian" outlook.

Lithuania, before World War II, was home to several illustrious Talmudic academies, which stood as bastions against the Haskalah and against secularization throughout Eastern Europe. After the Shoah, and in commemoration of the victims, the Lithuanian yeshivas and intellectual tradition flowered, both in Israel and in the Diaspora — including the United States, Canada, Mexico, South Africa, France, England, Switzerland, post-Soviet Russia and several other countries (Helmreich). Rabbis who survived the Shoah imbued their students with a strong commitment to Talmudic studies, which continues to be handed down from generation to generation. The movement has also attracted thousands of recruits among young people of African or Asian origin, as well as of German and Alsatian origin. The Lithuanian tradition, historically opposed to Zionism, has two centers: Bnei-Brak, a suburb of Tel Aviv, and Lakewood, New Jersey.

A third group consists of the various Hasidic movements that emerged from the rabbinical dynasties of what are today Ukraine, Poland, Hungary, Slovakia and Romania. Hasidism itself, an eighteenth-century Jewish mystical renewal movement, gave rise to a variety of trends structured around influential and often charismatic *rebbes* — heads of rabbinical dynasties. Though engaged primarily in the study of the Talmud, the Hasidim also devote particular attention to sources of Jewish mysticism, as well as sayings of earlier rebbes. The most significant Hasidic movements in terms of their critiques of Zionism at different periods of the twentieth century are those of Belz, Lubavitch, Munkacz, Satmar and Vizhnitz.

Outside of Russia, Zionism encountered the sharpest Orthodox resistance among the Hasidim of eastern Hungary and western Galicia. There, even marginal sympathy for Zionism was forbidden. The opposition included all Orthodox institutions, including the Beth Jacob girls' schools, established only a few years before World War I. The Hungarian Jews, particularly those from Satmar, achieved major stature among the bastions of anti-Zionism. The Satmar Hasidim who survived World War II settled in Williamsburg, in Brooklyn, where they founded the Yetev Lev D'Satmar

(Good Heart of Satmar) congregation in 1948, with a scant dozen members. Several years later, the congregation had grown to more than one thousand families (Rubin, 40). Satmar groups soon sprang into existence in Jerusalem and Bnei-Brak in Israel, in Antwerp, London and Montreal, as well as in several Latin American cities. Now global in scope, the group has established links with other organizations, including the *Neturei Karta*, which is made up principally of the descendents of the Jerusalemites of the nineteenth and the early twentieth centuries who looked to the Satmar Rebbe as one of their spiritual leaders.

Virulent opposition to Zionism and to the State of Israel is the hallmark of several Orthodox Jewish movements. They consider Zionism to be a heresy, a denial of fundamental messianic beliefs and a violation of the promise made to God not to acquire the Holy Land by human effort. The Satmar intensified their activism after the Shoah, which they interpreted as punishment for "the Zionist heresy" (Rubin, 95). The Satmar openly attack the Zionist claim to represent all Jews. It should come as no surprise that in North America, the Satmar, along with other anti-Zionist groups, while living in peace with their non-Jewish neighbors, suffer occasional hostility from Jews who sympathize to varying degrees with the State of Israel. Opposition to Zionism was also important among the disciples of Rabbi Samson Raphael Hirsch (1808–1888), leader of Orthodoxy in Germany, who articulated a vision of a religious Jew in modern society that remains important to a significant segment of world Jewry.

While united in their opposition to Zionism and the State of Israel, these groups differ in their approach to modernity, to history and to the interpretation of divine attributes. Some see the hand of God in the workings of history; others are much more cautious about attributing theological meaning to historical events. However, this diversified group constitutes a unified category — the Haredim — in the eyes of outside observers. Indeed, they share one fundamental characteristic, whether they reside in Jerusalem, New York, Bnei-Brak or Montreal: they continue to live in exile. Where anti-Zionist activists see the State of Israel as an obstacle to messianic redemption, non-Zionist Haredim simply attribute no metaphysical significance to either Zionism or to the state. All Haredim have remained faithful to the Jewish tradition that generally does not recognize the possibility of gradual evolution from exile to redemption. The two states of the world remain qualitatively distinct, and the passage from one to another can only be abrupt and discrete, a quantum leap of sorts. Exile is by no means a simple matter of a postal address or of political sovereignty; it is a theological and cultural concept that refers to the state of the world as a whole. Redemption signifies a radical change that brings harmony to all humanity and goes far beyond the strictly Jewish realm. For most observant Jews, including the Haredim, exile is a divine decree visited upon the Jews as punishment for their transgressions against the Torah. The Hasidim, more inclined to mysticism, see themselves as invested with the mission of gathering in sparks of the divine that are as dispersed throughout the world as are the Jews themselves.

The Haredim have not been alone. Reform Jews have also formulated Judaic critiques of Zionism, drawing on their own interpretation of the Torah. Like virtually all the currents of Judaism in the early twentieth century, the Reform movement was firmly opposed to Zionism. Reform Judaism sought to adapt Jewish rites and customs to the modern world. The reforms advocated by the new movement, which originated in northern Germany at the beginning of the nineteenth century, included a weakening of the ethnic dimension of Judaism, whose followers became "Germans of the Mosaic persuasion." Its adherents abandoned all reference to the return to Zion just before the Reform movement branched out to the United States in the mid-nineteenth century. Today, the majority of American Jews are members of Reform synagogues.

Prior to the rise of political Zionism in Europe, the program of Reform Judaism adopted in Pittsburgh, Pennsylvania, in 1885, rejected all forms of Jewish nationalism (Mezvinsky, 315). Reform Jews were thus prepared to refute Herzl's Zionist theory, which postulated the absolute existence of anti-Semitism that would justify a state for the Jews. They "detested both the premise and the conclusion of Zionism, i.e., that anti-Semitism was an absolute condition in all nation-states wherein Jews constituted a minority, and that a separate nation-state was a necessity" (Mezvinsky, 319). Mocking "Zionomania," they considered it every Jew's duty to join in against Zionism. "A sober student of Jewish history and a genuine lover of his co-religionists sees that the Zionist agitation contradicts everything that is typical of Jews and Judaism," noted, in 1899, a professor of Hebrew Union College, the Reform movement's rabbinical academy in Cincinnati, Ohio. The president of the College added in 1916: "Ignorance and irreligion are at the bottom of the whole movement of political Zionism" (Brownfeld 1997, 2).

In the 1930s, the Reform movement softened its opposition to the transformation of traditional Jewish identity into a national identity and went on to adopt an even more conciliatory approach after the Shoah and the Six Day War. Principled anti-Zionism in the ranks of Reform Judaism has survived mainly within the American Council for Judaism, but the synthesis of Reform Judaism and Zionism remains conceptually difficult. "Reform Judaism is spiritual, Zionism is political. The outlook of Reform Judaism is the world. The outlook of Zionism is a corner of western Asia," declared Rabbi David Philipson in 1942 (Brownfeld 1997, 9). Some even asserted that the Reform movement had rejected the philosophical basis of Reform Judaism by accepting Zionism. For Reform Judaism, Zionism is as much of a departure from tradition as it is for Orthodox Judaism. Even within the National Religious movement, whose *raison d'être* (as its name indicates) lies in its commitment to Zionism, there has been criticism of today's Zionism and the State of Israel (Burg). The specter of withdrawal from Gaza has sharpened divisions within the National Religious movement and has lead to widespread disillusionment with the state and, for some, with the ideology that underpins it.

Critics of Zionism face caustic and hostile reactions. Epithets such as "traitor," "anti-Semite" and "self-hating Jew" are routinely applied to those who question the legitimacy of Zionism and the Zionist character of the State of Israel. In a recent newspaper advertisement, the Bnei Brith Organization in the United States asserted that "anti-Zionism reveals its true colors as deeply-rooted anti-Semitism" (Cohen, R.). Rabbi Elmer Berger (1908–1996) of the American Council for Judaism observed that: "from the beginning, therefore, Zionism attempted to avoid debate of the *issues* by impugning *motives* of the anti-Zionists" (Berger 1957, 46). One can understand Zionist sensitivity, for to criticize Zionism raises questions of the highest humanitarian, political and religious magnitude. At the beginning of the twenty-first century, in spite of the military and political power of Israel, the Zionists have little patience with anyone who casts doubt upon the moral legitimacy of the State of Israel.

There is a broad spectrum of Judaic trends among those who, because of their religious convictions, reject Zionism. As a Reform rabbi once noted, these critics use Judaism to examine Zionism; they do not use Zionism to examine Judaism (Berger 1957, 32). Appreciation of this variety, without necessarily favoring one tendency over another, should help the reader understand the extent and the origins of the rejection of Zionism in the name of the Torah. Certainly, Zionism — and, moreover, the attraction of Zionism — has evolved over the last century. As the secular left has lost much of its pioneering spirit, National Religious Jews, for whom possession of the Land of Israel occupies the center of their worldview, have now joined forces with right-wing secular Israelis as the most devoted Zionists. The Judaic opposition to Zionism and to the State of Israel reflects this evolution, without altering the nature of its objectives.

Notes

1. The term "secular" does not entirely correspond to "hiloni," which has been used to designate those Jews who have completely abandoned the practice of Judaism. In the Israeli context, the term has acquired a more militant connotation, and now tends to mean "anti-Judaic," or occasionally, "anti-Semitic."

2. The term "gratuitous hatred" appears to be applied exclusively to the Jews. An Internet search for gratuitous hatred produced several hundred references, all to Judaic texts.

Chapter 2

A New Identity

I am, and there is none but me… (Isaiah 47:8)

Emerging from the world of European Jewry at the end of the nineteenth century, the Zionist movement appeared at first as a paradox, incongruous and yet threatening. For, while it claimed to be a force for modernization against the dead weight of tradition and history, it idealized the biblical past, manipulated the traditional symbols of religion and proposed to transmute into reality the millennia-long dreams of the Jews. But above all, Zionism put forward a new definition of what it means to be Jewish.

Israeli historian Yosef Salmon, in charting the variations of opposition to Zionism in the name of the Torah, delivers a concise assessment: "Put briefly, the general Haredi conception of Zionism was of a secularizing force in Jewish society, following in the footsteps of its predecessor, the Haskalah movement. Since its major programs were associated with the Holy Land — the object of traditional messianic hopes — it was infinitely more dangerous than any other secularizing force in Judaism and, accordingly, it had to be attacked" (Salmon 1998, 32).

From Messianism to Nationalism

Longing for the Messiah has been a constant in Jewish history. When from time to time this longing has been stirred awake, rabbinical authorities would attempt to moderate the flights of enthusiasm that, in their eyes, could rapidly turn to disenchantment and alienate Jews from Judaism. The story of Sabbatai Tzevi (1626–1676), the false messiah of Smyrna, who carried with him numerous Jewish communities in fervent anticipation of imminent deliverance before converting to Islam, is often cited by way of warning. The cautionary tale of Tzevi, and its sequels in Europe and elsewhere, traumatized the Jewish world and sharpened its sense of caution with regard to acting upon messianic aspirations of whatever shape or form.

Nevertheless, the emancipation of the Jews by Napoleon reawakened such aspirations. Entire communities, particularly those of the Low Countries and the Rhineland, welcomed the French army as the redeemer who would set them free and lead them to the promised land of liberty, equality and fraternity. Jews even composed messianic hymns in honor of their liberators. But, when Napoleon, campaigning in the Levant in 1799, called upon all the Jews to gather under his banner and to re-establish a Jewish state in Palestine, his invitation, though it was accompanied by a promise to reconstruct the Temple, generated a good deal less enthusiasm (Kobler, 55–57).

This transfer of the concept of redemption from the exclusive domain of God to that of worldly political action constituted a break with tradition that was to be echoed a century later in Zionist ideology. It had become clear that the messianic expectations of the Jews for a new and perfect world could never be realized in the prosaic context of the political and social shifts that, taken together, had brought about the emancipation: these expectations underlay the disenchantment felt by many Jews, including Herzl himself, in the aftermath of the Dreyfus Affair.

The emancipation of European Jewry, as a process, lasted from the end of the eighteenth to the early twentieth century, only to suffer tragic reversals before and during World War II. The emancipation offered the Jews equality before the law and removed political, social and professional restrictions that most of the Christian countries of Europe had for centuries applied to the Jews. Now emancipated, the Jews joined the modern world as full-fledged citizens. To anti-Semites, their doing so appeared, and continues to appear, subversive. The trial for espionage of Captain Alfred Dreyfus in France crystallized these fears. Dreyfus, a Jew of Alsatian ancestry (France had, a few years earlier, lost Alsace to Germany) was accused of spying for Germany in 1894. He was court-martialed, found guilty but pardoned by the president of the French Republic and finally rehabilitated in 1906.

In his intellectual history of Zionism, Avineri observes:

> Jews did not relate to the vision of the Return in a more active way than most Christians viewed the Second Coming. As a symbol of belief, integration, and group identity it was a powerful component of the value system; but as an activating element of historical praxis and changing reality through history, it was wholly quietistic. (Avineri 1981, 4)

Sincere secular commentator that he is, Avineri acknowledges that it would be, to use his own words, "banal, conformist and apologetic" to link Zionism to the Jewish tradition's "close ties with the Land of Israel." One must instead speak of a transformation of Jewish consciousness and surely not of the triumphal conclusion of centuries of yearning for the Holy Land. The transformation was to be all the more radical in that it took place at perhaps the most surprising of historical junctures. Avineri writes:

> From any conceivable point of view, the nineteenth century was the best century Jews had ever experienced, collectively and in-dividually, since the destruction of the Temple. With the French Revolution and emancipation, Jews were allowed for the first time into European society on an equal footing. For the first time Jews

enjoyed equality before the law; and schools, universities, and the professions were gradually open to them.... Until 1815 hardly any Jewish person had had a major impact on European politics or philosophy, finance or medicine, the arts or the law. A history of Europe at that time need not contain more than a passing reference to the existence of the Jews, individually or collectively. By 1914 the intervening hundred years of emancipation had shifted Jewish life from the periphery to the centre of European society. (Avineri 1981, 5–6)

The conservative forces in Europe saw the emancipation of the Jews as emblematic of the Napoleonic chaos they so deeply deplored. But they were not the only ones to deplore it. When Napoleon invaded Russia in 1812, the Lubavitch Rebbe called upon his Hasidim to resist the invader and to collaborate with the Russian army. His motivation derived neither from an upsurge of patriotism, nor a sudden outburst of gratitude for the benefits to be gained under the empire of Alexander I. The Rebbe had undoubtedly evaluated the impact of the emancipation on the Jews in Europe and found it wanting: derived from the Napoleonic "chaos," it had driven Jews away from the Torah and its commandments. Hence his unconditional support for the tsar's army, whose victory over Napoleon the Rebbe had already predicted, based on the complex permutations of several Biblical verses. So powerful was the wish to escape the emancipation among some Jewish circles that, in 1870, a Hungarian rabbi called for "the Jews to depart for Palestine, in order to reconstruct traditional civilization far from emancipatory Europe" (Kriegel, 164).

Similar reactions could also be found in Germany. With the hindsight of several decades, one commentator deplores that "the historic rubble of the crumbling ghetto walls was soil for the lethal seedlings of assimilation. This pestilence ravaged the flowering future of Israel, leaving only a wretched remnant. Shameful perfidy against God's Torah seemed to be the price for civic equality" (Schwab, 11).

We must therefore correct Avineri's observation that "from any conceivable point of view, the nineteenth century was the best that the Jews had ever experienced, individually and collectively, since the destruction of the Temple." Rather, this historical transformation was warmly greeted mainly by those who welcomed the emancipation and sought only to improve their social, economic and political status. But from the perspective of the Lubavitch Rebbe, as well as for a wide spectrum of European rabbis from different countries, the emancipation constituted above all else a grave threat to the Jews. The freedoms that Napoleon's armies carried with them were to bring about enduring transformation of European societies, but their impact on the Christian population was far less dramatic than it was upon the Jews. An emancipated Jew would have to change his language (from Yiddish to the local tongue), his dress, which would henceforth follow European fashion, even his trade. While not dismissing the emancipation as a whole, a substantial number of Judaic thinkers and rabbinical authorities worried about the breadth and the depth of the changes confronting European Jews in the nineteenth century. Zionism, the State of Israel and the ensuing turmoil in the Middle East stem directly from the transformation of Jewish identity touched off by the French Revolution (Hertzberg).

The emergence of ethnic nationalism in Europe at the end of the nineteenth century weakened political liberalism without seriously undermining its achievements for the Jews of Western Europe. Conversely, in twentieth century Central and Eastern Europe, where Zionism was to draw its principal strength, organic nationalism tended toward intolerance, exclusivity (of the "zero sum game" variety) and assertiveness. National revival required sacrifice, primarily from those who did not belong to the dominant nation, all of which seemed quite normal at the time (Sternhell, 11).

The internationalism of the Bolsheviks and the promise of a new world once again awakened the messianic expectations of the Jews, many of whom participated enthusiastically in the "building of socialism." But the longing for political redemption that inspired secularized Jews in the late nineteenth and early twentieth centuries could only increase the scepticism of the rabbinical authorities: some warned against the inevitable disenchantment that must follow political projects with messianic overtones. Zionism itself was one among many of the nationalist programs that were to inspire millions of people throughout Europe in the twentieth century.

A striking example of the way in which Jewish nationalism came to substitute for Judaism was the call issued by a young Jew to Vladimir Jabotinsky (1880–1940), a Russian author and Zionist leader: "Our life is dull and our hearts are empty, for there is no God in our midst; give us a God, sir, worthy of dedication and sacrifice, and you will see what we can do" (Schechtman, 411). The response came swiftly and took its inspiration from the mass movements that were then appearing in many European countries: *Betar*, a para-military youth organization that mobilized tens of thousands of young Jews. Even though it replaced Judaism, Betar was just as exclusive in its requirement of whole-hearted, unswerving devotion to the Zionist cause. Its members subscribed to a slogan borrowed from the Russian Jewish poet Haim Nahman Bialik (1873–1934): "There is only one sun in the heavens and one faith in the heart — and none other." To buttress the legitimacy of his approach, Jabotinsky recounted his conversations with Joseph Trumpeldor (1880–1920), a veteran of the Russian army who fought with the Jewish Legion at Gallipoli during World War I and in the Russian Revolution of 1917. Trumpeldor confided in him that the Jews must become a people of iron:

Iron, from which everything that the national machine requires should be made. Does it require a wheel? Here I am. A nail, a screw, a girder? Here I am. Police? Doctors? Actors? Water carriers? Here I am. I have no features, no feelings, no psychology, no name of my own. I am a servant of Zion, prepared for everything, bound to nothing, having one imperative: Build! (Schechtman, 410)

There is a utopian political flavor to this rhetoric: iron and steel were the Bolsheviks' and later the Fascists' metaphors of choice. Stalin (whose *nom de guerre* means "man of steel") used his private conversations with Lenin to legitimize his own policies of mass mobilization. The Soviet young pioneers were trained to serve the cause; their only response was *"vsegda gotov!"* (always ready!). Other mass movements in Europe, such as Romania's Iron Guard, adopted similar methods and rhetoric.

The language of redemption is omnipresent in most versions of Zionist ideology. Ben-Gurion's Laborites made a particularly coherent use of redemptive imagery, using the expression *geulat haaretz* (redemption of the land), to signify the purchase of Arab land by Jews. The Passover *Haggadah*, a seminal formative Judaic text about redemption, also became an instrument of secularization, undergoing major changes at the hands of Zionist educators. While references to God disappeared, the Haggadah read in certain leftist kibbutzim replaced God with Stalin, "who led us out of the house of slavery." This transubstantiation of the language of redemption, of religious values into secular concepts, infused the Zionist pioneers, who saw themselves as the vanguard of the Jewish people, fashioning history with their own hands. They used Judaic terms familiar to the Jewish masses of Eastern Europe to facilitate the propagation of their ideology, which, though radical, retained some traditional forms in order to appease widespread apprehension.

This instrumentalization of religion, writes Israeli historian and political scientist Zeev Sternhell, is not specific to Zionism, but can be found in many varieties of organic nationalism propagated in Europe from the mid-nineteenth century onward. While keeping intact the social function of religion in order to unify the people, Zionism eliminated its metaphysical content. In the same way religion became a vital element of many varieties of nationalism; for example, neither the Polish variant nor l'Action française (in spite of the atheism of some of its leaders) made any effort to disguise their Catholic traits. Sternhell defines this trend as "religion without God," religion that has preserved only its outward symbols (Sternhell, 56).

Berl Katznelson (1887–1944), the Russian-born leader of the Labor Zionist movement, applied this radical principle by simply rewriting the text of the *yizkor* ("He shall remember") commemorative prayer. The original prayer implores God to preserve the memory of the deceased without mentioning cause of death; the Zionist version calls upon the Jewish people to remember its heroes "who have given their lives for the dignity of Israel and the Land of Israel." As in other European nationalisms, the memory of fallen heroes became a weapon in the struggle for political independence, thus transferring to the political sphere a religious symbol borrowed from Judaism.

Most Zionists, irrespective of their practice of Judaism, used the Torah to justify Zionist claims to the Land of Israel. Another of Zionism's leading Russian-born theoreticians, Aaron David Gordon (1856–1922), explicitly denied the divine origin of the Torah while using it to justify the conquest of the Holy Land.

> "We in this country," said Gordon, "created the saying 'Man is made in the image of God,' and this statement has become part of the life of humanity. With this statement, a whole universe was created." From this he drew the following political conclusion: "With this, we gained our right to the land, a right that will never be abrogated as long as the Bible and all that follows from it is not abrogated." (Sternhell, 56)

An assertion of this kind, which postulates a Torah written by the Jews, is in the eyes of any practicing Jew, a heresy. Gordon's "tribal nationalism" stands at farthest remove from rabbinical thought, which strongly opposes any such notion. The same could be said of another of Gordon's ideas, that of "recycling" in a nationalist sense the blessing offered by Jews on certain holidays: "Blessed be Thee who chose us from among all nations." Where the blessing refers to having been chosen to accomplish the obligations imposed by the Torah, Gordon reinterprets it to mean that Jews have been "chosen" to acquire the Holy Land. In his view, the principal danger was European liberalism, which offered each Jew an individual choice and thus produced in the Diaspora a national life "that is not worth living." Devaluation of the absolute value of human life lay at the heart of several European radical nationalisms, including German National-Socialism.

It was easy for Gordon to influence Russian Jews in Palestine — the future Zionist elite — since most of them had little prior intellectual training, either in Talmudic studies or in European culture (Sternhell, 52). Gordon's thought took shape in the course of his career as an administrator of a landed estate in Russia and became an essential ingredient of the Zionist ideology that would eventually reshape a significant part of the Middle East — and the consciousness of an even greater segment of the Jewish people.

The Zionists' redefinition of the Jewish people, with pride of place to the national dimension of Jewish identity, provoked an outcry among rabbinical thinkers. For them, the concept of nation must be based on allegiance to the Torah rather than identification with an ethnic group or a given territory. Belonging to Judaism contains an objective dimension: those born of Jewish mothers remain Jews even though their loyalty to the Torah may leave much to be desired. But most rabbis, in Europe and elsewhere, concluded that in the Zionist version of Jewish identity "a total inversion of traditional values takes place: what until now was regarded as mere means to an end becomes the object, and that which was formerly the object becomes the means" (Zur, 111). Nonetheless, Zionist ideas continue to find adherents, most recently among the post-Soviet immigrants, who, while estranged from Judaism, belong to a "Jewish nationality" introduced under Stalin and still in use in Israel today.

The survival of the Jews through nearly two thousand years of exile is yet another of the questions that sets the Zionists apart from Jewish tradition. For the Zionists, the Jews had simply used religion as a means of realizing their "will to exist"; Judaism, in other words, was little more than an instrument of survival. Seen from this perspective, the Torah would have been granted in order to preserve the unity of the people. But, once they had returned to their land, the Jews would no longer have any need of its commandments, for a new national conscience shaped in the Land of Israel would be sufficient to maintain that unity (Salmon 1998, 30). Such explanations and particularly the expression "will to exist" are repugnant to the traditional Jewish sensibility. The idea itself gained popularity, of course, in those European nationalist movements that affirmed the will of peoples dispersed throughout the Russian and Austrian empires to survive and to establish a nation-state of their own.

We must bear in mind that Zionism takes as its example the organic nationalisms of Central and Eastern Europe, where nationalists were struggling to create a state, to set up legal and political structures for an already existing nation. Contacts with the exclusive aspects of German, Polish or Ukrainian nationalism were to exert a long-term influence on the Zionist movement and Israeli society. But few Zionists were aware of a countervailing reality, such as that of France, where, in a slow and deliberate process, the state made use of an existing legal and political framework to create a nation. They had never experienced the kind of tolerant nationalism that could allow for a clear distinction between nation, religion and society — the model that enables large Jewish communities to thrive in France, England and the United States today (and where a substantial number of rabbinical critics of Zionism can be found). In fact, once they discarded Judaism as the cultural foundation of the Jews, the Zionist movement and the State of Israel had no choice but to promote a national identity based on ethnicity and consolidated by the Arab threat. The survival of a "secular Jewish people" is therefore contingent on the perpetuation of the Zionist state.

The historians of Zionism emphasize that the founders of the movement were assimilated Jews. Avineri writes:

> They did not come from the traditional, religious background. They were all products of European education, imbued with the current

ideas of the European intelligentsia. Their plight was not economic, nor religious.... They were seeking self-determination, identity, liberation within the terms of the post-1789 European culture and their own newly awakened self-consciousness. (Avineri 1981, 13)

Zionism must be seen as a response, first and foremost, to the challenges of liberalism and nationalism, rather than as a reaction to ambient anti-Semitism. Again according to Avineri, Zionism could not have appeared before the French Revolution, no matter how dire the anti-Jewish persecutions of the preceding centuries. In this perspective, there can be little doubt that Zionism constitutes the most radical revolution in Jewish history (Avineri 1981, 13).

Opposition to this nationalist conceptualization of the Jew and of Jewish history was as intense as it was immediate. Even those rabbis who at first encouraged settlement in Palestine in the closing decades of the nineteenth century felt obliged to turn against the Zionists. What made the Jews unique, they declared, was neither the territory of Eretz Israel nor the Hebrew language, but the Torah and the practice of mitzvahs. The pious Jews of Palestine — the only kind before the Zionist settlement — enjoyed a certain degree of autonomy granted by the sultan. They had never contemplated national status, a concept as foreign to the Palestinian Jews as it was to the Ottoman authorities in Istanbul.

Judaic anti-Zionists abhor the nationalist conceptualization of the Jew peculiar to both Zionism and to the racial anti-Semitism from which the Jews suffered so much in the twentieth century. One of the most outspoken adversaries of Zionism is Rabbi Israel Domb. A Polish Jew who lost part of his family in the Shoah, he came to decry the Zionist enterprise when he migrated first to Israel and later to Britain. Like many others, he affirmed that the Jewish people constitutes neither a racial nor an ethnic entity. Their Covenant with God, contracted on Mount Sinai, makes them unique. It is this Covenant, and more specifically their fidelity to it, rather than their political or military prowess, that alone governs the destiny of the Jews.

Rabbis sensitive to the influence of European nationalism on Zionism have voiced sharp disapproval of its emphasis on the role of the "Volk" as the exclusive subject of Jewish history:

> There is no Jewish nation. The Jews form, it is true, a separate stock [*Stamm*], a special religious community. They should cultivate the ancient Hebrew language, study their rich literature, know their history, cherish their faith, and make the greatest sacrifices for it; they should hope and trust in the wisdom of divine providence, the promises of their prophets, and the development of humankind so that the sublime ideas and truths of Judaism may gain the day. But for the rest, they should amalgamate with the nations whose citizens

they are, fight in their battles, and promote their institutions for
the welfare of the whole. (Wistrich, 145)

In full awareness of Zionism's anti-Judaic content, the influential Viennese
rabbi and historian Moritz Güdemann (1835–1918) rejected, as early as the
first Zionist congress in 1897, any attempt to separate the Jewish nation
from its monotheistic faith (Wistrich, 151). In his view, the Torah must
be free of territorial, political or national considerations. Ever since the
Babylonian captivity, the Jews had, he believed, become a "community of
believers"; Jewish nationalism would, in spiritual terms, be a step backward
with regard to the sublime vision of the messianic realm that the Jews had
developed in the Diaspora. To return to a pagan concept that would confer
exclusivity upon Jewish nationality would be a self-destructive form of collective assimilation for the Jews. For him, the nationalist approach stood
as a contradiction *in adjecto*: one cannot be both Jewish and an atheist,
that is to say, Jew and non-Jew, at the same time. Rabbi Israel Meir Kagan
(1838–1933), best known for his book, *Hafetz Haim (He Who Desires Life)*,[1]
identified the same contradiction a few years later; it was to remain a vital
component of the Judaic critique of Zionism.

   We find the same categorical rejection from Rabbi Joseph Samuel Bloch
(1850–1923), a native of Galicia. During parliamentary debate in Vienna,
he compared the Zionist project with the false messiah Sabbatai Tzevi and
underscored the supranational character of Judaism. Citing a wide range
of sources, Bloch also explained to Herzl the Talmudic prohibition against
returning *en masse* to Palestine before the arrival of the Messiah. Later, in
the aftermath of the 1917 Balfour Declaration, Bloch warned the Zionists
that they were playing with fire, that they did not grasp the grave danger
for the future of the Jews posed by political Zionism and their concomitant
conversion to secularism. Shortly before his death, he encouraged the creation of a "Jewish anti-nationalist movement" to oppose the Zionist venture
(Wistrich, 150).

   The new Israeli identity, breaking sharply with Jewish tradition, sparked
a unanimous reaction among religious critics, who liked to quote two key
passages from Leviticus:

> So let not the land spew you out for defiling it, as it spewed out the
> nation that came before you. (Leviticus 18:28)

> You shall faithfully observe all My laws and all My regulations, lest
> the land to which I bring you to settle in spew you out. (Leviticus
> 20:22)

   Why two solemn warnings in the space of two chapters? According to *Or
ha-Haim*, a classical commentary written by the Moroccan Rabbi Haim Ben

Attar (1696–1743), the first is addressed to sinners, whom the land would spew forth. But the second warning is directed at those pious, practicing Jews, who would also be spewed out because they failed to protest against the sinners.

The responsibility of elders toward the rest of the people is a central theme in Jewish tradition, one that encourages religious Jews to oppose the transgressions committed against the Torah, Zionism being deemed a particularly grave one (Becher). The predictable result of this transgression would, they predicted, be the wholesale abandonment of Judaism. A recent survey showing that two-thirds of young Israelis would have preferred not to be Jews had they been born outside Israel seems to confirm the conclusion of anti-Zionist thinkers. In the same vein, anti-Zionists quote Leah Rabin (1928–2000), the widow of the Israeli Prime Minister assassinated by a National Religious Israeli in 1995, who would have preferred that her sons become Arabs rather than Orthodox Jews (Bell, 35). The critics of Zionism assert that the Israeli identity is nothing more than a means of divesting the young of their Jewish identity.

For Rabbi Shalom Dov Baer Schneerson (1860–1920), the fifth Lubavitch Rebbe, whose influence in Russia extended well beyond the Hasidic community, to seek freedom from the yoke of exile is as pernicious as to seek freedom from the yoke of the Torah. In order to escape their fate as Jews, the Zionists must abandon the Torah and the faith of Israel:

> In order to infuse our brethren with the idea of being a "nation" and an independent polity... the Zionists must give nationalism precedence over the Torah because it is known that those who cling to the Torah and the commandments are not likely to change and accept another identity, especially such as is implied in leaving exile by force and redeeming themselves by their own power.... Hence, in order to implement their idea, the Zionists must distort the essence [of Jewishness] in order to get [the Jews] to assume a different identity. (Ravitzky 1996, 16)

Moreover, Schneerson is unapologetic for the Jewish tradition of political accommodation (see Chapter 4), which he finds praiseworthy. For him, in addition to being a guarantee of survival, it constitutes an active commitment to the idea of divine redemption. Jehiel Jacob Weinberg (1884–1966), a rabbinical authority who bridged Lithuanian Judaism and German Orthodoxy, affirmed that "Jewish nationality is different from that of all nations in the sense that it is uniquely spiritual, and that its spirituality is nothing but the Torah.... In this respect, we are different from all other nations, and whoever does not recognize it, denies the fundamental principle of Judaism" (Shapiro, 98–99). Jews should thus be viewed as a unique people, which shuns political reality the better to flourish in the practice of Judaism, "in the four cubits of Jewish law, all that is left to God since the destruction of the Temple" (*BT* Berakhot 8a).

The Birth of the Secular Jew

Unlike the Reform movement in Central and Western Europe, which modified Judaism but did not abolish it, the Jewish radical movements of Eastern Europe sought to eliminate every notion of religious responsibility. By the latter decades of the nineteenth century, they had come to see themselves as the first generation to have cast off the yoke of the Torah, a conviction reflected in the Israeli national anthem, *Ha-tikva*: "Our hope is not in vain, two thousand years of longing, to be a free people on our land, the land of Zion and Jerusalem." The expression "to be a free people on our land" contains an element that never fails to elicit a fierce response from the rabbinical authorities, who take it to mean "free from the yoke of the Torah," not only "free from oppression." Even Hafetz Haim, a recognized authority in the laws of proper speech, attacks the concept in the most categorical terms:

> I fail to understand the expression "free Jews" used today. What does it mean? True, they may be free, but they are not Jews. The two contradict one another, for the Jew is not free, and he who is free is not a Jew.... They [the free Jews] are like the dead extremities of our nation, which cause the entire body to rot. Even though they call themselves Jews, they inveigh against the Torah, an opinion based on the false concept according to which one can be a Jew without the Torah and its commandments. But this opinion uproots the Torah in its entirety. (Wasserman 1986, 7)

The Jewish tradition traces the origins of the Jews to the shared experience of the epiphany of the exodus from Egypt and the giving of the Torah on Mount Sinai. As a group, the Jews are defined by their commitment to the Torah. Even though the Torah abounds in episodes of transgression and disregard for divine law by the children of Israel, the normative bond with the Torah remains the determining factor. It is precisely this bond, which obliges them to follow the commandments of the Torah, that makes Jews the "chosen people," a status that implies no intrinsic superiority.

In Western Europe, where Jews came to identify with the state following the emancipation, Jewish identity assumed a form close to that of the Christian identities recognized in those countries: it retained only its religious aspect, though often diluted in comparison with earlier centuries. Emancipation dissolved community structures and made available to Jews a national identity shared with their non-Jewish neighbors (e.g., French, German, Italian). At the same time, it introduced national differences within the Jewish people, and even within families. For example, a Jewish family that for centuries had lived along the Rhine suddenly found itself split between two, often conflicting, national identities — German and French. Still, the distinctive trait of the Jews remained their commitment to Judaism, though it now became private and therefore optional. In Western Europe, some Jews converted to other religions; others became atheists and no longer considered themselves Jewish. They assimilated, often leaving no trace of Jewishness after a few generations. In several European countries the term "Jew," with its often negative connotations, had practically vanished from polite speech before World War II. Jews became French Israelites, Germans of the Mosaic faith or Americans of the Hebrew persuasion.

Inspired by the new European reality, one of the leading theoreticians of Zionism, Ahad Ha-Am, pseudonym of Asher Hirsch Ginzberg (1856–1927), a Russian Jew from Odessa who made his livelihood as a tea merchant, insisted that Judaism was nothing more than an optional aspect of Jewish national identity. But when adapted to the situation of the Jews of the Russian Empire, where the emancipation had been slow in coming and where Jews lived in relatively compact communities, the idea of an "optional Jewish religion" produced an entirely different effect. The Haskalah undermined the practice of Judaism without diluting the Jews' sense of cultural belonging. Compared to Jews in France and Germany, the Jews of Russia had fewer opportunities to assimilate into the surrounding society, which remained largely unreceptive to them.

Thus crystallized the concept of the "secular Jew." The new concept, which quickly gained popularity in Eastern Europe, and particularly in the Russian Empire, eliminated the religious — and thus normative — dimension of the Jewish identity and retained only its biological and cultural dimensions. At the same time, most Jews were estranged from the Imperial State, particularly following the assassination of Alexander II in 1881. The impact of pogroms and socialist doctrine forced the secular Jews of Russia to define themselves in a radically different way, both in relation to Judaism and the Russian Empire, where Jews were officially one group among many *inovertsy* (those of different faith, heterodox) and thus conferred upon them, as Western Europe had done, religious minority status.

It was only under Stalin that the Jews ceased to be defined by Judaism and became a "Jewish nationality," marked in their identity cards, quite like the Armenians, the Uzbeks or the Russians. Within a few generations, this line entry, the notorious "fifth point" of the Soviet internal passport, had become the last factor that preserved the distinctive "national" identity of the Soviet Jews. This identity was largely devoid of any positive content and as such became both a burden and an obstacle to social and professional advancement. So it was that secular Jews in Russia acquired an objective identity free of normative content, that is to say, free of any connection to Judaism. Jewishness did not depend on what one did, but on what one was.

Certain rabbinical thinkers have asserted that racial anti-Semitism raised its head in Europe a few years after the emergence of a secular Jewish identity, thereby intimating a cause-and-effect relationship between the two. In fact, when the Zionists received the support of non-Jewish politicians, this support was often embarrassing. One of the first to express his enthusiasm for a Jewish State in Palestine, in a speech to the Hungarian parliament in 1878, was, in fact, an inveterate anti-Semite (Wistrich, 145). Herzl's contacts with the tsarist authorities and those cultivated by Vladimir Jabotinsky with the Polish anti-Semites underline the conceptual compatibility of Zionism and anti-Semitism. The anti-Semites wished to be rid of the Jews; the Zionists sought to gather the Jews in the Holy Land. A recent study of the history of Palestine under the British Mandate has pointed up the assistance provided to Zionism by the anti-Semites in the Colonial Office both in London and Jerusalem, and the efforts of the Zionist leadership to cultivate the myth of a world Jewish plot (Segev 2000). Several Judaic thinkers looked upon this coalition of interests with a heavy heart. (Chapter 6 elaborates on the connections they draw between Zionism and Jewish suffering in the twentieth century.)

The secular Jewish identity thus assumed a sociocultural coloration: it could be applied only to those who had consciously rejected Judaism while preserving linguistic (Yiddish and, later, Hebrew) and cultural traits. The identity that took shape was channelled into a diversity of political options, often inspired by socialism and nationalism. The concept of the secular Jew, the very antithesis of the traditional Jewish concept, became the cornerstone of Zionism.

The Judaic notions of "nation" and "people" have little in common with these concepts as they applied to the European societies of Christian origin in which the Jews lived. This fact enabled Orthodox Jewish leaders in Germany and other European countries to combine their traditional Jewish identity with unconditional allegiance to the modern state.

"National feelings result only from subjectivity, that is to say, of human desire," notes Yeshayahu Leibowitz (1903–1994), a Jewish thinker and professor at the Hebrew University of Jerusalem. As an Orthodox critic of Zionism and Israel, Leibowitz often found himself in a minority position. He can be compared to another dissident, Andrei Sakharov, who like Leibowitz was educated at home and had his first experience with public school only in adolescence. The two preserved their independence and intellectual honesty until the end of their lives. Leibowitz maintains that it is particularly difficult to define the Jewish people, for, since the nineteenth century, the majority had lost most of the common traits that had once made up its primary identity (Leibowitz, 26). He is referring, of course, to the practice of the Torah commandments, which, unlike faith, can be observed in the daily life of the pious Jew. For example, in order to respect the dietary code that is integral to Judaism), Jews must abstain from foods that are not kosher.

Each time they abstain, they make a gesture that all, themselves included, can easily recognize. The observable nature of the practice of a substantial number of commandments has a feedback effect on the Jew, thus reinforcing allegiance to the Torah. As the *Pirke Avot*, a collection of Jewish maxims drawn from the oral tradition, puts it: "One good deed leads to another" (*Pirke Avot* 4:2).

Taken together, the commandments constitute the traditional framework of Jewish identity. But the assimilation of many Jews has come to mean that these very commandments now have a divisive effect and constitute barriers between Jews. The question thus arises: do they belong to the same people? For an answer, let us turn once more to Leibowitz:

> The historical Jewish people was defined neither as a race, nor as a people of this country or that, or of this political system or that, nor as a people that speaks the same language, but as the people of Torah Judaism and of its commandments, as the people of a specific way of life, both on the spiritual and the practical plane, a way of life that expresses the acceptance of the yoke of the Kingdom of Heaven, the yoke of the Torah and of its commandments. This consciousness exercised its effect from within the people. It formed its national essence; it maintained itself down through the generations and was able to preserve its identity irrespective of times or circumstances. The words spoken by Saadia Gaon more than one thousand years ago, "Our nation exists only in the Torah" had not only a normative, but also an empirical meaning. They testified to a historical fact whose power could be felt up until the nineteenth century. It was then that the fracture, which has not ceased to widen with time, first occurred: the break between Jewishness and Judaism. The human group recognized today as the Jewish people is no longer defined, from the factual viewpoint, as the people of historical Judaism, whether in the consciousness of the majority of its members, or in that of the non-Jews. There indeed exist within this people a substantial number of persons who strive, individually or collectively, to live the Judaic way of life. But the majority of Jews — while sincerely conscious of their Jewishness — not only does not accept Judaism, but abhors it. (Leibowitz, 44)

An Incomplete Transformation

Imposing a modern national configuration on Jewish identity has not been an easy task. For those Jews who felt, or who wished to feel, integrated into the nations of the West, the new Zionist identity was as threatening as it was unacceptable. Even in the Russian Empire, many Jews who suffered from systematic discrimination at the hands of the state were not at all interested in embracing Zionism and even less prepared to emigrate to Palestine.

Among the millions of Jews who did emigrate from Russia in the early years of the twentieth century, only a handful were to travel to and settle in the Holy Land, and fewer still were to remain.

Avineri emphasizes that the Jews who left for America or Australia were faithful to the traditional Jewish response to the adversities of life: they relocated from one place of exile to another. To a surprising extent, this faithfulness to the tradition of exile survived even the abandonment of all Judaic practices. Thus, when the doors of the Soviet Union opened, the great majority of migrating Jews preferred to establish themselves anywhere else than in Israel, which, unlike Ottoman Palestine, which had proved so unattractive to their grandparents, could offer all the services of a modern state in order to attract and to accommodate immigrants. The State of Israel felt obliged to launch a diplomatic offensive against its staunchest allies — the United States and Germany — in an attempt to convince them to forbid or at least restrict access to Soviet Jews. When the number of ex-Soviet Jews settling in Germany exceeded the number of immigrants to Israel, the German government succumbed to Israeli pressure (*Deutsche Welle*).

The same behavior was observed in North Africa. A majority of those Jews who were able to settle in France, Canada or the United States did so, turning their back on the absorption mechanisms designed by the State of Israel. In fact, although the country has filled up, ideologically motivated immigration to Israel was never significant. The acceptance of a new national identity by the Jews required a radical change in their worldview.

Distinct from the Russian Zionists, most of whom were driven by rejection of Jewish tradition, Herzl's attitude was more pragmatic. While personally estranged from, and ignorant of, Judaism, he recognized its utility as bait, particularly with respect to those Jews "still sunk in the old ways," precisely those who have, indeed, turned out to be susceptible to Zionist overtures. On the political level, Herzl conceived Judaism as a useful tool for state building, very much along the lines of clericalism in Christian lands (Reinharz, 125). The rites of the Hasidic courts fascinated him, and, with a degree of cynicism, he hoped one day to be able to make use of them. If Herzl was aware of the opposition his approach had provoked among western rabbis (*Protestrabbiner*) concerned with preserving the social and political achievements of the Jews in the wider societies that surrounded them, he underestimated the intensity of the hatred and indignation Zionism called forth among the Orthodox rabbis to the East. Though Zionism found its most fervent devotees in Russia, its fiercest, most stubborn opposition likewise came from Russia, and from the Jewish communities on its borders.

The Lubavitch movement, culturally the most Russian of the Hasidic groups, took intransigent positions, particularly since Zionist ideas affected first and foremost the Russian Jews. At the beginning of the twentieth century, Rabbi Shalom Dov Baer Schneerson accused Zionist publications of promoting a Jewish identity completely devoid of all allegiance to the Torah

(Schneerson, 19–24). His attack was directed primarily at the nationalist interpretation of the Torah as propagated by the Zionists.

The secularization of the Jews entailed a much more radical transformation than that experienced by other national groups, whose characteristics remained intact irrespective of religious observance. Despite the violent secularization carried out in the name of Communist ideology, a Russian remained a Russian. Little changed in relations with other peoples or national groups, even though the disintegration of the Soviet Union was to present Russians with far greater challenges than it would the other peoples of the now-defunct empire. Paradoxically, the vital role of Russian language and culture in the construction of the new Soviet identity had diluted the properly Russian identity by integrating into it a wide diversity of peoples, including most Soviet Jews. Even after the collapse of the USSR, Russian national identity remained more inclusive than the identities of the other nations of the former Soviet Union.

The French-Canadian identity in Quebec may well be another example of the thoroughgoing transformation brought on by a change in terminology: Quebecois identity. The province, long dominated by the Catholic Church, underwent rapid secularization in the 1960s. The power of the Church collapsed, but identity survived due to a nationalist movement that carried out a fundamental change: where before, "language was the guardian of faith," an inversion took place, and language, and to a lesser extent, territory, became the alpha and omega of a new identity that gradually opened itself to other ethnic groups. The term "Canadian," which had previously meant "French Canadian," in current Quebec usage, has usually come to mean "English Canadian."

The Quebec and Russian examples illustrate the extent of change that national identities may undergo. But neither required a transformation as radical as the secularization of the Jews. Jewish identity, for many Jews, has today become secular, but this separate secular identity does not easily mesh with another nationality. Hence the maintenance, even though tenuous, of the Judaic component in most countries. Only Israel gives Jews the ultimate liberty to reject completely their spiritual heritage and to become a "normal people." The new Israeli identity would appear to facilitate collective assimilation without feeding the sense of personal betrayal connected to individual assimilation, and most of all, to conversion to Christianity. Language and territory are the fundamental signposts of the new identity, while the traditional Jewish identity is rooted in a religious consciousness without a common language or territory.

The transformation of identity was all the more difficult to bring about in that it entailed adapting Judaism to western conceptual frameworks. The fundamental distinction between the religious and the secular had only arisen, as far as the Jews are concerned, since the nineteenth century, and then only in Europe. Muslim societies were to experience modernization of Muslim and Jewish identities almost a century later.

It is hardly surprising that the anti-Zionist argument often resembles that of the Israeli supporters of a more "oriental" society, one more culturally anchored in the Middle East. In fact, the anti-Zionist discourse could easily be confused with that which brands Israel's Ashkenazi elites as the common foe of both Jews from Muslim lands and Arabs. "The authentic Jew and the Arab have much in common. This is why they can understand each other. Both are Orientals, and both are sensitive to spirituality. As for the Zionists, they have lost their Jewish authenticity, and become Westerners, materialists. This is why they cannot understand the Arabs" (Blau, R., 276–77). In such a context, it is easier to see how Rabbi Amram Blau (1894–1974), a renowned anti-Zionist of Ashkenazi ancestry, would overcome apparent cultural differences and establish close relations with the Black Panthers, a protest movement that arose among Jews of North African origin. Such social links are rare, but as we shall see throughout this book, affinities between the anti-Zionist Haredim and the radical left are often substantial.

Ruth Blau (1920–2000), the widow of Rabbi Blau and an anti-Zionist activist in her own right, analyzed the situation of the North African Jews in Israel in the early 1970s. Her evaluation was similar to that of mainstream sociologists, differing substantively only in its conclusions:

> They grow up resembling Palestinian children, nourished on the bitterness of their parents. Without the Torah, which was the source of their grandparents' dignity, they became revolutionaries. Their parents fell silent in resignation. They understood that they had been brought there to serve as unpaid soldiers. To risk their lives. To defend a state governed by Ashkenazim for Ashkenazim. From the Zionists they learned revolt. Taught to hate, they came to loathe their Ashkenazi masters. (Blau, R., 275)

In Rabbi Blau's eyes, Zionism had inflicted worse harm upon the Jews than upon the Arabs. The Arabs may have lost their land and their homes, but the Jews, by accepting Zionism, had lost their historical identity (Blau, A., 2–3). His wife, who had visited the Jews of Morocco before their exodus to Israel, continued to ask the same question decades later:

> All their faces shone with goodness, simplicity and great purity. These Jews, whose relations with their Arab neighbors were excellent, lived a modest, happy life centered on their rabbi.... Ever since, I have often thought of the Jews of that lost village in the Atlas [Mountains]. Where are they now? Were the Israeli agents successful in uprooting them? Are they in the Land of Israel? Do they still look, simply, like Jews. (Blau, R., 187–88)

The pain one reads between these lines suggests that the struggle of the rabbinical critics is not the same as that of the Black Panthers in Israel. For the anti-Zionist Haredim, the state itself is an abomination, while the protestors sought only to improve their lives in Israel. The rise of the oriental religious movement Shas, under the leadership of Rabbis Eliezer Menahem Schach (1898?–2001), one of the heads of Lithuanian Judaism, and Ovadia Yosef, former Sephardic Chief Rabbi of Israel and a leading authority on Jewish law, was to build a bridge between the two: the movement's ideologists — at the same time penitents and revolutionaries — sharply criticize Zionism and the state. But in contrast to the anti-Zionists who did not even recognize the state, Shas today criticizes Zionism from within the Knesset, where it fielded a stronger parliamentary representation than any other religious party at the beginning of the twenty-first century.

The majority of Russian rabbis, closer to the reality that had fuelled Zionism's popularity, relegated the Zionist movement to the same category as earlier efforts to eradicate the Torah. Rabbi Elhanan Wasserman (1875–1941), a disciple of Hafetz Haim and a pillar of Lithuanian Judaism, compared Zionists to the members of the *Yevsektzia*, the Jewish section of the Soviet Communist Party (Wasserman 1986, 3). Wielding their own version of secularized messianism, the Jewish Communists attacked traditional Jewish life with extraordinary vehemence. Wasserman states that the situation of Jews in the Soviet Union was far worse than under the tsars, which points to a traditional scale of values: the abolition of the Pale of Settlement and the opening up of new professions to Soviet Jews could not compensate for their transformation into mere bearers of a Jewish nationality. How, asks Wasserman, can a state that styles itself Jewish accommodate Jews better than a non-Jewish regime? This approach raises a series of questions touching on cooperation with the secular, which Chapter 5 explores in greater detail.

Wasserman remains tolerant of people that had strayed because of the incitements of their leaders, who bear the brunt of his sharpest, most unrelenting condemnation. For Wasserman, the Zionists have placed iron bars between the people and its God and made it impossible to bring the masses back to the Torah:

> Through their medium of a new Torah and new precepts they cause darkness in the mind and in the heart. It is also noteworthy that when a real opportunity is given the masses to hear the words of the true Torah they drink in its words eagerly. But the leaders bring the people stones instead of pearls. In place of Torah ideals they give their readers and hearers ideas of atheism. Levity, scorn, and a more than liberal portion of obscenity form the material of their chief writings and speeches. (Wasserman 1976, 17–18)

The principal quality that he attributes to the new Jewish leaders is their arrogance: "one needs only *chutzpah* (insolence) to be considered as a leader." Such leaders, he contends, seduce the masses with tender illusions that nationalism will bring redemption. It follows that the product of these efforts will be the antithesis of all that the Torah seeks to inculcate in the people of Israel. "All that is required of the Jew is national feeling. He who pays the Shekel [symbolic contribution to the Zionist movement] and sings the *Ha-tikva* is thereby exempted from all the precepts of the Torah" (Wasserman 1976, 23).

Tradition holds that the Jew has been granted a strong, even aggressive nature ("*oz*" in Hebrew); the Torah is meant to control that nature, for it requires the Jew to be bashful, merciful and charitable. Other laudable qualities include humility, introspection and the capacity for self-doubt and for self-correction. The daily prayer book clearly identifies what hinders communication with God and impedes one from being a good Jew:

> May our prayer come before You, and do not ignore our supplication for we are not so brazen and obstinate as to say before You... that we are righteous and have not sinned — rather, we and our forefathers have sinned. (*Complete ArtScroll Siddur*, 119b)

Tradition likewise instructs Jews to be mindful of the impression they create upon others, even upon those who have persecuted Jews in the past. Moses, for example, is concerned with how the Jews would be perceived by the Egyptians (Exodus 32:12), even through the Egyptians exploited his people during more than two centuries of slavery. In a deliberate break with Jewish tradition, the Zionist educational system has, from its inception, promoted the qualities of strength, self-affirmation and combativeness. It teaches young people to disregard the impression that they, and the state that they defend, create on the rest of the world. Ben-Gurion reportedly used to say: "What matters is what the Jews do, not what the *goyim* think."

Though they often express themselves in different ways, Zionism's foes tend to agree on the nature of the dangers it represents. First among them is, not unexpectedly, the internal dimension: the conversion of the Jews into members of a secular nation. Identification with the State of Israel has, they argue, substituted for the value system specific to Judaism — compassion and humility — the kind of ideals common to most nationalisms — egotism and national pride. For the Zionists of the Diaspora, this danger extends to the reduction of Jewish identity to that of a vicarious "Israeli" one, a fragile identity that could not survive the demise of the State of Israel. For these critics, to mortgage the future of Judaism to the fate of a fragile state is rather short-sighted.

In the Diaspora, the pride in Israel's military victories felt by many Jews accounts for the massive support for Zionism in the last decades of the twentieth century. Both critics and supporters of Zionism agree that this moral shift, resulting from the mutation of the humble Jew into the proud Zionist, has been the main impact of the State of Israel upon the Jews.

Jew, Hebrew, Israeli

The Zionists were not the first Jews to settle in Palestine. The Jewish presence in the Land of Israel has been uninterrupted since the destruction of the Temple. The Old Yishuv, as the settlements of pious Jews are usually known by history, existed in Jerusalem and in several other Palestinian towns when the first Zionist settlers arrived. The Old Yishuv had been able to survive primarily due to charitable contributions from the Diaspora. Certain philanthropists in mid-nineteenth century made it possible for its inhabitants to leave their old quarters and to take up residence in more modern, healthier districts, one of which was known as Meah Shearim ("hundredfold," often erroneously translated as "one hundred doors"), which harks back to the harvest of Isaac, who "sowed in that land and reaped a hundredfold the same year and the Lord blessed him" (Genesis 26:12).

Though the Arabs remained receptive to the economic overtures of the Zionists for some time, Palestinian Jews reacted with fear and even horror at the arrival of secular Jews from Russia. The legendary "Jewish solidarity" reviled by so many anti-Semites was nowhere to be seen. These Palestinian Jews would certainly not have responded in the same way to an invasion of Palestine by a foreign power, which, from a theological point of view, would have changed little for them. True to the particular responsibilities Jewish tradition imposes upon the Jewish inhabitants of the Land of Israel (see Chapter 3 for more details), they lashed out at the new settlers in dramatic terms: "They do not walk in the paths of the Torah and the fear of God... and their purpose is not to bring the redemption close but to delay it, God forbid" (Salmon 1998, 28). But the new settlers gave no indication of repenting, and worse yet, began to attract the youth of the Old Yishuv to Zionism. Thus began the conflict between Judaism and Zionism in the Holy Land, a conflict that, more than a century later, has not yet played itself out.

When the first "proto-Zionist" settlements of Hovevei Tzion were established in Palestine in the early 1880s, largely in reaction to the pogroms that had swept Russia, several rabbis gave public support to the newcomers. However, their enthusiasm quickly turned to dismay when they realized that many of the settlers were not practicing Jews. Rabbi Lapidos (quoted in Chapter 1) is only one of many Judaic authorities who protested the new trend and issued a warning against its dangers.

The creation of Rishon LeTzion, a settlement on the coastal plain, in 1882, marked a break with what had up until then been traditional Jewish communities. The new settlement was headed by Maskilim and was linked to the secular settler center of Jaffa, rather than to Jerusalem and Safed, the historical centers populated by religious Jews. In other settlements, such as Petah Tikva, the break was less apparent: the settlers received assistance from the *halukah* (the system for distribution of charity among pious Jews) and traditional Jewish education was dispensed alongside the secular Zionist curricula, which would later gain the upper hand.

The Old Yishuv continued to oppose the Zionist settlers, who, for their part, quickly turned the presence of pious Jews in the Land of Israel to their advantage. In 1911, a Zionist emissary, disguised as a representative of the traditional communities of Jerusalem, traveled to Yemen to recruit immigrants. The expedition, and the subterfuge that it represented, bore fruit. The Zionists' success in driving the Yemenite Jews away from the Torah was to remain a source of bitter recriminations for several decades. The secularization of Jews from the Muslim countries where the impact of the Haskalah had been minimal, has divided Israeli society to the present day and has given rise to protest movements such as Shas.

Zionism's critics often quote the Zionists themselves to prove their misdeeds, particularly with regard to the forced secularization of the immigrants. Indeed, Zionists openly debated the transfer of hundreds of thousands of Jews to Israel just in order to populate the country:

> There was an indiscriminate piling in of immigrants, which was neither Zionism, nor rescue. An artificial stampede was imposed on top of the natural one, and swept along tens of thousands of Jews, who did not have to come to Israel at this time, and without excessive provocation and cajolery would not have come. *Kibbutz Galuyot* [the Zionist operation to stimulate *aliya* after 1948] proclaimed, moreover, that Jews ought not to want to live anywhere but in the Jewish state, and Jews who did not pull up stakes, wherever they were, and head for Israel, were letting their people down.... We needed the maximum number of additional Jews in the minimum amount of time in order to discourage the Arabs from attempting a second round. By doubling our numbers from 700,000 to 1,400,000 in three years without regard to the quality of the new human material, or the effect on the economic and productive structures of the country — not to mention its morale — was not a guarantee of optimum increase in strength. (Samuel, 63 and 67)

The term "human material" was quite common in the vocabulary of the Zionist leaders of the day, including Ben-Gurion. The collectivist term, which reduced humans to the status of raw material to be shaped at will, has always been offensive both to religious and to secular liberal Israelis, who consider the individual unique and inimitable — and not an anonymous cog in the Zionist machine. This attitude would appear to characterize the Zionist movement from its beginnings, well before the Russian socialists became dominant in it (Rose, 91–92).

To this day, the Judaic critics of Zionism point to the excesses of enthusiastic Zionists during the first decades of Israel's existence. The Zionists may even have kidnapped hundreds of immigrant children from Yemen in order to transform them into "true Israelis." The government apparently assured the parents that their children had died. It was not until many years later, when some of the parents received military call-up notices for their children, that they began to smell a rat (Halevi, Y.K., 14–19).

The Yemeni Jews, well known for their devotion to the Torah and for their Judaic erudition, were subjected upon their arrival in Israel in the late 1940s to secular re-education campaigns, often in isolated camps. This measure was aimed primarily at the young, who, while not actually kidnapped, were nonetheless forced to endure ideological pressures designed to estrange them from tradition. Many sources concur: physical violence was employed, particularly when the young secular camp commanders forbade access to young religious Jews who wished to assist the internees. In the Knesset, an Israeli parliamentarian issued the following statement:

> I cannot employ any other terms to describe the situation in these camps than those of spiritual constraint and inquisition against the Jewish religion. I see nothing in what is being done in these camps but the cultural and religious murder of the tribes of Israel. (Blau, R., 271)

Their Zionist educators apparently forced the young Yemeni Jews to harvest oranges on the Sabbath, to walk about bareheaded and to cut off the side-curls the Yemeni Jews had worn for centuries. For many Yemenites, the contrast with their native land could not have been starker:

> The Arabs among whom we lived did not bother us, not even in the most insignificant of our religious observances. Quite the contrary, the government recognized our religion, our rights and our faith. If an official or a police officer were to come among us during the Sabbath, he would not dare to smoke, or to profane the Sabbath in any way. And here, they treat us with contempt, and force our people to profane the Sabbath. They mock us; laugh at our traditional beliefs, our prayers and the religious observances of our Holy Torah. (Blau, R., 271)

The issue of maltreatment of Jews in the Arab countries has, meanwhile, become a major controversy: the Zionists produce accounts of atrocities allegedly committed against the Jews, while their opponents assert that Zionism has been the cause of deteriorating relations with the Arabs. From the Zionist perspective, Jews living in the Arab countries had no alternative but to save their lives through precipitous emigration to Israel. This would make them refugees quite like the Palestinians who fled their homes in 1948 and would mean that an exchange of populations had taken place, a kind of rough retroactive justice. However, the anti-Zionists continue to publish eyewitness accounts of the neighborly relations between Jews and Muslims in all the countries of the Middle East, including the Holy Land. They accuse the Zionists of having provoked anti-Jewish riots, both by their overt aggressiveness in Palestine and by their covert activities in several Arab countries.

Hatred of Jews in several Arab countries is a recent development and is therefore reversible. This view is shared by more than a few Jewish historians, both inside and outside Israel, and is grounded in neutral sources such as the memoirs of a German military observer during World War I (see Chapter 5), according to whom relations between Arabs and Jews were excellent prior to the arrival of the Zionists.

New immigrants from the Arab countries were often assigned to border regions, where they were to acquire a Zionist identity predicated on an Arab threat:

> [Zionism] had been conceived in Europe by utopian colonizers yearning to till the land, like the Boers in South Africa or the Pieds-Noirs in Algeria. Militarily well-equipped…, the military and paramilitary organizations that had driven back the Arab armies… had been given or taken upon themselves the mission of "cleansing" the conquered region of its Palestinian inhabitants…. The Arab houses and villages thus emptied of their population were given on a priority basis to Jewish immigrants from the Arab countries whose messianic dream of the "return to Zion" was rapidly to evaporate… in the face of systematic exploitation. (Abitbol 1998, 15–16)

But socialization into the new society did not end there; the state allocated significant resources to re-make the culture of the immigrants. Several observers decried the fact that entire populations drawn from the Muslim countries suffered a "deculturation" marked by severance, often forcible, from Jewish tradition (Schonfeld 1980).

The Zionist re-education campaign was inspired by pedagogical experimentation undertaken throughout the twentieth century in several socialist countries: isolate the children from their parents and shape them to match the officially approved model. Indeed, the various forms of nationalist socialism employed psychological and cultural models to homogenize and control society; this was also the objective of Ben-Gurion and his associates (Sternhell, 27). Thousands of orphans and children of "enemies of the people" were assigned to re-education camps dispersed across the entire Soviet Union, in order to create "the new Soviet man" (Heller). In Israel, kibbutz members, most of them Ashkenazim, would often decide to leave their children's education in the hands of the collective. But the more traditional, non-Ashkenazi parents, mostly from the Islamic countries, were often forced to allow the state to take charge of their children. As a policy, it contributed to secularization, but it also contributed to the delinquency that flourished amid conditions of poverty and family disintegration (Menahem). The Judaic critique of Zionism focuses, among other things, on this attempt to separate the young from their families and from tradition.

The institution of *Aliyat Hanoar*, the aliya of the young, was the instrument of choice in the campaign designed to attract immigrants from almost every country. Adolescents, removed from their families and inspired by the grandiose vision of Zionism, would be assimilated into the dominant culture and thus become the vector of the future absorption of their families into Israeli society. Predictably, *Aliyat Hanoar* became the target of virulent attacks by religious Jews, who resisted the secularization campaign and the breakdown of the family that it was based on.

The struggle against Judaism has long since lost much of its drive, since many observant Jews from the Islamic countries are now firmly established in Israel. Today, *Aliyat Hanoar* deals with young people from the former USSR, whose allegiance to Judaism is weaker even than in Israel. Unlike their Yemeni or Moroccan predecessors, most Russian Jews do not carry with them a single memory, not a single attribute of Judaism. While the original Zionist emissaries were expected to convince the young "Orientals" heading for Israel to cast their phylacteries into the sea, later arrivals from the "first socialist state" would not even recognize the word "phylactery."

The new Israeli identity's opposition to Jewish tradition is amply documented; it explains why the hostility to Judaism often encountered in Israel is unparalleled in the Diaspora. This hostility to Judaism found diverse expressions among the founders of the state, including the choice of new, Hebraized names: the father of a member of the Knesset gave himself the name *Kofer*, heretic (Klein). The categorical rejection of Judaism can also be explained by the climate of religious coercion that results from the need of secular Zionist parties to ensure support or at least neutrality of the religious non-Zionists. This coercion weighs heavily on all aspects of life: from the prohibition of bus service on the Sabbath to the Orthodox rabbis' monopoly over weddings and burials. The Israeli press regularly reports incidents of anti-religious hostility. In one such case, the pupils of a secular high school, having completed their final — and obligatory — examination on the Torah, stacked up their copies in the schoolyard and set them afire, to the delight of all present. Let us remember, by contrast, that traditionalist Jews usually kiss the Torah upon closing it after study, and they certainly kiss the book should it inadvertently fall to the floor.

It would seem that the anti-religious enthusiasm that once galvanized the secular Jews of Russia produced long-lasting results for Jewish immigrants, mostly in Israel. The Zionists were by no means the only ones caught up in the secularizing urge. When they migrated to North America in the early twentieth century, Russian Jews also promoted a new secular identity and established secular socialist schools in major cities like New York and Montreal. Several decades later these self-same "people's schools," originally anti-religious in outlook, began to teach the fundamentals of Judaism. With the triumph of capitalism, they began to attract well-to-do bourgeois families. Today, the prosperous descendents of the Russian Jewish proletarians of yore have become regular synagogue-goers; some of them have even become Orthodox. Anti-Judaic fervor is but a distant memory.

However, in Israel the gulf that separates the secular from Judaism in all its forms has widened. Israeli newspapers are full of caricatures of Haredi Jews, not unlike the anti-Semitic stereotypes current in Europe in the nineteenth and twentieth centuries (Efron 1991, 15–22; 88–90). The Israeli historian Noah Efron writes: "This kind of hostility is not novel. Nowhere are Haredi Jews as feared and hated as in Israel. Israel is a bastion of a classic sort of anti-Semitism, aimed not against all Jews, but against the ultra-Orthodox, the overly *Jewy* Jews" (Efron 1991, 16). This should come as no surprise, for the image of the "New Hebrew," in reaction to European anti-Semitism, denies the image of the traditional Jew, who is depicted as a degraded, degenerate being. In fact, Zionism's promoters have simply refined the hateful image of the traditional Jew as painted by Voltaire and Fichte:

> One need not search hard to find denigrating images of the *Altjude* [traditional Jew] in Zionist rhetoric and pamphletry. Herzl had already noted in 1894 that Jews had "taken on a number of antisocial characteristics" in the ghettos of Europe, and that Jewish character was "damaged." [The poet David] Frishman [1859–1922, of Russian origin] opined that "[traditional] Jewish life is a dog's life that evokes disgust." [Another Russian poet,] Joseph Haim Brenner, [1881–1921] likened Jews to "filthy dogs, inhuman, wounded dogs." [Yehuda Leib] Gordon [1831–1892, an active opponent of Judaism, also of Russian origin] wrote that European Jews were parasites. [Micha Joseph] Berdyczewski [1865–1921, a poet and a philosopher born in the Russian Empire] christened traditional Jews "spiritual slaves, men whose natural forces had dried up and whose relation to the world was no longer normal," and elsewhere, "a non-people, a non-nation — non-men, indeed. (Efron 1991, 88-89)

The secular majority, claims Efron, have a deep fear of the Haredim:

> Several friends and colleagues have independently told me about nightmares in which they are captured and held by Haredim and, in some instances, tortured. [The secular] feel squeezed between two burgeoning enemies — the Palestinians on the one hand and

the Haredim, on the other…. More importantly, there is a feeling
that one is never safe, that no matter how rationally children are
raised, they may ultimately be lured into the Haredi camp. (Efron
1991, 16, 18–19)

It hardly comes as a surprise that secularist Israelis can experience something
close to visceral hatred. During the Gulf War, as dozens of Iraqi missiles
rained down on Israel and the threat of a chemical attack was acute, most
Israelis experienced a renewed sense of solidarity with one another. But
Efron reports a comment overheard during the war from a group of social
science students at Tel Aviv University. They were of the opinion that "the
best thing for the country would be if there were a chemical attack in Bnei-
Brak [bastion of Haredi Judaism] now, before they get new masks [adapted
for bearded men]. That would rid of all of them at once" (Efron 1991, 16).

Such intense hatred for Judaism would be difficult to imagine among
the most assimilated Jews of the Diaspora. Assimilated Jews in Canada,
France or Russia are conscious of their distance from their "Jewish roots"
and — should they feel the need — can search them out in Judaism. They
can join a synagogue, become members of a beginners' Torah study group
or come to participate discreetly at Yom Kippur services — all gestures that
can bring them closer to a Jewish way of life. To take this step in Israel is
far more difficult, for it means betraying one's secular identity and "going
over to the enemy."

The estrangement of Israelis from Judaism manifests itself both in the
Holy Land and beyond the borders of Israel. For example, on the day of
Rosh ha-Shana, the Jewish New Year, upon which Jews are called to examine their lives, repent and draw closer to the Torah, certain emigrants from
Israel who have never set foot in a synagogue organize dance parties not
unlike Christian New Year's Eve celebrations. Emigrants from Israel often
settle far from Jewish infrastructures and neighborhoods. Their integration
into their new country takes place outside of Judaism. This trend reflects
the feelings of two-thirds of secular Israelis, who, as we have seen, would
have preferred not to be Jews had they been born outside of Israel. A Jewish
educator in Toronto has noted that Judaic outreach is particularly difficult
among immigrants from Israel and the former Soviet Union — two groups
that share one important trait: a secular national identity that is a potent
deterrent against embracing Judaism.

The elevation of secular identity to the status of an ideal has not eliminated the sacred; it has transferred it instead from Judaism to other areas that
then become sacralized. An exposition at the Israel Museum in Jerusalem
eloquently underscored the transfer of sacred meaning from Judaic to secular
national symbols. Though Zionism draws frequently from Jewish tradition,
it is not the only domain to have drawn upon the Jewish idealism that had
been previously focused on the Torah; science, literature and the struggle

for social justice and peace can also become "sacred." This is how a secular
Israeli describes the peculiar relationship with poetry maintained by his
mother, the sister of Israel's national hero, Moshe Dayan (1915–1981):

> But my mother's love for poetry was not just a passing fancy; it
> was a way of life. If you ask me, the sickness of my mother and of
> many of her generation of reciters and declaimers was this: they
> did not only love poems, they believed them.... My poor mother
> took poems as an option, as a way of life. She quoted endlessly and
> believed in rhymes and in her notebook the way a religious person
> believes in mitzvahs and bible stories.... The poet Natan Alterman
> [1910–1970, a leading poet and pillar of the Israeli cultural estab-
> lishment] was to my mother as the author Leo Tolstoy was to my
> grandmother Dvora. When we were children, my mother used to
> cut out his weekly column from the Friday edition of the newspaper
> Davar. (Geffen, 14)

The sacralizing of culture has become an integral part of the Israeli
secular identity. At a marriage celebrated in a secular *moshav* near Netanya, I
struck up a conversation with the couple that shared my table. They were left-
ists, disgusted by the bellicose nature of Israeli society; they had attempted
to establish themselves in Europe, only to return to Israel. "People like you
have no problem adapting," they told me in terms bordering on reproach.
"You can settle in any country you like, find a synagogue, a Jewish school
and a kosher bakery, and there you are, all set! But we no longer have any
of that. We are tied to the land and the language; we're trapped here. We're
the hostages of our grandparents who wanted to create the New Hebrew
Man, and deprived us of everything Jewish."

Their analysis was as laconic as it was insightful. After all, "Zionism
had claimed: 'no more tradition's chains shall bind us,' and consigned to
oblivion all that had been so unfortunate as to precede it" (Barnavi, 220).
The Israelis I met, born of the policy of "no more tradition's chains" resented
their estrangement from Judaism, which they attributed, with some bitter-
ness, to the socialist Zionism of the founders. But at the same time, they
would not turn back to the Torah. To abandon their secular identity would
have been, for them, a betrayal of their very self, perhaps much more serious than the abandonment of either their land or their language. For this
very reason neo-Haredi preachers, such as Amnon Itzhak and Uri Zohar,
who appeal to thousands of potential "converts" to Haredi Judaism, openly
mock the idea of identification with the state and call upon their recruits to
cast it off in order to become "true Jews."

My encounter at the moshav reminds me of a critical remark made
a century earlier by Rabbi Haim Soloveitchik (1853–1918), a renowned
Talmudic scholar: "The Zionists do not drive away Jews from the Torah in

order to get a state. They need a state in order to drive the Jews away from the Torah" (Rosenberg, 269).

Leibowitz, in his critique of Zionism, notes that without the markers of Judaism, the existence of such Jews — now a majority of the Jewish people — represents a departure from the preceding millennia. These Jews, he argues, are seeking a national identity that exists only in and for itself, for they no longer have any concrete, empirically observable ties with Judaism. For Leibowitz,

> The danger is that [national identity] be transformed into statism and will to power; into a national identity in the Mussolinian sense.... Nonetheless, a portion — a minority, but a significant one — of the human group heretofore considered as the Jewish people insists on keeping alive its historical religious heritage by rejecting both this national identity and its symbols. Suddenly, it becomes clear that the notion of "Jewish national identity" today possesses two meanings, and, moreover, two contradictory meanings. (Leibowitz, 111)

Through the prism of Leibowitz's analysis, we can grasp the extent of the identity crisis fomented primarily by the very existence of the State of Israel, which lends legitimacy to a national identity whose main content is the state. While the Italians had developed a culture — language, literature, political tradition, intellectual heritage — that reflected their national consciousness centuries before finally creating a state of their own, the national consciousness of the Jews had only Judaism as a shared basis, and the state's founders openly opposed it.

Rabbi Jonathan Sacks, Chief Rabbi of Britain, singles out the lack of a commonality among today's Jews:

> The events of the past century — persecution, pogroms, the rise of racial anti-Semitism and the unfolding of the Holocaust, followed by the birth of the State of Israel and the constant fight it has had to undertake to survive against war and terror — have immeasurably deepened the *brit goral*, the covenant of fate that still continues to unite Jews in the face of the hostility of the outside world. We are, and remain, a *mahaneh*, a camp.... But we are no longer an *edah*, a congregation. Instead we have fissured and fractured into different *edot* [congregations]: Orthodox and reform, religious and secular, and the many subdivisions that continue to atomize Jewish life into non-communicating sects and subcultures. (Sacks)

Leibowitz, who like Sacks is certainly not an anti-Zionist, identifies an important focus of the religious critique of Zionism:

If the Jewish people as a bearer of the historical heritage of certain values no longer exists, there is no reason to create another by synthesis, by giving a state framework to a population whose national character is not defined by anything but that framework itself, that apparatus of power.... But I am no anarchist, and I affirm that such a framework is necessary, and must exist. And we wish to bring it into existence. But it does not exist for itself, nor is it a value of such worth that men invest all their efforts in it, let alone sacrifice their lives so that it can exist. The state exists to serve men; men do not exist for their State. (Leibowitz, 151, 214)

The inversion of values described by Leibowitz was precisely what the critics of Zionism had feared most. Their number included, at the end of the nineteenth century, a majority of the rabbinical authorities, and their fears were to prove well founded. It was exactly those Jews farthest removed from Judaism who found in Israel their last hope to remain a part of the Jewish people. Ironically, thanks to the religious coercion that so antagonizes secular Jews, Israel has remained the ideal, if not the unique, place in the world where one can preserve one's secular identity while believing oneself part of Jewish continuity. Secular Israelis do not lament the lack of a relationship with Judaism. Their self-image replicates their surroundings: they live in Israel, speak Hebrew and, unlike the Haredim, serve in the armed forces. They feel themselves much better Jews than those Jews with long beards and wigs they occasionally encounter in the streets.

Several Judaic critics emphasize that the threat posed by Zionism is particularly grave for those Jews who have become estranged from Judaism, because Zionism has cut off the road to repentance. Those who embrace Zionism see themselves as "good Jews," deplored the Lubavitch Rebbe at the beginning of the twentieth century. He went on to note that Zionism has never brought a single Jew closer to Judaism but, on the contrary, has driven many further away from the truth. Zionism casts itself as a replacement for Judaism, which it recognizes as a respected but by now obsolete predecessor. The analogy with Christianity is clear, and Schneerson draws upon it more than once (Schneerson).

The Rebbe acknowledges Zionism's immense power of attraction over the Jews. Zionism speaks a modern tongue, appeals to Jewish symbols on the emotional level and provides meaning for the life of a Jew whose attachment to the Torah is either weak or non-existent. But, as Schneerson reminds us, appearances can be deceiving. He compares Zionists to the pig. The pig is cloven-hoofed — a sign of a kosher animal; when it lies down and extends its legs, it would appear to be kosher. But, he cautions, the Torah forbids pork: "it is unclean for you" (Leviticus 11:7).

The majority of immigrants from the former USSR, even though a third of them could not be considered Jews under rabbinical law, are quite aware of their predicament. The paradox of the situation has not escaped the new Israelis, who paraphrase the words of Alexei Nekrasov, the nineteenth-century Russian poet: "You may not be a poet, but you must be a citizen." These words have acquired a new form in Israel: "You may not be a Jew, but you must be a Zionist." Indeed, immigrants from the former USSR, for whom belonging to the Jewish nationality is natural enough, correspond perfectly with the image of the secular Zionist as both pillar and *raison d'être* of the State of Israel. Created for the most part by Russian Jews, the State of Israel continues to resonate among those Russian Jews most estranged from Judaism.

Still, Rabbi Abraham Isaac Kook (1865–1935), a Russian rabbinical authority whom the British would appoint as first Chief Rabbi of Palestine, hoped that the return to the Land of Israel would bring the new secular Hebrew back to tradition. Inspired by the romantic nationalism in Russia, he anticipated that their love of the land would have a mystical influence on the intrepid pioneers. Now, nearly a century later, such hopes do not seem justified. While some National Religious Jews have become stricter in their observance of Judaism, the secular have remained secular, and the land has had no demonstrable spiritual impact on the majority of Israelis. Neither the language nor the Land of Israel appears to have strengthened Judaic consciousness. Indeed, according to many observers, it is only in Israel that 'dejudaization' has been so thorough. Some Zionist pioneers, while quite foreign to the Haredi camp, have reached a similar conclusion: "'It's hard to be a Jew' — would complain the Jew who used to live among the Gentiles. [But] It is now even harder to be a Jew faithful to the spirit of Israel among those new-fashioned Hebrews" (Berger 1957, 32).

The leaders of the National Religious movement sadly conclude that Rabbi Kook's optimistic forecasts have not been borne out by Israeli reality. In the absence of any other unifying factors, the common Arab threat can only produce a national identity that Leibowitz terms "Mussolinian." The behavior of many *yordim* — expatriate Israelis — eloquently illustrates the warrior mentality. In the event of a war in Israel, many would hasten to join their army units. An Israeli living in Boston ruefully quipped: "It is easier to die for Israel than to live there."

Rabbi Adin Steinsaltz, Israel Prize winner, thinker and distinguished translator of the Talmud, considers the Israeli nation to lack a specifically Jewish character. Judged by its outlook and lifestyle, he argues, it has become less Jewish than any other non-Jewish nation. "Will we be able to preserve ourselves and to survive in that quality of Israeli non-Jewishness?" (Steinsaltz).

The substitution of a new Israeli identity for the traditional Jewish one raises important questions about the value of the national preservation of the Jew no longer grounded in Judaism. Though himself not a religious Jew, the author of a psychohistory of Zionism asserts that complete severance of the relationship with God eliminates the sole distinctive trait of the Jews (Gonen, 334). The new Jewish identity must thus devise another common denominator. The unending concern for the security of the State of Israel has today assumed that role, both in the Diaspora and in Israel.

Modern-day pluralism allows for multiple identities, such as those of Irish Americans or Germans of Turkish origin. So it is that many Jews identify with Israel, attend concerts by Israeli singers, defend Israel — all without ever setting foot there or learning so much as one sentence of Hebrew. For three decades, Zionist organizations have been inculcating belief in the centrality of Israel in most non-Haredi Jewish schools of the Diaspora. This vicarious "Israelism" replaces the traditional Jewish identity all the more easily because the new identity makes far fewer demands. Since Jewish identity is based on obedience to the Torah and to the commandments that it articulates, it affects both the most intimate of precincts (such as food and sex) and public behavior (such as the non-use of automobiles on the Sabbath or dressing modestly). Contrariwise, Israelism imposes no particular obligation, while at the same time transmitting a feeling of belonging. "I identify with Israel because it is the last refuge of the secular Jew," a friend confided to me one day. While interested in Judaism he denies it any normative significance. "Without Israel I would be obliged either to observe the Torah commandments or to stop being a Jew." When I passed on his remark to Rabbi Moshe Dov (Baer) Beck, perhaps the most prolific of the anti-Zionist thinkers, he replied, to my astonishment: "What's wrong with being a non-Jew?" In other words, why would those who do not observe the Torah insist on remaining Jewish? A secular Jewish identity is obviously nonsensical for Rabbi Beck.

The existence of a state with a national flag, a powerful army and a prospering economy confers a certain sense of security. One might well ask if the creation of a national state in a heterogeneous region has contributed to the security of the Bosnians or the Ukrainians. But the existence of the State of Israel does make many Jews feel secure.

According to Avineri:

> Zionism was the most fundamental revolution in Jewish life. It substituted a secular self-identity of the Jews as a nation for the traditional and Orthodox self-identity in religious terms. It changed a passive, quietistic, and pious hope of the Return to Zion into an effective social force, moving millions of people to Israel. It transformed a language relegated to mere religious usage into a modern, secular mode of intercourse of a nation-state. Pious reiterations of the links of Jews to Palestine do not suffice to explain the emergence of Zionism when it did. (Avineri 1981, 13)

Indeed, for those who reject it in the name of the Torah, Zionism constitutes a clean break with both Judaism and Jewish history. Why then, the emphasis on discontinuity that we encounter in Avineri and other Zionist authors? Are they attempting to break down a wide-open door? In fact, theirs is a reaction to a massive body of *engagé* literature produced by Jewish and non-Jewish intellectuals, which presents Jewish history in teleological terms: all Jewish history leads to its Zionist culmination. Israeli historians of the first generation did so without hesitation: their Zionist allegiance came before all else. They were first propagandists, certainly more subtle than their Soviet counterparts, but just as devoted to the cause. When Mikhail Gorbachev launched the process known as *glasnost* in 1986, he invited historians to "fill in the blanks" left by the official historiography of the regime. Curiously, at the same time, young Israeli historians and journalists began to challenge the founding myths of the regime. They exposed the Zionist treatment of the Arabs and of the Jews brought from the Arab countries; they winnowed the archives of the army and the personal files of the fathers of Zionism. Their writings touched off torrents of protest, which continue down to this day. It must be remembered that the re-writing of Soviet history finally undermined the ideological underpinnings of the Soviet state and helped speed its collapse. The Israeli New Historians have likewise succeeded in undermining Zionist ideology and in turning a substantial portion of Israeli youth away from the ideological foundations of Zionism.

The chasm that, with only a few exceptions, separates the world of the Haredim from academia makes their critique of Zionism all but inaudible in university lecture halls. In like manner, the post-Zionist and the New Historians, products of Israel's secular milieu, remain largely invisible to the Haredim, who might otherwise find in their work many points of convergence.

Communication is not always easy, even within Haredi circles. Those Haredim who identify with *Agudat Israel*, founded in 1912 as an anti-Zionist movement, criticize the messianism of the National Religious, without, however, embracing the positions of Neturei Karta. Many Haredi thinkers have remained non-Zionists and refuse to admit that the establishment of a large number of Jews in the Holy Land is connected with messianic redemption. They reject all manifestations of Zionist ideology and state-related rites: everything that the sociologists label "Israel's civil religion" (Liebman 1983). Their critique of Zionism centers on those institutions that encourage behaviors at variance with Jewish law, but it does not condemn the very existence of the state as opposed to the Torah. The arguments put forth by these critics reflect both their collaboration with the state and their theological reluctance to interpret the modern Jewish settlement of the Land of Israel. They claim to have received no divine sign that would suggest that Israel constitutes a step towards redemption. When I asked the question of Yeshayahu Leibowitz he responded, with typical sarcasm, that God had not yet sent him a registered letter detailing his plans for redemption through the agency of the State of Israel: "But I check my mailbox every day!"

As we will see in the following chapter, while consciousness of exile remains unshaken in all Haredi circles, Aguda refuses to assign any Jewish value — negative or positive — to the Zionist enterprise. Unlike their predecessors, who decried Zionism vehemently as long as it remained an ideological movement, contemporary Aguda leaders, while continuing to reject Zionism, prefer to avoid theological interpretation of the unique impact of the sovereignty of mostly Torah-free Jews over the Land of Israel. The state provides for the religious Jews who live there; thousands of Talmud students study there at the feet of their masters, and yet, for them, the state possesses no particular Jewish significance.

Some criticize the anti-Zionist Haredim for having accorded too much significance to the state. A Talmudic scholar, witnessing in a Jerusalem street a Neturei Karta demonstrator decrying the very existence of the State of Israel, accused him of being a Zionist: "In Poland or in Russia would he thus curse the authorities? Would he act like this in America?" The demonstrator, because he treated the State of Israel differently, was considered a Zionist (Ravitzky 1996, 155). Indeed, the Haredim do not recite the prayer for State of Israel, an exception to the rule, for in all other countries Jews recite such prayers for their respective states. But when Neturei Karta condemned an Aguda activist for using an expression from the exodus from Egypt — "This is the finger of God" (Exodus 8:15) — in speaking of the proclamation of the State of Israel, Aguda issued a prompt denial. The apparent drift toward collaboration with the Zionists has also touched off criticism from within the movement (Weinman), some of whose members insist on avoiding all collaboration (Grozovsky). They remain convinced that the perpetuation of the State of Israel "is not good for the Jews," but this is clearly no longer the position of Aguda, which has often supported right-wing nationalists in Israel. Its concern is technically about the Jews of Israel, rather than about the state as such.

Modern Hebrew and Secular Identity

Language is one of the key ingredients of organic nationalism. It assumes greater importance still when the other elements of collective identity begin to wane, leaving something of a vacuum. Modern national identity often rests upon a sense of — frequently romanticized — belonging to a linguistic group and to a territory. The creation of Modern Hebrew is an unprecedented historical achievement. It came about far from a shared territory and represented a break in the status of Hebrew as one of prayer and Torah study (*leshon ha-kodesh*).

While a few rabbinical authorities supported the Hebrew revival, which began in the mid-nineteenth century, it is noteworthy that they invoked European nationalism rather than the Jewish tradition in the process (Avineri 1998, 3). The revival of Romanian, Polish and Lithuanian strengthened hopes of hammering out a modern language based on biblical and rabbinical Hebrew. The Zionists were not the first to insist upon using the national language in their homes. Inspired by Johann Gottfried Herder (1744–1803), the ideologue of the eighteenth-century German cultural renaissance, several members of the nationalist elites of Central and Eastern Europe sought to transmit the national language to their children, their native languages having been abandoned in favor of a universal vernacular, either German or Russian. Their aim was to create a literature in the national idiom, in order to develop a sense of common history, a "national spirit," indispensable for the nation-state to come. Nationalist elite intellectuals in the Austro-Hungarian and Russian empires felt obliged to learn the national language of the peasants, who were the only ones to speak it on a daily basis, and then to enrich it for use in the sciences, philosophy and politics. The enthusiastic supporters of Hebrew as a modern vernacular needed only to look around them for encouraging experiments and examples to be emulated. The challenge of Hebrew however was quite the opposite: it was necessary to revitalize the language of the rabbis and other intellectuals, and to adapt it for use in society, agriculture and industry. The challenge was all the more daunting in that, at the end of the nineteenth century, there existed no societies, farms and industries where the new language could be used.

The first novel written in Hebrew retraces the biblical story in a format reminiscent of other European nationalist movements (Aberbach). It was written within the borders of the Russian Empire, in Lithuania, where two nationalisms — Polish and Lithuanian — were locked in conflict, each glorifying its past in modern literary forms and, of course, in its own national language. Secular literature in Hebrew spread throughout nineteenth-century Europe, but the Russian Empire, with a Jewish male population more at home in biblical Hebrew than in Russian, provided the most fertile ground for the propagation of Modern Hebrew. Several former students of the famous Lithuanian yeshivas, that of Volozhin for example, abandoned the practice of Judaism and became the pillars of the new Hebrew literature and cultural icons of Zionism. A portion of the Jewish intelligentsia would also employ Hebrew in journalism.

For the critics of Zionism, the Hebrew revival had nothing to do with Jewish continuity but represented what they saw as another revolt against tradition. Some protested against the profanation of the sacred tongue; others saw it as a Zionist plot to take over, then deform, a language that had been the bearer of tradition. The secular revival of Hebrew soon drew the wrath of many rabbinical authorities, who saw it as a particularly pernicious attack on Judaism, singling out as it did yeshiva students, perhaps the only ones who could have access — and thus succumb — to this new literature.

Zionist literature and journalism also developed in the two imperial *linguae francae*: German and Russian. Both tongues were accessible to the more assimilated Jews, among whom, as many Zionist and anti-Zionist authors would later point out, could be found almost all the leaders of the Zionist movement. A particularly creative literary school took shape in the city of Odessa (Gurfinkiel). Several Jewish writers — including Ilya Ilf, Isaac Babel and Mikhail Svetlov — chose Russian and went on to fame in the Soviet Union.

Vladimir Jabotinsky also chose Russian and became a master of the language, but unlike other members of the same circle, achieved fame as a Zionist. Maxim Gorky, the future dean of Soviet literature, regretted that Zionism had won such a promising writer away from Russian *belles-lettres*. Known principally as the founder of the Revisionist movement in Zionism and as the theoretician of its political and military doctrine, Jabotinsky was also the author of several plays and historical novels, which often drew on his rather literal reading of Jewish lore. It is quite revealing that this ideologist of Jewish military power should write a work of literature based on the story of Samson, who, having been blinded, kills himself and brings down his enemies in death along with him. It was this heroic spirit that the founders of the State of Israel would strive to inculcate in youth. Similarly, it was at Masada, where an act of mass Jewish suicide had taken place in Roman times, that future Israel Defense Forces (IDF) officers would swear their oath to the state.

As rabbinical tradition values life above all and condemns suicide, it follows that many rabbis reject both the heroic novels and the Zionist indoctrination as alien and contrary to Judaism. The Zionists, except for a growing National Religious minority, are proud to have forged a new nation, by causing millions of Jews in Israel, and in the Diaspora, to abandon tradition while learning the Modern Hebrew language.

The victory of Hebrew over Yiddish was not the triumph of one language over another, but rather that of an ideology that rejected exile and sought to create a "New Hebrew Man." According to the Israeli intellectual Boaz Evron, "Zionism is indeed the negation of Judaism" (Leibowitz, 133). From the earliest days of secularization, rather than uniting the Jewish people, Judaism has divided it. "Ben-Gurion saw Judaism as the historical misfortune of the Jewish people and an obstacle to its transformation into a normal nation" (Leibowitz, 144). Having known the founder of the State of Israel well, Leibowitz affirmed that Ben-Gurion enjoyed with the Bible "a selective relationship, in the spirit of Christian criticism: hostility toward the Law and the Commandments, and admiration for the Prophets (whom he did not understand at all)" (Leibowitz, 145).

This selective relationship also held within it a negation of Jewish tradition, whose "exilic"[2] character the Zionists have so frequently derided. This approach to the Jewish past also had an impact on the nature of the archaeological explorations that the founders of the state used in order to develop the new national consciousness: vestiges of the Hebrew-speaking

Biblical period received virtually all attention, while official archaeology ignored Jewish monuments of the polyglot post-Biblical era, when the rabbis of the day lived in harmony with the Romans and laid the groundwork for the tradition of non-violence and compromise typical of rabbinical Judaism. The creation of Modern Hebrew has, of necessity, been accompanied by the emergence of an historical narrative adapted to the needs of Zionism.

The creators of the new vernacular transformed the language by assigning a secular meaning to traditional Judaic concepts. Eliezer Ben Yehuda (1858–1922), the instigator of the Hebrew revival, had studied at a traditional Jewish school in the Russian Empire. At age seventeen, he experienced a heavenly vision: that of a national revival in the Land of Israel. The creation of a national language became his overriding objective. Upon settling in Jerusalem in 1881, his home became the first to use Modern Hebrew as a vernacular. In open revolt against Judaism, he promoted the secularization of the language as a means of creating the "New Hebrew Man." Thus the word *bitahon*, which means "trust in God," came to mean "military security." The shift was far from innocent: the effect was to distance the new Hebrew language from traditional sources and, at the same time, to approach and win over traditionalist Jews, who were drawn by terms familiar to them. The process of distancing concentrated on the meanings of words precisely because the words themselves retained their original form. Thus the messianic term *kibbutz galuyot*, the "in-gathering of exiles," came to mean, in the new context, "immigration"; the Mishnaic term *keren kayemet*, "permanent fund," which originally meant the accumulation of merits in this life to be "expended" in the world to come, was transformed into the name of the Jewish National Fund, the financial arm of the Zionist movement. Another example is the word *agadah*, which denotes the ethical and inspirational — and non-legal — parts of the Talmud. In Modern Hebrew, *agadah* has taken on the meaning of legend, made-up story. Such shifts in meaning have been the object of strong Judaic criticism, for they tend to undermine the meaning these words enjoy in Jewish tradition and thus undermine tradition itself.

Yet these references to the Judaic heritage paved the way for Modern Hebrew and the Zionist worldview. Vladimir Jabotinsky, for instance, entitled his beginner's textbook of Modern Hebrew *Tariag Milim* (*613 Words*), an allusion to the 613 *mitzvahs*, which, according to Jewish tradition, is the total number of the Torah commandments (Jabotinsky 1950). Moreover, Jabotinsky's beginners' Hebrew text uses the Latin alphabet, making it possible for the learner to communicate in the language but not to access most of the Jewish heritage, which uses the Hebrew alphabet, even when the language written is not Hebrew: e.g., Aramaic for the Talmud, Arabic for most of the treatises of Maimonides (1135–1204), the Sephardic philosopher and codifier, and Yiddish for the *Tsena u-rena*, the "Women's Bible" published in the eighteenth century. Jabotinsky's approach was similar to that of his contemporary, Kemal Atatürk. Atatürk's reform of the Turkish language abolished Arabic script and, as a result, severed the overwhelmingly Muslim Turks from direct access to their Islamic heritage. But, several decades later, another beginners' textbook was entitled *Elef Milim* (*One Thousand Words*), since the Jewish masses for whom the new manual was written, most of them of Soviet origin, no longer recognized the number 613, for all its established place in Jewish tradition.

In this way, a Zionist interpretive framework replaced the Judaic one in Israeli literature, opening up new opportunities to denigrate Judaism. In this spirit the poet Alterman borrowed a part of the Jewish holiday liturgy: "You have chosen us from all peoples. You loved us and found favor in us" as inspiration for the title of his poem, "Of All Peoples," which deals with the Shoah. The poem, which suggests that God had chosen the Jews in order to kill them, to destroy them in the gas chambers, has been used in official celebrations of Independence Day (Geffen, 11–15).

The transformation of the "language of holiness" into a national vernacular remains a brutal affront to many religious Jews. The Haredim recall that, when the Zionists took control of a number of religious schools in the 1920s, they contrived, under the pretext of providing teachers with a greater mastery of Hebrew, to introduce Zionist ideas. Hebrew rapidly became the symbol of Zionism and, as a result, many Haredi yeshivas and *hadarim* (elementary schools) continue to offer instruction in Yiddish (some of them even in English) rather than adopt Hebrew as the language of instruction. In truth, for some Haredim, Modern Hebrew is nothing more than a "language created by the Zionists" (Steiner, 37). It should be noted as well that the very idea of creating Modern Hebrew and of devising an artificial language accessible to all, Esperanto, emerged at the same time in the minds of two young Jews from the same region of the Russian Empire — Lithuania and Eastern Poland. It was in this region that five languages — Russian, German, Yiddish, Polish and Lithuanian — coexisted in everyday use.

Even the phonetics of Modern Hebrew has irritated some critics, who accuse the Zionists of bastardizing the language by lending it an artificial pronunciation corresponding to none of the traditions of Israel (Zimmer, 34–41). Ben Yehuda drew Modern Hebrew away from the Ashkenazi accent, which disgusted him, because he associated it with the exile he knew all too well. He lent it instead "the Sephardic accent," which, in his eyes, reflected the exile he knew not and which thus appeared more acceptable. Abandoning the Ashkenazi accent was to deprive the new language of vital distinctions with respect to both vowels (the diacritical signs, *patah* and *kamatz*, could no longer be distinguished from one another when spoken) and consonants ("tav" is always pronounced the same way, while in Ashkenazi and Yemenite traditions, there may be variations: "t", "th" or "s"). However, the new pronunciation also overlooked several phonemes used by the different Sephardic communities: for example, the sound "het," which can no longer be distinguished from "khaf," the "ayin," which becomes "aleph"; those "Orientals" who continued to differentiate them in their speech were seen as "primitives." Only the affirmation of pride in Sephardic identity in the two last decades of the twentieth century began to pay homage to the Sephardim and their way of speaking the language.

Most anti-Zionists refuse to speak Hebrew, a fact that was to complicate my interviews with them. As I could not speak Yiddish, the language spoken by the majority of these pious Jews, I had to induce them to conduct our interviews in *leshon ha-kodesh*. They explained their refusal to speak the Israeli vernacular by way of a more general observation about the State of Israel: "Rather than sanctifying the profane — which is our principal role in this world — the Zionists profane the sacred." Otherwise quite distant from the Haredim, an academic philosopher of Judaism refuses to speak the modern vernacular Hebrew for his own reasons:

> Is this the innovative aspect of modern Hebrew in its transposition from the liturgical sphere to the nation-state, that it is used less as a praise of God's presence than as an instrument to project state power?... Is "our" language spoken with such vehemence – the language of power and might — that it marks a return to the Jewish ghetto mentality, now armed with nuclear missiles, a nuclearized ghetto, if you will? (Ellis, 6)

Thus, this critical attitude encompasses not only Modern Hebrew, but the entire Zionist enterprise.

Neologisms often invert traditional meanings. Though it has a pejorative connotation today, the word "totalitarianism" had a positive, proud meaning in fascist Italy. The origin of the term "State of Israel," when introduced by an anti-Zionist, was openly sarcastic. It was only later that the Zionists took it up, infusing it with positive meaning. According to Ravitzky, the term first appeared in a rabbinical diatribe of the early twentieth century, against the secularism of the Zionist movement and against the very idea of Jewish nationalism, which would remove the Jews from the Torah and the mitzvahs. The prospect was so terrifying that the writer compared it with the threat of total extermination of the Jews, as related in the Book of Esther: "For how can I bear to see the disaster which will befall my people! And how can I bear to see the destruction of my kindred?" (Esther 8:6) This is how the term "State of Israel" was apparently used for the first time:

> For I know the devastation they are wreaking upon the Congregation of Israel. My heart sinks within me, my eyes grow dark, and my ears wax heavy at what is being done and said. Their valor in the land is not for the sake of the true faith, nor is it for this that they wave their banners (while we raise the banner of God). What sort

of "nation" can they have if they throw over our holy Torah and its precepts (perish the thought)? How can I bear that something be called "the State of Israel" without the Torah and the commandments (heaven forbid)? (Ravitzky 1996, 4)

On the other hand, Rabbi Kook, one of the few rabbis to declare support for Zionism, praised the expression, giving it a radically different interpretation from the avowed intentions of Israel's secular founders. He looked forward to "an ideal state, upon whose being sublime ideals would be engraved," a state that would become "the pedestal of God's throne in this world." For him, the state would be the earthly expression of a messianic "Kingdom of Israel," a Jacob's ladder uniting earth with heaven (Ravitzky 1996, 131–37). The term underwent a radical transformation, setting up a tension between two connotations, the one pejorative and the other superlative and messianic. Both would assume their original power, derived from the Torah, in the language of the religious anti-Zionists (who, like most Haredi Jews, refrain from uttering the words "State of Israel"), but also in the language of the National Religious, inspired by Rabbi Kook's vision of redemption. Attitudes toward the state were to divide the various factions of Orthodox Jews as much as their attitude to modernity.

Ravitzky lists a whole range of terms used by the Orthodox. The State of Israel is described as "a Satanic State," an "anti-Jewish State," a "regime which calls itself Israel," a "State ruled by Jews," "the State of the Jews," "the State of the Jewish people," "the State of the Congregation of Israel," "the pedestal of God's throne in this world" and, finally, a "divine State" (Ravitzky 1996, 7). But among the Orthodox, only the National Religious would see the state as the fulfilment of the messianic promise.

Many historians attribute the success of the propagation of Modern Hebrew to the revolt against Judaism. In discussing the anti-religious generation of the founder of Modern Hebrew, Eliezer Ben Yehuda, they note:

> Only for them could the Hebrew language become a national language and virtually lose its religious value.... Only for them could the collective Jewish identity be considered in historical terms, utterly devoid of a religious burden. Only for them, at this or any stage in the evolution of Jewish national thought, could Eretz Israel be thought of in political terms and viewed through the glass of romantic nationalism, while the Orthodox attitude was set aside. (Bartal, 21)

The Hebrew language, which, in theory, should have given Israelis access to the classics of Judaism, has sometimes proved to be a barrier. They have discovered that their language is not equal to the task, that it would have to be enriched by other words and other concepts. What proved to be most difficult was the re-learning of an entire Judaic vocabulary, which had been either discarded altogether or transformed by the early Zionists. Devised for everyday usage, with modified and updated meanings of Judaic terms, Modern Hebrew is, today, of limited use to an Israeli who opens the Torah. At a concert in Tel Aviv to which I had invited a friend living in Israel for thirty years, a member of the country's cultural elite, I found my guest unable to understand a Hebrew song and offered my services as amateur interpreter. At the end of the song, he asked me how it was that I had been able to translate even before the words had been sung. I explained that the song was based on one of the Psalms of David, which I knew by heart. For him, the words of the Psalms had the resonance of a foreign tongue.

Paradoxically, the vernacular introduced by the early Zionists to create national unity has had the effect of dividing Jews. Most Haredim avoid Israeli Hebrew and continue to use their traditional pronunciation during prayers. Though these are recited in Hebrew, a secular Israeli would only be able to understand a few words in a Yemenite, Hasidic or Lithuanian synagogue.

For Zionism's opponents, the Land of Israel and the Hebrew language are not "national treasures," as the founders of Zionism assert in the manner of European nationalists. The neologism *moledet*, "motherland," represents for the anti-Zionists an imitation that undermines the very foundations of Judaism. The early Zionists naturally saw the Land of Israel as did the Russian romantics, with their earthy vision of Mother Russia. The dozens of Russian songs translated into Hebrew in the first decades of Zionist settlement were to instill the love of the *moledet* in the new arrivals. The "motherland" was so named because she would always welcome her prodigal sons, for whom her love was generous, unconditional and natural. The mother is the ultimate refuge, and, in fact, the State of Israel has often been presented as the Jews' ultimate guarantee of security. But this romantic image is quite foreign to Jewish tradition, though the Land of Israel is described once as "mother" in the Talmud: "The mother of a man degrades him while the wife of his father honors him: Where should he turn?" The story is about a rabbi badly treated in Israel but highly respected in Babylonia (*JT* Berakhot 2.8). Despite its ironic context, this reference is used in the Hebrew title, *Em Ha-banin semeha* (The mother of the children is happy), a passionate plea for the aliya composed during the Shoah (Teichtal, 33–36; 192–203). It pleads to "leave the land of exile and return to the bosom of the mother that is Eretz Israel" (Teichtal, 229). Jewish tradition did not take up this metaphor but left it anchored in its original context, which does not relate to settlement in the Land of Israel. "For us, Eretz Israel is not a homeland.... It is inconceivable that the simple possession of the Land of Israel might make of us a nation," stated Rabbi Wasserman (Sorasky, 224).

According to the Pentateuch, the Jews, or more precisely, the children of Israel, did not originate in the Land of Israel. They appear for the first

time as a people in exile, in Egypt. They were then granted recognition as
a people at Mount Sinai when they accepted the Torah, the act that distinguishes them from all other peoples. "Promised land" can thus be understood as not belonging to those who have received the promise, but to Him
who has given it. A classic commentary on the first verse of the Pentateuch
clearly illustrates the point: The Torah begins with the story of creation,
in affirmation that the entire world, including the Land of Israel, belongs
but to God Himself (Leviticus 25:23). Tradition defines the relationship to
the Land in explicitly conditional terms.

A portion of the prayer *Shema Israel*, which the Jews recite thrice daily,
is a good example of their conditional relationship to the Land:

> And it will come to pass that if you continually hearken to My
> commandments that I command you today, to love the Lord, your
> God, and to serve Him, with all your heart and with all your soul
> — then I will provide rain for your land in its proper time, the early
> and the late rains, that you may gather in your grain, your wine,
> and your oil. I will provide grass in your field for your cattle and
> you will eat and be satisfied. Beware lest your heart be seduced and
> you turn astray and serve gods of others and bow to them. Then
> the wrath of the Lord will blaze against you. He will restrain the
> heaven so there will be no rain and the ground will not yield its
> produce. And you will swiftly be banished from the goodly land
> which the Lord gives you. (*Complete ArtScroll Siddur*, 93)

The relationship has often been compared to that of a married couple: it
lasts as long as the spouses obey certain rules. Failing that, divorce ensues.
The term *moledet* eliminates the subtle sensitivity with which Jewish tradition relates to the Land of Israel.

Those familiar with the function of Hebrew as the vector of traditional
thought had begun to warn, as early as 1926, that "the Land is a volcano."
Some feared that the language, even secularized, would awaken among the
Israelis — unbeknownst to them — feelings deeply buried in Jewish tradition:

> [But] what will be the result of the updating of Hebrew? Will the
> abyss of the holy tongue which we have implanted in our children
> not yawn wide? People here do not realize what they are doing. They
> think they have made Hebrew into a secular language, that they
> have removed its apocalyptic sting. But that is not so.... Every word
> which is not simply made up but taken from the treasure house of
> well-worn terms is laden with explosives.... God will not remain
> dumb in the language in which He has adjured so many thousands
> of times to come back into our lives. (Ravitzky 1996, 3)

In truth, the explosive character of the language has been felt particularly among National Religious Jews, whose ardent messianic feelings are further stimulated by the use of Hebrew.

Notes

1. Observant Jews often refer to prominent rabbinic authorities by the title of their best known book, e.g., Hafetz Haim in lieu of Rabbi Kagan.
2. The neologism *galuti*, or *exilic*, reflects a disdain for life in the Diaspora, presented as a life with neither roots nor vigor; the term was introduced into Modern Hebrew by two nationalist authors: Itamar Ben-Avi, son of Eliezer Ben-Yehuda, and Uri Zvi Greenberg. It can be compared to the term "rootless cosmopolitan," introduced into Russian during the anti-Semitic persecutions that took place under Stalin and which also has a pejorative connotation, though more limited than the Hebrew neologism. Both terms reject and condemn cosmopolitanism.

Chapter 3

The Land of Israel: Exile and Return

> It is your iniquities that have diverted these things, your sins that
> have withheld the bounty from you… (Jeremiah 5:25)

Jewish tradition tends to interpret any calamity, even the most minor of accidents, as a consequence of the shortcomings in a Jew's behavior. The verse from Jeremiah quoted in the epigraph remains key to the Jewish tradition. The consequences become more serious still when the transgressions are committed in the Land of Israel. The normative, contractual relationship with the Land of Israel has an impact on the behavior of nearly all groups of religious Jews, whether supporters or adversaries of Zionism. The Jew's relationship with Israel thus becomes qualitatively different than a German's with Germany or a Russian's with Russia.

Between spiritual symbol and historic praxis in the relationship of Jews with the Land of Israel lies a gap, a cultural gap that can best be understood as a conceptual incompatibility difficult to bridge. Traditional Jewish culture discourages political and military activism of any variety, particularly in the Land of Israel. Those who do not (or no longer) share this cultural identity, see in this abdication of power, nothing but a "theoretical construct aimed at legitimizing this passivity by a very strong skepticism about any active intervention in the divine scheme of things" (Avineri 1981, 4). Pious Jews who remain loyal to the tradition of exile consider the abdication of political power to be as much a part of Judaism as is the prohibition of pork. Many religious Zionists, on the contrary, consider that a new "Torah of the Land of Israel" has taken precedence over the old tradition. This innovation sets them apart, and this difference is not lost even on secular Israelis, who occasionally come to appreciate the Haredim's apolitical tradition in comparison with the National Religious public they accuse of believing that "by getting the rabbis to join their cause, they would have God himself on their side. This custom of enlisting rabbis in political battles is unheard of in Judaism. Look at the Hasidic leaders and the rabbis of black-hat yeshivas. We haven't seen them plotting to turn the State of Israel into Khomeini-land" (Marcus).

The National Religious accord great importance to "the Jews' return to history" and take pride in the normalization of the Jews whom Zionism has freed from their "age-old passivity." But, contrary to Avineri's claim, what is at issue is not a transcendental principle of passivity, but one of resistance, often difficult and courageous, against the sense of national

solidarity, a feeling so natural that some Jewish thinkers have character-
ized it as "today's evil inclination number one." Two visions, each activist
in its own way, collide; and this collision explains many of the critiques of
Zionism formulated in the name of the Torah.

Zionism's opponents cannot bring themselves to admit that the Zionists
might truly love Israel. The Belz Rebbe, Issakhar Dov Rokeah (1854–1927),
relates a story to illustrate the point:

> One day, a man and his son paid a visit on the [previous] Rebbe.
> The son was preparing to make aliya to the Land of Israel. How
> did he intend to behave once there, asked the Rebbe. Where will he
> live? Will he observe the Sabbath and the other Jewish laws? The
> father replied that love for Israel had swept over his son. Do you
> speak of love for the Land of Israel? asked the Rebbe, indignantly.
> Go into my house of study and you will find assiduous youths who
> are exploring the Torah. In each of their hearts there is more love
> for Israel than among one thousand Zionists. Love for Israel is of
> no matter to the Zionists; they wish simply to free themselves from
> the yoke of the Torah and the mitzvahs: it suits them to act without
> any moral constraints. The Zionists go into the land of Israel, kick-
> ing out the Torah and committing forbidden acts. Is that what they
> mean by "love for the Land of Israel?" Love for the Land of Israel
> is tied up with love of God and love of the Torah. They cannot be
> kept apart. (Rosenberg, 386)

From the beginning, Zionism has encouraged love of the land, a love
that has taken political and ideological forms. The nature hikes that were
intended to impart an intimate knowledge of the terrain have been, since
the early years of the twentieth century, an integral part of the Zionist educational program. This intimate knowledge had near-sexual connotations:
the Hebrew term employed, *yediat ha-aretz*, alludes to the Biblical verses that
describe how man acquires carnal knowledge of woman. Love of the land
has provided fodder for more than a few psychological analyses (Gonen;
Rose). The normative relationship with the land that the mitzvahs imposed
upon the Jews who inhabited it gave way to a pseudo-sexual relationship
that transformed the land into a virgin longing for the arrival of the Zionists, who desire her and yearn to make her fruitful by shaking her out of
her age-old lethargy.

In political terms, this love was presented as knowledge of nature, but at
the same time, it effaced and in fact refused to recognize the Arab presence
in Palestine. In their enthusiasm, the Zionists would describe the flora and
fauna around them in minute detail, while ignoring the Arab villages and
their inhabitants. We have seen that the same selective vision was reflected
in archaeological research, itself central to the Zionist vision of love of the

land, that drew both professionals and amateurs, such as General Moshe
Dayan. During Israel's first decades, they sought to create virile, heroic
images of the Biblical era. Expressed in these terms, love of the land had
little to do with Jewish tradition, which sees it above all as a unique place
to live life according to the commandments of the Torah.

For Rehavam Zeevi (1926–2001), a general, ardent nationalist and
advocate of the deportation of all Arabs, the relationship with the land is
a mystic one: "this nation's homeland is this Land destined for us in the
depth of its experience [sic] as in the Bible" (Benvenisti). For the Zionists,
love of the land is possessive: it can tolerate no other claimant. The land
cannot truly be home to another people that had long inhabited it. They
tend to "nationalize" both physical and spiritual space, and to reserve it
exclusively for the Jews, with not the slightest relation to Judaic practices, a
fact deplored by traditional rabbis, who, like some secular Israeli observers,
see it as a form of idolatry.

> The cult of "Love of the Land," in which so many take part, is not
> — and never has been — innocent efforts meant only to provide
> aesthetic experiences, or a research field unto itself. It has always
> been a means for political enlistment and a propaganda agent for
> establishing and proving the claim of ownership over the redeemed
> Land of Israel. (Benvenisti)

Leading rabbinical authorities condemned the attempt to reconcile
Zionism with Jewish tradition by the Mizrahi movement, created a century
ago within the Russian Empire. In the early twentieth century, the principal
of the yeshiva of Slobodka, one of the empire's most prestigious, severely
reprimanded his students for attending a lecture promoting a synthesis
between Judaism and Zionism. He threatened to expel any student who associated with the Zionist movement and to revoke the rabbinical ordination
of any student who had already received it (Shapiro, 12).

Sounding a note of caution, Rabbi Rokeah declared that one should
be more vigilant toward the Mizrahis than toward the atheists (Rosenberg,
379). In his view, the secular Zionists openly profaned the Torah, while the
Mizrahis kept up the appearances of religious practice. Like the Lubavitch
Rebbe, he compared the Mizrahis with the pig, which possesses certain signs
of kosher animals and often displays them as if to mislead the innocent.
According to Rokeah, this "hypocrisy" explains the particular repugnance
of the Jews for swine, more than the hare or the camel, both of which are
equally prohibited in Jewish Law.

In the same vein, several rabbis emphasize that the problem is not that
non-practicing Jews founded the Zionist movement. It would have been far
worse had it been created by rabbis and Torah scholars, for it is the Zionist idea that is totally false. Haim Shaul Dawik (1861–1932), a Sephardic

cabbalist of Jerusalem, considered observant Zionists hypocrites capable of leading more Jews into error than could the secular Zionists, while Hafetz Haim compared them to armed bandits (secular Zionists were, for him, unarmed bandits) (Rosenberg, 505). This school of thought clearly rejects Zionism for intrinsic reasons totally unrelated to the status of religion in the Zionist enterprise. Rabbi Rokeah made it a point of principle to refuse to sit at a Sabbath table with a relative who had become rabbi of a Zionist organization: "Had he come dressed in a modern suit, I would not have done it," he explained. "But since he came in Hasidic dress, with his beard and his *peyes*, I did not want people to think that Haredim will have anything to do with Mizrahis" (Rosenberg, 375–76). Rokeah was expressing an idea current in Jewish traditional circles at the time: Zionism posed a mortal threat to the Jewish soul, and war against Zionism had become a vital necessity (Rosenberg, 480).

Transgression and Exile

Traditionally, the Land of Israel is considered more fragile, more sensitive, than any other. The transgressions of Jews in other lands might have no serious repercussions, but in Israel they would cause a major calamity. The responsibility that accompanies living upon the land lends any attempt to settle it enormous potential consequences. For the historian Yosef Haim Yerushalmi, tradition prescribes that:

> In the interval between destruction and redemption the primary Jewish task was to respond finally and fully to the biblical challenge of becoming a holy people. And for them that meant the study and fulfillment of the written and oral law, the establishment of a Jewish society based fully on its precepts and ideals, and, where the future was concerned, trust, patience, and prayer. (Yerushalmi, 24)

This traditional vision must be seen in the context of a broader attempt to "normalize the Jewish people." The Jews would simply live their lives with no further obligation to obey the commandments of the Torah and with no concern for the impact of their behavior on others. The liberation of the Jew — the essence of the Zionist dream — was, in fact, diametrically opposed to Jewish tradition.

In the traditional view, settlement in the Land of Israel will be brought about by the universal effect of good deeds rather than by military force or diplomacy. It will follow the advent of the Messiah, unlike the biblical conquest under Joshua, which was achieved by the use of power. And since it will be the work of God, it will be final and permanent. To better grasp this vision of the future, which has been a part of Jewish tradition for centuries, we must first sketch out the history — and the normative outlines — of

Jewish settlement in the Land of Israel, and of the departure of the Jews as presented by Jewish tradition.

The logic of the anti-Zionists is simple enough:

> We did not go into Galut because we did not possess a *Hagganah* [pre-1948 Zionist militia] and because we had no political leaders of the Herzl and Ben-Gurion type to guide us along the same paths. But we are exiled just because we did possess them and did follow their lead. And certainly Jewish Salvation will not come through such agencies. (Domb, 20)

Hafetz Haim, one of the leaders of Lithuanian Judaism, reminds us of the causes of exile, invoking the written Torah: "And the heathen shall know that the House of Israel went into captivity for their iniquity: because they trespassed against me, therefore I hid my face from them, and gave them into the hand of their enemies, so fell they all by the sword. According to their uncleanness and according to their transgressions have I done unto them, and hid my face from them" (Ezekiel 39:23–24). Hafetz Haim points to the grave danger of living upon the land while setting aside the Torah and the mitzvahs; he compares the Land of Israel to a royal palace where the slightest transgression takes on enormous proportions. The fear of violating the Torah commandments in the Holy Land is another of the substantive reasons that was to dissuade simple Jews, those more likely to sin, from settling in Israel before the advent of the Messiah.

Far more than a recurring argument used by the Jewish critics of Zionism, the destruction of the two Temples of Jerusalem lies at the core of their narrative. The secular make ample use of it as well. For example, a play entitled *The Pains of the Messiah*, staged at the end of the twentieth century, presented the zealots of the first century in the uniforms of the IDF and abounded in parallels between the confrontational spirit of the zealots and that of today's settlers. The latter could hardly have missed the point: young settlers from the Occupied Territories protested in front of the main entrance to the Jerusalem Theater, handing out leaflets denouncing the production.

Haredi rabbis, who would never set foot in a theater, came to the same conclusions:

> These Zionists claim to be the proud descendants of the infamous hoodlums who were responsible for the genocide of the Jewish people and the time of the First Temple. The prophet Jeremiah pleaded with them to lay down their arms in the face of insurmountable odds and certain defeat and surrender the city to Nebuchadnezzar, King of Babylon. Jeremiah proclaimed it was the will of God that the city of Jerusalem and the Holy Temple be destroyed as punish-

ment for their sins and if the "people of Israel" accepted this decree then their lives would be spared. Jeremiah was labelled a traitor by these hoodlums and as a result not only was the Temple destroyed, but almost the entire population slaughtered....

These Zionists also claim to be the proud descendants of the infamous hoodlums who were responsible for the destruction of the Second Temple. Rabbi Yohanan Ben Zakkai, leader of the Jewish people, called upon them to lay down their arms and surrender to the Romans. They refused and brought upon the Jews the calamity of the destruction of the Second Temple and the exile which followed. (Blau, A., 2–3)

The Zionist narrative also resorts to using history for its own ends, appropriating the Maccabees or Bar Kokhba, whom they transform into romantic resistance fighters against the foreign invader. The Zionist use of history is at the same time a rejection of the rabbinical interpretations, which remain the focal point of Torah anti-Zionism. The Zionist moral of the story is also opposed to the Jewish tradition: the Jews should have fought harder and better. The Zionists found inspiration in the "dizzying pretension that they could build a bridge as long as exile itself, between the hired killers of Masada and the soldiers of the IDF" (Barnavi, 219). From the Zionist perspective, which reproduced European nationalist values in often-violent terms (see Masada website), it was far better to seek honorable death in battle, if not an act of collective suicide such as Masada or Gamla, than to compromise with the invader. It should be remembered, though, that Jewish Law allows Jews to expose themselves to mortal danger in only three situations: if they are required, under threat of death, to practice idolatry, kill another human being or engage in sexual relations forbidden by the Torah.

"How much Jewish blood must be spilled in order for them to maintain their goal of a so-called 'Jewish State'?" indignantly asks Rabbi Blau of Neturei Karta. "Our fears are therefore at the height whenever the Zionist state is engaged in warfare. Convinced as we are of its eventual dissolution, we can only pray that its inhabitants may be spared suffering now and then" (Marmorstein, 4–5). In reiterating their unconditional submission to God, to the "King of Kings," the traditionalist rabbis confirmed: "...our concern for the honor of our King makes us more and not less sensitive to the fate of victims of the rebellion in the very precincts of the Royal Palace" (Marmorstein, 6).

Thus was opened a deep rift between the historical sensibility of the Jewish tradition and that of political Zionism, born of European romantic nationalism. It should come as no surprise that the anti-Zionist rabbinical authorities attempted, in the 1920s and 1930s, to conclude separate agreements with the Arab leadership. Later, during the bitter fighting that took place in Jerusalem following the declaration of independence by Ben-Gurion in May 1948, they organized demonstrations under white flags. The Zionists considered their "treacherous" behavior to be a vestige of exile. They were certainly right, insofar as exile has remained central to the Judaic sensibility and tradition.

Twenty-five centuries earlier, only a minority of the Jews of Babylonia had returned to the Land of Israel with Ezra and Nehemiah, there to establish limited political sovereignty after the destruction of the First Temple. The destruction of the Second Temple, which took place five centuries later, reinforced the exile-bound mentality among the Jews. For the Jewish people had experienced only sporadic episodes of what the Israeli historian Boaz Evron defines as "political crystallization": the Hasmonean Kingdom, the Khazar Khanate and the Jewish principalities of Yemen and Morocco (largely based on conversion) (Leibowitz, 128–29). The extreme marginality of the Jewish people to the political history of the world contrasts sharply with its centrality to the world's religious and spiritual development.

With respect to the state, Jewish tradition is lukewarm at best: God, should He wish to do so, can destroy it or banish its inhabitants from its territory without annihilating them or bringing their history to an end. It is a commonplace that the history of the Jewish people transcends any state framework. Or, as Leibowitz puts it:

> The historical Jewish people, despite all its contradictions and despite all the divisions that arose within it, never considered the state apparatus — that is, the force of organized power under which the people live — as one of the constitutive elements of its national essence. The same holds true with regard to the land. Contrary to what is claimed in our Declaration of Independence: "The Jewish people has emerged in the Land of Israel," eighty or one hundred generations have kept, rooted in their consciousness, the memory of the fact that a people — which already existed — had invaded the land of Canaan and had made of it the Land of Israel.... In its historical consciousness, the people existed outside all territorial attachments. It remembered — and was reminded — that it had been a stranger in the land of Egypt.... Later it was to become independent, not in a State, but in a desert, something without defined borders.... The historical image is clear: it is the people who have created the State, and not the State, nor the land, which has created the people.... It is thus quite clear, with respect to the Jewish people, that it was not a state apparatus, nor a framework for the wielding of power, nor a given territory, not even a language that brought it into being and kept it in existence. Its national identity is incarnated in one specific, immanent element — Judaism. (Leibowitz, 95–96)

He goes on to stress that the prophets who threatened the state with destruction would not have done so had it meant the disappearance of the people.

Reservations about the state are an integral part of Jewish tradition. Even many of the rabbis who accept or tolerate the State of Israel often warn that its existence as a state is not guaranteed in perpetuity, and for this reason, the State of Israel cannot presume to ensure the protection of the Jewish people for all eternity (Ben Hayim).

Zionism, on the other hand, underscores the importance of the state as a national value, the center, the very essence of the people. The sharp disparity in worldview colors all discussion of Zionism and criticism of it.

The destruction of the Temple and exile from the Land of Israel can be seen as less radical breaks than the emergence of a secular Jewish identity in the nineteenth century. "Most surprising of all is the fact that the destruction of the Temple, the loss of independence and the subjugation to Rome had no effect upon the nature of the Jewish people, nor upon its national identity, nor upon its consciousness of itself, nor upon the Jewish religious way of life (to the extent that it did not depend on Temple services)" (Leibowitz, 113). Even though Zionism and the State of Israel appear to hold out the promise of safe haven after two thousand years of exile, the critics of Zionism assert that they have instead provided a last refuge and a uniquely propitious environment for a secular Jewish identity. The creation of the State of Israel, they insist, by no means eliminates the condition of exile.

Messianic Caution

Jewish tradition postulates that salvation can only come about through messianic intervention. But the same tradition is extremely cautious with regard to the form of such an intervention: warnings against "forcing the end," that is to say, attempting to hasten redemption, can be found in several classical sources, particularly in the *Midrash*. During the exodus, the children of Ephraim, who attempted to go out of Egypt before the appointed time, perished as a result of their haste (BT Sanhedrin, 92b). The wording of the daily prayer underlines both the time factor and confidence in an ultimate redemption: "Sound the great shofar for our freedom, raise the banner to gather our exiles and gather us together from the four corners of the earth. Blessed are You, the Lord, Who gathers in the dispersed of His people Israel" (*Complete ArtScroll Siddur*, 107). The call for liberation could come from God alone, and only He could bring an end to exile.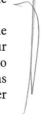

The Talmud (BT Ketubot, 111a) relates the three oaths sworn on the eve of the dispersal of what remained of the people of Israel to the four corners of the earth: not to return *en masse* and in an organized fashion to the Land of Israel; not to rebel against the nations; and that the nations do not subjugate Israel exceedingly. The oaths underlie the debate over the Judaic acceptability of the use of force (see next chapter). The Talmud does take up the right of individuals to settle in Israel, but there is a consensus against collective settlement. Several rabbinical sources through the centuries have interpreted these oaths to assert that even if all the nations were to encourage the Jews to settle in the Land of Israel, it would still be necessary to abstain from doing so, for fear of committing yet other sins and of being punished by an exile even crueler still. This interpretation stands at the heart of opposition to Zionism among many rabbis at the beginning of the twentieth century (Steinberg). The injunction against violating the oaths maintained its central position throughout the century, particularly in the thought of Rabbi Teitelbaum, head of the Satmar Hasidim and, more generally, standard-bearer of Haredi anti-Zionism. Any premature activism, according to this messianic logic, is to be proscribed:

> Even if the king of the Turks — may he be honored — or any rulers should permit the people of God to go up to their holy land, their patrimony, as was the previous redemption in the time of Ezra; if this redemption will not stem from the Great Redeemer Himself in His Glory… we shall say: This is not the path to the true salvation, or the long-desired goal. We shall not even consider it for temporal and incidental redemption, but only as a fly in the ointment. (Ravitzky 1996, 19)

Though the three oaths have been part of Jewish continuity, their relevance waxed as the possibility of settling in the Land of Israel increased and waned when that possibility receded. The oaths dampened any enthusiasm for a mass return to Israel, something that tradition considers illegitimate in any event. Even in critical circumstances, many pious Jews remained faithful to the three oaths. "Even though I might witness all the Jews leaving for the Holy Land, I would only go there if accompanied by the true Redeemer (*Goel tzedek haemeti*)" (Rosenberg, 356).

The concept of the "Land of Israel" may well rouse the enthusiasm of the masses, but it cannot be found in the Pentateuch, which refers only to the "Land of Canaan," "Land of the Amoreans" or "Land of the Hebrews" (Leibowitz, 161). Moreover, the borders of Israel, in these sources, vary substantially. The idea of return to the Land of Israel achieved by political means is alien to the idea of salvation in Jewish tradition. As Leibowitz puts it:

> Not a single program, or even the idea of a Jewish government of any kind in the Land of Israel could be found "in our times" [the pre-messianic period]. Needless to say, no attempt at restoration had been made [while] the intellectual and sentimental attachment to the Land of Israel — whether real or imaginary — persisted with

vigor. Midrashic literature and other later sources contain strong expressions of these feelings of affection, of esteem, of admiration — sometimes excessive — of its particular significance with respect to the Torah and to faith. Religious value is granted to the fact of living there, as opposed to existence in the land of exile. Nonetheless, all this remains part of the realm of consciousness, of feeling, and of literature, without ever being given concrete form in reality. Over these many generations, these feelings, and these words never materialized, no one single flare-up of mass migration took place, even during those periods when such a thing would have been possible. When the Land of Israel and Babylonia belonged to the same political world, that of the power of the Caliphs, only a few meager communities and Talmudic schools could be found there, while large population centers and major Torah institutions flourished in Babylonia. There was no immigration from there toward the Land of Israel, and it never occurred to the Jewish leadership to transfer the [Talmudic] academies of Surah and Pumbedita to Jerusalem (they would be later moved to Baghdad). (Leibowitz, 169)

So it was that the German pietists of the medieval period (*Hasidei Ashkenaz*) sounded the alarm against the aliya of the Jews who were then settling in the Land of Israel. Rather than expiating their sins, they were at risk of multiplying their transgressions. Other rabbinical authorities affirmed that whoever hastened to live in the Land of Israel before the final redemption would have no life at all (Ravitzky 1996, 24).

According to Leibowitz, the classical commentator Moshe Nahmanides (1194–1270) touched off a furor among his colleagues, the cabbalists of Gerona, when he settled in the Land of Israel a few years before his death. They insisted on the fullest application of the three Talmudic oaths and thus upon the injunction against settling there. "Nahmanides," Leibowitz argues, "is undoubtedly the only one of the masters to lend practical significance to the commandment to settle in the Land of Israel and to conquer it" (Leibowitz, 171). But his opinion on the matter apparently had no echo in the world of rabbinical legislation. A recent edition of the *Babylonian Talmud*, in response to the controversy that the question continues to generate, cites numerous sources that hold that settlement in the Land of Israel does not constitute a *mitzvah* (*Babylonian Talmud*, 110b1-2, note 15). It is usually assumed that the three oaths had acquired legal (*halakhic*) status toward the end of the Middle Ages. Rabbis Isaac Ben Sheshet Perfet of Barcelona (the Ribash, 1326–1408) and Salomon Ben Simon Duran of Algiers (the Rashbash, 1400–1467) invoked the three oaths to restrict the application of the commandment to inhabit the Land of Israel (Ravitzky 1996, 211–34). Though it might be argued that the three oaths are invoked more often when aliya emerges as a viable social option, Ravitzky demonstrates that their strict judicial application precedes by several centuries the rise of political Zionism and cannot be seen as an anti-Zionist innovation. A recent edition of the Talmud provides detailed references to the rabbinical prohibitions to transgress the three oaths (*Babylonian Talmud*, 111a2, note 13).

The three oaths are also invoked in warnings issued in fifteenth-century Spain, in the context of the Christian reconquest of the peninsula and of the expulsion of the Spanish Jews. There, the oaths had a particular resonance on the eve of the massive dispersal of the Sephardic Jews throughout the Ottoman Empire and the Mediterranean basin, as well as to England and the Low Countries. A small number of exiles from Spain did settle in the Land of Israel (then under the rule of the Ottoman Empire, which welcomed them generously). However, the attempt by Joseph Caro (1488–1575), author of the definitive code of Jewish Law, to restore the practice of rabbinical ordination that had existed at the time of the Temple of Jerusalem, met with little support from the rabbinical authorities of the day. The principal motive for their refusal was the fear of stirring messianic enthusiasm. A subsequent attempt by Don Joseph Nasi (1524–1579) to restore a collective Jewish presence in Galilee in the sixteenth century elicited no response from the Jewish world. The idea of restoring rabbinical ordination following the declaration of the State of Israel in 1948 was also quickly abandoned, for the same reasons.

Aware of the damage wrought by the movement led by the false messiah, Sabbatai Tzevi, Rabbi Jonathan Ebyeschütz (1690–1764), a renowned Talmudic scholar in Germany, condemned any attempt to hasten divine redemption:

> The congregation of Israel shouted out their vow — "Lest you arouse and awaken love" [Song of Songs 2:7] — against the ingathering of Israel. For even if the whole people of Israel is prepared to go to Jerusalem, and even if all the nations consent, nevertheless, it is absolutely forbidden to go there. Because the End is unknown, and perhaps this is the wrong time [Indeed,] tomorrow or the next day they may sin, and will yet again need to go into exile and be forced into exile, heaven forbid, and the latter [exile] will be harsher than the former. (Ravitzky 1996, 229)

In this perspective, the physical reconstruction of the land by the impious would lead the whole people of Israel into a cruel exile, one far crueler than the two that preceded it. This warning is often reiterated in contemporary anti-Zionist literature.

Despite his fierce opposition to certain of Ebyeschütz's positions, the German Rabbi Jacob Emden (1697–1776), an authority whose impact is still felt in Judaic jurisprudence, also refers to the three oaths as he formulates his reproaches toward Sabbatai Tzevi's messianic movement. Emphasizing that the times were those of grace and that redemption was indeed close at hand, he accused the false messiah of having attempted to hasten the process and in doing so, of bringing upon the Jewish people a great tragedy. Indeed, the oaths are even invoked in the writings of those such as Rabbis Zvi Hirsch Kalischer (1795–1874) and Yehuda Alkalai, whom the Zionists consider their spiritual forerunners. These authors lend their support to the settlement of the Holy Land but draw a distinction between it and the mass activism that the oaths are meant to restrain.

Sephardic rabbis were just as adamant as their Ashkenazi counterparts in their rejection of all attempts to speed the redemption. Hakham Yosef Haim (Ben Ish Hai) of Baghdad (1834–1909), considered to this day a major authority whose rulings are followed by many Sephardic Jews, makes an elaborate commentary on the fate of the tribe of Ephraim (see above), which, in a midrash on the story of exodus, brought disaster upon itself by attempting to hasten the redemption (*Yedei*, 47). In passing, he refers to the three oaths that forbid such activism.

There thus exists a solid consensus that the idea of a return to the Land of Israel brought about by political means is at variance with the vision of salvation found in Jewish tradition. Leibowitz, among others, considers erroneous "the fundamental thesis of Zionism, according to which the Jewish people is a people tied to a territory, that had been driven from it and for generations has aspired to return.... The singularity of the Jewish people is manifested in the length of its existence in exile over many centuries, that is to say, deprived of any territorial or political unity" (Leibowitz, 28, 41). The Jewish people's remembrance of the land has come to define it. In keeping with his sense of humor, Leibowitz notes that the Jews had never been "a people of the land," using the Hebrew expression *am ha-aretz*, meaning "ignoramus."

This vision, which might appear at first glance to be extreme, unrealistic, perhaps even anti-existential, is deeply rooted in tradition. Contrary to what we might believe, it was not formulated in reaction to the growth of political Zionism. Several decades before the first, halting steps of the Zionists, Rabbi Moshe Sofer (1762–1839) of Pressburg (Bratislava), one of the pillars of Jewish Orthodoxy in the nineteenth century, well known by his book, *Hatam Sofer*, states that it is preferable for the people of Israel to suffer a lengthy exile, the better to achieve final salvation (Ravitzky 1996, 2). From this point of view, messianic hopes must be kept alive, free from all compromise, until the arrival of the Messiah himself, the redeemer of Israel.

The messianic consonance of the return to Zion makes any Zionist, or even "proto-Zionist," attempt suspect of messianism, Sabbateism and the like. From its earliest days, the Russian movement, Hibbat Tzion, faced near-unanimous rejection by the rabbinical authorities. Rabbi Joseph Baer Soloveitchik (1820–1892) of Brisk (Brest-Litovsk) designated it in 1889 a "a new sect like that of Sabbatai Tzevi, may the names of evil-doers rot" (Ravitzky 1996, 13). His son Haim, one of the greatest masters of Talmudic studies, was even more forthright. Eight years after the condemnation of Hibbat Tzion by his father, he lashed out at the Zionist movement, which was gaining strength in Russia:

> Regarding the "Zionist sect," which has now banded and united together by force.... Have they not a bad reputation in their own places, and is not their purpose to uproot the fundaments of [our] religion — and to this end to take control of all the Jewish communities.... The people of Israel should take care not to join a venture that threatens their souls, to destroy religion, and is a stumbling block to the House of Israel? (Ravitzky 1996, 13–14)

The reference to force is clear: it alludes to a commentary by Rashi (Rabbi Solomon, son of Isaac [1040–1105], a classic of Jewish exegesis) on one of the oaths registered in the Talmud, "Do not go up [immigrate to Israel] together by force!" (BT Ketubot 111a).

Avineri describes the relationship between the Jews and the Land of Israel as paradoxical. While emphasizing its crucial function as a component of Jewish identity, he admits that never in pre-Zionist history did the Jews ever make the slightest effort to settle there *en masse*:

> The fact remains that for all of its emotional, cultural, and religious intensity, this link with Palestine did not change the praxis of Jewish life in the Diaspora: Jews might pray three times a day for the deliverance that would transform the world and transport them to Jerusalem, but they did not emigrate there; they could annually mourn the destruction of the Temple on *Tishah be-Av* [ninth of the month of Av according to the Jewish calendar] and leave a brick over their door panel bare as a constant reminder of the desolation of Zion, but they did not move there. (Avineri 1981, 3)

I recall celebrating a Jewish festival with a friend in Boston in the 1970s. In the afternoon, we joined a group of Hasidim, who, in a public park, were dancing and singing with radiant joy and confidence: "Next year in Jerusalem!" "But all they have to do is buy an airline ticket, and there they are!" exclaimed my friend, now a professor at Berkeley. The behavior of the Hasidim might well appear curious to an observer unacquainted with Jewish tradition. My friend was interpreting the desire articulated by the Jews for two millennia as formalistic ritual, or worse, as hypocrisy. But he did not realize that it is improper to interpret literally the Jews' prayer for the return to Jerusalem; what they are seeking is messianic perfection, the advent of a better world, which would encompass, among other things, the return — wrought by God — of the people of Israel to the Land of Israel.

This faith in redemption, which today may appear fatalistic, had become one of the essential characteristics of Jewish life in pre-messianic times, alongside those of obedience to Jewish law and to the law of the land in which they lived. The Jewish tradition had formulated the strategy of return to the promised land through the agency of spiritual effort, in order to do so in peace. Many threads of tradition warn against any worldly effort, which might delay redemption and bring down unprecedented calamities upon the Jews. The military conquest of the Holy Land and the ingathering of the Jews there constitute, from this perspective, an act of blasphemy, a usurpation of the divine prerogative, which undermines the Covenant of the children of Israel with God. It is therefore hardly surprising that rejection of Zionism can assume apocalyptic dimensions.

Tradition portrays the Messiah as relatively powerless, lest the people take him for the true source of their salvation and forget that God has assigned him his mission. Comparison is often made with Moses, the only person whom the Pentateuch describes as humble. Tradition stipulates that the Messiah must make his arrival astride an ass, a modest form of transportation if ever there was one, the better to point up his humility before God, He who must accomplish the ultimate redemption. Another interpretation (BT Sanhedrin 98a) suggests that if the people of Israel is worthy, the Messiah will arrive "with the clouds of heaven" (Daniel 7:13); if not, he will be "lowly, riding upon an ass" (Zechariah 9:9).

In his commentary on Zionist religious activism, Rabbi Moshe Sober, a National Religious rabbi and one of the translators of the Talmud into English, lashes out at the usurpation of divine will that he has encountered in National Religious circles, where the Judaic concept of providence is employed to justify any Israeli action:

> The notion that we can do whatever we please, succumb to any kind of temptation, or engage in any form of foolish self-aggrandizement without fear of penalty because we have an inside track to the Almighty is the plain opposite of religious faith. It is in fact an affront to the Divine, whose authority to determine the course of history we are usurping. The traditional penalty for this sin is to be sent to face a hostile world with no lucky breaks, no Divine assistance whatsoever, until we learn that only those who are performing God's will can count on Him for assistance. Such blind faith is not really a faith in God at all, but rather faith in ourselves. It makes a tool out of the Almighty. It turns him into a kind of "secret weapon" whose purpose is to guarantee our success at whatever we fancy. It is an idolatrous concept that masks what is actually an irrational belief in our own invincibility. (Sober, 30–31)

His warning comes as a reaction to the increasing tendency to "recruit God" for military ends, particularly among the Jewish settlers in the West Bank, who continue, in spite of the evacuation from Gaza, to remain defiant and to seek to expand Jewish settlements in the name of their version of Judaism, ignoring the three oaths that enjoin patience upon the Jews.

A classic case of lack of patience leading to violation of the oaths is the revolt of Bar Kokhba, whose history is often evoked to warn against the dangers of Zionism. The revolt against the Roman invader lasted three years, from 132 to 135, and its leader was proclaimed Messiah by one of the great rabbis of the era, Rabbi Akiva (50–135). The uprising, which had awakened the highest hopes, ended in unprecedented tragedy. Like the destruction of the First Temple and the Babylonian captivity, the destruction of the Second Temple at first appeared to have had a merciful outcome. Just as the Emperor Xerxes had ordered it to be rebuilt less than a century after the captivity in Babylonia had begun, the Roman Emperor Hadrian granted permission to the Jews to rebuild the temple. When the imperial decision was revoked some years later, certain Jews gave way to indignation and called for revolt. The rabbinical authorities were able to calm the hotheads, but they could not entirely control the situation. Isolated attacks on Roman military units began in 123. Hadrian turned against Judaic practice, allowed by his predecessor, and caused a temple to Jupiter to be built upon Temple Mount. Tensions remained high, but the emperor's presence in the region dampened hostilities. Only in 132, when he departed Palestine, did revolt break out in earnest.

Enthusiasm soared; much of the Land of Israel quickly fell under the control of Bar Kokhba, who issued new currency bearing Judaic symbols and the legend "Freedom for Israel." But, having attested to the "pitiless nature" of Bar Kokhba, the rabbis abandoned him. They did so in full recognition of the danger of annihilation that hung over the city of Betar, because the false messiah "represented a graver danger for the Jewish people" than did any military defeat. In the interim, the Roman army received massive reinforcements from other provinces of the empire and set about crushing the revolt. The final battle at Betar gave the *coup de grace* to the rebels' attempt to gain independence. The punishment and exile that ensued were far harsher than those that followed the destruction of the Temple several decades earlier, a detail that recurs frequently in contemporary religious critiques of Zionism. As a result of intensified oppression by the Roman authorities, itself a reaction to the revolt of Bar Kokhba, Rabbi Akiva, among many Judaic scholars, met a cruel death, the land was laid waste, and the center of Jewish life definitively transplanted to the Diaspora.

Jewish tradition has drawn from these events an unequivocal lesson: the revolt led by the false messiah was a revolt against God and his decrees; as such it brought consequences both grave and inevitable. "The kingdom of [Bar Kokhba] was, after all, ruled by the Torah... and his contemporaries were all saints.... Yet see how grievously they were punished, heaven spare us the like, for [their actions in rebelling against Rome] amounted to a forcing of the End before the appointed time" (Ravitzky 1996, 69). The story thus functions as a cautionary tale to all those who might be tempted to ignore the three oaths and attempt to hasten redemption.

Ironically, the very same story was to provide inspiration for the Zionists, right-wing Zionists in particular, who sought revenge through military means and strove to restore national freedom. Overturning tradition, Jabotinsky and his allies gave the name Betar to their youth movement, and later to a soccer team, and to a settlement established in the West Bank after 1967.

The Torah and Jewish tradition have often been used to justify Zionist claims to the Land of Israel. Some go so far as to compare the frequency of references to Jerusalem in the Torah and in the Koran. Others invoke Judaic ritual, the daily prayers and grace said after meals in an attempt to demonstrate that for centuries the Jews have dreamed of the return to Jerusalem. But the critics of Zionism detect a deliberately falsified reading of tradition: every reference to the return is an appeal to God to bring back the exiles, rather than a call to Jews to wilfully appropriate the land. The text of the prayer that every practicing Jew recites three times daily contains several relevant references: "Blessed are You, the Lord, Who gathers in the dispersed of His people Israel. Restore our judges as in earliest times and our counsellors as at first" (*Complete ArtScroll Siddur*, 107). Grace said after meals contains powerful and apparently fitting passages on the return to the land. On the Sabbath and the holidays, recitation begins with Psalm 126, which conveys the feelings of the exiled:

> When the Lord will return the captivity of Zion, we will be like dreamers. Then our mouth will be filled with laughter and our tongue with glad song. Then they will declare among the nations, the Lord has done greatly with these, the Lord has done greatly with us, we were gladdened. O, Lord — return our captivity like springs in the desert. (*Complete ArtScroll Siddur*, 183)

Having praised God for nourishing his creatures, the text turns to supplication:

> Have mercy, the Lord, our God, on Israel, Your people; on Jerusalem, Your city, on Zion, the resting place of your Glory; on the monarchy of the house of David, Your anointed; and on the great and holy House upon which your name is called. Our God, our Father — tend us, nourish us, sustain us, support us, relieve us; Lord, our God, grant us speedy relief from all our troubles. Please, make us not needful — Lord, our God — of the gifts of human

hands nor of their loans, but only of Your hand that is full, open, holy, and generous, that we not feel inner shame nor be humiliated for ever and ever. (*Complete ArtScroll Siddur*, 189)

The graces culminate in an ardent appeal: "Rebuild Jerusalem, the Holy City, soon in our days. Blessed are You, the Lord, Who rebuilds Jerusalem in His mercy." (*Complete ArtScroll Siddur*, 191)

While the Zionists add up the number of times Jerusalem is mentioned in an attempt to legitimize Israeli control over the holy city, the followers of the Jewish tradition see in these words an expression of messianic hope, the abdication of all pretense to terrestrial power and an appeal for compassionate mercy. Salvation is to be expected only from God, and never from "flesh-and-blood beings." To interpret the texts as a call for a war of national liberation would seem to do violence to their explicit content. The Zionists' claim has been repudiated by several Haredi authors, who deplore distortion and instrumentalization of the meaning of the daily prayers in the interests of a political cause.

The adversaries of Zionism often experience a sense of revulsion at the way Israeli elites use the Torah and the concept of the promised land. But they are not alone in their revulsion. Leading academic observers have noted that reference to Judaic concepts is by no means indicative of a commitment to Judaism or loyalty to the Torah:

> A key institution of Judaism, the Sabbath, is praised by a secular thinker in these words: "More than Israel has kept [the verb *shamar* in Hebrew means 'keep,' 'preserve' and 'practice'] the Sabbath, the Sabbath has kept Israel." That is, the Sabbath is treated as instrumental, Israel the secular group as principal. But in Judaism, the Sabbath is a holy day, sanctified by Israel, the holy people, and not a means for some ethnic goal of self-preservation. (Neusner, 4)

The philosopher Leibowitz becomes more indignant still at the nationalist instrumentalization of Judaism:

> But there is worse, a sort of disqualification at once religious and moral, a spiritual corruption at the hands of lies and hypocrisy that borders on blasphemy, in the fact that a people could make use of the Torah to strengthen its national pretensions, while the majority of its members, as well as the social and political regime that it has adopted, have no connection with religious faith, and see in it nothing but legends and superstitions. This is a kind of prostitution of the values of Judaism, which amounts to using these values as a cover for the satisfaction of its patriotic urges and interests. And if there exist Jews willing to join the national-occupationist trend,

and go so far as to make a "Greater Israel"... the essential element of their faith, a religious commandment, well then, these people have become the heirs of worshippers of the golden calf who also proclaimed: "Behold your God, O Israel." The golden calf need not necessarily be made of gold. It may also be called "nation," "land," "State." (Leibowitz, 176)

The appropriation of Judaic concepts for secular ends — and thus at odds with Judaism — has nonetheless proved quite effective. It successfully attracted the Jewish masses of Russia to Zionism, the most popular Jewish movement in the heady days of the Russian Revolution. Similar political use of Judaic concepts was later to prove effective in attracting Jewish immigrants from the Arab countries, who, unfamiliar with intra-Jewish ideological conflicts, could not easily distinguish between Zionism and Judaism.

The Zionist Idea

In its negation of traditional Judaism, the Zionist outlook is often seen as a clean break with Jewish messianic yearning. It is also sometimes associated with "messianic activism," reminiscent of an entire history of false messiahs (Ravitzky 1996, 79–144; Rose, 1–57). Theodor Herzl, in his visit to Jerusalem in 1898, personified this break and naturally enough unleashed a storm of criticism. Not only did he transgress the Sabbath but also ascended Temple Mount, formally forbidden to Jews by Jewish law. The Lubavitch Rebbe of the day condemned him categorically: "He desecrated the Torah and Mitzvahs in public. He entered the holy city of Jerusalem on Sabbath and he went to the Temple Mount. Even from a humanistic point of view he should not have done so. He violated the Sabbath in public in the holy city, and in the holiest place of God, whereby, he was just doing evil in the eyes of God. His purpose was to emphasize and flaunt their impure and corrupt ideology that Judaism is nationalism. The leader of the Zionists raised the idol of nationalism, which is a rebellion in [sic] God, and the disbelief in Torah and Mitzvahs, in above all places, the palace of God" (Schneerson, 19–24). His condemnation refers the reader to the books of the prophets, which relate several episodes in which the Temple was contaminated by idolatry, often at the direct command of Jewish kings.

The reaction to Zionism among the emancipated Jews of Central and Western Europe was predictable. Western Jews easily grasped to what extent the theories of the Zionists played into the hands of their worst enemies, the anti-Semites. Rabbis in Germany, France, Austria and Great Britain — those countries in which Jews enjoyed full civic rights — were virtually unanimous in their rejection of Zionism. In France, Zionism attracted primarily Jewish intellectuals of Russian origin, the same group that dominated the Zionist movement in Palestine and formed the avant-garde of Zionism in most countries. Despite the pronounced differences between the social acceptance of the Jews in Western and Eastern Europe, the opinions of the rabbis reflected a consensus, which can be more readily explained by the universality of the Jewish tradition than by the circumstances of their respective communities. The question raised by France's Grand Rabbin Zadoc Kahn in 1897, shortly after the first Zionist Congress has, a century later, lost nothing of its pertinence: "But none of its laws, neither civil, political or religious, is Jewish; why should the new state call itself Jewish?" (Abitbol 1989, 39).

The French rabbis were unanimous: Zionism was "narrow-minded and reactionary." They refused to recognize the Jews as a separate political nation. "We, the French Israelites, have a fatherland, and we intend to keep it" (Nicault, 21–22). Moreover, Herzl and his associates were seen primarily as "*Boches*," a disdainful French term for Germans popular in the early twentieth century. Identification with France and its national values was incontestably dominant, but it existed alongside a strong sense of communal solidarity in such matters as aid to the Jews of the Arab countries and Russia. On the other hand, "the Jews of France always took great pains to draw a distinction between their dislike of the nationalist [Jewish] ideology and their attachment to the Holy Land" (Abitbol 1989, 43).

In Germany, as we have already seen, opposition to Zionism was successful in uniting the various Jewish groups that had otherwise been in conflict. Orthodox and Reform Jews discovered, to their surprise, common ground from which to oppose a movement — Zionism — that could only undermine their situation in Germany. The question of dual loyalty was hotly debated in the Jewish press, which openly discussed the support Zionism provided for the worst forms of anti-Semitism. It was often underlined that the Zionists and the anti-Semites saw eye-to-eye on three key issues: 1) the Jews were not a religious group but a distinct nation; 2) the Jews could never integrate into the country in which they lived; and 3) the sole solution to the Jewish problem was for them to leave.

Though articulated before the formal emergence of the Zionist movement, the work of Rabbi Samson Raphael Hirsch has fuelled opposition to the principles of Zionism to the present day (Liberles; Rosenbloom). His analysis of the messianic project was shared by the German Jews, natural enough considering Hirsch's contribution to the consolidation of Orthodoxy in Germany, and by several Hasidic groups, even though they did not share his educational or social outlook (Hirsch, S.R., 461). Hirsch encouraged integration into the wider society, appreciation of German and, more generally, Western culture, while strengthening Orthodox Jewish discipline on the personal level. For Hirsch, Jewish nationalism could only be a transcendental idea, which did not depend on settlement in the Land of Israel and even less so on political sovereignty over it. The veritable return to Zion lay, for him, in the creation of circumstances that would allow the Jewish people to accomplish their true destiny: the life of Torah and mitzvahs. "The Torah does not exist for the state but the state for the Torah" (Zur, 111). In a Europe caught up in a web of conflicting nationalisms, Hirsch restated the classic concept: the Torah, and only the Torah, makes of the Jews a collective entity.

In a letter to the secretary of Rabbi Elhanan Spector of Lithuania, a major Torah authority of the late nineteenth century, Rabbi Hirsch clearly outlined his position on Jewish nationalism. He recounted how he had refused support, which Rabbi Kalischer was then seeking from him, to the Hibbat Tzion movement. The latter even accused Rabbi Hirsch of "delaying the redemption." "I was categorically opposed to Rabbi Kalischer of blessed memory on this issue. What they consider a great mitzvah, is in my eyes a not insignificant transgression" (*Shemesh Marpe*, 215). He further clarified his ideas in a commentary on the verse: "Moses commanded us a Torah, the inheritance of the congregation of Jacob" (Deuteronomy 33:4). For Hirsch, this inheritance consists of the Torah, and not of the land it promises. The teachings of the Torah constitute a national inheritance; land and power could only be the conditional attributes of this treasure.

As the Zionist movement consolidated itself, the opposition of the German rabbinical authorities became firm. The national organization of German rabbis condemned the Zionists, who were then preparing for their first Congress: "The efforts of the so-called Zionists to establish a Jewish national state in the Land of Israel… [are in conflict with] the messianic goals of Judaism, as these are expressed in the Scriptures and in other religious sources" (Ravitzky 1996, 14). In their concern for preserving the traditional, millennia-long relationship of the Jews to the Land of Israel, the German rabbis also wished to put to rest all suspicions about their loyalty to Germany. In their opposition to the nationalism and separation promoted by the Zionists, they often invoked the prophet Jeremiah; he had called upon the Jews to seek the well being of their country of residence and not to allow themselves to be excluded from the obligations that the country imposed. "We are required to accept the yoke of exile instead [of finding ourselves, at the end of days in] hell," warned a Hasidic commentator at the beginning of the twentieth century (Rosenberg, 361).

The secular nature of the settlement of Palestine led the few rabbis who supported or tolerated the enterprise to emphasize its purely practical, and non-messianic nature, rather than a pathway toward redemption. In fact, they were able to support it only because they did not foresee either the eventuality of the use of force or the possible linkage between the settlement of the Land of Israel and final redemption. In stark contrast with the Zionist messianism that reigns today in National Religious circles, the precursors of religious Zionism took explicit precautions against precisely such a turn of events. Rabbi Nephtali Zvi Yehuda Berlin (the Netziv, 1817–1893), an outstanding rabbinical figure and dean of the distinguished Volozhin Yeshiva in Russia, feared an adverse reaction from "the nations" if ever the Jews were to conflate messianic visions with politics. While he fully respected the intellectual stature of Rabbi Kalischer, the Netziv rejected his messianic expectations: "All of this [messianic] talk came to pass only because the Gaon [Kalischer] thought that the light of redemption had begun in his day; but in our own time, in which we are subjugated in Exile and subject to new edicts, we must not bring up any idea of redemption in connection with the settlement of the land" (Ravitzky 1996, 32–33).

Though it may seem surprising today, Rabbi Isaac Jacob Reines (1839–1915), founder of the Mizrahi movement, which is nowadays imbued with the spirit of imminent redemption, inveighed against confusing settlement with messianic expectations. Well aware of the rabbinical consensus that rejected the very idea of Zionism as heretical and dangerous, he affirmed that: "Zionist ideology is devoid of any trace of the idea of redemption.... In none of the Zionists' acts or aspirations is there the slightest allusion to future redemption" (Ravitzky 1996, 34). One could detect defensiveness in a joint declaration signed by Reines and other Zionist rabbis in 1900: "Anyone who thinks the Zionist idea is somehow associated with future redemption and the coming of the Messiah and who therefore regards it as undermining our holy faith is clearly in error" (Ravitzky 1996, 34). It is clear that to locate the Zionist enterprise in an eschatological perspective was unthinkable, even for its most ardent defenders. They insisted that it was nothing but a movement that sought to improve the collective welfare of the Jewish people.

In fact, one of the rare ideas shared by the earliest Zionist ideologues and the rabbinical majority was the negation of any messianic dimension in Zionism. The secular sought to distance themselves from Judaism and the expectation of the Messiah, of which they spoke with irony and condescension. "Israel has no Messiah, so set to work!" proclaimed the poet Brenner in 1910 (Ravitzky 1996, 35). One of the ideologues of Hibbat Tzion in Russia, Peretz Smolenskin (1842–1885) warned, in 1881: "If you strive to establish colonies in the Land of Israel, may you go from strength to strength!... But if your intention in doing so is to clear the way for the Messiah, you will be attacked by both the believers and the enlightened" (Ravitzky 1996, 36).

The messianic aspect of the Zionist project worried a broad range of rabbis as it did their German counterparts, for all their distance from the Hasidim, who, aside from their traditional Talmudic approach, had come to focus on the theological dimension and the deeper significance of events. The Hasidim made messianic redemption and the unique character of the people of Israel the central elements of their opposition to Zionism.

Contrary to other historians, Ravitzky asserts that the Hasidic critique draws on a deep-rooted tradition that antedates Zionism. In his view, resistance to Zionism reflects the thought of a long line of Hasidic rabbis. Drawing on this tradition, the fifth Lubavitch Rebbe, Shalom Dov Baer Schneerson,

began his frontal attacks on Zionism as early as 1899. At the core of his opposition lies the centrality of exile. Even were all the Zionists to turn pious
and their undertaking suddenly to become feasible, tradition would still
forbid any attempt to hasten redemption. It even prohibited praying too
vocally, for only God can decide upon the propitious moment.

It should come as no surprise, then, that tradition also rules out the use
of force to hasten deliverance. The quality of deliverance is yet another vital
consideration: it will be complete; it will entail no further enslavement. It
will be a redemption far superior to those brought by Moses and Aaron in
Egypt and by Hanania, Mishael and Azariah in Babylonia. Messianic expectations are formulated in such categorical terms that no human action
could possibly replace them. According to Rabbi Jacob Isaac Rabinowitz
of Biala (1847–1905), the Biala Rebbe:

> The Zionists likewise wish to join together and to unite against
> God and his Messiah. In fact, Israel have no greater foe and enemy,
> who wish to deprive them of their pure faith, that our salvation and
> redemption transcends the way of nature and human intelligence;
> that He, may He be blessed, watches over us with a sharp eye in our
> exile, and, "In all their afflictions he was afflicted" (Isaiah 63:9) so
> to speak. (Ravitzky 1996, 18)

The refusal to follow along behind the Zionists in reconstructing the
Land of Israel in association with the secularists is categorical:

> Heaven forbid that we walk in the way of these sinful people, who
> strive for natural redemption. This striving is forbidden.... The act
> of *teshuva* (repentance) alone is a legitimate means to hasten the End,
> but acts of ingathering [the exiles] and of bringing [Israel to their
> land] depend solely upon the hand of God. (Ravitzky 1996, 18)

Rabbi Isaac Yeruham Diskin (1839–1925), who presided over the
Jewish Law Commission established to deal with the exploitation of the
Land of Israel, in 1917 virulently denounced the Zionist movement,
which was then in the process of establishing its control over all the Jews
of Palestine:

> The eyes of all Jews behold that God has not chosen the Zionists
> to build upon His Land and to cultivate His inheritance. For it is
> incumbent neither upon us, nor upon them [the Zionists] to build
> the House of God. Moreover, it cannot be "built"; on the contrary,
> they [the Zionists] are actively destroying and demolishing, wreak-
> ing great damage, and conspiring against God the better to eradicate
> completely the religious foundations. Like the accuser can never

become the advocate, thus will the enemies of Zion never become
its admirers. (Rosenberg, 368)

Hasidic symbolism tends to downplay the centrality of physical Palestine in comparison with the Land of Israel as a spiritual concept. The
Rebbe and his court stand symbolically for the Land of Israel and Jerusalem
in the imagination of the Hasidim, who, in their rejection of modernity,
remain largely impermeable to Zionism. For these detractors, Zionism is
truly satanic: it had replaced the supernatural by the natural, the religious
by the secular, patience and trust in God by political and military activism.
Rejection of the Zionist experiment can be expressed in allegorical language
of great power. Rabbi Haim Elazar Shapira, the Munkacz Rebbe (1872–1937),
described in these words his visit to Palestine, during which he observed
the effects of the Zionist enterprise:

> When I journeyed to the Holy Land I said to the Adversary before
> embarking at Istanbul, "A berth costs a great deal of money.... You
> decide: either you go to the Holy Land and I stay here... or you
> stay here and I go alone to the Holy Land...." And he chose to
> stay there.... And I rejoiced in my voyage. But when I reached the
> Holy Land I immediately caught sight of the Adversary standing
> in the port, and I cried out in anguish, "What are you doing here?
> Did I not leave you in Istanbul with the understanding that you
> would stay there?" And he answered, saying, "you ask me what I
> am doing here? 'The fellow came here as an alien, and already he
> acts as the ruler' (Genesis 19:9, paraphrase). Why, this is my regular
> abode, and the one with whom you spoke in Istanbul was... just
> my overseas emissary." (Ravitzky 1998,41)

It is striking to note that the Munkacz Rebbe equates Zionism with
Satan, and reinterprets the biblical verse "The Lord rebukes thee, O adversary; even the Lord who has chosen Jerusalem rebukes thee" (Zechariah
3:2) to mean "The Lord rebukes thee, O adversary; the Lord rebukes thee
who has chosen Jerusalem." His absolute rejection of Zionism includes
just as absolute rejection of all those who collaborate with "this satanic
work." And, like other rabbis, he identifies Zionism as the gravest danger,
which, in creating the false impression that Jews who espouse Zionism may
remain Jews, runs the risk of turning Jewish masses away from the path of
the Torah.

The Munkacz Rebbe's conclusions reinforced the traditional view that
redemption would come not through natural means, but through miracles.
Drawing on a tradition under which only the just may inhabit the land of
Israel, he postulated that its material reconstruction would necessarily lead
to a spiritual decline and, ultimately, to destruction. This point of view, even

more frequently articulated in rabbinical circles after the Shoah, apparently reflects a constant in the interpretation of the relationship with the Land of Israel. The Zionists were accused of "defiling of the land by any form of material thing, stores, workshops, and factories!" (Ravitzky 1996, 173).

The Zionist Enterprise

Zionism being a movement of European origin, imitation of "the nations" becomes a recurring theme in Torah-based critiques of Zionism. The German Jews' sudden rediscovery of Zionism in the wake of the Nazi takeover of their country brought forth an outburst of bitter sarcasm from Rabbi Simon Schwab, who would later work to re-establish German Orthodoxy in Manhattan.

> Today the liberal Jew who once considered Stuttgart "his" Jerusalem subscribes to a Zionist sheet which preaches a different kind of assimilation: complete national equality with the other nations, in other words, just the same old assimilation, a sham solution which engenders arrogance and which, since in neither knows nor respects the will of God, does not interfere in any manner with our comfort. Zion, which has been erased from the prayer book, has now been restored to the emigration passport.... The grandchildren of those who once banished the remembrance of Jerusalem from their synagogues are now pressing in front of British consulates. (Schwab, 15)

In the face of the Nazi threat and the Zionists' enticements, Schwab calls on his fellow Jews to "return to the fatherland of Torah" (Schwab, 123).

Between the world wars, Hafetz Haim warned that, if Jewish leaders did not follow the counsels of tradition, they would gravely endanger the entire people of Israel. He reminded them that the rabbis of the Roman era studied the biblical story of Jacob's meeting with his brother Esau in an attempt to determine the proper way of approaching the imperial authorities:

> In our time, the Torah has been grossly dishonoured; people come to the Torah only regarding questions like the saying of the Kaddish. In political matters, that is, in matters affecting the whole people, reliance is not placed on the Torah-words; those who are entrusted with clarifying these issues are professional politicians and writers. These are the leaders of this generation. From which spring do they draw their political theories? From their own Torah: "Let us be like all the nations." They despise God's Torah. (Wasserman 1976, 26)

"If we do not preserve the Torah, neither the State nor the language will save us," Hafetz Haim wrote. "Has our blood been shed for eighteen centuries in order to catch up with Bulgaria?" he asked sarcastically (Rosenberg, 476). Bulgaria's accession to political independence in 1908, after centuries as part of the Ottoman Empire inspired many Zionists, particularly Eliezer Ben-Yehuda, the founder of modern Hebrew and a sworn opponent of Judaism (Kuzar; Ben-Yehuda). Rabbi Domb, a veteran of the anti-Zionist struggle, took up the theme in his book, *Transformation*:

> It manifestly is absurd to believe that we have been waiting for 2000 years in so much anguish, with such high hopes and with so many heart-felt prayers merely in order to finish up by playing the same role in the world as an Albania or a Honduras. Is it not the height of futility, to believe that all the streams of blood and tears, to which we ourselves can bear witness in our own time apart from the testimony of our ancestors, should have been fated to the acquisition of this kind of nationhood which the Rumanians [sic] or Czechs, for instance, have achieved to a *greater extent* of success without all these preparations? (Domb, 14–15)

By insisting that the return to the Holy Land can only be accomplished by divine will, Rabbi Wasserman, a disciple of Hafetz Haim, likewise pointed out that Jewish nationalism was certainly nothing new, but rather an imitation of the Balkan (which Rabbi Alkalai, who lived in the Balkans, knew well) or German (which surrounded Rabbi Kalischer in Prussia) models. Those familiar with European history would have had little need of Wasserman's warning note; it was directed to the majority of Jews, whose innocence and messianic faith could well, in his view, make them vulnerable to a Zionist propaganda, which often employed the traditional terminology of Judaism. There is nothing unusual about such usage. Italian nationalism drew its inspiration from Roman history; reference to ancient Greece was used to legitimize the formation of the modern Greek state.

Another of Wasserman's commentaries sought to clarify the aims of Zionism. First, he brought out the respect that the Torah accords to the non-Jew. He referred to thirty-six verses in which the Torah enjoins the Jews to treat with deference, and respect, all strangers, even the descendents of Haman, that sinister personage of the Book of Esther. On the other hand, the Torah is quite severe with regard to Jews who do not obey its commandments. "He is worse than the dog.... We see, therefore, that one's origin alone without Torah is valueless, so that the National idea is nothing but a modern idol..." (Wasserman 1976, 30). This condemnation of Zionism, formulated only a few years before the Shoah, aimed at the very nature of the Zionist enterprise.

The strategy for the return to the Land put forward by Hafetz Haim unfailingly resembles the general outline to be found in Ezekiel:

> For I will take you from among the nations, and gather you out of all countries, and will bring you into your own land. Then will I sprinkle clean water upon you, and you shall be clean: from all your uncleanness, and from your idols, will I cleanse you. A new heart also will I give you, and a new spirit will I put within you: and I will take away the stony heart out of your flesh, and I will give you a heart of flesh. And I will put my spirit within you, and cause you to follow my statutes, and you shall keep my judgments, and do them. And you shall dwell in the land that I gave your fathers; and you shall be my people, and I will be your God. (Ezekiel 36:24–28)

A moral transformation and a return to the proximity of God would be both the means and the objective of the return to the land. It is in these terms that the classical tradition of Judaism envisions the coming together of the Jews in the Holy Land. Hafetz Haim is simply reiterating this tradition, while stressing that the Zionist temptation is a trap that would prolong exile, rather than end it.

Hafetz Haim illustrated his point by quoting the Passover Haggadah, known to most Jews. The Passover meal includes songs praising divine providence and His generosity. The song "Dayenu" ("It would have been enough") proclaims: "Had He only given us the Torah, and not brought us into the Land of Israel, it would have been enough for us" (*Shalom Hartman Institute*, 103). Hafetz Haim points out that the Haggadah does not say "had He only brought us into the Land of Israel and not given us the Torah, it would have been enough for us." He concludes that, whatever efforts the Zionists might make, it would be impossible for the Jews to establish and sustain themselves in Israel without living by the Torah. His students have noted that it was their teacher who identified this basic impossibility, which explains the chronic violence surrounding the Zionist enterprise. "Without the Torah we cannot exist as Jews even decades, yet, we have existed without Eretz Israel for two thousand years" (Wasserman 1976, 33). This vision of Zionism as an obstacle on the path to redemption preceded by several decades the sense of impasse that now looms over Israel.

The great majority of rabbis (and, needless to say, secular Israelis) rejected the efforts of Rabbi Kook to present the Zionists as the "white ass" that will carry the Messiah into Jerusalem. Some underlined the dangers, both spiritual and physical, that they saw in the Zionist enterprise. In an article published in the course of debates over the fate of Palestine in the mid-1940s, one can read:

> Over Israel there have arisen Zionists who adopt gentile notions in an attempt to force the End, using a false note of worldly redemption through power and the kindness of the other nations.... They have come to the Holy Land and raised the flag of rebellion

against the kingdom of heaven.... They have connived by the most horrendous means to uproot our holy Torah, as well as all human morality.... They have become entangled with our Arab neighbors to the point where the Yishuv is being subjected to riots and Jewish blood is being shed, heaven forefend.... Our Holy Torah teaches that we should take no interest in the political realm while in exile, until the coming of the Messiah, may he come speedily and in our own day, and there is nothing in this position to antagonize our Arab neighbors. While in exile we wish only to live and to fill the commandments of our Creator, may his Name be blessed; and we have no interest in living in our Holy Land except to imbibe its holiness and to full the commandments, which can only be fulfilled here. (Ravitzky 1996, 62)

As Ravitzky notes, the concept of "exile in the Land of Israel," shared by many Haredi circles today, is not of rabbinical origin. It was introduced by one of the ideologues of the Haskalah, the Russian Jewish journalist Yehuda Leib Gordon, who advocated freeing Zionist settlement from any trace of Judaism, which for him was a heavier burden than the yoke of the nations. He warned his followers, that "the exile under Israel is more difficult for us than the exile under the nations of the world" (Ravitzky 1996, 150). It is curious that the term Israel — understood as the corpus of Judaic laws and customs — takes on, in his secularist vision, a thoroughly negative connotation.

Life in Israel has never been easy. The existence of the *yordim*, a term that became pejorative when applied to the Jews who have left Israel, confirms that the Diaspora has always represented a legitimate option for Jews. Avineri reminds us:

the Jewish Diaspora was created not only by the forceful expulsion of Jews from their country by Nebuchadnezzar, Titus and Hadrian; the flourishing Jewish communities in Alexandria and Babylon owed at least part of their origin to processes similar to those that led to the concentration of so many Israelis in certain areas of New York and Los Angeles. Now as then, life in Israel may be hard, the burden of maintaining a commonwealth is not easy; living in Exile frees one from many of these onerous burdens. (Avineri 1981, 226)

He readily concedes that life in the Diaspora is not to be disdained and that it has been recognized as an easier, more comfortable option for the Jews. He recognizes as well that the Diaspora offers models — cultural, social and economic — that Israeli society is increasingly eager to imitate. For Avineri, this reversal of the Zionist scheme means: "bringing Exile back to the Jewish State." For the critics of Zionism, it is above all a process that marks the end of the ideological illusions that have cost the inhabitants of the Holy Land so dearly.

At the same time, the number of ideologically motivated immigrants has remained modest throughout the history of Zionism.

> It is a remarkable fact that the "ingathering of the exiles" which Ben-Gurion has proclaimed, appears to have attracted *only* those Jews whose naïve minds rendered them an easy prey to their highly coloured tales, but somehow *failed* to elicit a response from those Jewries living in civilized countries such as Great Britain and the U.S.A. etc., to whom Zionism could not offer anything, in exchange for the material advantages which they already enjoyed in a *greater* and more *secure* form. (Domb, 17–18)

The immigration of nearly a million Soviet Jews at the end of the twentieth century confirms this diagnosis: they were fleeing political uncertainty and the privations brought about by the collapse of the Soviet system, while the State of Israel actively hindered other countries from accepting them.

But the secularizing impact of Zionism remains the gravest accusation formulated by its critics. Zionism, they say, has made it easy and natural to disregard Judaism. Some insist that the assimilation of Jews in Israel is profound and thus irreparable: for many secular Israelis, to be Jewish is a simple matter of speaking Hebrew and residing in Israel. These critics believe that Zionism, by appearing "Jewish," has undermined the foundations of Judaism even more effectively than the Haskalah before it (Domb, 7).

In tradition, exile had a therapeutic, even cathartic function. A parable attributed to Rabbi Joseph Haim Sonnenfeld (1848–1932), one of the pillars of anti-Zionist resistance in Palestine, exhibits the logic that lies beneath the yearning for messianic salvation. "There was a king's son, perfect in every quality, the only, beloved son of his father. One day, the son fell ill. The king immediately summoned the finest physicians to his son's bedside. Could it be that this brilliant son ask his father and the doctors to remove him from the hospital and take him home? Whatever their compassion, they would not allow him to leave until he was completely cured."

"This is what has happened to us," continues Sonnenfeld:

> The people of Israel find themselves in such a situation. God has exiled us on account of our sins, and exile is as a hospital for the Jewish people. It is inconceivable that we take control of our land before we are completely cured. God keeps us and protects us, and administers to us His "medicinal" trials in perfect measurement and dosage. We are certain that when we our completely healed

of our sins, God will not hesitate for a moment, and will deliver us Him self. How could we be in such haste to leave hospital in the face of mortal danger, a worldwide danger that hangs over our heads, God forbid? What we seek of deliverance is that our cure be complete; we seek not to return in ill health to the royal palace, God forefend. (Rosenberg, 441)

The passivity of which pious Jews are accused exists primarily in the eyes of those who are not familiar with their beliefs. Many of them must constantly call upon all their spiritual resources to ward off the temptation of nationalism. To reaffirm their trust in divine mercy, they strive to live Torah life, for Jewish tradition considers that each good deed has an effect on the entire world. Good deeds (as prescribed in the Torah) are all the more important in that every Jew is obliged to look upon the world as half guilty, half innocent. Each deed, no matter how minor, will be weighed on the balance of divine justice, for ultimate redemption. "It should not be thought that the inferiority of the nation of Israel among the nations, and its prostration in exile, can be attributed to ill fortune." Rather than seeing the history of the Jews as part of the fatalistic turnings of the wheel of history, tradition affirms that the "fate" of the Jews depends only upon heaven's assessment of their deeds (Rosenberg, 361). Against all stereotypes, the Judaic approach appears in this light as resolutely anti-fatalist.

From this perspective, religious Jews are active in the world, even if, from a political standpoint, the effect may remain invisible. But the Zionists, whose reading of Jewish history is modern and European, come to radically different conclusions. The Jews were exiled from their homeland in an historical accident; Zionism thus proposes to redress what it perceives as an historical injustice in historical, rather than religious terms. There lies the core of the conceptual conflict over Jewish return to the Land of Israel. For many pious Jews, Zionism appears as an obstacle to redemption of Israel. Rather than relying on "prayer and the plea for mercy," the Zionist pioneers resorted to physical labor and armed struggle.

Chapter 4

The Use of Force

> ...for it is not by strength that man prevails. (Samuel I 2:9)

Force, and its use, is no stranger to the Torah. The Pentateuch and several of the books of the prophets, such as Joshua and Judges, teem with violent images. Biblical Israel was conquered under conditions that could hardly be described as peaceful. But far from glorifying war, Jewish tradition identifies allegiance to God, and not military prowess, as the principal reason for the victories mentioned in the Bible. After the Romans' destruction of the Second Temple of Jerusalem, Jewish life underwent a metamorphosis, which included a principled rejection of the use of force. In theological terms, the loss of the Temple spelled the end of an entire decision-making system that had made military action legitimate. Viewed in the context of Judaism, the annihilation of Jerusalem has defined the normative Jewish attitude toward force, resistance and the Land of Israel ever since.

Codified Pacifism

Jewish tradition over the last two millennia can only be described as pacifist. Tradition interprets the Temple's destruction and the ensuing exile as divine punishment for transgressions committed by the Jews. This interpretation holds that the Temple was razed by the Romans because of gratuitous hatred among the Jews; the first exile to Babylonia because of illicit sex, murder and idolatry.

According to the Talmud, the Roman siege of Jerusalem in the first century divided the city's population. The scholars of the Law tended to favor negotiated compromise, while the zealots organized a forceful response. Following a logic that has changed little over the centuries, these rebels took their own camp hostage by burning the city's granaries, because the grain in them, according to the Talmud, would have allowed the city to survive for twenty-one years:

> The Rabbis said to the zealots: Let us go out and make peace with the Romans. The zealots would not let them do so; they said to the Rabbis: Let us go out and wage war against the Romans. The Rabbis said: It will not be successful. The zealots arose and burned down those storehouses of wheat, barley and wood, and there was famine in the city. (*BT* Gittin 56a)

Tradition also condemns the proponents of armed struggle. Instead, it praises a group that set itself apart from the defenders of the city. The Talmud, as well as several classical exegetes — such as the Italian Ovadia Seforno (1470–1550) — reproached the advocates of armed struggle in particularly severe terms: "If the Zealots had heeded Rabbi Yohanan Ben Zakkai, the Temple of Jerusalem would not be destroyed" (Seforno). Considering the central position held by the Temple in Judaism, the accusation was indeed serious. It has stood for centuries as a warning against any collective temptation to use force.

Seforno's commentary reveals an important viewpoint found in the oral Torah. The Mishna defines a strong man as someone who succeeds in controlling his own inclinations, passions and urges (*Pirke Avot*, 4:1). This definition reflects a worldview that places total confidence in Providence and disdains the use of physical force. For example, take the dominant attitude to iron, the instrument of murder *par excellence*. Iron tools would not be used to hew the stones of the Temple, because iron is seen as an instrument of war and murder. In many Jewish households, before reciting grace after the meal, the families remove all knives from the table, which the Jewish tradition associates with the altar of the Temple of Jerusalem. King David himself was never able to build the Temple because he had shed blood in the wars he fought, even though they were waged with God's sanction. This attitude to war was known even by Napoleon. When he issued a proclamation inviting the Jews to re-establish a Jewish State in Palestine at the end of the eighteenth century, he took pains to reassure the Jews that they would not have to conquer the promised land; they only had to keep it once it had been occupied by the French army.

The revulsion caused by war is clear and repeatedly stated. "God did not send us into exile because we had no army, but because we had sinned" (Blau, R., 249). The oral tradition interprets allegorically the Biblical verses that mention the instruments of war: the sword and the bow used by Jacob the Patriarch against his enemies (Genesis 48:22) become prayer and supplication (Bereshit Rabbah 97:6); the victory of Benaiah over Moab (2 Samuel 23:20) now stands for Torah study (BT Berakhot, 18b). Tradition locates Jewish heroism in the house of study, not on the battlefield.

The holiday of Purim, related in the Book of Esther, provides an ideal model for conflict resolution. The story is as simple as it is prophetic. Haman, the Persian vizier, has planned a total massacre: "to destroy, to kill, and to annihilate, all Jews, both young and old, little children and women, in one day" (Esther 3:13). The response of the Jews was to proclaim a fast of repentance, but at the same time to find a way to influence the king and thereby circumventing the vizier and his decree. Queen Esther intervened, revealed to the king her Jewish origins and convinced him to stop the planned genocide. "But it did not occur to any of the Jews to use physical means against Haman," noted Rabbi Elhanan Wasserman in his commentary on the history of Purim written at the end of the 1930s (*Jewish Guardian* 1977, 8–9). And the violence of the Jews against their enemies that occurs in the finale has been explicitly authorized by the king.

Still, the use of force cannot be separated from the story that lies at the heart of another holiday, Hanukkah, which also celebrates deliverance from a collective threat. The difference between the two threats to the Jewish people explains the differing relationship to force expressed in the stories. If Haman's threats of destruction induced the Jews to repent, King Antiochus, who had outlawed Judaic practice and forced the Jews into idolatry, sought their spiritual destruction. Under such a threat, concludes Wasserman, the use of force becomes legitimate: a Jew is duty-bound to sacrifice his life rather than worship idols. This history of the Maccabees is also used by those who wish to draw practical conclusions, all the while bypassing the traditional vision of the event:

> [F]or a Jew who reflects, Hanukkah is nothing more than the day of commemoration of the heroes of Jewish self-defence. No miracle fell from the sky.... But the sword had created one: a dead people had been resurrected. The Torah could not save the fist; it was the fist that saved the Torah. The sword, and not the skullcap, will protect the Jew in the blood-soaked lands of his enemies. (Rozenfeld)

Ironically, glorification of force reverses the significance of the holiday, which celebrates allegiance to the Torah against Hellenistic influence. What is the Judaic reference to Hanukkah? A passage from the daily prayer reveals its meaning:

> In the days of Mattisiahu, the son of Yochanan, the High Priest, the Hasmonean, and his sons — when the wicked Greek kingdom rose up against Your people Israel to make them forget Your Torah and compel them to stray form the statutes of Your Will — You in your great mercy stood up for them in the time of their distress. You took up their grievance, judged their claim, and avenged their wrong. You delivered the strong into the hands of the weak, the many into the hands of the few, the impure into the hands righteous, and the wanton into the hands of the diligent students of Your Torah. (*Complete ArtScroll Siddur*, 115)

The war that the advocates of the use of force were to invoke as a precedent for martial heroism turns out to have been, in Jewish ritual, a victory of God and not of humans. Tradition emphasizes that the decisive factors were loyalty to the Torah and moral purity, rather than the number of soldiers and the fighting strength of the army.

With regard to Hanukkah, the Talmud relegates the hostilities to a secondary position. It focuses instead on the miracle of the oil that burned for eight days in the Temple that the Maccabees had liberated and purified. Tradition links the purity of the oil untouched by the Hellenizers and the purity of heart all Jews must keep in order to fight idolatry.

Indeed, the frontal attack on the Torah had made the use of force possible. But ever since, the image of the Jew that has most inspired rabbinical resistance to Zionism has been presented in these terms:

> Condemned by God to exile but armed with their faith, the Jewish communities under the leadership of their rabbis never looked upon the land where they had settled as being definitively theirs. Over the centuries, the Jews had led a silent, religious life, observing the laws of the country where they resided. Praying for the well being and the prosperity of their non-Jewish neighbors at the same time as for their own,... their only wish, their only demand was to be left in peace to lead their lives according to the Law of the Torah. And when, for one reason or another, life became impossible and their departure was desired, they bowed their heads and departed. Such was the law of exile, and the Jews accepted it, until the advent of the Messiah and Final Redemption. (Blau, R., 277)

The secularized image of the Maccabees was to provide a prototype for several modern Jewish authors, including Jabotinsky, who used it to stimulate national pride among the Jews. The desire to acquire respectability by setting up a state "like all the nations" (Samuel I 8:5) explains the cult of the Maccabees so frequently encountered in Zionist circles. It goes without saying that the Zionist interpretation of the story of the Maccabees, and of the holiday of Hanukkah, raised the ire of many rabbinical authorities in Europe. These rabbis deplored the "neopaganism" that they saw in the secularization of Hanukkah and protested against the cult of force that accompanied it. While the Hanukkah blessing contained in the Sephardic prayer books does not refer to any war whatsoever, the Ashkenazi version does. This is the version that the Zionists interpreted, transforming the Maccabees into "the patriotic victors of war of national independence. It is a travesty of history," protests an anti-Zionist activist, who reminds us that the *casus belli* of the Maccabees was quite precisely the intention of the Hellenizers to "tear the people away from its Torah and to impede the people from following its commandments. However, the name of these champions of the struggle for Judaism is often used by its modern-day adversaries to designate athletic clubs" (Blau, R., 199).

Many European rabbis were well aware that "hearts and emotions are ruled by Hebrew culture, Judaic chauvinism and 'Maccabean' athletic trivia" (Schwab, 41). Even the looming Nazi threat did not blind them to the nature of the new Zionist society, which they continued to condemn.

A striking model for relations with the nations compares the Jew in exile with the sheep surrounded by seventy wolves. "In such a position, the wisest policy for the sheep is to endeavor to become forgotten by the wolves. No good can come to the Jews unless the nations of the world apply themselves to other matters and pay no attention to them," writes Rabbi Wasserman. "At a time when the peoples talk increasingly about us, great is the danger which threatens" (Wasserman 1976, 24). In the context of the ceaseless media coverage of the conflict in the Holy Land, it is easy to understand why a number of anti-Zionist sources insist that all aggressive behavior must be avoided, for it can only be counter-productive.

This sensibility, and the humility that flowed from it was, as we shall soon see, precisely what led many secularized Jews to revolt in the early twentieth century. Patience in the face of injustice and persecution filled them with shame and impelled them to take fate in their own hands. Inspired by European ideological trends the new sensibility first triumphed in Russia, then spread, though to a lesser degree, to other Jewish communities. But the older tradition, the source of inspiration to those who oppose Zionism in the name of the Torah, has endured.

In Jewish tradition, two outstanding figures are credited with transforming a Temple-centered Judaism into a Judaism that was at once more personal and more cosmopolitan. The first is Yohanan Ben Zakkai, a Torah scholar who, trapped in Roman-besieged Jerusalem, contrived to flee the rebels hidden in a coffin. Tradition holds that he gained permission from the Romans to teach the Torah at Yavne, a small town southwest of Jerusalem. He thus became an emblematic figure in the emphasis on Torah study, as opposed to the struggle for political independence. The Torah replaced the land in its physical sense and became, to use the expression of Rabbi Weinberg, "the national territory" (Shapiro, 99). The philosopher George Steiner echoes him: the Book itself is the homeland of the Jews. Henceforth, the Jews were to be known as "the people of the book"; their standard-bearer would be the scholar, the wise man, the *talmid hakham*, rather than the conquering general. In today's nationalistic context, a figure like Yohanan Ben Zakkai would likely be seen as a "traitor to his country," who abandoned his brethren in their struggle against the foreign invader. But, Ben Zakkai's attitude toward military power continues to inform the Judaic critique of Zionism.

The second outstanding figure was Judas the Prince (Yehuda Ha-Nasi, 135–219), revered by Jews as the compiler of the Mishna. According to tradition, he had the clairvoyance to write down the oral Torah in the conditions that arose after the destruction of the Temple, when geographical dispersion of the Jews threatened to disrupt word-of-mouth transmission. A signal aspect of the life of Judas the Prince, as preserved in the Talmud, was his friendship, even intimacy, with Antoninus, the Roman Emperor of the day. Judas the Prince had settled in Tzipori (Sephoris), the Roman administrative center in Galilee; his residence, which has recently become a tourist attraction, was located in the center of the Roman town. Tradition relates that in his relationship with the Roman authorities, Judas the Prince drew inspiration from the Biblical verses that describe the encounter between Jacob and his brother Esau, whom Jacob feared. In them, Jacob places his trust in God. But at the same time, he divides his family into two camps: "If Esau comes to the one camp and attacks it, the other camp may yet escape" (Genesis 32:9). This approach, meant to minimize potential damage, warned the Jews against concentrating in any single place or any single country.

> That which the Zionists considered negative was indeed positive, for thanks to exile, Israel survived. Its dispersion meant that its enemies were never able to exterminate it totally. When the Jews were persecuted in one country, they sought refuge in another with well-established Jewish communities. Concentrated in one place, the Jewish people are vulnerable. This is why the collective return to Israel should not take place before the arrival of the Messiah. At that time, anti-Semitism will no longer exist, all the nations will be favorable to Israel, and there will be no risk of extermination. (Lévyne, 256)

In all matters not involving idol worship or the profanation of Judaism, all attempts must be made to avoid conflict between the Jews and the societies in which they live. Judas the Prince's definition of a strong man — he who can control his impulses, including his warlike impulses — must be seen in this light.

Both figures, Yohanan Ben Zakkai and Judas the Prince, embody a conciliatory attitude toward any occupying power and point up the sharp difference between the patriots who perished in armed struggle or collective suicide, e.g., at Masada and Gamla, and the rabbis who fled confrontation, preoccupied as they were by the survival and development of Judaism and, by extension, of the Jewish people. There can be little doubt that the survival of the Jewish continuity owes much to these two "collaborationist" rabbis, who hold such a prominent place in tradition.

Should the inhabitants of a town populated by Jews be endangered, Jewish Law allows for self-defense, even on the Sabbath. It draws on the Talmud, which enjoins the Jew: "He that comes to kill you, rise up and kill him" (BT Yoma, 85b). Tradition, nonetheless, remains far removed from violence in any form, laying down the three character traits that distinguish the Jews: they must be bashful, compassionate and charitable (BT Yevamot, 79a). The Talmud accords supreme value to peace, while downplaying the use of force (BT Perek Hashalom, Derekh Eretz). Interpreters of the verse "seek peace and pursue it" (Psalms 34:15), postulate it is the only precept that obliges the Jew to "pursue the commandment" (BT Perek Hashalom, Derekh Eretz) in order to discharge it. In contrast, the commandment to rise to one's feet in the presence of an elder does not oblige one to seek an elder in order to accomplish its injunction. However, if peace is not present it must be sought, with no regard for the effort to be made or the distance to be traveled. This remained the dominant tradition until the twentieth century, when Zionism resorted to military heroism. It is not unusual to encounter Israeli politicians who consider peace less important than the military control of certain historical sites such as Temple Mount. "[Even today] we must understand that without Jerusalem and without our historical roots the Zionist project will not be able to survive" (Sharansky, 32M).

But are these pacifist values firmly anchored in the Jewish worldview or are they simply the creation of historical circumstances? In a work of religious polemic, the Spanish poet and scholar Yehuda Halevi (1080–c.1141) presents a dialogue that was to assume its full force almost one thousand years later:

> The Rabbi: I see thee reproaching us with out degradation and poverty, but the best of other religions boast of both. Do they not glorify Him who said: He who smites thee on the right cheek, turn to him the left also; and he who takes away thy coat, let him have thy shirt also. He and his friends and followings, after hundreds of years of contumely, flogging and slaying, attained their well-known success, and just in these things they glorify. This is also the history of the founder of Islam and his friends, who eventually prevailed, and became powerful....

To which the King of the Khazars, who is about to choose between the three monotheistic religions, responds with a touch of cynicism: "This might be so, if your humility were voluntary; but it is involuntary, and if you had power you would slay" (Halevi, J., 78).

The Jews of Russia: Frustration and Violence

In the event, the shift took place well before the Jews gained any kind of power. It happened in Russia, a country that was home to millions of Jews concentrated in the Pale of Settlement and ruled by a cruelly punctilious bureaucracy. The great majority felt both impatience and exasperation at the restrictions and persecutions they were forced to endure. In the nineteenth century, the Russian government busily promulgated new laws to integrate the Jews, but still the restrictions remained. At the same time, educational opportunities, as well as Russification, were surging ahead: in the 1880s, the absolute number of Jews in Russian universities exceeded the number of Jews studying in the yeshivas of the empire (Stampfer, 224). The gap was all the more significant in that university access for Jews was limited by the *numerus clauses* (quota), which did not apply to the yeshivas. But opportunities for social promotion remained proportionally scarce for Jewish university graduates, amplifying their frustration — and accelerating the spread of ideas that embraced political violence.

Two decades were to prove critical. In 1861, the liberal reforms of Alexander II opened the doors to the integration of the Jews and, as in Germany and Austria, gave every appearance of leading them to identification with the empire. Jews flocked to the universities, into new trades and rapidly became a significant portion of the Russian intelligentsia. But when a terrorist bomb killed the tsar in the center of Saint Petersburg in 1881, the period of liberalism came to an end, and, for the first time in more than two centuries, a wave of pogroms swept across Russia. This wave had been gathering force within a wider context of conservative rejection of all political opposition. One of the prime causes of the pogroms was said to be the visibility of the Jews in oppositionist movements.

Reactions among Russian Jews were anything but uniform. The rabbinical authorities, in their majority, opposed political violence (Lederhendler, 67). Traditionalists, motivated above all by concern for the future of their families, sought escape via emigration to the United States. But the most Russified Jews, who identified with modern, European values, could not be satisfied with individual solutions: they perceived a collective "Jewish problem" and sought a large-scale remedy.

The new feeling of self-confidence and of belief in armed force that had arisen among Russia's radical Jews cannot be compared to Jewish participation in the armed forces of their own countries in the nineteenth and twentieth centuries. Joining the military was part of attempted social integration and not an aggressive challenge to non-Jews. Those who enlisted identified with their respective empire or republic and participated in military life, often with courage and ingenuity. For example, Fritz Haber, who synthesized the first poison gases, also supervised their deployment and use at the front, in the uniform of a German officer (Angerer; Goran). But such cases had little overall impact on the culture of non-violence that governed Jews' relationships with their non-Jewish neighbors.

Zionism must be seen in the context of several movements originating in tsarist Russia that attempted to "normalize" the Jew of the Diaspora. Zionism's contribution would be the transformation of the meek traditionalist Jew into a brawny, strong-arm Hebrew. The radicals proclaimed it necessary to straighten the spine of the Jew, long curved before oppressors and long bent beneath the weight of the volumes of the Talmud; to free the Jew from the burden of exile as well as from that of Jewish tradition, defined as "the yoke of the heavenly kingdom" — meaning loyalty to the Torah. Implicit in this process of liberation was an increased reliance on the use of force.

For Avineri this movement must be seen as "a clear break with the quietism of the religious belief in messianic redemption that should occur only through divine intercession in the mundane cycles of world history" (Avineri 1998, 3). Within a single century, the repugnance felt by Jews toward violence had been transformed, in some of them at least, into defiant militarism, no longer a concession to the imperatives of self-defense.

Zionism has never been a uniform ideology. While certain factions openly favored an "offensive ethos," a military approach to the Arab population of Palestine (Schattner), the dominant current until the 1980s, tracing back to Ben-Gurion's Mapai, preferred the "defensive ethos," which accepted the use of force only as a last resort, in reaction to living in a "dangerous neighborhood" (Shapira).

The earliest settlers had projected onto Palestinian reality the memories of bygone Russia: the Arab threat was often likened to the murderous shadow of the pogroms. But their actions were like those of all settler groups in a foreign territory: they took up arms to defend their settlements. The arrival of masses of European Jews following World War II and the Zionist interpretation of the Shoah (see Chapter 6) created a cultural fusion of immense power: a self-image of the just victim. In reality, that too was another inverted transposition from rabbinical tradition, which presents the Jews as weak in physical strength, but powerful in their trust in God. In the Zionist version, self-confidence takes the place of trust in God.

Most rabbis had reacted to Zionism with revulsion, as they had to the very idea of armed struggle. To defy the nations could bring nothing but fresh disaster, they warned and remained faithful to the tradition of compromise, or even emigration, rather than confrontation with the local population and government. But fewer and fewer Russian Jews heard their voices.

Like the majority of Jews in France and Germany, perhaps most Russian Jews at the turn of the century had begun to see themselves through the multi-faceted prism of non-Jewish society. This profoundly affected their consciousness and behavior. Many broke with Judaic practices entirely, identified with modernity and began to admire Europe, even though they were observing it from a distance. In the war with the Arabs in Palestine, the process acquired a significant ideological dimension: Jewish settlers, primarily of Russian origin, were now acting in the name of Western civilization. Their determination to protect civilization against "the Arab savages" has remained a major theme in the Russian-language press in Israel, which today boasts more than one million Russian-speaking inhabitants (Shumsky, 9).

This process of long-distance acculturation to an imaginary Occident had begun during the last half of the nineteenth century. Their shock, anger and frustration at the pogroms found an outlet in radical, often clandestine parties that preached the systematic use of violence (Tessendorf). Jews flooded into the Russian oppositionist movements. At the same time, they founded several specifically Jewish ones (including the Socialist Bund, anti-pogrom self-defense groups and various Zionist parties). The pervasive atmosphere of nihilism and contempt for human life (Landry) generated an upsurge of terrorism whose specter haunts the world to this day. Some observers have even drawn a connection between the Russian ideological heritage of the nineteenth century and the broader history of terrorist activity, including the Middle Eastern variety, up to and including the spectacular attack on the Twin Towers in Manhattan (Glucksmann).

While other Jewish communities the world over remained faithful to the tradition of non-violence and contemplated no armed action against the populations amongst which they lived, that tradition became ever weaker in Russia, as great numbers of Jews discovered the allure of political violence. Many Russian Jews supported the radical political parties through their periods of crisis and decline, due in part to their unshakeable idealism and to their use of smuggling networks for oppositionist political ends. Russian civil servants of the day saw Jews as the "most dangerous component of the revolutionary movement" (Haberer, ch. 12). Western historians have corroborated the observation: Jews were the dominant element among illegal opposition groups. In some organizations, Jews accounted for more than fifty percent of the membership. More than three-quarters of the members of a radical group uncovered by the police in 1889 were Jews (Haberer, 254). For example, 83 percent of political exiles in the Yakutsk region of Siberia were Jews.

The Socialist Revolutionary Party (SRP), undoubtedly the most violent of these radical movements, preached and practiced the systematic use of terror. Many Jews were party members, both in the leadership and among the rank-and-file. One of the last actions of the SRP, and certainly one of the most notorious, was the Jewess Fania Kaplan's attempted assassination of Lenin in the summer of 1918.

The Bolsheviks, whose doctrine also endorsed overt recourse to violence, boasted a strong Jewish contingent as well. In October 1917, six of the twenty-one members of the Central Committee of Lenin's party were Jews (Frankel, 294). There were more Jews in Lenin's first government than members of any other minority group. And Jews continued to serve the new regime, often in such key positions as Commissar of War or as head of the much-feared Cheka, the Soviet secret police. The members of the Jewish section of the Communist Party, all Jews by definition, employed organized violence against all manifestations of Jewish particularism, whether Judaism, the Bund or Zionism (Gitelman 1972). So great was their zeal that some of the Jewish Section's initiatives, which included destroying synagogues and burning Torah scrolls on Jewish holidays, drew a reaction from the Commissar of Nationalities, who, on more than one occasion during the 1920s, stepped in to calm their fervor. The Commissar at that time was a man whose name is rarely associated with moderation and tolerance: Joseph Stalin (Exhibition).

Jewish participation in the Socialist Revolutionary and Bolshevik parties was of a completely different order than their participation in political organizations in Germany, Austria or France. Russian Jews joined political parties to bring about a violent change in a society, which they felt had rejected and humiliated them, and threatened their physical survival. Whatever the Jewish consciousness of an individual member of these movements, it seems clear that Jews joined them because of their Jewishness, which had set them apart from Russian society in the first place. The radical parties sought out recruits on the margins of Russian society, which was populated by frustrated minorities such as the Poles and the Lithuanians, as well as Jews, who aspired to transform Russia totally so that anti-Semitism would disappear in a radiant, forward-looking social vision.

The choice of radicalism and violence was a logical one in a social context that excluded the Jews and, at least up until the 1905 revolution, had proscribed all political activity. Autocracy had driven the Jews to extremism, or certainly those Jews who, unlike their elders, were not at all inclined to interpret suffering as a stimulus to moral self-improvement. But in order to understand the origins of this massive shift among the Jews of Russia, we must examine how ideas of political violence penetrated the strictly Jewish movements of the day.

Pride and Self-defense

The pogroms of the late nineteenth century deepened the insecurity of the Jewish populations of the Russian Empire. The fear of violent death grew acute during the riots of 1881 and, a generation later, following the 1903 Kishinev massacres. This was a sudden dread of the non-Jew, of the neighbor who might, at any moment, kill, rape or kidnap. In contrast to Jewish reactions during the pogroms of the seventeenth century, which had been far crueler and more violent, for a growing number of secularizing Jews the insecurity and suffering they encountered at the end of the "century of progress" had lost all religious significance. Rather than scrutinizing their own behavior and intensifying their penitence while they fled the violence, they asserted their pride and called for resistance. It was a radical departure from tradition.

Assimilated Jews like Jabotinsky sought the respect of the society around them in response to the feelings of inferiority that had invaded their consciousness when they came into contact with European culture. In fact, one of the chief motives of Zionism's founders was to gain the respect of the larger non-Jewish society, a concern not foreign to Jewish tradition. Several verses of the Pentateuch refer directly to the kind of impression that the children of Israel must make upon the society around them. Invoking the commandments of the Torah, Moses exhorted the people: "Observe them faithfully, for that will be proof of your wisdom and understanding to other peoples, who on hearing of all these laws will say: Surely this great nation is a wise and understanding people" (Deuteronomy 4:6). In other words, only the Torah can make them "wise and understanding" in the sight of the nations.

Zionism emerged from a climate of shame, of insulted dignity. Even though the Torah, both written and oral, repeatedly cautions Jews against personal or collective pride, it was precisely in these traits that the Zionists sought the kind of respect that they defined in terms of the classic Western criteria for success: a country, an army, independence. What gave the Zionist movement its extraordinary vigor was not the suffering of pogrom victims, but the humiliation of the rejected supplicants, those whose hopes of integration into Russian society the pogroms had shattered. They felt themselves drawn by the doctrine of Herzl, another rejected aspirant, whose hope of becoming a full-fledged European was shaken by the Dreyfus trial. Yet the Dreyfus Affair, which caused in Herzl a feeling of profound rejection, remained, for French Jews, a French rather than a Jewish matter, which, in any event, had culminated in the victory of Dreyfus's supporters (Abitbol 1989, 33).

At first glance, it seems odd that anti-Jewish violence and anti-Semitism had a greater impact on acculturated Russian Jews than upon those who suffered its direct impact on their lives and belongings. But the traditionalists were staunch believers in the Judaic system of interpretation, which was capable of absorbing violent blows. They expected nothing of the tsar and his government and had little cause to be taken in by it. But Jews educated in Russian and integrated into urban life welcomed Alexander II's reforms with enthusiasm, fully expecting emancipation on the European model. Even though the vast majority of them suffered no physical consequences, the violence of the pogroms devastated them. The reaction of some of their associates, who appeared to see in the anti-Jewish riots the spark of a broader revolt against the regime (some Russian government experts had arrived at the same conclusion [Jabberer]), was particularly distressing to them.

Russian Jewish intellectuals, even those like Ahad Ha-Am, who had earlier expressed doubts about the use of armed force, now called upon the Jews to defend themselves. But it was Haim Nahman Bialik, a Russian author who later became a cultural icon in Israel, that stoked the fires of revenge and violence. In a poem written following the Kishinev pogrom of 1903, he castigated the survivors, heaping shame upon their heads and calling upon them to revolt not only against their tormentors but also against Judaism. Bialik lashed out at the men who hid in stinking holes while their non-Jewish neighbors raped their wives and daughters. The anger that had swept over many Jews caused Bialik, a former yeshiva student, to overturn the Jewish value system. He mocked the tradition that attributed all adversity to shortcomings in the behavior of the Jews: "let fists fly like stones against the heavens and against the heavenly throne." Bialik broke violently with Judaism and issued a ringing challenge: defend yourselves or perish!

Brenner, another poet and like Bialik the son of a pious Russian Jewish family, rebelled as well against Jewish tradition. He radically transformed the best-known verse of the Jewish prayer book "Hear, O Israel, God is your

Lord, God is one!" one of the first verses taught to children and the last to be spoken by a Jew before his death. Brenner's revised verse proclaimed: "Hear, O Israel! Not an eye for an eye. Two eyes for one eye, all their teeth for every humiliation!" He was to die a violent death during the Arab riots in Jaffa.

Pride, as a motive, had been invested with a new meaning. While Judaism, like all religions, considers it a vice, the secular Jews sought it at all costs, even at the cost of life. Heroic romanticism, in a clean break with Jewish tradition, put down roots in these new Jewish circles. It went hand in hand with Herzl's idea of legalizing dueling, the ultimate manifestation of noble honor, in his state of the Jews. Yet the idea of dueling would have occasioned nothing more than revulsion among those who clung to Jewish tradition, for whom life was too precious to sacrifice for an illusory honor. Honor, pride, the thirst for power and revenge: these were the new motives that swept into Jewish consciousness at the beginning of the twentieth century.

The shift in outlook that took place then among many Russian Jews was undoubtedly more significant than the real impact of Jewish self-defense in Russia. It radically modified the meaning of Jewish history in the eyes of the youth, who thirsted after a specifically Jewish activism. The secular version of Jewish history had eliminated the privileged relationship between God and his people and made the Jews the victims of an historical injustice. This view of history tends to stimulate a powerful impulse to action. In passing, it should be noted that several of the founders of armed Jewish units, both in Russia and in Palestine, recognized the importance of the use of force as a way of wrenching the Jew from his Judaic past.

Vladimir Jabotinsky's principal motivation appears to have been the affirmation of national pride. As an organizer of the Jewish Legion during World War I, he glorified the use of force as the most convincing way of bringing this affirmation about. It was not only a matter of self-defense, or even of offensive and terrorist operations in Palestine, as practiced by groups like Lehi and Irgun, all of which are well documented (Schattner). Making no direct reference to Palestine, Jabotinsky proposed that the British government use Jewish units in a potential conflict in Abyssinia in 1935. He promised to mobilize one hundred thousand Jewish men from different countries and place them at the disposal of Great Britain, undertaking to organize their military training in all the populous Jewish communities of the continent. On another accasion, Jabotinsky obtained the assistance of several governments, including that of Poland for infantry training and of Italy for naval training at the port of Civitavecchia. According to his biographer, "the Jewish Legion had become a cherished legend and an inspiring precedent" (Schechtman, 297). Militarism was a feature of many nationalist ideologies of the twentieth century; Zionism was no exception.

Large numbers of Jews overtly and defiantly broke away from the Jewish pacifist tradition. One of Jabotinsky's favorite poems clearly illustrates the total reversal that had taken place. The poem's hero is a Russian rabbi teaching little children the *Aleph-Bet* (alphabet). He begins with a groan and a sigh laden with four thousand years of pain and loneliness, and continues: "One has to be strong to survive all that we have borne.... consolation may only be found in strength... there is no other consolation but one's own strength." Thus does he turn Judaism on its head, telling the children that "each generation has its own *aleph-beth*"; that of their generation is as simple as it is concise: "Young men, learn to shoot!... Of all the necessities of national rebirth, shooting is the most important.... We are forced to learn to shoot, and it is futile to argue against the compulsion of a historical reality" (Schechtman, 445). In 1936, Jabotinsky proclaimed, loud and clear: "Jewish youth, learn to shoot!" a slogan that was to have a direct impact on the thousands of secular Jews influenced by strong-arm Zionism. This emphasis on the use of force was almost as common among the socialist Zionists. Ariel Sharon's father, a Russian socialist settler in Palestine, offered his son "an engraved Caucasian dagger" for his bar-mitzvah gift (Sharon, 23). Traditionally, for their bar-mitzvah, or confirmation, young Jews receive Judaica books, which embody the concept of mitzvah, or divine commandment, that they become obliged to perform. In this case, the bar-mitzvah was filled with new content, a dagger that may have predestined the young Ariel Schneiderman (Sharon's original name) to become an intrepid soldier.

Joseph Trumpeldor, a Russian veteran, is the incarnation of romantic heroism in the Zionist curriculum. Killed in a skirmish with the local Arab population, he allegedly managed to utter the last words: "How good it is to die for the fatherland." The phrase was to become, alongside the officers' oath at Masada, one of the symbols of the new determination to take up arms.

Trumpeldor's predecessor in the Diaspora was the Russian Zionist activist Pinhas Dashevsky (1879–1934), who held a central position in the Zionist education system. Dashevsky attacked one of the instigators of the 1903 Kishinev pogroms and went on to become "the first revolutionary manifestation of Jewish national consciousness." His terrorist act was an exemplary one, for "he understood the true nature of Zionism and adhered to it throughout his life" (Sternhell, 50).

The example of Trumpeldor, who had been decorated by the tsar for his bravery in battle, inspired Zionist youth throughout the former Russian Empire. Students from Riga had originally encouraged Jabotinsky, in 1923, to set up a Zionist activist organization that took the name *Brit Yosef Trumpeldor* (the Josef Trumpeldor Alliance), the acronym for which — *Betar* — harked back to Bar Kokhba's last stand. The organization quickly became a Zionist educational institution with a strong military component. Betar shock units drew stern opposition from many Jews in Palestine, who insulted the participants in a military parade organized by Jabotinsky in

Tel Aviv in 1928, one year before the massacre at Hebron. The spectators spat upon them, calling them "Militarists! Generals!" (Schechtman, 88).

Zionist youth mobilization led to another sharp break, this time with the pacific self-image of the Jews, whether practicing or non-practicing, and, naturally, it drew hostile reactions. Albert Einstein was among the Jewish humanists who denounced the Betar youth movement in 1935, describing it as being "as much of a danger to our youth as Hitlerism is to German youth" (Schechtman, 261). Reform Rabbi Stephen Wise expressed his indignation at what he saw as a slogan to fit the times: "Germany for Hitler, Italy for Mussolini, Palestine for Jabotinsky!" (Schechtman, 267). He considered Jabotinsky's philosophy to be militaristic, while "the whole tradition of the Jewish people is against militarism" (Schechtman, 269). An article published in Prague, in 1934, under the title "Brownshirt Zionists" accused Jabotinsky of direct links with the fascist dictatorships:

> His role became tragically grotesque as he, financed by the rising Italian and in particular German Fascism, started to form in Jewry a Fascist party, or to be more precise a more extremely anti-labor and anti-Arab, though naturally not anti-Semitic, brand of Hitler party. (Schechtman, 562–63)

The accusation may seem extreme, but a danger did exist: "deprived of its religious dimension, the dream of a 'Third Kingdom of Israel' could only lead to totalitarianism" (Barnavi, 225). Intense devotion to a cause, to a nation, to a leader, was far from unique at the time. Parallels could be found in many European countries, where youth was mobilized for military or civil service in the name of the fatherland.

In its Zionist version, the yearning for the Land of Holiness was expressed as the reduction of Jewish history to a continuum of suffering that could only lead to Jewish self-emancipation and to the enfranchisement of the Jews as a modern people on its own land. An expression frequently heard in Israel is *ein berera* ("we have no choice"), which dismisses any other option available to the Jews of the world. It follows that the State of Israel is the only place for the Jews, though ever since its creation, conditions have been more serene in the Diaspora. *Ein berera* can also mean that there is no other choice but the use of force. As we have seen, the roots of this radical shift in Jewish self-awareness can be located primarily in nineteenth-century Russia. There, in addition to setting up self-defense units in many cities, Jews carried out assassinations of Russian personalities accused of killing (in Kiev) or of publicly humiliating the Jews (in Vilnius). The appetite for political violence increased with use. Two motives merged: Jewish self-defense and the struggle for a just society. This merger took on particular importance in the early years of the twentieth century, when groups of Russian Jews migrated to Palestine where they would play a critical role in the development of the new Zionist consciousness.

One such Russian Jew was Israel Shohat (1886–1961). Faithful to his nationalist convictions, soon after his arrival in Palestine he proposed replacing the Arab guards employed by Jewish landowners with Jews. It was not long before the Holy Land's first armed group, Ha-Shomer (the Guard), also known as a "conquest group," was organized. Its members committed repeated acts of violence against the Arabs and forced the Jewish settlers to replace their Arab workers with Jews (Morris, 53). After World War I, Ha-Shomer was integrated into the Hagganah, which was formed in 1920. Left out of Hagganah, Shohat traveled to Moscow in an attempt to involve the Soviet secret services in the struggle against the British authorities in Palestine. After the declaration of the State of Israel, he reappeared as a high-ranking Israeli police officer (Shochat). His career demonstrated how prideful, pugnacious nationalism was transplanted from Russia to Palestine and then incorporated into the power structures of the newly created state.

The broadened legitimacy of the use of force set the Jews of Russia apart from those of other countries, where armed resistance against non-Jews was neither necessary, nor even conceivable. In only one other country did a Jewish self-defense initiative take place: it was during the collapse of the Austro-Hungarian Empire and was fully backed by the state authorities. But Russian Jews made up not only a majority of the founders of the State of Israel, they also became the most influential group within its military elite. The man who did more than any other Zionist to introduce terror into Palestine was the Russian, Avraham Stern (1907–1942), a member of several paramilitary groupings. Traces of the Russian cultural influence are likewise visible in recent history: Moshe Dayan, Ezer Weizmann, Itzhak Rabin (1922–1995), Rehavam Zeevi, Raphael Eitan and Ariel Sharon are all descendents of Russian Jews, whose propensity for the use of force can only be likened to their estrangement from Jewish tradition. The two things that set them apart were, at the time, closely related: only by completely rejecting Judaism and its cult of humility could the Russian Jews acquire a newfound confidence in their own strength and in their capacity to re-conquer and defend Israel.

The Russian dimension of Zionism cannot be overestimated. One telling indicator is the composition of the Knesset twelve years after the founding of the state. Despite the almost total prohibition of emigration from the Soviet Union for more than four decades, over 70 percent of the members of this political elite were Russian-born, while 13 percent were born in Palestine/Israel of Russian parents. The American Zionist elites, whose support was crucial for Zionism's success, were also composed primarily of Jews of Russian origin (Gilbert, 115). The replacement of the Jewish elites of German origin with those originating in Russia also contributed to the shift, between the two world wars, of Jewish public opinion in the United

States in favor of Zionism. Even in Morocco, Zionist ideas and activities were introduced almost exclusively by Russian Jews (Kenbib, 478–80). The essentially Russian character of Zionism stands revealed in its concepts, its methods and the support it drew from the most powerful section of the Diaspora, the United States.

A Russian weekly argues that the cruelty shown to the Chechens and the Palestinians accounts for the mutual sympathy that can be observed between Russia and Israel at the beginning of the twenty-first century. "It is not Dostoevsky's Russia that has opened its eyes, and come to adore Israel," but rather the Russian militarists who had suddenly discovered affinities with Sharon (Furman). Russian Jews form the most reliable electoral base for the Israel right wing. "It is quite natural for the Russians to belong to the right wing; it is a political camp that has long drawn sustenance from the ideological heritage of the great leaders of Zionism, Jabotinsky and Begin, both born in the Russian Empire," notes a Russian Israeli journalist obviously sympathetic to the Israeli right (Radyshevskii).

Israeli right-wing parties, which draw much of their support from voters of Russian origin, bear out the Russian dimension of the Zionist enterprise. Moledet (whose website in Russian modifies the World War II slogan, "For Our Soviet Fatherland," to read, "For Our Jewish Fatherland"), in its support for deportation of the Palestinians, has published an interview with a Russian Israeli journalist who affirms that without the historical experience of the Russian Jews, the Israelis will remain unable to attain their destiny. Israelis of Russian origin must guide the nation and purify it of its many illusions. In her view, the State of Israel is the advance guard of the Jewish people, itself threatened by total extermination in the world of the twenty-first century (Kaganskaya). Moledet's aggressive stance has won admirers in Russian nationalist circles, which lament that the Russian will to struggle has survived only in Israel, and primarily among Israelis of Russian origin (Rumiantsev). Incidentally, the URL for the Moledet site in Russian is almost identical to that of a Russian ultra-nationalist one (http://nasha-rodina.ru/ and http://www.rodina.org.il), and the two sites contain reciprocal links. Though all expression of Zionist feelings was proscribed throughout the long Soviet period, cultural ties have remained solid.

An Ambivalent Nationalism

Zionism is unique among nationalist movements: where most national liberation movements were pledged to set the people free and consolidate its control over a given national territory, Zionism set out to create a language, form a new national consciousness, transport the people that had been shaped in these new circumstances to another part of the planet, replace the local population and defend itself against the efforts of that population to take back the lost territories. In the words of Israeli historian Anita Shapira, "Zionist psychology was molded by the conflicting parameters of a national liberation and a movement of European colonization in a Middle Eastern country" (Shapira, 355). The use of force is indispensable for achieving these two objectives. As Israeli historian Benny Morris explains:

> Zionist ideology and practice were necessarily and elementally expansionist. Realizing Zionism meant organizing and dispatching settlement groups to Palestine. As each settlement took root, it became acutely aware of its isolation and vulnerability, and quite naturally sought the establishment of new Jewish settlements around it. This would make the original settlement more "secure" — but the new settlements now became the "front line" and themselves needed "new" settlements to safeguard them. After the Six Day War, a similar logic would underlie the extension of Israeli settlement into the Golan Heights (to safeguard the Jordan Valley settlements against Syrian depredation from above) and around Jerusalem (to serve as a defensive bulwark for the districts of the exposed northern, eastern, and southern flanks of the city). (Morris, 676)

At the beginning of the century Jabotinsky took part in the organization of Jewish armed units in Odessa. More than a half-century after his death, he stands at the center of the debate over the legitimacy of the use of physical force. Far removed — like the great majority of the Zionists — from Jewish tradition, Jabotinsky promoted the use of force as the only way to settle the land and to crush Arab resistance. Unlike many Social-Zionists who refused to recognize Zionism as a colonizing movement, Jabotinsky was proud to proclaim it. In truth, the leaders of the socialist movement shared Jabotinsky's views, without ever admitting as much. In a speech to a congress of his political movement in 1922, Ben-Gurion "declared the intentions which," says Sternhell, "he was to hold throughout his life":

> It is not by looking for a way of ordering our lives through the harmonious principles of a perfect system of socioeconomic production that we can decide on our line of action. The one great concern that should govern our thought and work is the conquest of the land and building it up through extensive immigration. All the rest is mere words and phraseology [parperaot u-melitzot], and — let us not delude ourselves — we have to go forward in an awareness of our political situation: that is to say, in an awareness of power relationships, the strength of our people in this country and abroad. (Sternhell, 20–21)

To better grasp Ben-Gurion's antagonism toward Judaism, we should note his disdainful dismissal of the yeshiva student, the figure he and his comrades knew so well, and so detested: "We are not yeshiva students debating the fine points of self-improvement. We are conquerors of the land facing a wall of iron, and we have to break through it" (Sternhell, 21).

Ben-Gurion's socialism, Sternhell reminds us, was inspired by the German nationalist socialism of the years immediately following the Great War. The Social-Zionists were quite close to the thought of Spengler, who in turn had paraphrased a remark by Heinrich von Treitschke: "Socialism means power, power and again, power." In the introduction to his book, Sternhell goes to great lengths to invent the term "nationalist Socialism" to avoid calling Ben-Gurion's political outlook National Socialism.

In the following year, 1923, Jabotinsky published in Russian an article that borrowed Ben-Gurion's expression, alongside his message affirming that all Zionists understand that victory can be won only by force (Jabotinsky 1923). An admirer of Mussolini, who reciprocated his esteem, Jabotinsky mobilized the Jews for war, revolt and sacrifice.

This transformation of identity reflected the growing estrangement of the Zionist leaders from Jewish tradition. It is instructive to examine the subject index of Jabotinsky's biography (Schechtman): it includes a substantial list of heroes of European nationalisms, leading figures of world literature and references to Russian obscene language but not a single reference to rabbis or Judaic scholars. The library of Israel's first president Haim Weizmann, preserved as a museum collection, displays the same trait: among the thousands of books in Russian and in European languages, those in Hebrew make up an infinitesimal minority, of which fewer still deal with Judaic heritage. The extent and depth of the break becomes even more striking when one realizes that Jabotinsky interpreted such Biblical figures as Samson to conform with the eastern European nationalist outlook that he knew and appreciated, but without the slightest reference to the Jewish exegetical tradition, to which he was a stranger (Schechtman, 529).

Jabotinsky was not apologetic when it came to his representation of Samson: "This novel is totally free of the Biblical frame of reference...." Indeed, Jabotinsky's Samson transgresses Jewish law and revels in the delights and the sophistication of the Philistines, while maintaining an alliance with his brothers from the twelve tribes of Israel. For their benefit he borrows from the Philistines the technology of iron, military discipline and other strategic knowledge that his brothers do not possess, treating them all the while with tender condescension. Jabotinsky's novel, one reads in the preface written by a British officer, is an expression of the political philosophy of militant Zionism:

> [Of] Jabotinsky's uncompromising revolt against the unorganized, formless Jewish dispersion with no state organization, no leadership, no discipline and no national policy.... He wanted for the Jews what they lacked most: a united nation with a central leadership; a

state with an army; "iron" for their defense in a hostile world, and a man who gives the signal and thousands lift up their hands.... (Jabotinsky 1945, 13)

Jabotinsky's influence has endured to this day. The leading elements of the Jewish terrorist organizations Lehi and Irgun emerged from the ranks of Betar. Many of them would meet death at the hands of the British authorities. Menahem Begin, Beniamin Netanyahu and Ariel Sharon can be counted among his most illustrious admirers and disciples. Yet the rabbinical circles of the day rejected his works. For certain Haredi commentators, the trail blazed by Jabotinsky led straight to destruction (Becher, 3–4). Returning to the story of Bar Kokhba, they reminded their followers that the rabbinical authorities condemned the chief of the rebellion against Rome to capital punishment, even though a majority of rabbis of the day had recognized him, however briefly, as a messiah. Jewish pacifist tradition would remain faithful to its historical origins. In so doing, it stood as an obstacle to Jewish nationalism.

Unlike Jabotinsky, who openly endorsed the colonialist and therefore violent character of Zionism, the majority of the Zionist pioneers refused to acknowledge conflict over the land between the immigrants and the local population. Jabotinsky derided the illusions of the Social-Zionists, who insisted on the "purity of arms," a concept the IDF was later to inherit.

The left, meanwhile, ignored the national character of Arab opposition to its colonizing efforts. A passage from the memoirs of Ariel Sharon, himself a product of the Israeli Labor Movement, is revealing. In speaking of his parents, who had come from Russia to settle in Palestine, he emphasizes that they supported equal rights for Jews and Arabs:

> My parents believed firmly that the Arabs had full rights in the land; "in the land" they would say, "ba'aretz." Jews and Arabs could be citizens side by side. But they believed without question that only they themselves have rights "over the land," "al ha'aretz." And no one was going to force them out, regardless of terror or anything else.... When the land belongs to you physically, when you know every hill and wadi and orchard, when your family is there, that is when you have power, not just physical power, but spiritual power. Like Antaeus, your strength comes from the land. (Sharon, 24–25)

The contrast with the commentary by Rabbi Hirsch quoted earlier is striking. For him, the Torah teachings constitute a national heritage; land and power are nothing but its conditional attributes. Sharon may be conscious of the Greek dimension of his attachment to the land, for he invokes the mythical figure of Antaeus rather than a Biblical character, whose relationship with the Land of Israel would be of an entirely different nature and would not resonate with the romanticism of the Zionist settlers.

The contradictory relationship with the Arabs underlies the systematic violence that haunts the Zionist enterprise to the present day. The prevalent defensive ethos made it possible to maintain a façade of hope for peace and fraternity, even if behind this façade the shadows of fear and suspicion were deepening. But the realities of the 1930s and 1940s, the Arab Revolt and, in the distance, the Shoah, generated cynicism and pessimism, and introduced an offensive ethos that recognized the inevitability of armed conflict with the Arabs. The new ethos also reflected the horror of the threat of total destruction, which despite Israel's incontestable military superiority, continues to dominate the collective consciousness.

The ethical heritage of the Diaspora, inspired by a millennia-long pacifist and moralizing tradition, slowly vanished under the impact of the Palestinian question. Writes Anita Shapira: "Zionist psychology was moulded by the conflicting parameters of a national liberation and a movement of European colonization in a Middle Eastern country" (Shapira, 366–67). The generation that followed the first settlers to Palestine mirrored the dream of the founders; the next generation saw itself as pragmatic, physically fit, aggressive and prepared to take up arms. Each succeeding generation was less ambiguous than the one before it about the use of armed force: "You can't build a state wearing white gloves," as Alterman would later put it (Shapira, 368). Even though the advocates of the defensive ethos at least outwardly abhorred Jabotinsky and his militarism, the realities of the conflict the Zionist enterprise had fostered in Palestine brought about the triumph of his doctrine, and his ideas were to remain popular in Israel in the early twenty-first century.

The term "security" has replaced the concept of self-defense, widespread before the creation of the state. As we have already seen, the Hebrew term *bitahon* was borrowed from the rabbinical literature, where it meant, "trust in divine providence." A Judaic concept was thus taken over by the modern language and given an opposing meaning: rather than putting his trust in Providence, the new Hebrew would henceforth rely on the force of arms. Security became the responsibility of the state, and for decades, everything related to security remained a sacred cow for Israeli society.

Innumerable contemporary rabbinical critiques of classical inspiration have dealt with this substitution of the sacred. The biblical verse most often cited is the following:

> Take care lest you forget the Lord your God and fail to keep His commandments, His rules, and His laws, which I enjoin upon you today. When you have eaten your fill, and have built fine houses to live in, and your herds and flocks have multiplied, and your silver and gold increased, and everything you own has prospered, beware

lest your heart grow haughty and you forget the Lord your God...
and you say to yourselves: "My own power and the might of my own
hand have won this wealth for me." (Deuteronomy 8:11–14, 17)

The work of providing Judaic legitimization for the use of force was left
to National Religious circles. But the task was not a simple one: two of the
precursors enlisted by Religious Zionism — Rabbis Zvi Hirsch Kalischer
and Yehuda Salomon Hai Alkalai — proved to be more inspired by the
heady atmosphere of nineteenth-century European nationalism than by the
Jewish tradition. Avineri notes that the call to arms that reverberates in the
words of these rabbis is based explicitly on the experience of the European
countries that had recently won their independence (Avineri 1998, 4). They
are rife with references to honor and pride, which makes them remote from
the discourse of Jewish tradition:

> Why do the people of Italy and of other countries sacrifice their lives
> for the land of their fathers, while we, like men bereft of strength
> and courage, do nothing? Are we inferior to all other peoples, who
> have no regard for life and fortune as compared with the love of their
> land and nation? Let us take to heart the examples of the Italians,
> Poles, and Hungarians, who laid down their lives and possessions
> in the struggles for national independence, while we, the children
> of Israel, who have the most glorious and holiest of lands as our
> inheritance, are spiritless and silent. Should we not be ashamed of
> ourselves? (Avineri 1998, 4)

Even among rabbis who supported the Zionist enterprise we can detect
stubborn traces of Jewish pacifism. For the two precursors of Religious Zionism, Kalischer and Alkalai, the use of force remained a foreign concept.
They continued to invoke the oath not to "rebel against the nations" (BT
Ketubot, 111a) and insisted that the return to Israel would by no means
involve military force: "and no sword shall cross your land" (Leviticus
26:6).

Rabbi Samuel Mohilever's address to the first Zionist Congress in 1897
illustrates this aspect of Jewish tradition. Mohilever (1824–1898), one of the
founders of Hibbat Tzion, called upon the Zionists "not [to] stumble with
their tongues, God forbid, to speak against our Holy Law or in opposition
to the secular governments that rule over us.... Allow them to find favor in
the eyes of Kings, Princes and Rulers before whom they stand to plead for
Thy people and Thy land" (Avineri 1998, 4). Mohilever's role as an emissary
to several governments and his support for the Zionist political program do
not appear to depart from the pacifist tradition that he so clearly enunciated
in his speech.

From the earliest days of Zionism, many rabbis had warned of the physical threat it posed. The members of the Old Yishuv feared that the nationalist ambitions of the new settlers would create tensions with Arabs, with whom their devoutly religious communities had always coexisted in peace. For these rabbis it was essential to protect themselves from the Zionists, whom they called "destroyers of the city." They grounded their arguments on a passage from the Talmud that was later to give its name to Neturei Karta, one of the most active groups in the anti-Zionist movement:

> Rabbi Yehuda the Patriarch sent Rabbi Hiyya, Rabbi Assi, and Rabbi Ammi to travel among the towns of the Land of Israel to provide for them scribes and teachers. They came to one place and found neither a scribe nor a teacher. They said to the people, "Bring us the guardians of the town." The people brought them the guardsmen of the town.
>
> They said to them: "Do you think these are the guardians of the town? They are nothing other than the destroyers of the town."
>
> They said to them, "And who are the guardians of the town?"
>
> They said to them, "The scribes and the teachers."
>
> As the Scripture puts it: "…unless the Lord watches over the city, the watchman keeps vigil in vain (Psalms 127:1)." (*JT* Haggiga, 1.7)

During the first decades of Zionism, the leaders of the Old Yishuv saw the Jewish settlers, and not the Arab population, as the looming threat. The Jews were the first to reject the newly arrived Zionist settlers in Palestine; only later did the Arabs follow suit. Rabbi Sonnenfeld of Jerusalem quoted the biblical verse, "I will assign the land you sojourn in to you and your offspring to come, all the land of Canaan, as an everlasting holding" (Genesis 17:8) to emphasize that God alone would give the Land to the People of Israel and that the Zionists could not acquire it by force (Rosenberg, 440).

The Palestinian rabbis left no doubt about the origins of the violence that has haunted the Holy Land: the Zionists and the State of Israel had needlessly provoked the nations. In fact, the emergence of Zionism and its rapid, extraordinary success emboldened these religious Jews in their rejection of military action. The critics of Zionism point out that in Hebron, where some sixty Jews were massacred in 1929, the Zionists had provoked the Arabs. The killers were not residents of the city but had traveled there in response to a campaign organized by the Zionist organizations of Jerusalem to appropriate the Wailing Wall. Spurred on by national pride — but without the slightest intention of praying there — thousands of Zionists had gathered in Jerusalem, chanting "The Wall to the Jews." Present was Rabbi Kook, one of the rare rabbinical authorities to have lent his support to the demonstration. Witnesses were to claim later that the massacre at

Hebron appeared to have taken place as a fallout from the tensions that had developed in Jerusalem and elsewhere. Most of the town's Jews had found refuge with their Arab neighbors, these same witnesses added (Segev 2000, 325).

To his followers who wished to establish themselves in the Holy Land, the Gur Rebbe wrote that the Arabs were a friendly, hospitable people. Recent works of history dealing with Palestinian society before the proclamation of the State of Israel also point to the relative harmony that prevailed at the time (Rosenberg, 1071; Segev 2000). The memory of cordial relations between Jews and Arabs continues to motivate the anti-Zionists, who question the strong-arm approach they attribute to the Zionist concept of the state: "The number of dead and wounded on the two sides has become intolerable. We believe it is time to contemplate a radical break with the fundamentals that have defined, and in reality have stifled, debate on this issue." The ideas expressed are thoroughly traditional and make no pretense of innovation: "Our perspective is far from new. It is the centuries' old view of the Torah. It was universally shared by all Jews and it is only our people's recent flirtation with assorted secularist dogmas that have caused it to be forgotten of late in some quarters" (Weiss 2001). They recall that the Jews have always interpreted exile from the Holy Land as divine punishment. Return can only be achieved by spiritual means; such means alone can have a lasting impact. The Judaic arsenal is a familiar one: repentance, prayer, Torah study and good deeds. From this perspective, the mighty Zionist arsenal has been counter-productive. Instead of bringing about salvation, say the anti-Zionists, it has perpetuated violence.

Israel's Victories

Some of the positions taken by the anti-Zionist Haredim are quite close to those of the Israeli "peace camp." A Neturei Karta document asserts:

> The Zionist movement was not only a heretical departure from Judaism.... It was monstrously blind to the indigenous inhabitants of the Holy Land. In the 1890s, less than 5% of the Holy Land's population was Jewish, yet, Theodor Herzl had the nerve to describe his movement as that of "a people without a land for a land without a people." Time and again both Revisionist and Labor Zionists, the former overtly and the latter under the clouds of deceptive rhetoric, have sought the elimination of the Palestinian people from their state. They have dispossessed thousands and refused them the right of return or minimum compensation.... This aggression has plunged the region into its never-ending spiral of bloodshed. (Blau, A., 2–3)

Unlike the National Religious, who encourage their children to serve in the armed forces, the Haredim, with a few exceptions, do not. The exemption from obligatory military service for thousands of Torah students dates back to an agreement between Ben-Gurion and certain Haredi rabbis at the foundation of the state itself. Ben-Gurion bought thereby domestic peace as the rabbis promised not to oppose publicly the proclamation of the State of Israel.

Both parties felt that the compromise, which applies to the great majority of Israel's Haredim, would be short-lived. In Ben-Gurion's eyes, the Haredim represented a mournful vestige, a remnant of the Diaspora fated to vanish in the whirlpool of the new Israeli society. From this perspective, religion could be made to serve the Zionist cause, preserving the Jewish people spread among the nations, but it certainly had no independent function. The Haredim, meanwhile, looked upon Zionism as a short-term aberration, as a revolt against the Torah and, at worst, as a false messiah. They certainly never anticipated that it would last.

Naturally enough, the secular majority thinks it scandalous that their sons should risk their lives while "the religious " continue in the safety of their houses of study. The Haredim, meanwhile, justify their exemption by affirming that the Torah protects the Jews in the Land of Israel far better than the state with all its weapons. The two viewpoints have remained as far apart as ever; there seems to be no possibility of dialogue, no common denominator. But, like any human reality, the army and war came in for rabbinical scrutiny.

The upshot was that contemporary rabbis further circumscribed the defensive ethos developed by the secular Zionists. Even those who belonged to the National Religious faction and who considered the State of Israel as the "beginning of the flowering of our redemption" tended to limit the application of force to self-defense, albeit defined in broader terms. Even though, with few exceptions, self-defense was the only possible justification for the use of force, the very definition of self-defense became an issue, above all for the defenders of the National Religious position, for there were few Haredim in the armed forces.

At the other end of the spectrum, Yoel Teitelbaum, in his *Va-Yoel Moshe*, the fundamental source of contemporary Judaic anti-Zionism, based on the three oaths taken on the eve of exile, grants no legitimacy to armed struggle. For him, any action by an illegitimate state must by definition be illegitimate. To buttress his conclusion he cites the Maharal of Prague, Rabbi Yehuda Loew ben Betzalel (1512–1609), who insisted that even under threat of massacre and torture, the Jews have no right to establish themselves in Israel and have even less right to use force against the nations to do so (Loew). In Teitelbaum's eyes the Zionists, by using violence against the Arabs, had violated the oath that enjoined them to not revolt against the nations (see Chapter 3) and had thus brought upon the Jews even worse persecutions and torments; it is clear that he is referring to the Shoah and to the chronic violence experienced by the State of Israel. Teitelbaum describes the wars waged by the state as "killings whose only aim is to sustain an impious Jew at the head of the government"; in other words, to sustain the Zionist structure of the state. He goes on to cite several judicial sources, such as the *Sefer Mitzvot Kattan* code, which omits, in its list of commandments practiced to the present day, all reference to situations of war (*Jewish Guardian* 1984a).

Another critic of the use of force, Rabbi Elhanan Wasserman, who perished in the Nazi camps, accused Zionism and the affront to the world that it represented, of being the direct cause of the Shoah (see Chapter 6). For Rabbi Wasserman, the Jews were nothing more than a lamb surrounded by seventy wolves; it might be able to bite one, but that would surely drive the other wolves into a frenzy.

Rejection of the use of force also applies to events of the past, glorified by the Zionists. Traditionalists challenge the heroism of the resistance fighters of the 1943 Warsaw Ghetto uprising. Though the revolt has been engraved upon Israeli collective consciousness as an act of courage and an example to be emulated, those who oppose violence have an entirely different vision:

> To die a hero's death just for the sake of dying a hero's death is not compatible with the Jewish faith, even if no one else is endangered by it — and certainly not if it stands to endanger the lives of others who value every minute and who do not stop hoping even in the most despairing circumstances for God's salvation, which can come as quickly as the blink of an eye.... Heroism in these times is to live like a hero in the ocean of suffering, and by doing such to fulfill the Divinely imposed role of heroism.... Let them not long for false heroism, which has no basis in Judaism. (Warsaw, 5–7)

In the midst of the War of Independence, touched off by the proclamation of the State of Israel in 1948, a group of native-born inhabitants of Jerusalem proclaimed:

> We will not allow ourselves, our wives and our children, to be led to our deaths, God forefend, in the name of Zionist idolatry. It is inconceivable that the impious, the unbelievers, the ignorant, and the irresponsible heretics lead an entire population of hundreds of thousands of Jews, like lambs to the slaughter, God save us, because of their false, demented ideas, and that an entire population, like an innocent dove, allows them to lead it to be killed. (*Jewish Guardian* 1984b, 17)

This attitude betrays not a trace of patriotism, of ethnic solidarity or even of the survival instinct. Against dominant opinion, the anti-Zionist Haredim perceived the danger as emanating from the Zionists and the

State of Israel itself: the five Arab armies that were marching on the young state were nothing more than the emissaries of divine anger awakened, in their view, by the insolence of impious Jews who had taken themselves for masters of the world.

Israel's spectacular victory in the Six Day War reinforced a sense of identification among the majority of the world's Jews, re-ignited the optimism of the Israeli population and electrified the National Religious, who saw in it a miraculous intervention and a sign of approval of the Zionist enterprise. The threat drummed up by the Israeli leadership on the eve of the war, which won the near-unanimous support of the Jewish world and aroused powerful sympathy in the West, turned out to have been a conscious manipulation. General Matti Peled (1923–1995), a member of the General Staff at the time, described the situation with typical Israeli outspokenness:

> Pretending that the threat of genocide hung over our heads in 1967, and that Israel had to fight for its physical survival was nothing but a bluff.... All the stories that were making the rounds about the immense danger confronting us because of the extreme narrowness of our territory were never once taken into account in our pre-war planning. (Kapeliouk)

The same article, published on an anniversary of the war, quotes several members of Israel's military and political elites, who agree that Israel's survival had not been in doubt before the IDF attacked in 1967. General Ezer Weizmann, then at the head of a right-wing nationalist party committed to Israel's territorial expansion, also shared that view.

Light-years distant from the General Staff, pious circles felt the same and saw nothing more than another example of Zionist belligerence:

> Who can forget the darkness of the six days [in 1967] when, under the pretext of the [closing of the] Straight of Tiran, the Zionists arose, surveyed the earth, and declared war.... And in the end they conquered all of Eretz Israel from the Arabs, reaching the place of our glorious Temple. And the thing led to confusion and uncertainty, which grew apace. During the first week after the conquest, the sages forgot their wisdom; the trail of successes and the [ostensible] miracles, as well as [their own] blindness, led them to dance around the [Golden] Calf. Perfectly pious Jews looked catastrophe in the face and could not cope with it. (Ravitzky 1996, 74)

The Satmar Rebbe likewise condemned the Six Day War, reminding his followers that the Zionists had sacrificed thousands of lives on the altar of the state that he considered to be the source of all violence in the region. Yet "there is no doubt that the Torah in no way permits the loss of one Jewish life for the sake of the entire Zionist state.... Even in a nation of *tzaddikim*, righteous people, there is no authorization in our era to subject Jews to war.... It is clear as day that the Torah obligates us to make every effort to mediate for peace and avoid war. These evil people, the Zionists, do the opposite of the Torah view and quarrel with the nations constantly" (*Jewish Guardian* 1984a). For the Satmar Rebbe, to draw the Jews into war without Torah sanction was tantamount to murder. The conclusion was as powerful as it was categorical; his remarks were widely circulated in Yiddish throughout the Haredi world (Teitelbaum 1983). Torah sanction for war cannot be obtained if a prophet has not first crowned a king whose behavior conforms to Judaic commandments, declared Teitelbaum. His ruling rejected the opinions of several Mizrahi rabbis who had conflated the State of Israel with the concept of kingdom as defined in Jewish tradition, and in particular by Maimonides. It was their way of enlisting Judaism in the Zionist enterprise, including its military aspects.

For the National Religious, the Six Day War pointed up the need to occupy and settle the land. But many observers outside the Mizrahi camp deplored what they heard and saw, accusing the National Religious of racism and intolerance (Rubinstein, ch. 7). In recent times, there have been signs of a growing sensitivity even among the supporters of the National Religious position, some of whom have formulated solid criticism of National Religious excesses, particularly among the militant settlers (Burg). Yitzhak Blau, a rabbi at a National Religious yeshiva located in the West Bank, has demonstrated how Judaic sources have been systematically deformed to derive from them warlike teachings (Blau, Y., 39–60). He shows that many National Religious rabbis have used the Torah to denigrate the value of compassion, to promote racism and to transform the occupation into the supreme good. Latent in their arguments he detects the influence of secular fascist-minded intellectuals like Berdyczewski and Uri Zvi Greenberg (1896–1981), who dismissed Judaic pacifism and rejected the entire rabbinical tradition.

The use of Judaic sources to legitimize belligerent, defiant trends in Zionism has had a powerful mobilizing effect. Those who today advocate such an approach are numerous and include rabbis of the National Religious persuasion. For them, "earthly military exploits are raised to a metaphysical plane and take on a universal, messianic meaning and validity. Note that in this instance religion is not lending its sanction to a conservative social structure but to an innovative one (i.e., Jewish political sovereignty), a structure that represents revolutionary change in the life of the people" (Ravitzky 1996, 85). This revolutionary consciousness that animates thousands of National Religious Jews makes some of them quite cynical about the Judaic heritage: "If Israel proves to be ten percent better ethically than the rest of the world, it will be 'a light unto the nations.' If it proves to be 25 percent better, it will bring the Messiah. If it is 50 percent better, it will be dead" (Fishman, 96). Yitzhak Blau notices that National Religious thought, like the secular

Zionists, glorifies concepts foreign to Jewish tradition, such as "national honor" and "national pride." "It would be quite an irony," concedes Blau, "to discover that a virulent critic of Judaism, Friedrich Nietzsche, indirectly influenced the religious Jewish community."

The resurgence of militancy among the National Religious took place in the aftermath of the Six Day War, in the wake of the conquest of the Biblical territories. Militant Islamism would arise two decades later.

Israel's 1967 triumph was a source of deep concern for Yeshayahu Leibowitz. He lashed out at the arrogance born of victory and at the feeling of omnipotence he interpreted as idolatry. He advocated restitution of the conquered territories. If this was not done, added this perspicacious observer, Israel would find them a source of constant concern. He expressed his opinion a few months after the Six Day War, at about the same time as did Rabbi Amram Blau, who also called upon Israel to return the territories without delay:

> If the Zionists had even an iota of common sense…, they would invite the Arab states to form, with them, a confederation that would embrace the Palestinians, who would thus recover their rights. Peace should be made when one is strong. Now, they [the Zionists] are strong. But they will not do it, because they are prideful, and will refuse to make the slightest concession. They prefer to place the lives of millions of Jews in jeopardy rather than ever see an Arab as president of such a confederation. By this spectacular, lightning war they imagine they have won. No one can doubt that today they are at the height of their power. It is at this point that their downfall will begin. It will not be long before they witness all the problems their conquests will bring. The hatred of the Arabs will deepen, and they will seek revenge. The Zionists now have hundreds of thousands of enemies within their borders. All of us who live here are now in great danger. (Blau, R., 234)

The suicide attacks of the al-Aqsa Intifada made Amram Blau's prognosis appear all too accurate. A man who would never once have opened a political science textbook, Blau based his assessment of any given situation on a Judaic interpretation and on a moral sensibility that recognized how the use of force could become a trap and a threat to the Jews. His widow added with approval, a decade after the Six Day War, that on the eve of the IDF offensive, Charles De Gaulle had warned: "Israel, following its brilliant military success, will become a prisoner of its victory" (Blau, R., 234). A broad spectrum of observers, ranging from an Orthodox academic through a Hasidic rabbi to a French general, have warned against the futility — and the danger — of the use of force. This meeting of the minds, insists Ruth Blau, demonstrates that the outcome was perfectly foreseeable and that only the Zionists' pride and the arrogance could have so blinded them to it.

In the aftermath of the capture of East Jerusalem by Israeli troops, Leibowitz proposed that worship at the Wailing Wall be forbidden, lest the wall be converted into an object of worship. At the same time, Satmar and Neturei Karta leaders also forbade their followers from praying at the wall, but for different reasons: no spiritual benefit can be obtained from a victory of the impious.

Even though the majority of Reform Jewish communities drew closer to Zionism following the Six Day War, several Reform rabbis protested against the wave of patriotism. They spoke out against the vicious circle of violence, which they accused the Zionists of having fomented, and recalled the tradition glorifying those who contrive to avoid war. John Rayner, a Reform rabbi in London, invoked the story of the two brothers, Esau and Jacob, to point out the futility of revenge (Rayner, 3–4). The Torah enjoins the descendants of the two brothers, the Edomites and the Israelites, to forgo armed conflict: "You shall not abhor an Edomite, for he is your kinsman. You shall not abhor an Egyptian, for you were a stranger in his land"(Deuteronomy 23:8). The Torah, speaking of Egypt, stresses the reasons for gratitude among the Israelities, and not revenge. Emphasizing that Jewish tradition disapproves of the use of force, Rayner recalled a slogan he had seen at the commemoration of the assassination of Israeli Prime Minister Yitzhak Rabin: "The best reprisal is peace."

Quite in tune — unbeknownst to them — with current political and historical analysis, the Haredi critics of Zionism draw no distinction between the two principal political movements in Israel, "the left" and "the right." In their view, the two camps are the same: Zionism cannot allow itself to become pluralistic. That which brings the two together — their conviction of the legitimacy of Zionism — must certainly be more substantial than the tactical or stylistic differences that divide them. In fact, Labor has been no less active in encouraging settlement in the West Bank than their Likud opponents. Among the political formations, only Meretz and Gush Shalom have consistently opposed settlement in the occupied territories. Indeed, the terms "left" and "right," regularly employed in Israel and outside, are quite relative. Those who vote for the left are generally better educated and better off than those who vote for the right. In Israel, it would be more accurate to speak of a division between tribal nationalism and liberal cosmopolitanism.

The consequences of the occupation begun in 1967 are as apparent today as they were during the days immediately following the Israeli victory. Predictably, as decision-makers failed to heed the calls of Leibowitz and Teitelbaum for the immediate evacuation of the settlements, Israel's attention has been monopolized by the challenge of maintaining them. Many American and Israeli rabbis have raised their voices against the occupation and supported those members of the armed services who have refused to perform their national service in the West Bank (*New York Times* 2002).

The withdrawal from Gaza in August 2005 struck many settlers and their opponents with the sense of futility of the settlement enterprise. It is hard indeed to find sense in the nearly four decades of violence, human sacrifices and material investment that the Israeli occupation of Gaza entailed. There are also rabbinical organizations, such as Rabbis for Human Rights, that defy the policies of the State of Israel, but without calling Zionism into question (Rabbis). Another group, Oz ve-Shalom/Netivot Shalom, which draws its inspiration from Judaism, displays its National Religious colors while protesting against specific actions of the Zionist State (Oz ve-shalom). Its members are drawn from modern American Orthodoxy and the Israeli National Religious, for whom commitment to Zionism is the cornerstone of their identity. They call attention to the acts of cruelty perpetrated by the Israeli army and police, but do not question the Judaic legitimacy of the state. Nonetheless, they are concerned that, "Ultimately, a society that does not tolerate any moral questioning of its ... policies will invariably turn corrupt. In contemporary Israel, unfortunately, there are too many strident, well-positioned religious voices arguing for just such a society" (Blau, Y., 57).

The Haredim condemned Israel's most controversial war, the invasion of Lebanon, in terms quite similar to those employed by the secular opposition. Some denounced it as a demonstration of cruelty that made Jews appear to be murderers, which in turn profanes the Holy Name: "Only by irresponsible killers have we heard such that they killed the men, women, and the children of their enemies in order to capture a State." All arguments about a clear and present danger to Israel were swept aside. "For everyone knows that the military strength of the army of the Zionists greatly surpasses that of the Arabs. It is known that they cannot win a war against the Zionists because they are not so advanced militarily" (Torat, 17–18). According to this view, it is impossible to have confidence in military men: "The reason for this is that a man of war by nature is bloodthirsty, likes the battlefield, and does not have the right perspective about the outcome of things" (Torat, 17–18). The allusion is to Ariel Sharon, then Minister of Defense, who had misled Prime Minister Begin before and during the war in Lebanon.

Israel's military victories raised new questions among critics of Zionism. How could the impious enjoy such martial success? In contrast to the National Religious, who saw the victories as miraculous and thus as a sign of divine benevolence, the anti-Zionist Haredim attributed the Israeli victories to the work of Satan. For them, it was inconceivable that God could have aided those they consider to be idolaters (Ravitzky 1996, 75). The contradictions were well delineated: the victories were either due to divine intervention or to the work of Satan, who creates mirages of redemption in order to mislead the just. In this polarized vision, no room has remained for a compromise interpretation. For its detractors, the victories are just other episodes in a continuum of destruction that begins with the rise of

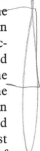

Zionism, includes the Shoah and leads to inevitable decline.

The Israeli operation at Entebbe, Uganda, in 1976, certainly one of the IDF's most spectacular — and least controversial — exploits, became an opportunity to warn against pride. The Israeli military had freed the hostages taken on an Air France flight from Tel Aviv to Paris. Many Jews felt a sense of relief, but also of pride in the Israeli armed forces. It was reported that a few days after the operation, the spiritual leader of a major yeshiva in Bnei-Brak warned his students against any feelings of conceit or pride associated either with Entebbe or any other Israeli military action: "Even a drop of pride is a sign of idolatry" (Moshe).

The identification with Jewish history in its Zionist version only reinforces the image of victimhood. Israel justifies its military operations with the words *ein berera*. Many Jewish organizations worldwide use the same terms to voice approval for Israel's military operations. The use of anti-Semitic clichés by a significant part of the Arab media has simply reinforced the emotional connection between anti-Jewish persecutions of centuries past and Israeli vulnerability to terrorist, and particularly, suicide attacks.

Several Israeli commentators have noted that Israel's military capacity — its army is far and away the most powerful in the region — has not altered its self-image as victim (Ezrahi). Nor has the shift in the balance of power in favor of Israel brought about, among Israelis, the expected change in the awareness of their power. As a result, the disparity between power as it is wielded and the sense of weakness has reinforced Israel's self-righteousness. "The whole world is against us," seems to be the dominant sentiment, particularly since Israel is increasingly isolated politically, able to count only on the United States and a handful of its most faithful allies. This sense of isolation and looming danger is almost automatically associated with the words that the Jews pronounce at the beginning of the solemn Passover meal: "For not just one enemy has stood against us to wipe us out. But in every generation there have been those who have stood against us to wipe us out. Yet the Holy One, Blessed be He, keeps on saving us from their hands" (*Shalom Hartman Institute*, 76).

But, as is so often the case when religion is used for political ends, only the first part of the phrase is cited, and the promise of divine redemption falls by the wayside. It was by such a device that the name of the first Jewish settlement movement in Palestine, in 1882, was derived. *Bilu* is the acronym of the first four words of the verse: "O House of Jacob! Come, let us walk by the light of the Lord" (Isaiah 2:5), from which the words, "by the light of the Lord" have been dropped. The same device was used in the campaign to help Soviet Jews to emigrate during the 1960s and the 1970s. The slogan, "Let my people go," drops the second clause of the sentence: "to worship me" (Exodus 90:13). In both cases, what disappears is the normative connection with God.

At the same time, rabbis in both Israel and the Diaspora have raised their voices against the culture of victimhood that is growing increasingly prevalent among the Jews. "Personally, remarked an American Jewish educator, I have never found this view of the eternally-hating gentile to have any resemblance with reality. It seems a myth, pure and simple, and an ugly one at that" (Schiller, 5–12). Another Judaic refrain that has often been invoked to justify resignation in the face of the eternal hatred of the nations is the Talmudic saying: "Esau hated Jacob." Yet some rabbis, including the Netziv, stress that in the future the two will love one another deeply, as did Rabbi Judas the Prince and the Emperor Antoninus (Berlin). In the light of this interpretation, it is easier to grasp why many rabbis sought inspiration in the story of Esau and Jacob before negotiating with the Roman authorities: they were attempting to transform an enemy into a friend.

Since the start of the second Intifada, Israeli society has fallen into crisis, a crisis of despair. Israel's military power has arguably brought Israelis neither peace nor security. Rabbis and generals alike have spoken of the ineffectiveness of the use of force against the Palestinians. The Palestinian tactic of suicide bombing has been linked to a verse from Deuteronomy: "Then the Amorites who lived in those hills came out against you like so many bees and chased you, and they crushed you at Hormah in Seir" (Deuteronomy 1:44). Rashi's commentary is quite specific: "Just as the bee that stings the human dies then and there, so do the Amorites who touch you die immediately." Rabbi Isaac Zeev Ha-Levi Velvel Soloveitchik (Brisker Rov 1886–1959), an innovator in Talmudic studies and eyewitness to the daring attacks of the Israeli military, added his own commentary to Rashi's, underlining the futility of going to war against the Arabs:

> They [the Zionists] think that by killing the Arabs they will frighten them,… but they will not cease attacking Jews right up to the end. The Arabs are attacking us because Heaven has sent them…. The Arabs do so not because they do not fear the IDF, but because someone has sent them from on high. "To the bitter end,"[1] means that a million Arabs will be prepared to sacrifice themselves to kill but a single Jew. (Liss, 2, 230)

The verse refers to the misfortunes that must surely afflict the children of Israel should they persist in their refusal to obey divine will. In the prophetic commentary of the Brisker Rov, it becomes an allusion to the young Palestinians who sacrifice their lives to kill Israelis. In another style, Moshe Sober, a Mizrahi rabbi who has since distanced himself from Zionism, commented in 1990:

> The Palestinians will indubitably suffer more than the Israelis. That is the usual pattern in insurrections. But every dead Palestinian will only serve to strengthen their organization and every dead

Israeli to weaken our establishment. It is a battle that cannot be won. (Sober, 91)

The Satmar Rebbe Yoel Teitelbaum is said to have often prayed for the disappearance of the State of Israel without any Jew suffering as a result. While he proposed no political solution, he looked upon the state as a serious threat to the Jews. Like many critics of Zionism, he declined to envisage scenarios. Faith in God, who alone could accomplish such a task, would suffice. Many of his disciples have since pointed to the peaceful collapse of the Soviet Union — its nuclear arsenal and its powerful conventional forces notwithstanding — as an example of the feasibility of such a miraculous transformation. Following in Teitelbaum's footsteps, many rabbis remain sceptical that the spectacular victories of the Israeli army can ensure the security of the Jews. This feeling of futility has now spread well beyond rabbinical circles.

A similar cautionary message emanates from a monumental work edited by Daniel Elazar (1934–1999), a pioneer of research into the Jewish political tradition in Israel:

With the benefit of historical hindsight 2,500 years later, we know that the visionary Prophets and not the practical politicians of the day, the kings and aristocrats, were the true realists in the international arena. It was Isaiah who urged neutrality in the face of the Assyrian crisis, not Kings Ahaz and Hezekiah, and who was vindicated by the course of events. A century later, the passion of the "patriotic" party at court, and not Jeremiah's counsel opposing rebellion against Babylonia, led to the destruction of the monarchy, the burning of the Temple, and the all-but-complete annihilation of the Jewish people. (Elazar, 49)

These observations dovetail with rabbinical opinions opposed to the use of force. It is all the more noteworthy that Elazar, founder of the Jerusalem Center for Public Affairs and former advisor to several Israeli governments, remained close to nationalist circles.

Militarism has long provoked strong reactions. In late nineteenth century Vienna, Rabbi Güdemann predicted that the Zionists would ultimately create a Judaism of cannons and bayonets that would invert the roles of David and Goliath and would end in a perversion of Judaism, which had never glorified war and never idolized warriors. Quoting an Austrian poet, he concluded that the Zionists were following a path that leads "from humanity through nationality to bestiality" (Wistrich, 152).

In the words of his contemporary, the Lubavitch Rebbe, the survival of the Jews could only be assured by patience and by "sweetness of soul." Physical inferiority must be seen as a source of strength and tenacity. His opinion is a classic one. Elements of it can be found several centuries previously, in the writings of the father of Maimonides: "While the current destroys walls and sweeps along rocks, the soft thing remains standing. Thus the Exile destroys and breaks and uproots great pillars and enormous walls, but the Holy One, blessed be He, saves the weak and soft nation, that the current not sweep it along" (Ravitzky 1996, 16).

Yet the National Religious see the state as the beginning of the messianic era, which leads in turn to radical conclusions:

> Once the doors of the Holy Land are thrown open, there is no further need to prolong exile, and from that moment on the protection of Providence abandons us, and we shall be treated henceforth according to the customary laws of the world, where minority nationalities find themselves in danger of extermination. If exile had once been our painful lot, it has now become our fault. (Polonsky)

It follows that it is necessary to rely upon armed force — which is indeed one of the basic tenets of Zionism. On this point, the National Religious have aligned themselves first and foremost with the secular Zionists who had been, from the very beginning, dedicated to the use of force. After the 1967 war, they were to become its most ardent advocates. Even though the enthusiasm of the young Zionists impressed some contemporary rabbis, they did not approve of their actions:

> But they seek recourse to military and political strategy with a view to recapturing Jerusalem by force, and thus rise up against the oaths sworn to God.... They insist that the gathering in of the exiles must precede the arrival of the Messiah.... And this is not the holy path... for it is not by force and not by power that we shall return to our land, and no political sophistication of any kind can return our State to us. (Rosenberg, 362–63)

As the twenty-first century opens, violence is no longer the exclusive realm of the military; it has become a part of daily life among the settlers of the West Bank, among whom the National Religious form the ideological hard core. They are now extending their strong-arm approach first to Arab civilians and later to all those whom they consider as obstacles to permanent retention of the territories. This is the context in which National Religious young people dressed as practicing Jews attack journalists and international observers in the streets of Hebron and elsewhere in the West Bank (Settlers). Political violence against their Jewish political opponents has become part and parcel of this belligerent group, which has also been accused of encouraging the assassination of Rabin in 1995.

The critics of Zionism see not only the cruelty that for them is the inevitable result of the discarding of tradition by the National Religious and their secularist compatriots. They judge the bellicose behavior of the National Religious even more severely, accusing them of pretending to keep the traditions while in fact rebelling against them. For them, the National Religious are committing a particularly grievous transgression: the profanation of the divine name. For anyone who sees televized images of ostensibly pious Jews abusing foreign journalists and Arab civilians can only conclude that Judaism inspires such cruelty.

In reaction to the violent images that have become a part of the second Intifada, anti-Zionist rabbis have redoubled their efforts to dissociate Judaism — and Jews in general — from the actions of the Israeli armed forces. They have purchased advertising space in English-language publications in Europe and North America to denounce the violence, which they unambiguously attribute to the ambitions of the Zionists in creating and perpetuating the State of Israel. At a demonstration organized by the Coalition of American Arab and Muslim Organizations in February 2002, a leaflet distributed by Neturei Karta argued:

> Its [State of Israel's] cruel treatment of the Palestinian people is against the Creator's imperative that we deal justly and kindly with all men.
>
> To all our Arab and Islamic brethren around the world, let the message go forth today, that your quarrel is not with the Jewish people, the people of the Torah. We stand with you in your suffering. We feel your pain. We are with you.
>
> Let there be no more innocent victims, neither Palestinian nor Jew.
>
> Let us pray that the Zionist state will, with God's help, soon become a distant and dismal memory. (The Cry)

Despite their rather modest numbers, the anti-Zionist activists have been successful in transmitting their message of reconciliation with the Palestinians and of condemnation of Israeli military operations to a huge Arab and Muslim audience. They have given interviews to the Al-Jazeera network, which are broadcast throughout the Arab-speaking world, on Iranian television and to innumerable newspapers and magazines. On the occasion of the holiday of Purim, which was marked by an outburst of violence in the Land of Israel in 2002, the anti-Zionists declared: "Purim is a holiday that commemorates the victory of faith over barbarity, of good over evil. It is fitting for us to repudiate the current heresy and violence of Zionism on this day." In several major cities they burned the flag of Israel, accompanied by the following commentary:

> The Zionist experiment has reached its inevitable conclusion.

Death tolls mount and no viable solution is in sight. Slowly the Jewish people are awakening to the reality of Zionism, its rejection of Torah views of exile and redemption, combined with its aggressive stand toward Gentiles in general and Palestinians in particular.

By burning the Israeli flag we are symbolically declaring that the Israeli state, contrary to its absurd claims, is not representative of the Jewish people. In fact, its denial of our faith and its brutalization of the Palestinian people, renders it antithetical to Judaism.

It is the task of world Jewry to remain patriotic citizens of the lands of their dispersion and pursue peace with all men. (Orthodox)

From within Reform Judaism, voices questioning the existence of a Zionist state and accusing American Zionists of hypocrisy are also being heard. The American Council for Judaism has held to a traditional anti-Zionist position even though Reform synagogues tended to identify more closely with the State of Israel in the wake of the Six Day War. Rabbi Elmer Berger, the organization's founder, underscored the lack of coherence among his rabbinical colleagues, who, while struggling for justice and peace, refuse to condemn Zionism, which, he sees as essentially militarist and oppressive. "I felt a strange combination of sadness and near-amusement as I witnessed their participation in the civil rights battles in the United States while they were silent — and perhaps ignorant, as well — about the near-apartheid practiced by the Zionist infrastructure in the Zionist state" (Berger 1978, 3). Alan Brownfeld, a prolific writer reflecting the old-style reform movement, reiterates a point of view widely shared by Jews at the beginning of the twenty-first century: "... the contradiction between Jewish values and the uses of Israeli power is becoming a reality recognized by more and more Jews who seek to restore the humane religious tradition of their faith and separate it from the nationalism which, all too often, has corrupted it" (Brownfeld *Washington*, 87–88). For Rabbi Leitner of the Satmar community in Williamsburg, the very presence of the State of Israel engenders violence. "It would be easier to bring the Messiah than to make peace between the Arabs and the Zionist State" (Leitner).

The Roots of Terrorism

The political assassination of Jacob Israel De Haan (see Chapter 5 for the context of this terrorist act) is often used by the anti-Zionists by way of illustrating the cruelty of the Jewish national liberation movement. De Haan (1881–1924) was the spokesperson of Agudat Israel, and his killing set in motion a wave of indignation among the religious Jews in Jerusalem and elsewhere.

Driven by his Zionist convictions, De Haan, a Dutch poet, journalist and barrister, had immigrated to Palestine. Jerusalem high society lionized him; he quickly gained entry among the most influential circles. His reports, published in the Netherlands, expressed his boundless confidence in Zionism. In 1920, he organized a spectacular defense of Vladimir Jabotinsky, who had been accused of anti-Arab violence. But his acquaintance with Jabotinsky and the other leaders of the future Israeli right wing, which was fascinated by the growing fascist movements of Europe (Schattner, 297), alerted De Haan to the threat that Zionism's violent side represented. He began to deplore openly the aggressiveness of the Zionist enterprise and allied himself with Agudat Israel, thus becoming a representative of religious anti-Zionism. He also became aware of the conflict with the Arabs that Zionist activists were fomenting through discriminatory hiring policies, moral laxity and nationalist aspirations that had until then been foreign to the region.

De Haan's dispatches, published in the Netherlands and in England, began to adopt an anti-Zionist tone. De Haan knew Zionist circles from within, as well as the Western audience to which his reports were addressed. He had begun to think seriously about setting up an anti-Zionist coalition that would have included Agudat Israel and other religious Jewish groups, as well as Arab notables. An alliance of Jews, Muslims and Christians for peace stood poised to discredit the minority Zionists, who, imbued with a sense of mission, insisted that they alone spoke in the name of the Jewish people. They ostracized, degraded and insulted De Haan. One incident illustrated the difficulties facing this Western, middle-class Jew who had taken an anti-Zionist position in a highly ideologized society built around fanatical left-wing Russian Zionists. A Dutch tourist related that in the course of a stroll with De Haan through the streets of Jerusalem, several passersby spat upon the ground as they passed: "Is this not a sign of disrespect?" asked the tourist. "Not at all, it's a sign of respect for you; had you not been with me, they would have spat in my face."

De Haan began to receive death threats, but refused either to leave Palestine or to abandon his anti-Zionist activities. Finally, when a newspaper publicized his intention to establish an anti-Zionist movement on his return from a trip to London, agents of the Hagganah shot De Haan down as he came out into the street after prayers. An historian of the Hagganah gave this explanation for the assassination:

> Agudat Israel had thrust itself into the midst of a communal struggle. Until the First World War, the *old yishuv* was in control. They had comprised the majority of the Jewish population and now felt like prisoners in their own home. The *old yishuv* refused to surrender and submit to secular domination.... When they broke away and formed an independent community... no one disturbed them. Were it not for De Haan, they would have organized their own small community devoid of any political or communal signifi-

cance. De Haan used his connections to move the struggle into the realm of international politics. He aspired to establish a political organization to rival the Zionist movement, which was still in its infancy and not yet fully established — this was the danger of De Haan. (Danziger, 443)

The Zionists feared that De Haan would succeed in setting up a rival organization comprised of leading rabbis who would reject the nationalist ambitions of the Zionist movement and establish cooperative relations with Arab leaders. Such an eventuality struck fear into the Zionists, who, in demographic terms, were still in the minority in Palestine.

David Tidhar (1897–1970), the British Police officer in charge of the De Haan murder investigation, was also a Hagganah agent. Only forty years later were the accomplices to admit the organization's role in what was a political assassination. Tidhar revealed his participation in a radio interview:

After he [De Haan] had done so much damage, it was decided in the Hagganah to remove him and not allow him to travel to London. If he would have continued to live, he would have caused trouble. I regret that I was not chosen to liquidate him. My job was to protect those who did. De Haan would come to *daven Minchah* [pray in the afternoon] in Shaarei Zedek's synagogue. I was the officer in charge of the Machane Yehuda precinct, most of whose policemen were Arabs. I was asked to insure that no Arab officers would be present in the station between three and five in the afternoon. I replaced the Arab officers with Jewish ones and informed them that if they heard gunfire they were not to move until receiving orders from me. After thus arranging matters with the police officers, I moved into the area and waited for the shots. (Danziger, 444)

The order to "eliminate the traitor" came from the highest echelons of the Zionist movement. The description of De Haan as a "traitor" shed light once more on the influence of the Russian terrorist movements, much of whose rhetoric was adopted by the Zionists. Like the Bolsheviks, the Zionists considered all opposition to their political goals as illegitimate. Though they might tolerate tactical divergences within the movement, they could not countenance principled opposition to the Zionist project. Intolerance necessarily legitimized violence.

The Haredi leader, Rabbi Sonnenfeld, quickly lashed out at the moral morass into which the Zionists, blinded by their political aims, had fallen:

This murder, perpetrated by the descendants of Jacob employing the tactics of Esau in order to still the voice of Yisrael and Yaakov [the two first names of the victim], must strengthen us in our struggle to guard our camp against influences alien to our spirit and our Torah. This pure blood which has been spilled cries out from the stained *talis kattan* [ritual garment]: "You shall see it and remember all the commandments of the Lord, and you shall not be led astray after your heart"[2] on which the Sages comment: "This refers to heresy" [Berakhot 12b]. See the abysmal depths to which the Zionist leadership has fallen and call out in a strong voice: "Separate yourself from this evil community" [Numbers 16:21]. (Danziger, 441)

The horror of violence felt by Rabbi Sonnenfeld and many others served to underline Zionism's innovative, aggressive nature, which made the pious Palestinian Jews feel like "prisoners in their own home." These rabbis rejected the use of violence and the glorification of armed force that distinguished the Zionists from the residents of the Old Yishuv.

For today's critics of Zionism, the sad tale of De Haan reminds us that the terrorism the Zionists brought with them from Russia to Palestine in the early years of the twentieth century would ultimately be turned against their descendants in the closing decades of that century. Indeed, aside from the Hagganah, which was responsible for the assassination of De Haan, several armed organizations — such as Lehi and Irgun — perpetrated terrorist acts. Their leaders, Itzhak Shamir and Menahem Begin, went on to become prime ministers of Israel. What united these military organizations was the conviction that it was necessary to inculcate fear and to terrorize the adversary, all in the name of establishing a nation. Ironically, the same approach was later to be adopted by the Palestinian terrorists.

The State of Israel is perhaps the only democratic country where, after World War II, a political assassination could be said to have achieved its objectives. If the assassination of Egyptian President Anwar al-Sadat caused barely a ripple in that country's stance with regard to Israel, the murder of Prime Minister Rabin in 1995 by a young National Religious Jew arguably brought a halt to the reconciliation with the Palestinians that had begun with Oslo, or at least postponed it. The first political assassination, that of De Haan, had also achieved its aim. His murder put a stop to contacts established between the anti-Zionist majority in the Holy Land in the 1920s and the world's great powers. In both cases, terrorism bore bitter fruit: discord among Jews and Arabs.

The Torah stipulates that if the impious persist in their errors and do not return to the Torah after the third or fourth generation, their descendents will be punished for all of the sins that have accumulated since the first generation. From this point of view, Palestinian terrorism is a punishment meted out for the continued transgressions of the Zionists. It is also a punishment for having taken God for granted, suggests Moshe Sober, who is sharply critical of the faith he often encounters in the National Religious circles to which he is close:

> Lack of faith in Israel's future is equivalent to lack of faith in God Himself and His assumption of control over history. Figuratively speaking, we have but to march forward and the Red Sea will once again part before us.
>
> ...As a rabbi, religious faith is a concept with which I deal regularly. Trust in God is a prime value in Judaism, as in any other religion. But it must be clearly understood that the Jewish concept of faith is not a blind confidence that everything will turn out right no matter what we do.
>
> Faith in God means that the universe is run by a just and loving God who is not out to get us and is ready to give us a break, who will treat us fairly and mercifully — *as long as we are doing what we are supposed to be doing.* If God occasionally pulls out chestnuts out of the fire when we do not deserve it, it is an act of Divine kindness, which we cannot rely upon in advance; it must be considered against such negative aberrations as the agonizing slowness of God's intervention against the Nazis a few decades ago. The fact is that God has his own agenda, His own plan of history, and occasionally it calls for people to be treated in a manner which appears to us unfair, in accordance with His inscrutable Will. (Sober, 30)

Both rabbis and secular Jewish intellectuals have often used the same arguments to condemn the use of force by the Zionists. Amram Blau of Neturei Karta in Jerusalem accuses the Zionists of having no respect for human life: "they have proven to be irresponsible, extended their rule over parts of the Holy Land, which had been inhabited by Arabs, and thereupon brought the entire Arab world into conflict with the Jewish community" (Blau, A., 2). The analysis of Hannah Arendt, a secular German Jew assimilated into Western culture, hardly differs:

> And even if the Jews were to win the war,... [t]he "victorious" Jews would live surrounded by an entirely hostile Arab population, secluded inside ever-threatened borders, absorbed with physical self-defense.... And all this would be the fate of a nation that — no matter how many immigrants it could still absorb and how far it extended its boundaries (the whole of Palestine and Transjordan is the insane Revisionist demand) — would still remain a very small people greatly outnumbered by hostile neighbors. (Arendt, 187)

Zionism also had an impact on support for the traditional Jewish attitude to war. Historical research, not to mention historical novels, have revealed the contrast between the values of romantic virility espoused by

Christian royalty and aristocracy, and the deep-seated pacifism of their Jewish counsellors (Feuchtwanger). In our day, however, many Diaspora Jewish leaders number among the most outspoken advocates of the strong-arm approach with regard to both the Arab-Israeli conflict and the American intervention in Iraq. What is not clear is whether these leaders represent a true shift toward pugnacity among the Jews. Reputable opinion polls taken after two years of the al-Aqsa Intifada (2000–2003) and hundreds of civilian victims among Israeli Jews, the percentage of American Jews in favor of force to resolve the conflict in the Holy Land hardly exceeds 8 percent (Arab). Revulsion at the use of force continues to hold a dominant position in Jewish life, despite the incontestable cumulative impact of, first, Zionism and then, the State of Israel, upon Jews for more than a century. The Jewish adversaries of Zionism, in their commitment to peace, remain rather close to the mainstream Jews of the United States and surely of many other Diaspora communities.

Notes

1.   The Hebrew expression *ad hormah* is translated in the verse as "at Horma" or "to the bitter end."
2.   The allusion here is to the Biblical injunction to add fringes to the borders of garments so that God's commandments be remembered. (Numbers 15:37–41).

Chapter 5

Collaboration and Its Limits

> Who may ascend the mountain of the Lord? Who may stand in
> His holy place? — He who has clean hands and a pure heart, who
> has not taken a false oath by My life or sworn deceitfully. (Psalms
> 24:3–4)

Most of those who inhabited the Land of Israel resented the arrival of the
Zionists in the late nineteenth century. The pious Jews of Jerusalem were, in
fact, the first to react to the newcomers, whom they saw as rebels against the
Torah and thus as persons both evil and dangerous. They called for "breaking off all relations, even to the detriment of family ties, with whomever
belonged to the Jewish community governed by the new Zionist institutions" (Kriegel, 159). At the very beginning of the twentieth century, the
Meah Shearim district became the center of resistance to the invaders and
has since, along with New York, Montreal, Antwerp and London, formed
the hard core of the movement against Zionism and, later, against the State
of Israel.

The Arab reaction to Zionism was slower to gather strength. At first,
the local Arab population enjoyed cordial relations with Zionist leaders like
Haim Weizmann, who held out to them the prospect of economic and even
political cooperation. Only when Arab leaders became fully aware of the
political ambitions of the Zionist movement did their views come around to
those of the pious Jews in taking a rejectionist stance, which has remained
dominant in the Arab world ever since.

Pious Jews rejected the newcomers without making the slightest attempt
to understand their political aims. The secularism of the Zionists made them
immediately unacceptable to the Jews who then resided in the Holy Land.
While Arab opposition remained primarily political, the rejection of Zionism and, later, of the State of Israel by traditional Jews was deeply rooted in
their Judaism and was hardly influenced by political considerations. While
the Arabs came to recognize the Zionists as colonialist intruders who would
endanger their political and economic well-being, the Haredim were alarmed
at the danger of the divine punishment that the actions of those whom they
viewed as miscreants threatened to bring down upon all the inhabitants of
the Land of Israel.

To transgress the Torah in the Holy Land and to incite others to do so
constitutes a sin of particular gravity. The prayer of *Amida*, which Jews recite
thrice daily, provides the framework that explains, and in fact determines,

their rejection of the newcomers:

> And for slanderers let there be no hope; and may all wickedness perish in an instant; and may all Your enemies be cut down speedily. May You speedily uproot, smash, cast down, and humble the wanton sinners — speedily in our days. Blessed are You, Lord, Who breaks enemies and humbles wanton sinners. (*Complete ArtScroll Siddur*, 107)

Some prayer books include commentaries and interpretations of the deeper meaning of the words to be recited. Among the Hasidim, the prayer quoted above is occasionally accompanied by the following note: "One should intend that the Zionist State disappear in our days as soon as possible, without either pain or damage for the Jews." The same explanatory note can be found accompanying one of the Rosh ha-Shana prayers:

> And so, too, the righteous will see and be glad, the upright will exult, and the devout will be mirthful with glad song. Iniquity will close its mouth and all wickedness will evaporate like smoke, when You will remove the kingdom of evil from the Land. (*Complete ArtScroll Siddur*, 679)

Accusations of the utmost gravity are brought against the Zionists, who are considered to be more dangerous than the Karaites or the followers of Sabbatai Tzevi, for they threaten to turn the Jews away from the straight path and corrupt their souls.

The Zionists were quickly to become, despite their initial numeric inferiority, the active party to the conflict with the Orthodox Jews. The memoirs of a German general attached to the Ottoman troops in Palestine during World War I present a point of view distant from intra-Jewish polemics:

> How curious that the war has brought about an upsurge in the struggle between the Zionists and the non-Zionists, a battle that has turned ugly and has done little to further the interests of the Jews in general. The non-Zionists, that is to say, those Jews who had no political objectives and who belonged to the Orthodox current, at the time formed the preponderant majority in Palestine. The Zionists residing there represented no more than 5 percent of the population, but were very active and fanatical, and terrorized the non-Zionists. During the war, the non-Zionists attempted to free themselves from Zionist terror with the aid of the Turks. They rightly feared that the activities of the Zionists would destroy their good relations that prevailed among long-time Jewish residents in Palestine and the Arabs. (Von Kressenstein)

Resistance to Zionism in the Holy Land

Opposed to the Zionist enterprise from the beginning, the Old Yishuv waged "the fight against Zionism when it grew to the point of invading the Holy Land" (Blau, R., 192). Its contacts with the earliest Zionist settlers were all but non-existent. The Zionist attempt to convoke a "Jewish National Assembly" in 1903 was received with indifference by the pious Jews of Palestine (Weinstock, 146).

The ideal of Jewish unity, severely tested by the split between the Hasidim and their opponents since the late eighteenth century, was further eroded under the impact of emancipation and the Reform movement. To preserve their particular interests, the Orthodox communities of Germany and elsewhere had established, as early as the nineteenth century, direct contact with government, sidestepping other Jewish representative agencies.

The person most responsible for the decision was Rabbi Samson Raphael Hirsch:

> I cannot understand how any straight-thinking Jew can belong to an organization established for Jewish purposes, whose founder and director is completely removed from anything Jewish.... In the end, the difference between he who serves God and he who does not is fast disappearing.... It seems to me, that if ever there was an age which needed clear thinking, the clear demonstration of adherence to Judaism by each individual, that is our poor and debilitated age. (Klugman, 182)

He also opposed the recently established Alliance israélite universelle and refused to support the Hibbat Tzion proto-Zionist movement. Rabbi Hirsch's categorical refusal to compromise would be later held up as a precedent by opponents of Zionism: "There is room in the Torah nation even for sinners and rebels, because, as the Sages taught, a Jew who sins is still a Jew. But institutionalized sin and organized heresy have no place in the Torah nation" (Klugman, 184).

Ever since the Balfour Declaration in 1917, the Zionists enjoyed the support of the British authorities, which were more than prepared to accept their claim to speak on behalf of all the Jews of Palestine. A mission in 1918 by the Zionist Commission, chaired by Haim Weizmann, marked the first attempt to establish Zionist control over Jewish life there. Rebuked by the rabbis of the Old Yishuv, Weizmann held out a carrot: funding for the yeshivas. This approach mollified certain critics; others remained intransigent, suspecting that Zionist aid would become a means of depriving the yeshivas of support in the long term.

In essence, the World Zionist Organization intended to centralize charitable fundraising throughout the world and extended support to certain yeshivas as a means of eliminating their own fundraising. The effort was only partially successful; Haredi circles, up to the present day, have maintained independent fundraising networks based on their own institutions rather than on central agencies like the United Jewish Appeal.

The rabbinical authorities of the Old Yishuv, while adamant in their opposition to Zionism, were institutionally divided. The British High Commissioner, Sir Herbert Samuel (1870–1963), launched an initiative to set up unified structures to govern the administration of rabbinical law. A rabbinical assembly, convened in 1921, adopted the new structures, which resembled those that had prevailed during Ottoman rule and introduced a significant innovation: two positions of Chief Rabbi of Palestine, one Ashkenazi, one Sephardic,[1] an innovation that still survives in Israel.

The first Ashkenazi Chief Rabbi of Palestine was Rabbi Kook, whose attitude to Zionism was more positive than that of most rabbinical authorities of his day. Nonetheless, the attempted unification was only a partial success. The thought of subordinating their rabbinical courts to a higher authority was unacceptable to many Jerusalem rabbis, who recognized no chief rabbi. A gap began to grow between the Haredim and the new rabbinical structures. The educational system would henceforth be fragmented; relations with the Zionists and, later, with the State of Israel would reflect the existence of this gap.

Agudat Israel refused to participate in the Jewish National Council, organized by the Zionists. The formulation of its refusal was telling: the organization refused to collaborate with a body that had issued "a solemn proclamation of the deposition of God and the Torah as sovereigns of the Jewish Nation" (Reinharz, 135). The reason was not political; it centered instead on principled opposition to the new Jewish identity promoted by the Zionist movement. Given its refusal to accept the new identity, Aguda, led by Rabbi Sonnenfeld, could not accept even a measure of control by a predominantly Zionist organization.

Rabbi Sonnenfeld made representations to the British authorities and, at the international level, to the League of Nations, in an attempt to gain recognition as an independent community. Aguda successfully blocked adoption by the British authorities of legislation intended to give the Zionists full control over religious life. It also established contact with influential European circles, thanks to the efforts of Jacob De Haan.

The traditional view of collective return to the Holy Land focused first and foremost on repentance and observance of the Torah. But, in the meantime, the rabbis of the Old Yishuv wished to ensure the security of the individuals who made up the community and established contact with Arab leaders, such as King Hussein of the Hejaz. Rabbi Sonnenfeld, who headed Aguda at the time, along with Jacob De Haan, in February 1924 submitted a petition to the king. It confirmed the pacific intentions of the Orthodox Jews and requested that they be represented in all discussions over the future of Palestine. "We assure His Majesty that the Jewish population relates to their neighbors with brotherly harmony wherever they exist, and also in the Holy Land we will adhere to that tradition and in the future will cooperate with all the inhabitants in the building and prospering of the land for a blessing and peace with all ethnic groups" (Memorandum, 5). Wary of the possible negative effects of Zionism on the Jews in Arab lands, the document concludes with a request "that His Majesty will do the utmost to use his huge influence for the benefit of the Jewish people which live in all Arab countries." The meeting strengthened the ties of cooperation that De Haan had earlier established with Emir Abdullah, Hussein's son. As a result, the Emir signed a document welcoming Jewish immigrants to Palestine, providing that they not evince any exclusivist political ambitions, such as setting up a Jewish state. Abdullah's letter was read out to the Congress of Agudat Israel held in Vienna in 1923. A document of highest significance, the letter accepted the idea of mass Jewish immigration and the peaceful settlement of Jews in the Land of Israel. But it excluded the concept of Jewish nationalism, which was foreign to both traditional Jews and to most of the Arabs themselves. The document vanished forever in the burglary of De Haan's house following his assassination by the Hagganah a year later. With it vanished the possibility of peace posited in terms of individual and equal rights. The nationalist objective of the Zionists was to prevent that agreement from becoming a reality, but the fact that such a document existed reminds us that peace between Jews and Arabs had been possible. The policy that would ultimately prevail reflected the outlook of the Zionist immigrants from Russia, who opposed the old-stock Jews of Jerusalem.

The Haredim insisted on being a part of any eventual political arrangement with the British authorities. For them, it was a question of legitimacy. The Zionists, meanwhile, took very seriously the threat posed by Jacob De Haan: had he traveled to London, he might well have undercut their strategy to position themselves as the exclusive representative of the Jews in Palestine in their relations with British decision-makers. De Haan enjoyed high-level contacts in the West and was prepared to activate them in an attempt to combat the Zionists and their designs on the traditional communities of Palestine. He would also have had to convince his interlocutors in London that the religious Jews, with whose leaders De Haan was in regular contact, represented no danger for the local Arab population. He underlined the absence of nationalist ambitions among the traditional Jews, a nuance that placed them in a favorable position in the increasingly distraught context of the national struggle in Palestine. It is a nuance that often eluded contemporary observers, who seemed to confound the Zionists with their most tenacious detractors because both groups called themselves Jews.

Even though many of them spoke Arabic and maintained cordial relations with their Arab neighbors, the majority of rabbis in Jerusalem and elsewhere in Palestine were not at ease with either Western languages or, worse yet, with Western concepts such as that of nation, a concept central to Zionism. The Zionists, on the other hand, felt much more comfortable with Europeans than with these rabbis clothed in their long black caftans. By the early 1920s, it had become urgent to find a credible advocate for the anti-Zionist Jews. De Haan filled the need brilliantly, but the aggressive atmosphere created by the Zionists around the Old Yishuv cast a threatening shadow over his activities.

Indeed, the old-stock residents of Palestine, Jews and Arabs alike, did not fit in with the image of a "land without people" cultivated by the socialist settlers from Russia who claimed to represent "a people without land." The Zionists had arrived in a land where for centuries Jews, Muslims and Christians had, for the most part, lived peacefully side by side. But for the ideologues of Zionism the Land *was* empty: the picturesque traditional communities they encountered were, for them, nothing more than a part of the landscape. Not only did the Zionists ignore the Arabs; they hardly noticed the traditional Jews, whose Sephardic majority was integrated into the Arabic-speaking local economy. These were the very Sephardim that the Ottoman regime had recognized as the representative of the Jews in the Holy Land, whose chief, the *Hakham Bashi*, held high rank in the bureaucracy of the Sublime Porte. The pious Ashkenazim had developed mutual aid and charitable funds to meet their needs, which to this day remain their main source of livelihood.

The Zionists looked upon these pious Jews as vestiges of a long-lost past condemned to vanish in the maelstrom of the Zionist enterprise. Faithful to the tradition of European political determinism, the Zionists cast a wide net. They styled themselves the vanguard of world Jewry: and since the return of the Jews was, for them, inevitable, only they, the Zionists, could represent "the true interests" of the Jews, even if some of those Jews were not aware of their existence, while others dared to oppose them.

The assassination of De Haan was probably the first terrorist act to be committed by the Zionists in Palestine. De Haan was about to travel to London, where he would have attempted to convince the British government to recognize the rabbinical authorities that refused to be represented by the Zionists. That would have deprived the Zionist movement of its claim to represent the Jewish people before British and international authorities. The threat of the emergence of an alternative Jewish organization, both anti-Zionist and pacifist, was more than the Zionist activists in Palestine could tolerate. The murder of De Haan destroyed the links that the traditionalists had sought to establish with both the Arabs and the great powers. There was no one to replace him. Given their suspicion of European education, religious Jews rarely produced individuals capable of communicating with the outside world. Thanks to their peculiar dress code, the Haredim were certainly the most visible Jews, but at the same time, the least audible and the least equipped to make their ideas heard in the wider world. But De Haan's dream has survived the man. Some Haredim, including a former member of the Knesset, compared it to the Rabin-Peres plan for a "new Middle East," put forward in the 1990s, after several wars had left tens of thousands of victims in their wake.

Driven by their unshakeable faith in the regeneration of the Jewish people by Aliya and by productive labor, the Zionists took over the Jewish structures of self-government that had been set up by the British mandatory authorities. The Jewish Agency, the executive arm of the Zionist movement, was given official status; Histadrut, the trade union founded by settlers from Eastern Europe, became the center of the labor movement in Palestine, providing employment via its network of enterprises and social services through a system of clinics, cultural clubs and the like (Lockman; Shalev; Karsal).

The rapid growth of the Zionist movement in Palestine could no longer be ignored. The Ashkenazi rabbinical authorities of the Old Yishuv entered into an alliance with their European counterparts. Rabbi Sonnenfeld broke with Agudat Israel and established Eda Haredit, "The Community of the God-Fearing" in 1927. The breakaway took with it close to half the Jewish population in Palestine, both Ashkenazi and Sephardic.

While most of the opponents of Zionism were Ashkenazi Jews, the Sephardim also formulated a strong critique of Zionism. The Hakham Salomon Eliezer Alfandari, "*sabba ha-kadosh*, the Holy Grandfather" of Istanbul (c. 1826–1930), was the living embodiment of the Sephardic opposition. He forbade all contact with Zionists and inspired other Jewish scholars to attack them publicly. He found few differences between the Mizrahi and Agudat Israel, which had originally been established to oppose the Mizrahi: "The Mizrahi and the Aguda differ in name alone; what binds them all together is money and power rather than [concern for] the honor of heaven" (Ravitzky 1996, 57).

Another Sephardic luminary, Hakham Jacob Meir (1856–1939), leader of the Sephardic communities in Palestine, publicly attacked Zionism in 1928, at the departure ceremony for Sir Herbert Plumer (1857–1932), the British High Commissioner. When the master of ceremonies presented Hakham Meir along with dignitaries associated with the Zionist apparatus, the rabbi protested vigorously and declared that he neither recognized nor belonged to that community. Moreover, he announced that all pious Jews must separate themselves from it. Along with Sonnenfeld, he drafted a letter to Plumer in which he condemned the Zionists and called upon the British authorities to free the traditional Jews from Zionist control (Danziger, 450). The League of Nations later authorized the Jerusalem Haredim to remain outside of the increasingly influential Zionist infrastructure.

Their isolation ("right of exclusion" in the language of the day) came formally to an end with the declaration of the State of Israel in 1948, but the anti-Zionists attempted to obtain at least equivalent status from the United Nations, successor to the League of Nations. They emphasized that they had never signed the Israeli declaration of independence, even though Agudat Israel had done so. Aguda, argued the most intransigent anti-Zionists, had thus "caused the death of thousands of Jewish souls in the ensuing conflict of 1948–49" (Statement). The refusal to recognize the State of Israel would deprive the anti-Zionists of all political or social rights. To remain independent of the "Zionist entity," as they and the Arab countries referred to the State of Israel, meant accepting total exclusion.

The Eda Haredit policy of self-segregation affected almost all areas of possible contact with the Zionists. Following the death of Rabbi Sonnenfeld in 1932, a smaller group split off to follow a stricter course, particularly with regard to education. Readers will recall that Rabbi Amram Blau was to emerge as the leader of the new group, known as Neturei Karta. In 1945, Neturei Karta took control of Eda Haredit and in 1953 elected as its president the Satmar Rebbe, Yoel Teitelbaum. Thus was established a broad anti-Zionist alliance that brought together Eda Haredit, the Satmar Hasidim and members of Neturei Karta throughout the Diaspora. Renowned rabbis were behind this alliance, which deeply opposed all cooperation with the State of Israel.

The funeral in Jerusalem of Rabbi Blau, the leader of Neturei Karta, a movement of modest institutional scope, showed the surprising popularity enjoyed by the anti-Zionists. The ceremony brought hundreds of thousands of Jews into the streets of Meah Shearim. The organizers of the funeral explicitly forbade from touching the coffin all those who participated in elections, whether municipal or national, or those who enrolled their children in schools, no matter how ultra-Orthodox, which received state support of any kind (Hirsch, M. 1974, 5). The deceased had refused to use either buses or trains, because they were associated with the State of Israel; he traveled only in taxis belonging to other Haredim or to Arabs.

Rejection of Zionism in the Diaspora

Pious Jews were quick to take a stand against Zionism for one simple reason: most of them saw in it a catalyst for the deliberate rejection of Judaism. As we have seen, a Zionist could abandon Judaism while still considering himself "a good Jew." Zionism, moreover, proclaimed itself to be the beacon and advance guard of the entire Jewish people, rather than one political option among many. Judaic opposition to Zionism was thus quite natural.

Many Haredim are well aware of, and concerned about, attempts to cast the State of Israel as "the vanguard of the Jewish people." One source deplores the Zionists' success "in all international assemblies to present themselves as trustees of the entire Jewish people, and to our shame and disgrace, all Jews appear haughty as the result of the activities of these heretics in the international arena" (Mavo).

Attitudes toward European culture had little impact on the rabbinical critique of Zionism. Hasidic rabbis, who were quite closed to Western culture, shared the anti-Zionist opinions with Orthodox rabbis, who accepted and even admired European culture, and even with Reform rabbis in Germany and in the United States.

Opposition to all forms of cooperation with the Zionists was particularly strong in Germany at the turn of the twentieth century. It should be remembered that German Jews refused to allow the first Zionist congress to be held in their country and that it was finally transferred to Switzerland (Zionist). Rejection of Jewish nationalism drew its inspiration from influential Judaic authorities like Rabbi Samson Raphael Hirsch:

> Not in order to shine as a nation among nations do we raise our prayers and hopes for a reunion in our land, but in order to find a soil for the better fulfilment of our spiritual vocation in that reunion and in the land which was promised, and given, and again promised for our observance of the Torah. But this very vocation obliges us, until God shall call us back to the Holy Land, to live and to work as patriots wherever He has placed us, to collect all the physical, material and spiritual forces and all that is noble in Israel to further the wealth of the nations which have given us shelter. It obliges us, further, to allow our longing for the far-off land to express itself only in mourning, in wishing and hoping; and only through the honest fulfilment of all Jewish duties to await the realization of this hope. But it forbids us to strive for the reunion or the possession of the land by any but spiritual means. (Hirsch, S.R., 461)

This explains his refusal to consider Hibbat Tzion as a partner in the return to the Land (see Chapter 3). It draws upon the refusal of the prophet Ezra to allow the Samaritans to participate in the construction of the Second Temple:

> It is not for you and us to build a House to our God, but we alone will build it to the Lord God of Israel, in accord with the charge that the king, King Cyrus of Persia, laid upon us. (Ezra 4:3)

It was thus preferable to abandon the Temple and the land precisely because the construction was sacred and all cooperation with the impious was proscribed. The Mizrahi party, putative Temple builders, was roundly condemned in Germany as it had been in Eastern Europe: "The commandments of the Mizrahi, as a party within Zionism, are irreconcilable with the fundamental principles of masoretic Judaism" (Zur, 109).

The verse from Ezra sheds light upon yet another aspect of the Zionist enterprise: the government and people of the day would in no way accept anything that exceeded the royal decree and would thus risk deteriorating into a perilous adventure.

During the first decades of the twentieth century, Orthodox circles in Germany viewed the battle against Zionism as more important than the struggle against Reform Judaism. While Reform Judaism was a religious movement in which the Torah, however re-interpreted, remained central to Jewish identity, Zionism denied the Torah that central position. "Zionism is the most terrible enemy that has ever arisen to the Jewish Nation. The anti-nationalistic Reform engages it [the Jewish nation] at least in an open fight, but Zionism kills the nation and then elevates the corpse to the throne" (Zur, 111), fulminated, in the wake of the Great War, Rabbi Isaac Breuer (1883–1946), one of the most eminent disciples of Rabbi Samson Raphael Hirsch. The two movements, Orthodoxy and Reform, appeared to have buried their differences and expressed principled opposition to Zionism. Thus the Haredim were not alone in rejecting the legitimacy of Zionism in the name of the Torah. The Reform movement, in Germany as well as in the United States, had formulated, particularly prior to World War II, a position that closely resembled the Orthodox critiques.

Reform rabbis emphasized the pre-eminence of religious identity and condemned the transformation of that identity into a national, or even a racial one. In rejecting the new nationalism, they proposed, in the mid-1940s, "the creation in Palestine of a democratic political structure in which neither religious faith nor ethnic derivation would be a deterrent to full participation in the national polity" (Berger 1978, 12). But the Zionist leadership opposed the Reform initiative because it threatened to undermine the plan for a Jewish nation-state. The opposition to liberal ideas was to have a profound effect on relations between the State of Israel and the Diaspora (see Chapter 7).

Reform anti-Zionism had reached its peak before World War II. It has since declined, in response to feelings roused by the Shoah and the humanitarian arguments advanced by the Zionists as well as in the enthusiasm of the 1967 Israeli victory. Despite the decline, some groups within the Reform movement continued to oppose the existence of the State of Israel for reasons quite similar to those invoked by Neturei Karta. In a speech to an Arab audience in Jerusalem before the Six Day War, Reform anti-Zionism's best-known representative, Rabbi Berger, asserted that the Zionist threat hung heaviest over the Jews, who "may be [its] last and most tragic victims" (Berger 1978, 57). The prophetic tone could well have belonged to the anti-Zionist rhetoric of the Hasidim, who stand far away indeed from Reform Judaism. The rejection of Zionism may well be based on a Judaic sensibility shared by a great many Jews, despite the persistent ideological divisions within Judaism.

Anti-Zionism also created a rallying point for the Haredim, whose isolation and sectarian subdivisions were and are proverbial. Hasidim and

Mitnagdim opposed to Zionism share space in anti-Zionist publications, where Haredim of different tendencies quote the words of the great scholars of Lithuanian Judaism. For example, the widow of Rabbi Blau of Neturei Karta, respectfully quotes Rabbi Haim Soloveitchik:

> Zionism calls for a Jewish state not because there must be a Jewish state in and of itself, but because it considers that a Jewish state is the most practical way to reach its goal: to break the Covenant entered into on Mount Sinai, and to turn a holy nation into an earth-bound people. As such, Zionism represents the collective evil inclination of the Jewish people. (Blau, R., 262)

Evil inclination is a central concept in Jewish tradition: "Who is strong? One who shows self-control, as it is said: 'One slow to anger [literally: controls his inclination] is better than a hero, and one who shows self-control than one who takes a city (Proverbs 16:32)" (*Pirke Avot*, 4:1). Once again, we can detect the contrast between military and Judaic heroism, which consists of striving for moral perfection. From this perspective, the evil inclination has impelled the Jewish people to embrace the mundane definition of heroism: to take cities and to control them.

But anti-Zionist rabbis remained divided over the question of collaboration with non-practicing Jews. Certain Haredim resisted for practical reasons: "How can we collaborate with people who only want to change the composition of the Israeli government? No sooner than a party chosen by them will be in power that they will cease all opposition. For us, even if all Israelis began to practice the Torah, the State of Israel should still not exist."[2]

Rabbi Schach saw the left as Judaism's greatest enemy. While his pacifist positions were unmistakable, and he often put forward policies that resemble those of the left (he never hesitated to declare that the settlements in Judea, Samaria and Gaza constitute a needless provocation to the nations), he vigorously opposed any political alliance with the left-wing parties. He had identified among left-wing ideologues a deep-seated propensity to tear the Jewish people away from its traditions and to transform it into a people like all others (Ben Hayim). For him, the question of identity remained more important than any short-term political advantage that might be obtained from collaboration with the left.

Most Haredi authorities wish to proclaim their opposition to Zionism because they are convinced that it is firmly rooted in the Torah. Any alliance with those who do not accept the authority of the Torah is automatically ruled out. Yet, some anti-Zionist Haredim are more open to short-term collaboration with secular anti-Zionist organizations. The Hasidim may not be prepared to modify their positions, but some among them have suggested technical cooperation, in recognition of the superior public relations and communications skills of the secular agencies. But the reticence remains substantial. British Rabbi Joseph Becher was to insist, in the mid-1980s, that his contribution to a collection of anti-Zionist essays by non-Haredi authors be published in insert form rather than as an integral part of the book (Becher).

Jewish opponents of Zionism are even more divided on the issue of collaboration with the Arabs. Certain anti-Zionists favor friendly relations with the Arabs, which once again brings them close to the Israeli left. "The Zionist analysis of the Arabs is an aberration for an Orthodox Jew who, like my husband, was born in the old city of Jerusalem at the beginning of the century," writes Ruth Blau. "As Rav Amram used to say, the Arabs have been transformed into a kind of universal enemy of the Jewish people. Nothing could be more false. The Jews and the Arabs lived side by side until the British, then the Zionists, decided that it was in their interest to sow discord" (Blau, R., 276).

Yet, the question of ethnic solidarity remains a thorny one. Some, like the Neturei Karta and Lev Tahor, a movement led by Rabbi Shelomo Helbrans, reject the very concept of solidarity with the Zionists and developed cooperation with Arab organizations and sometimes even with Arab states. Yasser Arafat appointed Rabbi Moshe Hirsch of Neturei Karta as Minister of Jewish Affairs in the government of the Palestinian Authority. Rabbi Helbrans has attempted to set up a Jewish Embassy that could represent Jews opposed to Zionism and would offer an alternative to the pro-Zionist positions of the majority of Jewish organizations. The embassy would negotiate with Arab representatives to bring about a peaceful transformation of the State of Israel into a state of all its citizens (Gruda).

However, the leaders of the Satmar Hasidic movement remain aloof from political activity and avoid contact with the Arabs. They publish paid advertisements in the world's leading daily newspapers to publicize their opposition to the very idea of a State of Israel. But, as one of the Satmar leaders confided to me, they would not accept any Arab contribution toward defraying the costs. "Political considerations most often sacrifice truth, which for us is central" (Meizels). The position of the Satmar Hasidim is sensitive to the feelings shared by many Jews. While affirming that it is the continued existence of the State of Israel, rather than the Palestinians, that threatens the survival of the Jews, they abstain from appearing to collaborate with Israel's Arab foes lest they be seen as partners with "those who kill Jews.... The wars that have been fought in the Holy Land are not our wars, no matter who wins. But we are against the sacrifice of Jewish lives," notes a Hasidic author in Williamsburg (Filop).

Williamsburg is also the home base of Rabbi Abraham Leitner, a respected disciple of Rabbi Joseph Zvi Duschinsky (1868–1948) of Jerusalem, who openly opposed the plans of the Zionists before the United Nations in 1947. According to Leitner, collaboration with the Arabs is possible, but only in the perspective of peacefully dismantling the State of Israel and of transforming it into a bi-national state. For him, blood must not be shed. Divine providence alone can resolve the matter.

Indeed, a faction of Neturei Karta in America has begun to emphasize the humanist critique of Zionism. Focusing on the Palestinian dispossession, exile and occupation, they have come to see the treatment of the land's earlier inhabitants as a very grave flaw of Zionism. This faction is sometimes criticized by other anti-Zionists who maintain a purely theological opposition to Zionism and Israel.

Judaic opposition to Zionism could not improvise in either political or intuitive terms. To be credible, it had to rest upon reasoned rabbinical arguments. This was what led Rabbi Yeshayahu Asher Zelig Margolis (1894–1969), who had organized the visit to Palestine of the Munkacz Rebbe in 1930, to encourage the Satmar Rebbe to draft a fundamental treatise that would set out a legal and theological framework for Judaic opposition to Zionism. Over time, Haredi activism against the Zionist enterprise was to develop a solid intellectual foundation, the pivotal work of which remains *Va-Yoel Moshe*, written by Rabbi Yoel Teitelbaum.

In his own writings, Margolis paints a picture of polarization: a Haredi minority besieged by the Zionist hordes. For him, separation from the secular constitutes an absolute principle and a practical need and, at the same time, acquires mystical significance. He does not recognize that the Zionists have "Jewish souls," and, like many rabbinical authorities, he attributes their origins to the tribe of Amalek, the eternal enemy of Israel (Ravitzky 1996, 55), a condemnation as severe as it is unusual.

Amalek intervenes for the first time in the story of the exodus from Egypt (Exodus 17:8–16; Deuteronomy 25:17–19). There he falls upon the rear-guard, despite having no material aims. The juxtaposition of the two biblical verses suggests that the attack was the consequence of the doubts expressed by the children of Israel immediately after the flight from Egypt: "Is the Lord present among us, or not?" (Exodus 17:7). The ensuing verse reads: "Amalek came and fought with Israel" (Exodus 17:8). Tradition suggests that Amalek was intent on defying God, whose message was to be borne by the children of Israel. The injunction to blot out the memory of Amalek thus remains in force, in symbolic terms, to the present day.

To portray the Zionists as Amalek is to exclude them irredeemably from the Jewish people. While Judaism holds out the possibility of repentance to almost all Jews, Margolis points out that it remains open only to those who transgress in the heat of a short-lived temptation. But the behavior and the ideology of the Zionists are, for him, grounded in the conscious, deliberate rejection of Judaism; the gates of repentance must therefore remain forever closed. Ravitzky confirms that the decision to cast the Zionists as a diabolical force was far from an improvised one: it drew instead on an entire legal and philosophical tradition (Ravitzky 1996, 56). While fiercely condemning Zionist leaders, Satmar Hasidim treat rank-and-file Jews who consider themselves Zionists with usual respect.

The Sephardic Jews, meanwhile, joined the anti-Zionist struggle mainly in the Land of Israel. The Sephardic Diaspora had by and large avoided the political divisions and the ideological conflicts that had shaken the Ashkenazi Diaspora. Their communities remained united; the process of modernization among the Sephardim appears to have been more harmonious (Stillman; Kaplan), because the affirmation of a secular Jewish identity was all but absent in the Sephardic Diaspora (see Chapter 2). Generally speaking, those Sephardim who transgressed Jewish law did not do so in defiance; they recognized the validity of the rabbinical tradition but looked upon themselves as "too weak" to withstand the many temptations of modern life. Even in Israel, the Sephardic immigrants have remained closer to Judaism and number few secularist militants. Unlike Ashkenazi Israeli emigrants, those Sephardim who enter the Diaspora integrate more easily into Jewish communities. Sephardic Jewish identity has remained more tradition-oriented, more moderate and further removed from the polarization between the religious and the secular that has marked the lives of the Ashkenazi Jews both in Europe and in Israel.

Though they were unfamiliar with the conflict between the secular and the religious, some Sephardim had protested against the very idea of the partition of Palestine proposed by the Peel Commission. Prominent Moroccan Jews signed, alongside their Muslim compatriots, a strongly worded letter to the Foreign Office. Dated August 9, 1937, just a few weeks after the publication of the commission's report, the letter warned "of disastrous consequences that would result in undesirable troubles between Arab and Jewish elements." The letter ends with a call for "an independent Palestinian state to be governed by democratic parliamentary institutions, the only regime that can ensure both groups in Palestine equal rights in the country so dear to them" (Kenbib, 557).

From an historical perspective, the rabbinical resistance to Zionism seems natural; what is less so is the cooperation between some Orthodox rabbis and the Zionists. "Orthodoxy's willingness to cooperate with those who, according to Jewish law, were sinners, constituted an unprecedented compromise," notes Israel Bartal, a specialist in the history of Eastern European Jewish responses to modernity (Bartal, 23). It should be remembered that the first to feel directly the impact of Zionism in their communities were the rabbis of Eastern Europe, primarily those in the Russian Empire. They understood, more rapidly than anywhere else, that the Zionists were intent on radically transforming Jewish life, that they were investing the relationship between the Jewish people and the Land of Israel with a radical new meaning.

In the Diaspora, opposition to Zionism has been, for the most part, the work of Ashkenazi rabbis, particularly those hailing from the former

Russian Empire. Only later did Hungarian rabbis join forces with them. As Zionism was, in practice, largely "a Russian phenomenon," it was only natural that it would encounter resistance from Russian rabbis.

That resistance was fierce. Many Russian rabbis, including Rabbi Haim Soloveitchik, a leading innovator in Talmudic scholarship, were quick to grasp that Zionism, which offered a national identity devoid of any normative content, provided balm to the conscience of those who wished to abandon what they saw as the strictures of Judaism. In Lithuania, large numbers of eminent rabbis, fearful of legitimizing a secular identity, broke off all contact with the Zionists, refusing outright to collaborate with those who had deserted Judaism. When, in 1884, the Hovevei Tzion movement appointed as its leaders two secularists, that is to say, sinners in the eyes of tradition, most of the rabbis who had initially supported the movement immediately dissociated themselves from it. The lifestyle of the Biluim and of Hovevei Tzion, the first Russian "proto-Zionist" groups to settle in Palestine, alarmed the rabbis to such an extent that one of them issued a warning of exceptional gravity: "Whoever gives money to Hovevei Zion forfeits his reward in the world to come, despite all the charitable deeds that he may have performed and may yet perform" (Salmon 1998, 33). Taken in the context of a well-known passage from the Mishna, "each Jew will have a reward in the world to come," the rabbi's solemn warning carried substantial weight among practicing Jews.

The Russian rabbis considered the formally religious rhetoric of the leaders of the Bilu movement as a diversionary tactic. Two of the most eminent, Elija Akiva Rabinowitz (1862–1917) of Poltava, a delegate to the Second Zionist Congress, and Judah Leib Zirelson (1860–1941), an advocate of opening yeshivas to Russian culture, set up an opposition movement to Zionism. Such influential figures as Rabbi Shalom Dov Baer Schneerson, the Lubavitch Rebbe, would later join this movement. The alliance of anti-Zionist forces produced, in 1900, a book entitled *Or la-yesharim* (*Light for the Righteous*), an anthology of rabbinical judgements drawn from both Hasidic and Mitnagdic authorities. It underscored the threat of Zionism for the survival of the Jewish people and rapidly became a leading reference for critics of Zionism (Landau). Two other major compendia presenting a cross-section of anti-Zionist Judaic opinions, *Orah le-Tzion* (*Light unto Zion*) and *Daat Ha-rabbanim* (*The Opinion of the Rabbis*), were published in 1902 (Weingott; Steinberg). Among Russian rabbis, the reaction was categorical:

> We are dumbfounded to learn that men who do not accept the yoke of the Kingdom of Heaven, who have never followed the path of our Holy Torah, who neither know nor truly love their brothers…, boast that they are able to bring salvation to the House of Israel. (Lévyne, 226)

Shalom Dov Baer Schneerson, the Lubavitch Rebbe at the turn of the twentieth century, analyzed Zionism through the prism of the Talmud, with reference to "that man," as Jesus is often called. Rather than rejecting "that man," the Talmud suggests that Jews should have welcomed him and thus avoided his separation from the Jewish community. But, wrote the Lubavitch Rebbe, this approach would be of no avail with the Zionists, for they rejected the very idea of God, something that Jesus, clearly enough, had never done. On the contrary, it was necessary to keep the greatest possible distance from the Zionists, who sought the support of the Judaic authorities to legitimize their movement (Schneerson, 19–24). For Schneerson, Zionism was a greater threat to Jewish continuity than Christianity, a particularly serious accusation coming as it did from a Hasidic leader of his stature. Zionism provided an apparently innocent way to drive a wedge between the Jews and Judaism, the long-standing goal of Christian missionary activity.

Some see in Schneerson's condemnation — issued a century ago — a foreshadowing of the unconditional support currently offered to Zionism by several Christian evangelical groups. Critics also point to Zionism's borrowings, not only from secular anti-Semitism, but also from Christian religious thought. Some Zionist thinkers openly asserted: "the Jew must negate his Judaism before he can be redeemed" (Efron 1991, 89). The massive support extended to the State of Israel by the millions of Christian supporters of Zionism is overtly motivated by a single consideration: that the return of the Jews to the Holy Land will be a prelude to their acceptance of Christ or, for those who fail to do so, to their physical destruction. In his book, *The End of Days*, Gershom Gorenberg, a religious Jewish author, deplores the messianic scenario dear to many Christian Zionists, which includes the conversion to Christianity of great numbers of Jews and the destruction of those who refuse. In his view, "the evangelical scenario is a drama in five acts, where the Jews disappear in the fourth" (Cypel).

For the evangelical preacher Jerry Falwell, the founding of the State of Israel in 1948 has been the most crucial event in history since the ascension of Jesus to heaven, and "proof that the second coming of Jesus Christ is nigh…. Without a State of Israel in the Holy Land, there cannot be the second coming of Jesus Christ, nor can there be a Last Judgement, nor the End of the World" (Tremblay, 118).

These groups have provided massive political and financial assistance to the most resolute nationalist forces in Israeli society. In their view, the principal function of the State of Israel is to prepare for the Second Coming of Christ and to eliminate Judaism and those who profess it. This would explain why Christian Zionists have come to play an increasingly significant role in the financial and political support of the State of Israel. Millions of evangelicals have taken up a commitment to Israel as that country's population has become less and less Jewish (with the arrival of many non-Jewish immigrants from the former USSR, contract workers, etc.).

Yet the nationalist rabbis who benefit from Christian Zionist assistance tend to turn a deaf ear to the apocalyptic pronouncements of Christian Zionism and its claims that the State of Israel "is more important for Christians than it is for Jews" (Edgbaston). A messianic vision also drives the National Religious faction, and particularly the settlers in the West Bank, perhaps today's most highly motivated Zionists. The most significant evangelical group, the Christian Coalition of America, maintains close ties to President George W. Bush.

The State of Israel also cultivates the Christian Zionists, who give it an unconditional base of support in many countries. "As soon as I say the word 'Israel,' they start singing 'Hallelujah!'" an Israeli diplomat in charge of such contacts assured me. "You cannot imagine an audience better disposed toward us." In the eyes of many anti-Zionists, such ties only confirm that Zionism is fundamentally anti-Jewish — that it represents a more serious threat than the Christian missionaries upon whom the Jews have always looked askance.

There is nothing new about the categorical rejection of Zionism in the name of the Torah. At the beginning of the twentieth century in Lithuania and in the Hasidic regions further to the south, the Zionists were described as "the evil men of this generation," and Zionism was presented as a greater threat than all the false messiahs who had appeared in Jewish history: "[Zionism alone was determined] to uproot all the laws of the Torah and the commandments" (Salmon 1998, 33). Such was the origin of the slogan, "Judaism and Zionism are diametrically opposed to each other," which one can still read on the walls of Meah Shearim, in Jerusalem.

In the face of the growing popularity of Zionism among the Jewish masses of Russia, some rabbis sought a compromise. We recall that Rabbi Reines suggested an accommodation and went on to form, at the beginning of the twentieth century, the Mizrahi movement. But most rabbis remained opposed to any form of compromise. No rabbi would then use the neologism "secular Jew." That would have lent legitimacy to those who sought to negate Judaism. Indeed, the usual terms for Jews who reject the Torah — *posh'im* (sinners), *avaryanim* (transgressors) or *reshayim* (evil-doers) — are terms of opprobrium, hardly conducive to collaboration. The alliance between rabbis and Zionists required a vocabulary that Jewish tradition did not possess. Wrote Rabbi Domb:

> Zionism is basically the reverse of our Emuna [faith] and religious ideology. To become a Zionist means to conceive Jewry as something temporal and earthly, *utterly divorced* from all the divine connections, upon which the whole of Emuna [faith] is based.... Paradoxically enough, it was not grasped by the founders of the Mizrachi [sic] movement. They, although driven by the Zionist hostility to Judaism to form their own group, nevertheless *preferred to believe*

that a synthesis of these two diametrically *opposed* conceptions could be worked out. (Domb, 22)

Compatibility with secular Zionism looked little better. According to Israeli historian Barnavi, "the indisputable pragmatism of the historical leaders of the National Religious party had long obscured the atypical nature of this group in the Zionist landscape" (Barnavi, 226). Reines explains the upsurge of secularism as a "passing illness" that the return to the Land of Israel should rapidly cure. This belief, often attributed to Rabbi Kook, had become essential to those rabbis who sought a rationale for their collaboration with the Zionists. Even though the Zionist press was full of rabbinical approval for the movement, "none of these came from the first rank of rabbinical leaders in Russia" (Salmon 1998, 33).

During the years between the two world wars, opposition to Zionism continued to be the rallying cry for the most eminent rabbis of the time. Wasserman, like Margolis, compared leaders and ideologues of the Zionist movement, but not their followers, to Amalek, the archetypal enemy of Israel (Wasserman 1986, 3). Jewish heretics are thus to be considered enemies, unlike the rest of humanity, which every Jew is obliged to welcome with benevolence (*Pirke Avot* 1:15).

Given that the Zionist enterprise invoked the concept of Jewish unity, it was precisely this theologically important concept that drew attacks of both Hasidic and Lithuanian rabbis. Wasserman categorically rejected any form of cooperation undertaken in the name of Jewish unity:

> We are far from recognizing and from understanding the truth of the Torah in this regard, and events are so demonstrating this to us with every passing day. For example, when we are asked to elect representatives to the Municipal Council or to the [Polish] Parliament, the Haredim also attempt to set up "the Jewish united front" against the non-Jews. But who are the "Jews" who are our partners? Are they not those Hellenizers who are not Jews at all, and who attack us and despise us? Do these people represent us better than the non-Jews?... We are but affirming and perpetuating the lie that they are Jews, and we are defrauding the authorities in suggesting that these elected representatives are legitimate, and are honest representatives of the Jews.... "He who flatters the vicious falls into his hands." And all this can be attributed to our illusions, to our desire to recognize them as Jews. What is the advantage of these futile dreams when reality lashes out at us at every turn? They do not hide their faces, and they struggle aggressively against the Torah. (Wasserman 1986, 8–9)

Several Hasidic rabbis were to echo his opposition to efforts to bring

about what the Zionists call national unity but which, for them, was nothing
but an ethnic power cult (Marmorstein, 6). They firmly rejected cooperation within such a national framework, whether in the Diaspora or in the
Land of Israel. They also challenged attempts to undertake shared initiatives, for they rejected the very existence of common interests between Jews
faithful to tradition and those who have abandoned it and who are, from
such a perspective, no longer legitimate Jews: "He who abjures it is like
an apostate who no longer has the slightest relationship with us. But those
who follow the National Religious faction think otherwise: 'He may well
have rejected the Torah, but thanks to his nationalist convictions, he is one
of us'" (Wasserman 1976, 31). In Chapter 7, we return to the question of
Jewish common interests, a subject of capital importance in the discourse
of anti-Semitism.

Opposition to the Mizrahi ideology among the Haredim was theological
rather than political, reflecting a strict reading of Jewish tradition.

> Instead of returning the sinners to the straight and narrow path, the
> National Religious faction has become the faithful disciple of the
> freethinkers who use all their energy and their strength, in private
> and in public, against those who carry the banner of the Torah. They
> indeed build bridges between those who practice their faith and
> those who do not, but on these bridges we see only those who are
> heading in one direction: no one returns. (Wasserman 1976, 32)

For Rabbi Meyer Weberman, one of today's leading anti-Zionist thinkers,
the Mizrahi movement has caused as much damage to Judaism as the secular
Zionists, for it has pretended to remain faithful to the Torah, all the while
falsifying its meaning (Weberman). One of the points falsified by the Mizrahis, according to the Haredim, related to the excessive trust the Zionists put
in their own power. For Wasserman, this constitutes a form of idolatry. The
Zionists must then be described as idolaters, for Wasserman reminds us that
all that appears to man to possess the power to do good or evil independent
of God becomes an idol. The definition of Zionism as idolatry was to have
significant consequences in discussing what lies in wait for the Zionist State
when peace is finally brought to the Holy Land (see Chapter 7). However,
well before the proclamation of the state, Rabbi Wasserman concluded that
the entire Zionist project was destructive, rather than constructive (Wasserman 1986, 11). He went on to say, quoting his teacher Hafetz Haim, that
history was accelerating and that "the danger that the earth vomit up [its
inhabitants] was closer at hand than in preceding generations."

Relations with the State

Elections to the Knesset provide an opportunity to protest the very existence of the State of Israel. The principal of the Torah ve-Yirah Yeshiva, a

bastion of Haredi anti-Zionism in Jerusalem, regularly organizes protest demonstrations prior to Israeli national elections, threatening those who participate in the elections that they must answer "to charges of murder before the Divine tribunal" (Milhamot).

Major Sephardic authorities have also taken Israeli elections as a symbolic *casus belli*. Yakov Mutsafi (1900–1983), a rabbi of Iraqi origin, joined the opposition to participation in Israeli elections, which he deemed "impure" (Naimi, 109). His opposition to the State of Israel included refusing social welfare payments from Israel's National Security Institute (Naimi, 133).

Yet the majority of the Haredim, while remaining opposed or indifferent to Zionism, came to moderate their attitudes following the proclamation of the State of Israel: it is clearly more difficult to elude an existing state than an ideology. The state provides services and requires financial and personal participation; it also imposes its own identity on its citizens, regardless of their opinions. Total rejection of the state, of its institutions, its currency, etc., may no longer be practiced except by a few Haredi groups, but it still remains multi-faceted.

The principal of a yeshiva warned his students, following the proclamation of the state, in these terms:

> The Amalekites, the "mixed multitude," take many forms.... What was once called Zionism and ostracized as such by all faithful Jews is now called a state.... The so-called pioneers, who were always considered beyond the pale, are now members of the Knesset. (Ravitzky, 66–67)

If collaboration with the state legitimizes it, religious Jews who collaborate with it will suffer a loss of legitimacy, notes Ravitzky. Haredi radicals often lash out at Aguda, which they accuse of having succumbed to the evil inclination of political realism. Aguda's collaboration with the state, which has been going on for several decades, has drawn fire from many anti-Zionist rabbis. Critics point to the financial advantages accruing to Aguda's schools and other institutions, which may, they intimate, hinder the judgement of its collaborators: "You shall not take bribes, for bribes blind the eyes of the discerning and upset the plea of the just" (Deuteronomy 16:19). Those among the Haredim who accept public funds are accused of hypocrisy (Philipof).

Haredi collaboration with the state encompasses a wide range of issues, most of which is limited and conditional in nature. The positions taken by Rabbi Schach illustrate how to reconcile ideological purity with circumspect pragmatism. On the ideological level, he favored uncompromising opposition to the State of Israel, which he called a "collective revolt against the kingdom of God." While taking care not to lend legitimacy to the official institutions of the state, on the practical level, he focused on an overarching goal: to safeguard the Jewish people through the survival of its Orthodox minority.

As a result of Rabbi Schach's pragmatism, participation of the Orthodox parties in political affairs increased during the years that he was their leader. His was an approach that could be traced to Rabbi Avraham Yeshayahu Karelitz (1878–1953), a major rabbinical authority better known as Hazon Ish. He permitted Jews to participate in the Israeli political system while denying its legitimacy: "If a highwayman falls upon me in a forest and threatens me with arms, and I begin a discussion with him, so that he spare my life, does that mean that I recognize his legitimacy? No; for me, he remains a highwayman" (Ben Hayim). This is the response to the criticism frequently directed at those religious Jews who collaborate with the state. And as a response, it touches on the fine line that divides the public from the private domain. While to become a member of a Zionist organization is a personal decision, participation in a state is, on the contrary, imposed and thus loses much of its normative value.

In the event, the majority of Haredi Jews and their rabbis accept the state *a posteriori*, and then only as a concentration of Jews in need of the social and other services normally provided by a state. The acceptance is the same as the principle that applies under Jewish Law when a forbidden act is committed in error or without the knowledge of the person responsible for it. It is forbidden, for example, to combine milk and meat. Jewish Law forbids the addition of even the tiniest quantity, whether out of the desire to improve the taste or for any other reason, but it is flexible if less than a sixtieth part falls into it by error. The broth is thus considered kosher *be-di-avad* or *a posteriori*.

Most Haredim, in fact, can only accept the State of Israel as *be-di-avad*. They reject Zionist thought, whether secular or religious; they do not celebrate Independence Day or any other holiday promoted by the state; they abhor many of the practices of the state and avoid contact with the secular majority. Their sons only very occasionally serve in the Israeli army, and their daughters perform the obligatory alternative service not at all. Many do not come to a standstill when, each year, the sirens call the population to observe a minute of silence in commemoration of the victims of the Shoah. While they may be citizens in spite of themselves, the Haredim avoid the official name of the state, preferring to say that they inhabit "the Land of Israel." It is easy to identify a non- or an anti-Zionist Haredi: such a person will avoid pronouncing the words "State of Israel" or even "Israel," and will instead employ traditional terms with an Ashkenazi inflection: *Eretz Yisroel*, "Land of Israel" or *Eretz ha-kodesh*, "Holy Land."

These same Haredim reject the National Religious approach, which tends to attribute to the State of Israel characteristics drawn from Biblical history. The presence of millions of Jews in the Land of Israel changes nothing in the situation of the Haredim, who, theologically speaking, remain in exile since their residence there has not acquired a legal status comparable to that of the Jewish kingdoms of the past. Accordingly, the last head of the Lubavitch movement, Rabbi Menahem Mendel Schneerson (1902–1994), avoided use of the term *memshala*, which means "government" in a Jewish normative sense, referring instead to the government of Israel as *hanhala*, "administration," which, in Hebrew, has an inferior connotation (Hus). Understandably, the Haredim never employ such terms as *malkhut*, "kingdom," and *bayit shelishi*, "Third Temple," which convey a sense of continuity with the eras of the First and Second Temples and thus would tend to legitimize the State of Israel.

The Haredim deal with the question of national security without reference to ideology: the only question that can be raised with respect to any particular state policy is to ascertain whether such a policy protects human life. But even with this limitation, there may be serious differences of opinion. Rabbi Schach, for instance, criticized the war in Lebanon as adventurous and provocative, while the last Lubavitch Rebbe became an outspoken supporter. Rabbi Ovadia Yosef approved the withdrawal of Israeli troops from such occupied lands as Hebron and the Sinai, while his successor as Chief Sephardic Rabbi in Israel, Mordekhai Eliyahu, opposed it, often slipping into rhetoric closer to that of the National Religious faction than to that of the Haredim. Yet these issues, for the Haredim, have no romantic or ideological connotations and remain clearly separated from the messianic project; they refuse to invoke the biblical promise to justify political control over the Land of Israel. A Haredi member of the Knesset is rather straightforward:

> Zionists are wrong. There is no need to foster love of the Land of Israel through political and military rule in the entire land. One can love Hebron even from Tel Aviv. By the same token, there is no need to link the attachment to Hebron by means of Israeli rule there; the city can be loved even if it is under Palestinian rule. The State of Israel is not a value. Only matters of spirituality belong to the family of values. (Segev 2005, 6)

Significantly, it was Ben-Gurion, a principled opponent of Jewish tradition, who liked pointing to a copy of the Pentateuch in order to justify the Zionist claim to the Land.

Haredi Judaic critics have repeatedly attacked the political and military positions adopted by the National Religious. Following the Six Day War, the Mizrahi movement, which had initially been a minor figure on the country's political scene, became much more self-assured, for it had interpreted the Israeli victory as a divine miracle and later as a sign of divine approval for the settlement of the lands conquered in 1967. The most outspoken advocates of Greater Israel, meaning the annexation of the territories seized by the

State of Israel, relied on their own interpretation of the Torah, which was to make them more resolute than the secular Zionists. Haredi critics have likened them to the false prophets, a well-established category in Jewish jurisprudence:

> The Holy Torah enjoins us to remove ourselves from false prophets, and not even to listen to them when they talk about the Commandments. Even though their words may be in the service of God, it is forbidden to listen to them, for the Torah forbids us from hearing false prophets, even when they defend a just cause. (Teitelbaum 1998, 56)

Worse yet, in the eyes of certain Judaic critics, the members of the National Religious movement are accomplices to murder, for they foment wars in which thousands die. "We must flee as far from them as we can, for to remain in their company constitutes a grave danger for the body and for the soul" (Teitelbaum 1998, 56). Aguda's participation in successive Israeli governments, including the one that launched the war against Lebanon, has drawn similar accusations. No one, the Judaic critics claim, has the right to send Jews to war, both because of the prohibition against the use of force and for humanitarian reasons: "They decided irresponsibly to send thousands of Jews to war without considering the anguish and sorrow of the mothers and fathers whose children would be killed" (Torah, 17).

Aside from the basic texts — the works of Rabbis Wasserman, Teitelbaum and Beck — a series of stories passed on by word of mouth have inspired Haredi rejection of the State of Israel. One of these stories relates that when the venerated Hazon Ish received Prime Minister Ben-Gurion, who was at the time attempting to integrate the Haredim in the newly founded state, the rabbi neither shook his hand, nor looked him in the eye. It was apparent that he was acting out of respect for the Talmudic prescription that forbids looking upon the face of an unbeliever (BT Meggila, 28a).

Agudat Israel, the veteran Haredi party, recognizes the State of Israel, but with significant reservations. The Party encourages pious Jews to settle in Israel and strives to protect their interests. Aguda has participated in several Israeli governments; its members hold key positions in the administrative machinery all the while projecting the image of non-participation by their refusal to accept ministerial portfolios. In fact, when an Aguda member is promoted to ministerial rank in Israel, a legal fiction is employed. The Prime Minister appoints the Aguda member as deputy minister, while leaving the ministerial position vacant. In this way, Aguda shows due consideration for its anti-Zionist tradition, while promoting the political and economic interests of its members.

Despite the substantial divergence between Satmar and Lubavitch Haredim, and between them and the supporters of Aguda, all concur in

denying the state Judaic legitimacy. Aguda, certainly the most accommo-
dating of the Haredi groups with respect to the state, has found itself in the
midst of a controversy concerning its formal recognition. On the occasion
of its world congress, celebrated in Jerusalem in 1979, the organizers failed
to invite the president of Israel and took care that not a single Israeli flag
appear in the hall. The critics of this symbolic ostracism of the state were
quick to observe that "the refusal to invite the President was not a rejection of the man alone but of the entire State of Israel" (*On the Essence*, 4),
to which Aguda tacitly agreed, quoting Maimonides, who had forbidden
the appointment of an impious Jew to administrative positions of any kind
(Maimonides, Hilkhot Melakhim 1.7). While the Mizrahis see the state as
the work of God Himself (*On the Essence*, 7) and any insult to it as sacrilege,
Aguda followed the customary reasoning of the religious Jews:

> Zionism was dangerous when it was a dream and aspiration, but it
> is manifold more dangerous when it became embodied in the form
> of an independent state. This state has strength, it has means of
> influence and is likely to blind people with its charm and might.
> The danger of Zionism has not become less because a man who
> invokes the Name of Heaven stands at its helm [Menahem Begin].
> On the contrary: when the Prime Minister has a positive attitude
> toward religion and Agudat Israel is in the coalition — the chance
> of error is greater. People may think that things have changed.
> Therefore, it is imperative that we carry on our historic struggle
> against Zionism in all its forms, both the Jabotinsky brand and
> that of the Labour Front, for in this sense there is no difference
> between them. (*On the Essence*, 9)

Yet again, religious opposition to Zionism demonstrates how much it
has in common with that of the Palestinians, who also insist that the Zionist
consensus has obliterated all differences between the two foremost political
parties in Israel. For example, Aguda, during its 1979 Jerusalem congress,
took care not to make the slightest reference to the Biblical borders of the
country so as to avoid endorsing the National Religious position of holding
onto all the lands occupied in 1967. The congress declined to endorse the
prohibition, which the Knesset had just adopted, on contacts with the Palestine Liberation Organization (PLO); neither did it rule out the eventuality
of a Palestinian state. Despite the centrality of Jerusalem in Jewish spiritual
life, Aguda also abstained from endorsing the Israeli law that proclaimed
Jerusalem as "the unified and eternal capital of the State of Israel." All that
Aguda was, in fact, prepared to show in return for state financial support
for its institutions was a moderate degree of tolerance.

Religious opposition also appears to have smoothed over the deep doctrinal differences between Hasidim and Mitnagdim. When, after a demon-

stration, Rabbi Amram Blau was arrested and taken to prison, he received a visit from the Hazon Ish, who made two journeys in order to meet him. Upon his release, Blau commented: "it was well worth going to prison to have had the honor of such a visit" (Blau, R., 265–66). The Haredi approach, adds Ravitzky, and particularly that of the Lithuanian tradition, of which the Hazon Ish was a part, has displayed remarkable consistency (Ravitzky 1996, 176). The opponents of Zionism are well aware of the fact and appear to take pride in their fidelity to tradition. As Rabbi Schach commented wryly:

> When I am asked by the heavenly court why I did not identify with the Zionist idea, I will unhesitatingly place the blame for this on the Hafetz Hayim and the other leading scholars who preceded me, and they will already know what answer to give. (Ravitzky 1996, 176)

Prominent Sephardic rabbis have also taken strong anti-Zionist positions, despite the more conciliatory attitudes of their followers. Rabbi Israel Abuhatsera, better known as Baba Salé, (1889–1984), a Moroccan mystic revered by many Sephardim and quite a few Ashkenazim, praised Rabbi Teitelbaum's anti-Zionist activities and particularly his book, *Va-Yoel Moshe.* He had studied the book alone for several days, he said. When he had completed his reading, he organized a festive meal similar to those that mark the conclusion of the study of a Talmudic tractate. "This book is a great and important tractate for our generation, and Rabbi Yoel [Teitelbaum] is a pillar of light whose radiance should lead us all to the arrival of the Messiah." During the festive meal, Baba Salé recited several passages from the book, pointing out that Rabbi Teitelbaum had answered all his questions about Zionism "truthfully, without compromise." And on learning of Rabbi Teitelbaum's death, Baba Salé remarked that "the world had become empty" (Yehudiof, 217–19).

The refusal to attribute Jewish value to the State of Israel has allowed some Haredim to deal with it as they would with any other state. Following this logic, some Haredi leaders justify participation in governmental affairs, but do so in terms applicable to exile. Jews, they reason, have always sent representatives to political leaders in order to protect the interests of the community. In like manner, the Haredim justify the practice of appointing delegates to the Israeli government as a way of safeguarding the interests of observant Jews.

For those who, while rejecting Zionism, have not committed themselves to opposing it, the state is an institution that must be assessed on its merits. Those who tolerate the State of Israel and give it *de facto* recognition use, whenever possible, institutions that are independent of the state, for example, community-based rabbinical arbitrators rather than the Israeli judicial system. On the theological level they, like the majority of practicing Jews, consider themselves in exile. The question of collaboration remains a knotty one; many rabbinical authorities have pondered the question, often on a case-by-case basis.

As the Haredim's principal interest lies in maintaining and expanding their yeshivas, the decision of whether or not to collaborate with the government depends almost exclusively upon its generosity toward these educational institutions. Housing is another benefit that Haredi families, often indigent and numerous, can obtain from the state. All other considerations are, by definition, ruled out. The Haredim remain aloof from the definition and resolution of major national issues. From a Zionist point of view, such a position seems perfectly cynical; the Haredim are accused of parasitism, of profiting from the state while contributing nothing to it. They retort that it is not the tanks and the fighter aircraft of the IDF that protect the Jews of the Holy Land, but the study of the Torah, to which thousands of young people devote themselves instead of joining the army. Their argument only serves to underscore once more the cultural abyss that separates the Haredim from the rest of the population. But it also reflects an approach that has been developed over time with respect to collaboration with the state: the "father-in-law model."

In traditional Jewish families, especially in Eastern Europe, the best Talmudic students were married to the daughters of the wealthiest families. The pre-nuptial arrangements specified that the fiancé's father-in-law would underwrite the needs of the new family in order that the young husband might pursue his Torah study. The Haredim often conceptualize their relationship with the State of Israel in these terms. Without making a significant contribution either in fiscal or military terms, all the while consuming resources in the form of family allowances and funding for religious schools, the Haredim feel that they are offering a true protection to the population because they live Torah life in the Holy Land. The many sins against the Torah that have been committed under the State of Israel would have long ago brought about divine punishment, they argue, suggesting that they have assumed the role of the righteous for whom Abraham searched in vain in Sodom (Genesis 18:20–33).

Independence Day is, for the adversaries of Zionism, an occasion to display their true colors with regard to the State of Israel. Some, the most radical, burn the Israeli flag and don the sackcloth and ashes of the penitent. According to *Va-Yoel-Moshe*, the cardinal source of rabbinical anti-Zionism, to celebrate Independence Day,

> [is] worse than to accept idolatry; it is not only that they accept, but that they celebrate and rejoice in the terrible insurrection against God and His Holy Torah. There are many sinners, and even miscreants, whose hearts are troubled because they do not serve God, but they are incapable of resisting the temptation of

the false ideologies that have confounded them. But those who rejoice in their sin are guilty of something graver still: blasphemy. (Teitelbaum 1985, 2, sec. 157)

Most Haredim deliberately ignore all aspects of the national holiday. The daily prayers of penitence are recited, and daily routines proceed unchanged. Across the Haredi spectrum, attitudes on the whole are uniform. The following comments from a leader of Belz, one of the most conciliatory of the Hasidic movements with respect to the state, do not differ significantly from the passage from *Va-Yoel Moshe*:

> You should refute the heretics and the defiant ones who seek to uproot our holy Torah, saying to them: your rejoicing is our mourning and despair. To the innocent, unsophisticated ones among them, however, we are obligated to tell the story of our exile — the State of Israel within the Land of Israel. For this exile is the most difficult of all exiles; it is founded in that very declaration of he who declared the creation of the State. (Ravitzky 1996, 148)

The statement contains several meaningful allusions. "He who declared the creation of the State" is, clearly enough, its founder and prime minister, Ben-Gurion, who is seen in Haredi circles as an ominous, malevolent figure. But still more significant is the reference to exile. It alludes to the Passover Haggadah — the account of exile in Pharaonic Egypt — and it is to this tragic page of Biblical history that the leader of the Belz Hasidim compares the experience of life in Israel. The feeling of living under siege "in one's own house" is typical of the lives of the Haredim in Israel, who continue to exist in a kind of internal exile, identifying neither with the symbols nor the ideology of the state. They reject the very idea of the secular rebuilding of the Holy Land and above all, of Jewish nationalism. For them, living in Israel surrounded by the "impious" and led by "arrogant sinners" constitutes a double exile and is thus doubly painful. These feelings, however, are not merely the result of their experience of life in Israel; they reflect, above all, their relationship with the ideology that gave rise to the state. Rabbi Wasserman, as if anticipating the rise of a state conceived in accordance with the Zionist doctrine, foresaw in 1937 "the beginning of a new exile," of an "exile amid the Jews," of an "exile of the Yevsektzia" (Ravitzky 1996, 149).

A deep sense of alienation is felt on both sides, for confronting one another are two radically different, even opposing, identities and behavior patterns. The secular in Israel are repelled by the Haredim's large-scale exemption from military service and by what the secular see as religious coercion, while the Haredim feel they are constantly on the defensive in the face of a permanent assault by permissiveness on all that the Torah prohibits (Cohen, A.; Liebman 1990). Even the Arab threat, while strengthening ties among Jews, has stoked the fires of conflict: the Haredim stay at home, while the secular and the National Religious are mobilized in the defense of the state.

We know that, while the Haredim have remained impervious to the ideological arguments of the Zionists, they have proven far less so to the material blandishments of the state, such as subsidized housing. Haredi families have more children than their fellow citizens and, at the same time, are too poor to purchase apartments on the open market. The economic vulnerability of the Haredim has become an effective tool for bringing a portion of the community under Zionist influence. When Ariel Sharon, then housing minister, offered to build a Haredi city in the territories occupied in 1967, some Haredi leaders forbade their followers from accepting his offer while others remained silent. Thus, paradoxically, the town of Emmanuel became a bastion of non-Zionist Haredim in the midst of hard-core Zionist settlements. Emmanuel soon became a target for Palestinian terrorist attacks, transforming its inhabitants into hostages of a political situation in which, despite their nominal anti-Zionism, they found themselves allied with the West Bank settlers.

The imperative of preserving Emmanuel and a few similar settlements in the West Bank has encouraged some Haredim to participate in right-wing secular parties, and in particular, the Likud. Once Haredi rabbinical authorities had authorized their followers to vote for a secular prime ministerial candidate, nothing could stop the Haredim from playing a more active role in the secular parties and from voting for them. As they considered the Israeli left more anti-religious than the right, the Haredim began to vote massively for the Likud candidate, even though in his personal behavior he could be seen to transgress openly several fundamental commandments of the Torah. The *rapprochement* with the Likud detected by some observers (Dayan) may well prefigure the integration of a large number of Haredim into the political mainstream, easing the traditional reliance on specifically religious parties. In that event, a gap would open between those Haredim who continue to reject Zionism and the State of Israel, and those who feel obliged, for fear of the Palestinians, to participate more actively in the political life of the state.

As a result, several of the communities associated with Agudat Israel have tempered their criticisms of the state, while formally continuing to reject Zionism. Recent books published in the ArtScroll History series exemplify the tendency to accept some of the basic postulates of Zionism and to encourage a certain degree of patriotism and even political and military activism (Goldwurm; Holder). The Arabs are often presented as the enemy, "Jewish nationalism" becomes an acceptable, even positive term, the word "Zionist" is less and less used, and the dichotomy increasingly spoken of is that between the religious and the secular, rather than the Haredim and the Zionists.

Unlike Aguda and the other anti-Zionist Jewish parties that benefit from the resources provided for them by the State of Israel in return for their political support, the most intransigent of the self-excluded anti-Zionists receive neither state subsidies nor family allowances. At the same time, they continue to seek a political framework that would exclude them from Israeli rule, but would nevertheless recognize their right to reside in the Land of Israel. Before the end of his life, Rabbi Amram Blau of Neturei Karta requested a meeting with President Nixon in an attempt to ensure anti-Zionist Jews with the protection of any other country than Israel (Rosenberg, 912). The attempt proved fruitless; the anti-Zionists lacked the know-how, the means and the cultural affinity with the Western governments they hoped to convince to support their cause. While pro-Israel organizations, particularly in the United States, have developed effective long-term political alliances, often on issues unrelated to Israel, the anti-Zionist Haredim venture into the political arena only sporadically.

The State and Judaism

For many of Zionism's opponents the problem, as we have seen, is less the secular character of the state than the fact of establishing one in the first place. When people usurp a messianic prerogative, they commit a grave transgression against divine will. This rabbinical dictum should be seen as a reaction to the Zionist program for the ingathering and national self-determination of the Jews in Israel, with no regard for either their way of life or their relationship with the Torah. On this issue, the Satmar Hasidim and the secularists who struggle against religious coercion share the same opinion: "the state has no business in the synagogues of the nation." While for the Satmar Hasidim the state is simply illegitimate, for the secularists the state may not impose a religion upon the population. The separation of synagogue and state is the shared aim of both groups — based on diametrically opposed principles: opposition to the anti-Judaic character of the state for the Satmar, defense of liberal pluralism for the secularists. Prominent Haredi scholars published reasoned arguments for the separation of Judaism from the State of Israel (Vainfeld).

The state, in other words, should not be involved in determining who is a Jew or prohibit the raising of pigs. Legislation passed by the Knesset may reflect the Orthodox criteria of Jewishness, but many critics have cast doubt upon the legitimacy of parliamentary incursions into religious law. If the Knesset, they say, were one day to pass a law making individual Sabbath observance compulsory, this would only make Judaism appear to be created by people. Will Jews respect the Sabbath because they recognize their Creator and obey His laws or, as a conscientious citizens, will they simply be abiding by the law of the land? Any Knesset legislation may well include certain aspects of Jewish law, while ignoring others. Confusion between Jewish law and the law of the land would soon arise, leading those who observe the law of the land to believe that they are acting in conformity with Jewish tradition. Seen from this perspective, the secularization of Jewish Law would signify its profanation as divine revelation. However, most of Aguda followers are in favor of a state enforcement of Jewish law.

The National Religious, who cooperate on many issues with the secular Zionists, are concerned by the potential impact of the secular and their institutions on its young people. This concern, voiced by Rabbi Reines, at the beginning of the twentieth century, remains alive today. For example, the number of religious young people serving in the military who abandon the practice of Judaism has reached such a point that specialized institutions have been established to segregate them from secular soldiers. These National Religious young people divide their time between the army and a network of specialized yeshivas (called *hesder*). The effect has been to lengthen their military service substantially. Collaboration with secular Israeli soldiers remains a source of concern, because of their "contagious" lifestyle, but also because of political divergences.

National Religious youth is, on the whole, driven by messianic doctrines encouraging the settlement of the biblical Land of Israel in its entirety. The most enthusiastic, most intransigent settlers are to be found among those who profess National Religious beliefs. While many non-religious soldiers resent orders to serve in the territories occupied in 1967, refusing to protect those who, in their opinion, are little better than a gang of fanatics, National Religious soldiers refuse to obey orders to evacuate parts of the territories conquered in 1967. Conscientious refusal has now become common on both ends of the political spectrum.

Both National Religious and secular soldiers must also be protected from the influence of the Haredim. More than a few officers have left their military service to engage in full-time Torah study after attending lectures given by Haredi educators. In accordance with Israeli practice, Haredi students are exempt from military service. Some suspect that the exemption from military service may reflect the military's determination to protect its young soldiers from Haredi influence, as such influence could endanger their Zionist beliefs. The army has forbidden access to military bases to several Haredi groups that lecture regularly on Judaism. The Haredim, indeed, attract the youth by their apparent authenticity and their disregard for the Israeli mainstream, particularly in matters of dress and behavior. Even when they manage to penetrate army bases, the Haredi educators avoid using the expression "State of Israel." Privately, they display awareness of the subversive effect of their lectures on the young recruits. "We are against Zionism and its state," a Lubavitch Hasid told me. "But we have different approaches. The Satmar favor a frontal attack. We use the side door to introduce our ideas" (Hus).

Teshuva, as the return to the Torah is known, channels these young penitents almost exclusively toward the Haredi camp. Zionist Judaism, for all its openness and modernity, offers little attraction for those who seek a spiritual dimension in their lives and wish to become a part of the Torah-observant community. Secularists who embrace Judaism favor the more traditionalist, almost always non-Zionist, if not anti-Zionist, trends.

One of the Hasidic groups most opposed to Zionism, Lev Tahor, the headquarters of which was transferred to Canada in 2000, is largely made up of former IDF officers who have embraced Hasidic Judaism, leaving behind both the army and later, the State of Israel. Where once they wore green uniforms, they now wear black frock coats and have grown long side-curls; even their body language no longer resembles their former military bearing. Significantly, several members of this group have been drawn from National Religious circles. They have even learned Yiddish in order to avoid using Hebrew in daily life. Settled in the Laurentian Mountains, north of Montreal, they no longer teach modern Hebrew, which for most is their mother tongue, to their children. Artificial though it may be, their determination can be seen as a reaction to the efforts undertaken, more than a century ago, by Ben Yehuda when he abandoned his homeland, Russia, and his mother tongue, Yiddish, for Palestine and for the Hebrew that he had "desanctified" and transformed into a vernacular. Today, the Hasidim of Lev Tahor are restoring the "heavenly status" of Hebrew by using it exclusively for prayer and the study of the Torah, but insist upon speaking Yiddish among themselves. On my few visits to their rural settlement, their Rebbe granted them permission to use "the Zionist language" to discuss with me their anti-Zionism. In and through their lives they have turned back the clock, obliterating a century of Zionism as if it had never existed. Today they embody, both collectively and individually, the undoing of Israel called for by their spiritual leader (see Chapter 7).

The feeling that the Haredi variety truly represents authentic Judaism in terms of commitment to the Torah is quite widespread among the National Religious. At a symposium organized in Jerusalem in September 2001 by the New York-based religious Zionist group *Eda*, several Israeli educators and spiritual leaders admitted that more and more of those who held National Religious beliefs considered their path to be one of compromise, but that the Haredi worldview seemed preferable because of its authenticity. Indeed, when National Religious Jews change allegiance and integrate into Haredi society, they define themselves as *baalei teshuva* — penitents — despite the fact that they too have been reared in families that practiced the Torah, observed the Sabbath and the holidays, and enrolled their children in state-run religious schools. With messianic salvation through Zionism growing ever more remote, feelings of inferiority *vis-à-vis* the Haredim appear to be on the upswing in the National Religious camp. Hundreds of copies of anti-Zionist classics such as the abridged version of *Va-Yoel Moshe* were reportedly purchased among the settlers in Gaza and the West Bank (Hirsch, M. 2003).

At the same time, the Haredim continue to avoid association with "State Judaism." The use of the Star of David, considered the quintessential Jewish symbol the world over, illustrates the tension that exists between the state and Judaism, and of the alienation of the Haredim from Zionism and the State of Israel. Synagogues built before World War II often incorporated a Star of David into their decor, though its use as a symbol began as recently as the emancipation (Scholem, 243–51). Yet since the proclamation of the State of Israel, the Star of David is found mostly in synagogues that are openly associated with Zionism. Many synagogues that have remained non- or anti-Zionist, both in Israel and elsewhere, avoid using the emblem as a decorative element precisely because it has become a symbol of the state. They have taken their inspiration from tradition, which relates that the Jews had ceased to use a certain kind of monolith because miscreants had also begun to use it ([Rashi on] Deuteronomy 16:22). Other religious Jews avoid the emblem in protest against the behavior of the Israeli armed forces, which "are staining the Star of David with blood" (Brownfeld *Issues* 2002, 1–10).

Even more explicitly, one of the leading contemporary rabbinical authorities, Rabbi Moshe Feinstein (1895–1986), who moved from his native Russia to New York, discourages displaying the Israeli flag — "a foolish and meaningless object" — in synagogues. The State of Israel, he argued, represents no Jewish value and could not be associated with a Jewish house of worship (Feinstein, 105). Perhaps, the most prominent Sephardic legal authority, Rabbi Ovadia Yosef of Jerusalem, upholds Rabbi Feinstein's verdict and, in his comment, specifies that "those who chose this flag as a symbol of the State were evil-doers." Emphasizing that removing the flag, "a vain and useless object," from the synagogue should be done in harmony and peace, he recommends "uprooting all related to the flag so that it should not constitute a reminder of the acts of the evil-doers" (Yosef, 429). Rabbi Yosef's stance illustrates the original anti-Zionist position of Shas, the party that he co-founded with the late Rabbi Schach.

The Hazon Ish took an even more intransigent position, forbidding entry into a synagogue decorated with an Israeli flag even if there is no other synagogue in the vicinity. A Jew asked the Hazon Ish if it included the only Sabbath of the year when every Jew, man and woman, is obliged to attend services and to listen to the biblical verses mentioning Amalek. And yet, the Hazon Ish insisted that it was forbidden to enter such a synagogue even on this occasion (Steiner, 36–37).

The contrast with the nationalist feelings espoused by the secularist immigrants from Russia or Argentina, for whom Israel represents the promise of freedom and a full, meaningful life, could hardly be more eloquent. The new immigrants identify with the structure and the ideology of the state, with its political parties and, unlike the Haredim, many of whom have been residing in Israel for generations, feel quite at home there (Gitelman 2002;

Lewin-Epstein). But for the Haredi Jews associated with Satmar, Neturei Karta or Lev Tahor, any form of collaboration with the State of Israel is illegitimate. A key reason for this rejection is the responsibility they attribute to Zionism for the suffering of the Jews in the twentieth century, particularly with respect to the Shoah.

Notes

1. The Ottoman authorities had created the position of Rishon LeTzion, the Chief Sephardic Rabbi, in 1827.
2. Interview with a rabbi who asked to remain anonymous, Monsey, NY, November 12, 2002.

Chapter 6

Zionism, the Shoah and the State of Israel

> I shall hide my face from them and see what their end will be.
> (Deuteronomy 32:20)

The Shoah, the industrialized massacre of millions of Jews during World War II, holds a central position both in the Zionist discourse and in that of its Judaic detractors. The Zionists can rightly claim that some of them, such as Jabotinsky, foresaw the murderous tragedy and called for a massive migration to Palestine. For the overwhelming majority of Zionists, the Shoah stands as ultimate proof of the threat that hangs over the head of every Jew in the Diaspora. In their eyes, it lends full and irrefutable legitimacy to the establishment of the State of Israel. In the aftermath of World War II, the Zionist movement presented its political project as a reaction to the Shoah and, a mere two years after the fires of the crematoria had been extinguished, prevailed upon the United Nations to establish a Jewish state. Consistent with this argument, prevention of another Shoah also justifies the military hegemony the new state acquired early on and has steadily reinforced ever since. Among those who reject Zionism and the State of Israel are to be found both Haredim, who suffered proportionally far more than any other group of Jews during the Shoah, and Reform Jews in the United States, who were spared the tragedy. Many of the arguments of religious anti-Zionist thinkers are likely to bruise current sensitivities. Many may be troubled by the perception of some rabbis of the Shoah as a tragedy that summons the Jews to repent of their sins, and in particular of their support for Zionism. Irrespective of the vantage point from which it is discussed, the Shoah remains an emotionally charged subject.

The Catastrophe and Its Causes

Each time calamity has struck the Jews they have turned their eyes to the destruction of the Temple of Jerusalem, the event that Jewish tradition has ever since invoked to interpret tragedy. The traditional dictum, "All is in the hands of heaven except for the fear of heaven" (BT Berakhot 33b), means that every human being is endowed with free will. Free will is seen as a gift, whose misuse may well provoke God's wrath. A distinction is often drawn between a tragedy inflicted by God (such as the destruction of Sodom and Gomorrah) and a tragedy that results from the withdrawal of divine providence. In this interpretation, God punishes only the guilty; but when God withdraws ("hides His face") and humans inflict punishment, then the innocent also suffer.

From the Judaic point of view shared by most pious Jews (Soloveitchik), the tragedy of the Shoah calls out for the closest scrutiny of one's own behavior, for individual and collective atonement. It is not an occasion for accusing the executioner and even less an attempt to explain his behavior by political, ideological or social factors. The executioner — be he Pharaoh, Amalek or Hitler — cannot be anything but an agent of divine punishment, an undoubtedly cruel means of bringing the Jews to repentance (BT Meggila 14a, Sanhedrin 47a). In like manner, one of the songs sung at the end of the Passover meal, *Had gadya*, reminds those present at the festive table that the deliverance they are celebrating can come from one source alone: divine providence (*Shalom Hartman Institute*, 160–64).

Following this same logic, only divine providence can explain the catastrophes that have afflicted the Jews, affirmed Rabbi Wasserman, only a few years before his own death at the hands of the Nazis. His brief text, *Ikveta de-Meshiha* (*The Epoch of the Messiah*), remains one of the fundamental sources in the Judaic critique of Zionism. Wasserman was fully conscious of the danger that German National Socialism represented for the Jews. But he saw in it no innovation, no exception to the divine order.

We find a similar interpretation in the writings of his German contemporary, Rabbi Schwab, a prominent disciple of Rabbi Samson Raphael Hirsch. Schwab clearly describes the Nazi anti-Jewish legislation as punishment for the Jews' abandonment of the Torah. "God is calling them now, and they make no reply. People whisper to one another, with a furtive side-long glance at the forces which God has unleashed upon us for our chastisement, that this is not the time for making accusations. They glance into the harsh distorting mirror held up by the messengers of God, and believe that not they, but the others are to blame" (Schwab, 5). The German rabbi was remarkably prescient, writing as he did only a few months after Hitler's ascent to power: "God has smitten you, measure for measure.... The God of history reveals himself in the crisis and chaos of our age. Does my people know this?... Only one tenth will remain" (Schwab, 7, 13). He held fast to his views even after the Shoah. In a later English translation, he did not see fit to modify that part of his 1934 book that called on the Jews of Germany to repent in the face of the impending catastrophe.

For Wasserman the Nazi persecutions, of which he was soon to become a victim, were the direct consequence of Zionism. Of all the "isms" to which Wasserman had been a contemporary witness, he accused Jewish nationalism for fomenting war between the Jewish people and the heavenly kingdom. For him, the goal of Jewish nationalism was to banish God from the hearts of the children of Israel. As long as the Zionist leaders refused to foreswear their actions and did not repent of their sins, there could be no salvation. In singling out socialism, which had inspired much of the Zionist enterprise in Palestine, Wasserman saw an instance of divine justice in the fact that a combination of nationalism and socialism, both idols worshipped by the East-European Zionists, had engendered precisely the National Socialism that was to inflict such fury upon the Jewish people of Europe:

> Nowadays, the Jews have chosen two "idols" to which they offer up their sacrifices. They are Socialism and Nationalism…. These two forms of idol-worship have poisoned the minds and the hearts of Hebrew Youth. Each one has its tribe of false prophets in the shape of writers and speakers, who do their work to perfection. A miracle has happened: in Heaven these two idolatries have been merged into one — National-Socialism. There has been formed from them a fearful rod of wrath which hits at the Jews in all corners of the globe. The abominations to which we have bowed down strike back at us. (Wasserman 1976, 23)

He remained convinced that the Shoah, the extent of which he had intuited, could be nothing but punishment for the abandonment of the Torah that had been for so long encouraged and practiced by the Zionists. By this logic, as long as the Zionist enterprise should last, the Jewish people would continue to pay in human life for the transgressions inherent in Zionism. The violation of the three oaths was to cause the blood of the Jews to flow as freely as "the blood of the deer and the antelope" (Wasserman 1976, 23). The violence from which the Israeli population has suffered for more than a century would be, in this view, an ongoing punishment for the very creation and perpetuation of the State of Israel.

Both the Zionists and their detractors agree that the hostility encountered by the Jews through the centuries well exceeds all normal bounds: it is, in fact, a hostility quite unlike all others. But while the Zionists habitually attribute the phenomenon of intense hatred to the political and military powerlessness of the Jews, pious Jews tend to locate its root in the seriousness of the sins committed by the Jews:

> Whenever, in the course of history the Jew loses consciousness of his heritage and mission in life, it becomes necessary that his enemies rouse him and restore him to the possession of his faculties. The magnitude of his enemies and the severity of the methods they employ in awakening the Jew depend entirely on the intensity of the latter's lethargy.
>
> An analogy may be found in the case of a man who is asleep in a burning house. If he sleeps lightly a gentle nudge may suffice to make him aware of the danger; however, if he has sunk into an extremely sound and deep slumber it may be necessary to strike him hard in order to save his life. Similarly when the Jewish people are on the whole conscious of their Jewishness, anti-Semitism expresses

itself in minor annoyances which suffice to prevent the Jew from forgetting his destiny. However, when the Jew completely ignores the covenant which God made with his ancestors and desires to live like other peoples of the earth, then hordes of beastly anti-Semites swoop down upon him with terrific force and fury, as is the case in our own day. (Wasserman 1976, 44–45)

Wasserman's explanation, given before the Shoah, remains to this day an eloquent condemnation of Zionism. Like many others, he saw it as a sharp break with Jewish continuity. Quoting the verse: "Take care not to be lured away to serve other gods and bow to them" (Deuteronomy 11:16), he cites Rashi's commentary: "No sooner does a man turn aside from Torah than he embraces idolatry." In other words, the slightest distancing from the Torah presages a total break that would then justify a corresponding punishment intended to return to the path him who has strayed. Quoting Hafetz Haim, for whom "where there is no Torah, there can be no faith in God," Wasserman, his disciple, categorically concludes: "the reason for our present plight, unparalleled in Jewish history, must be attributed to the abandonment of the study of Torah" (Wasserman 1976, 46).

Rabbi Wasserman's last words, spoken as he was arrested, cast another light upon his interpretation of the Shoah:

> In Heaven it appears that they deem us to be righteous because our bodies have been chosen to atone for the Jewish people. Therefore, we must repent now, immediately. There is not much time. We must keep in mind that we will be better offerings if we repent. In this way we will save the lives of our brethren overseas. Let no thought enter our minds, God forbid, which is abominable and which renders the offering unfit. (*Jewish Guardian* 1977, 8)

The Judaic literature that presents this particular vision of the Shoah is abundant, draws on classical sources and begins well before Auschwitz. The political and military interpretation of exile by the Zionists is seen as an important cause of the catastrophe. As Zionism's transgression was a collective one, so too would the punishment be collective, recalling the responsibility of the Torah sages for the Jewish people as a whole: "On the road to Auschwitz, a Jew asked Rabbi Shelomo Zalman Ehrenreich, known as the Shimlauer Rov (1864–1944), why the Blessed One had caused this catastrophe to befall the Jews of Europe. He answered: 'We are being punished because we did not sufficiently combat the Zionists.' For, any offence against the Torah, even by an individual, will fall upon the community as a whole" (Blau, R., 259).

The Talmud warns: "Once permission has been granted to the Destroyer, he does not distinguish between righteous and wicked" (BT Baba Kama

60a). Warning that the righteous may be the first to suffer, it articulates the idea of communal responsibility, noting that God may punish one Jew for another's transgressions (BT Sheviot 39a). The death of six million Jews during World War II is thus interpreted as a punishment for the violation of the universal order committed by the Zionists, a punishment that was to sweep away even those who had never known sin.

On the other hand, Rabbi Issakhar Shlomo Teichtal, in a book written in Budapest in 1943, accused the Haredi leadership of having discouraged emigration from Europe to the Land of Israel between the two wars. Originally an anti-Zionist, he changed his mind and wrote this book before dying in the Shoah (Teichtal). Largely ignored in the Haredi circles (even though he remained a Haredi all his life), it became a basic text in National Religious schools. From his perspective, God used the suffering of exile to encourage the Jews to migrate to the Holy Land. For him, they would not be able to justify themselves after the Shoah by saying: "Our hands did not shed this blood" (Deuteronomy 21:7). As the verse refers to the absolution of the sages of the town from the responsibility for a murder committed in its vicinity, the accusation is a serious one, even though his analysis remains the exception in the Judaic literature dealing with the Shoah (Schindler; Schwartz and Goldstein).

Indeed, it is impossible to grasp the theological mechanics of cause and effect that determine survival. But for the Haredim, there can be no other means of explaining the powerful, irrational hatred that the Jews have suffered throughout their history. In the eyes of Rabbi Domb, the causes of this hatred elude even those who are its victims. He goes on to quote a rabbinical student imprisoned in Auschwitz who asked his SS torturer why he hated him so. "I am only following orders," came the response. But when he asked the reasoning of those who gave the orders, he was told that even they did not know why. "After that I could no longer see SS and gas chambers in Auschwitz, but I could only see verses, Psukim [verses] from Tnach [written Torah], moving in front of my eyes in the full living horror of their *fulfilment*" (Domb, 12).

Hitler dispatched to their deaths millions of individuals who could have been used in the Nazi war machine. During the last three years of the war, Germany suffered from a growing labor shortage, but Hitler, blinded by a hatred that can only be described as obsessive, acted against the immediate interests of his country. The railway system was mobilized to carry the Jews to their death; for him, it was a higher priority than his army's need for rail transport. Thousands of soldiers and officers of the SS, who would have been far more useful at the front, were assigned to tasks connected with the extermination of the Jews. Rabbi Domb — and he is only one among several Orthodox Jewish thinkers — sees in this inexplicable hatred scriptural confirmation of the special connection between God and his chosen people (Domb, 10), quoting the Pentateuch in support of his stance: "For a fire has flared in My wrath and burned to the bottom of Sheol, has consumed the earth and its increase, eaten down to the base of the hills" (Deuteronomy 32:22). In the same vein, Teitelbaum, the Satmar Rebbe, who was himself rescued from the Shoah, wrote:

> Because of our sinfulness we have suffered greatly, suffering as bitter as wormwood, worse than any Israel has known since it became a people.... In former times, whenever troubles befell Jacob, the matter was pondered and reasons sought — which sin had brought the troubles about — so that we could make amends and return to the Lord, may He be blessed.... But in our generation one need not look far for the sin responsible for our calamity.... The heretics have made all kinds of efforts... to go up by force and to seize sovereignty and freedom by themselves, before the appointed time.... [They] have lured the majority of the Jewish people into awful heresy, the like of which has not been seen since the world was created.... And so it is no wonder that the Lord has lashed out in anger.... And there were also righteous people who perished because of the iniquity of the sinners and corrupters, so great was the [divine] wrath. (Ravitzky 1996, 65)

In Poland, rabbinical thought was no different. The second Gur Rebbe, author of the notable *Sefat Emet* (*The Language of Truth*), Rabbi Yehuda Leib Alter (1847–1905) identified the then-nascent Zionism as a serious threat to the Jews well before the Shoah:

> Jacob [the Jewish people] wished only to live in peace when he was struck down by the calamity of the Zionists. Thanks to the mercifulness of the Lord, our situation in the world has improved considerably... but lo, Satan has come to spread confusion in the world. The Zionist leaders proclaim that we are threatened by a grave danger hidden behind the walls, and that the power of the enemies of Israel is at its height — God forbid! For this reason, our greatest duty is to protect ourselves from this confusion lest it take root among the masses. He who has a brain in his head must understand that, by their absurd writings, the Zionists will only increase hostility, if they continue in their impudence, to spread the defamatory rumor that we are in revolt against the peoples, and that we are a danger for the countries in which we reside. Their prophecy of misfortune may well come true. (Blau, R., 176–77)

Still others saw Zionism as one of the principal causes of the Shoah, but from a different perspective. Only a few years before the rise of the Nazi threat, which was to be turned against the Jews and against those of Jewish origin, Rabbi Sonnenfeld diagnosed the return to Israel in a state of acute illness, by which he meant secularization and Zionism, as an unprecedented danger for the Jewish people as a whole (Rosenberg, 441).

Written after the Shoah, Rabbi Blau's commentary is no less categorical, though more concise: "if it were not for Zionist sinning, the tragedy of Europe would never have happened" (Hirsch, M. 1974, 5–6). Blau firmly opposed the suggestion, widespread among the partisans of Zionism, that had the State of Israel existed in the 1930s, it would have been able to absorb the Jews of Europe: "This is outright heresy. I repeat that the Holocaust came as a retribution for Zionist sinning. They violated the three oaths mentioned by the Talmud as God's orders against working for a Jewish state, and thus brought upon Jewry such a calamity in which Jewish bodies were turned into Nazi soap. In all such matters what seem to be questions for non-believers are actually answers for us" (Hirsch, M., 1974, 6).

Rabbi Blau's widow would later add an historical footnote to the cause and effect relationship between Zionism and the Shoah. Recalling the message that Theodor Herzl and Max Nordau were actively propagating in the early twentieth century among European leaders that "the Jews constitute a foreign, destructive element for the countries in which they live," she quoted a minister of Emperor Franz-Joseph's government: "If the malicious propaganda that would cast the Jews as a danger to the world and as revolutionaries continues, instead of establishing a Jewish State the Zionists will bring about the destruction of the Jews of Europe." She concluded: "Hitler, less than fifty years later, unfortunately would make the Austrian minister's fear a reality" (Blau, R., 296).

Rabbi Joseph Zvi Duschinsky, representing the traditional Ashkenazi community before the United Nations in 1947, declared that Zionism had been the root cause of violence and friction with the Arabs, which forced the British government to limit Jewish immigration to Palestine from 1930 on. Zionism is thus presented as an obstacle to the salvation of millions of Jews from the Shoah:

> the colossal massacre of millions of our brethren at the hands of Nazism during the Second World War might have been averted to a very substantial degree for many of them might have been able to live peacefully in the Holy Land as there would have been not the slightest justification for the limitations of Jewish immigration as have in fact been enforced during the last decade. (Statement, 4)

Duschinsky had unerringly singled out Zionist militancy, holding it responsible for the White Paper adopted by the British authorities that imposed severe restrictions on Jewish immigration to Palestine on the eve of World War II. In other words, the rabbi concluded that, if the Jewish communities in Palestine had been in the hands of traditional leaders with no nationalist ambition, the customary harmony with the Arabs would have made it possible to open the country's doors to the threatened Jews of Europe. This conclusion bolsters the theological argument put forth by Amram Blau among others, which sees the Shoah as divine punishment for Zionism.

The lesson drawn from the Shoah by the Zionists brought forth stinging criticism from several Haredi thinkers. According to Rabbi Domb:

> Instead of drawing the right conclusions and accepting the mani-festation of God's will as a rebuke, they deliberately took advantage of the confusion which reigned after the stunning blow, to exploit it for their own political ends which are, in fact, the very reverse of those designed for His people. The mighty Zionist propaganda machine set to work soon after the conflagration to distort and mis-interpret the meaning of the event by allegedly logical reasoning. "This happened," they shouted from the roof-tops, "because the Zionist idea was not accepted long ago; because we did not have the means to defend ourselves and to fight back; we must therefore arm ourselves on a territory of our own, and once our Zionist nation has been established, our future will be secure." (Domb, 13)

Wasserman, meanwhile, notes that ignorance of the Torah and the ex-tinction of faith among many Jews had made them "the most unfortunate of men. They do not know the reason for their suffering; they have no one to turn to in time of trouble. Who can imagine the extent of their despair and disillusionment?" (Wassermann 1976, 24). Today, few Jews are aware of this Judaic vision of history. Wasserman believed that the loss of this traditional framework for interpreting adversities had left secular Jews helpless and driven them to violence, against others and against themselves.

The Zionists and the Shoah

Coordinated Jewish opposition to the German National-Socialist regime was an idea shared by many Zionists, whose thought naturally tended to function by national categories. Though some of Jabotinsky's supporters believed that "Hitler saved Germany" and would only oppose the Nazi ideol-ogy because of its anti-Semitism (Segev 2000, 23), it was the more militant wing of Zionism that took an aggressive stance toward the new German government. Jabotinsky acted as though he were the supreme commander of the Jewish Armed Forces. In his broadcasts over the official Polish radio and in articles published in the press in several countries, he lashed out at Germany. Nazi leaders mentioned his articles and speeches as those of someone who had quite openly "revealed the plans of his race" and who, "to the horror of the other Elders of Zion, spoke more plainly than they would have liked" (Schechtman, 214–17).

Indeed, his speeches referring to a unified Jewish nation played directly into the hands of those who threatened the German people with tales of a world Jewish conspiracy. It was precisely because of this attitude, which they saw as provocative, that many Haredi rabbis criticized the defiant Zionists. In fact, rabbinical criticism of the intransigence and the defiance of Jewish organizations toward Nazi Germany, was frequent throughout the 1930s. They accused these organizations — linked primarily to the Zionist movement — of dangerous and irresponsible behavior following the adoption of anti-Jewish measures in National-Socialist Germany. Wasserman reminds his readers that "the Jews must not combat their adversaries:... the Torah and prayer are our only weapons" (Wasserman 1976, 28). He condemns the "new leaders" who prefer struggle and demands. Sarcastically, he asks: "Whom must we fight? The strongest powers in the world. We must boycott them, and assemble at congress to shoot at them with newspaper articles, and thereby bring fear and trembling into their hearts" (Wasserman 1976, 28). While mocking their campaign, he protested against the anti-German mobilization of which the Jews appeared to have taken the leadership.

Rabbi Simon Schwab also sided with the traditional Jewish attitude of compliance and compromise. In 1934 he wrote: "the Jew must loyally serve any state into which God's historic providence has placed him, regardless of forms or changes of government in these countries." He must "go about his business quietly and honestly" and "strive to be correct in his dealings with whatever government is in power, but who for the rest devotes all his efforts to the inner religious consolidation of his Judaism" (Schwab, 20–21).

For several rabbinical authorities, in fact, the sin that led to the Shoah was Zionism itself. The Zionists, they insisted, had provoked "the nations" by their arrogance, had disturbed the quietude of the Jews of the Diaspora and had interfered with negotiations to save the Jews during World War II. The Zionists had, in their view, declared war on Hitler and his country well before the outbreak of hostilities. They had called for an economic boycott of Germany and thus provoked the dictator's rage.

Several influential rabbis, including Weinberg, who taught at the time at the prestigious Berlin *Rabbinerseminar*, opposed the boycott and the anti-German propaganda that accompanied it, both of which they saw as dangerous and irresponsible. The American historian Marc Shapiro writes that a considerable number of rabbinic authorities, including Haim Ozer Grodzinsky (1863–1939), Elhanan Wasserman and Yoel Teitelbaum, rejected the boycott as an attitude contrary to Jewish tradition (Shapiro, 117). Two irreconcilable approaches had taken shape: the traditional one, which favored negotiation and compromise, and the new attitude, which cast itself as a defense of honor and made no attempt to avoid conflict.

The conciliatory position may well seem incomprehensible in today's world, where bellicose and defiant assertiveness has become the rule. But it did correspond to the pragmatic approach that had emerged over the centuries in the Diaspora and which had become the object of Zionist disdain. Seen from the traditionalist perspective, any arrangement, even the most difficult one, is preferable to confrontation, particularly since the confrontation being stoked by the Zionists could not even be taken seriously. In fact, the Zionist strategy appeared rather like propaganda designed for internal use. Even the United States, where the Jewish community was relatively influential, was to bide its time even after Pearl Harbor, until Nazi Germany finally declared war. The impact of Jewish activism on the actual conduct of the war would, in any event, remain minimal.

In prophetic times, Wasserman noted, false prophets were more numerous than genuine ones, who were denigrated and held up to ridicule and calumny. But such prophets did not fear to risk their lives:

> The function of the true Prophets was to awaken Israel from its slumber. The false prophets fulfilled the reverse aim: to lull Israel with sweet dreams. All this is clear: It is easier to swim with the current than against it. Nowadays, we have no true Prophets; of false prophets we have more than enough... and just as Israel has paid the fearful price of listening to the false prophets in the past, so do we today pay this penalty.... So long as we are guided by misleaders who have brought us into a state of war with God, there can be no hope that our position will improve. On the contrary, it will worsen from day to day. There is only one way left for our deliverance — to make peace between ourselves and our Father in Heaven, the Guardian of Israel. Only then can peace be upon Israel. (Wasserman 1976, 29)

Even though some Jews saw the Zionists as "false prophets" and "deceivers," the nature of the Zionist movement remained ambiguous. Zionist activity in the West, particularly between the two wars, had emphasized the vocation of Palestine as a place of asylum for persecuted Jews. It did so because political ambition, and particularly the intent to create a Jewish state, by no means enjoyed the unanimous support of Jews in the United States and in other countries where Zionist fundraising campaigns were the most important. Indeed, internal debate clearly revealed that Zionism was above all an ideological movement for self-determination rather than a pragmatic plan to rescue Jews in distress. Russian-born Haim Weizmann is claimed to have said: "Nothing can be more superficial and nothing can be more wrong than that the sufferings of Russian Jewry ever were the cause of Zionism. The fundamental cause of Zionism has been, and is, the ineradicable national striving... to have... a national centre" (Rabinowitch, 10). Ideology would then explain the indifference of which both historians and rabbis accuse the Zionists. The Shoah reinforced the political determination of the Zionist leaders to set up a Jewish state; it was also to provide them with an argument of unusual power.

Shortly after the advent of National Socialism, the Zionists negotiated an agreement with the government in Berlin for the transfer of 60,000 German Jews and their capital to Palestine (Black). As in their contacts with anti-Semites elsewhere, Zionist emissaries in Germany established a smooth working relationship with the Nazi authorities, in particular Adolf Eichmann, who was then in charge of Jewish emigration. In the opinion of Howard M Sachar, a widely read American historian sympathetic to the Zionist movement, Eichmann "dealt cordially and cooperatively with Zionist representatives from Palestine. When the Zionists sought permission to open vocational training camps for future emigrants, Eichmann willingly supplied them with housing and equipment" (Sachar, 197).

Following the conclusion of the accord and facing British-imposed restrictions on immigration to Palestine, Zionist organizations undercut efforts to welcome Jews anywhere else but Palestine. In doing so, they drew sharp criticism from Reform and Haredi rabbis and, much later, from a significant number of Israeli intellectuals. All the critical voices concurred in accusing the Zionist leadership of being much more concerned about the future state than the fate of the Jews in the extermination camps. The upshot was that several planned attempts to save the Jews, in Hungary and elsewhere, appear to have encountered resistance from the Zionist leadership. Incriminating evidence can be found in anti-Zionist sources: in response to an appeal to come to the aid of the Jews of Europe, one Zionist leader allegedly replied: "One cow in Palestine is more important than all the Jews in Poland." Yet another, underlining the importance of acquiring a state after World War II, argued: "If we do not have enough victims, we will have no right to demand a state.... It is as insolent as it is ignominious to raise funds for the enemy in order to preserve our blood, for it is only through blood that we will obtain a state" (Rabinowitch, 11).

The negotiations between the Nazis and a representative of the Jewish Agency, Dr. Rudolf Kasztner (1906–1957), became the focus of a well-publicized trial in Israel. Kasztner, the court found, had agreed to a compromise: he assisted the Nazis in calming the Jews in the camps on condition that he select a few thousand Jews to be allowed to leave Nazi-occupied Europe. When exposed in Israel, he sued for libel, lost in a lower court but then won at the Supreme Court after an appeal by the government. In an atmosphere of public indignation, especially among the families of victims of the Shoah, Kasztner was shot to death on a Tel Aviv street (Sachar, 373–6).

In anti-Zionist circles, the verdict was clear: "In the twentieth century, the blood of six million Jewish victims, men, women, children, the elderly, had been traded for a state by its founders and leaders. What normal human being could be capable of imagining such a monstrosity?" (Blau, R., 184–85). Some even wondered aloud if Ben-Gurion was truly "human." In 1938, following the *Kristallnacht*, which unleashed physical violence against the Jews of Germany, Ben-Gurion is reputed to have said: "If I knew that all Jewish children could be saved by having them relocated to England, but only half by transferring them to Palestine, I would choose the second option, because what is at stake would not only have been the fate of those children, but also the historical destiny of the Jewish people" (Porat, 120). Consistent with his vision, Ben-Gurion "was opposed… to the creation of a strong, competent official agency with the necessary resources to undertake rescue operations, as well as to the use, for such operations, of funds raised by Zionist organizations. Nor did he call upon the American Jews to raise significant funds to be used for this purpose" (Porat, 128). On another occasion, after the deposition on the extermination of the Jews of Europe in Yiddish by a survivor of the Vilnius ghetto, Ben-Gurion is reported to have said in a "cold, even hostile manner" that the woman had used "a foreign, rough-sounding language" (Porat, 121).

Ben-Gurion's personality aside, the Zionist movement stands accused of turning a blind eye to the fate of the European Jews, except when the Shoah might serve the objectives of Zionism, and to torpedo rescue efforts that did not correspond with its political objectives (Kranzler). The Zionist leadership is accused of "blocking attempts to allow European Jews to immigrate to other parts of the world, in order to force them to emigrate to Palestine" (Porat, 122). Made by Israeli historians at the end of the twentieth century, these observations confirm what the rabbis in black frockcoats had long been asserting. What might be described as the Jewish consensus had not previously taken these rabbis seriously. And it was probably not a matter of their cultural distinctiveness. Accusations of this gravity were ignored, even when they emerged from culturally like-minded Reform circles that were thoroughly integrated into American society.

Following a visit to the Jewish communities of Europe before World War II, Rabbi Morris Lazaron (1888–1979), a representative of American Reform Judaism, protested against the concentration of funding on projects in Palestine to the detriment of efforts to rescue the Jews of Europe, then under direct threat from the Nazis. He went on to criticize the Zionist assertion that only Palestine could become a safe haven for the Jews. He lashed out at the Zionist propaganda that sought to convince Jews that, sooner or later, the entire world would reject them because of their Jewishness. In his opinion, there was no reason to undermine the confidence of American Jewry by inviting them to abandon all confidence in emancipation because of German policy (Greenstein, 79).

Another Reform rabbi, Elmer Berger, attributed to the Zionists the same crime of which the Haredim accused them: that of sabotaging any initiative for the rescue of the Jews of Europe, including the decision by President Roosevelt to find, during the earliest days of the war, countries that would offer the refugees asylum. The president, it appears, had grasped the Zionist logic:

"Well, they're right from their point of view. The Zionist movement knows that Palestine is, and will be for some time, a remittance society. They know that they can raise vast sums for Palestine by saying to donors 'there is no other place this poor Jew can go.'" "But," said Roosevelt, "if there's a world political asylum for all people irrespective of race, creed or color, they can't raise their money. Because the people who don't want to give the money will have an excuse and say, 'what do you mean there's no place they can go but Palestine?' They are the preferred wards of the world." (Berger 1957, 57)

Morris Ernst (1888–1976), a human rights activist with close ties to Roosevelt who reported the president's remarks, set out to test the veracity of what he had heard and informed his Zionist friends of the White House initiative. "I assure you that I was thrown out of parlors of friends of mine. And they said very frankly, and they were right from their point of view. 'Morris,' they would say, 'this is treason — you're undermining the Zionist movement.' I'd say, 'Yes, maybe I am. But I am much more interested in a haven for a half a million or million people — oppressed throughout the world." The *New York Times* editorialist went on to comment: "Why in God's name, should the fate of all those unhappy people be subordinated to a single cry of Statehood?" (Berger 1957, 57).

Following the Six Day War, Ruth Blau drew attention to the difference between the massive support given to Israel on the eve of hostilities, for which she held the Israeli leadership fully responsible, and the indifference of Jewish leaders that met a proposal to pay $50 per capita to rescue hundreds of thousands of Jews from the Shoah: "What a contrast between the tumult of 1967 and the deathly silence of the Zionist chiefs concerning the holocaust of 1940–45, that they knew all about" (Blau, R., 235).

Several sources accuse the Zionist movement of applying a policy of "selection," that is, of admitting to Palestine only those most likely to make an active contribution to the Zionist enterprise, from a political or economic point of view. The term "selection" has particularly ominous resonance: as Jews stepped from the trains that had brought them to the extermination camps, the SS selected those who might, for a period of time, contribute to the economy of the Reich through forced labor, while the non-selected were immediately dispatched to the gas chambers. A 1938 speech given by Haim Weizmann, the future president of Israel, is often cited in this respect:

Palestine cannot absorb the Jews of Europe. We want only the best of Jewish youth to come to us. We want only the educated to enter Palestine for the purpose of increasing its culture. The other Jews will have to stay where they are and face whatever fate awaits them. These millions of Jews are dust on the wheels of history and they may have to be blown away. We don't want them pouring into Palestine. We don't want Tel Aviv to become another low-grade ghetto. (Bell, 35)

It is unlikely that Weizmann's remarks were a slip of the tongue; a year earlier, he had used similar terms: "The elderly will disappear, their fate awaits them. They have no significance, either economic or moral. The elderly must reconcile themselves to their fate." His attitude, frequently denounced by the religious anti-Zionists, did not escape the attention of the Western press. Shortly after the war, a human rights advocate wrote: "Who can tell how many thousands of Jewish lives might have been saved from Hitler's claws if these anti-Jewish pressures exerted by Jews had not been effected?" (Sussman, 428).

In Israel, some historians seem to confirm the accusations of historical responsibility for the Shoah leveled against the Zionist movement by Haredi and Reform rabbis alike. Though they express themselves in different language, they concur in their assessment that Ben-Gurion and his circle hindered attempts to save the European Jewish communities from extermination. The Zionist leadership, they argue, did its utmost to subordinate rescue efforts to their primary objective, which was the creation of a New Hebrew people and the establishment of a Jewish state. It treated human beings as "human material," reducing the survival and the death of millions to a matter of political expediency (Segev 1993). The anti-Zionist critique can be better understood when one reads in a scholarly work that:

> The Jewish communities scattered across Central and Eastern Europe were important to the founders chiefly as a source of pioneers. They were considered to have no value in themselves. Even at the height of the Second World War, there was no change in the order of priorities: it was not the rescue of Jews as such that topped Berl Katznelson's order of priorities but the organization of the Zionist movement in Europe.... Thus, every event in the nation's life was evaluated according to a single criterion: the degree to which it contributed to Zionism. (Sternhell, 50)

The Zionist movement, like so many of the twentieth-century movements that promised social transformation, had adopted the principle of functional morality — yet another instance of cultural affinity with the Russian Bolsheviks. A few months after seizing power in Russia, Lenin called upon a congress of young Communists to abandon the old morality and to shape a new, class-based morality that would have only one criterion: its utility to the struggle of the working class. The Zionists' relationship to the Shoah reflected a similar conviction: "as they saw it, Zionism was an operation to rescue the nation and not an operation to rescue Jews as individuals" (Sternhell, 51). It was not the first time that individual interests were to collide with those of a state, but in this particular case, even though the state was nothing but an idea, the confrontation proved tragic in the extreme.

Those who draw a distinction between individual morality and that of the state appear to have departed from Jewish tradition: "Every Jew is born a subject of his king, and by the same token, a Jewish state... can exist and survive only if it is in accordance with the sovereign will of God the king" (Schwab, 32). An Israeli expert in political history sketches out the morality to which the opponents of Zionism were not alone in subscribing:

> For the Prophets and the Bible as a whole, the same standard of good and evil, right and wrong, applied to the behavior of God and man, the individual and the nation. Cruelty and injustice, violence and oppression were violations of the principle which for them was built into the structure of the universe — that doing right leads to well-being and doing wrong to disaster — both in the life of the individual and in affairs of state. This principle, which I have called "the law of consequence" can no more be violated with impunity than any fundamental law in the physical universe.... He who would argue for dichotomy between the ethics of the individual and the morality of government flies in the face of Jewish tradition; indeed, the tradition would insist that it runs counter to the testimony of human experience and is doomed to failure.... What is decisively ruled out is any approach — whether to the Arab-Israel problem or any other — that establishes a dichotomy between politics and morality. (Gordis, 49–50)

Fixation on the state had pushed aside traditional compassion, both in terms of the failure to rescue the Jews during the Shoah and in terms of relations to the survivors of the catastrophe. It was this moral re-conversion that drew the ire of the Judaic critics of Zionism. The Haredim and those belonging to Reform Jewish circles were undoubtedly the first to compare the Zionists to the Nazis on several levels: the definition of a Jew, the cult of strength and the worship of the state. They were quick to accuse them of the same cold indifference toward the victims as had been displayed by the Nazi officials (Schonfeld 1977). Such comparisons, frequently made at the time, lost some of their credibility after Soviet propaganda and later on some Arab media took them up.

Today, however, the indifference of the Zionist leadership toward the victims is well documented (Segev 1993). Survivors arriving in Israel after the Shoah encountered scorn and even hostility. The mistreatment of Shoah survivors touched off, at the time, sharp criticism in Jewish anti-Zionist publications. The State of Israel, whose interests took precedence, was accused of systematically undercutting attempts by other countries to take in the survivors or any other group of Jews. The Zionists were accused of instituting a "reign of terror" among Shoah survivors interned in the displaced persons' camps of Europe. Zionist emissaries reportedly used coercion, food deprivation and violence against Shoah survivors in order to extort money and draft them in the Israeli army. The Zionist leaders believed that "a survivor, a stateless Jew becomes ipso facto a citizen of the Jewish state, hence subject to the same rights and obligations as other Israeli nationals" (Grodzinsky, 230). In like manner, the Zionists intimidated and forced thousands of survivors to declare to the Anglo-American Commission of Inquiry that they wished to establish themselves in Palestine, despite the possibility of seeking a home elsewhere. No fewer than fifty thousand of these forced recruits were to leave Israel shortly after their arrival, including some who returned to Germany, while, one author sarcastically adds, no one had ever heard of Jewish immigrants leaving the United States or any other country of immigration (Domb, 17).

Judaic critics quote debates in the House of Commons in Ottawa to buttress their accusations of the Zionists. There, Canada's Minister of Immigration points to the Israeli government as an obstacle to greater Jewish immigration to Canada: "The government has made no progress in providing facilities for immigrants from Israel and has no intention of making any progress in that direction because the government of Israel, which is a country seeking immigrants, does not wish us to do so" (*House of Commons*, 1464).

Such accusations cast a revealing light on a constant in Israeli policy, that of viewing all Jews as potential citizens of Israel. The pattern of "appropriating" the Jews of the Diaspora, especially when they are in migration, has repeated itself, though in less tragic circumstances, throughout the history of the State of Israel. Israeli governments, irrespective of the party in power, have regularly attempted to channel the migratory flow of Jews toward Israel, opposing the relocation of Russian Jews to the United States and Germany, of Argentinean Jews to the United States and of North African Jews to France and Canada. The habit of treating the Jews of the Diaspora as state property and of placing the interests of the state above individual liberties reflects the voluntarism of many of the revolutionary political regimes of the twentieth century, including Zionism.

Miraculous Rebirth or Continued Destruction?

For the Zionists, the lesson of the Shoah is simple: a state must be secured at all costs; it must be strengthened and populated by the largest possible number of Jews against any possible Arab opposition. According to Leibowitz,

> The Shoah is an oft-used instrument. Speaking cynically, it can be

said that the Shoah is among the most useful objects for manipulat-
ing the public, and particularly the Jewish people, in and outside
of Israel. In Israeli politics, the Shoah is held to demonstrate that
an unarmed Jew is as good as a dead Jew. (Leibowitz, 61)

Others derive a different teaching from the Shoah: one must beware a
powerful state that claims to transcend individual morality, practices racial
discrimination and commits crimes against humanity. This is why most Jews
have remained strongly committed to equality and liberal democracy.

Everyone, including the anti-Zionists, recognizes the role of the Shoah
in the establishment of the Zionist State:

After the terrible destruction of the Second World War, European
Jewry had lost many of its great leaders. In addition, there was
a sense of confusion that permeated many survivors. The non-
Jewish world was anxious to make amends for its passivity during
the Holocaust. Hence, the Zionist triumph in 1948. However, a
dispassionate reading of Jewish history will yield the conclusion
that, since its inception, Zionism was opposed by the overwhelming majority of Torah-observant and believing Jews. (Central
Rabbinical Council)

The founders of Israel were able to convince the majority of the United
Nations member-states that the only possible reparation and, at the same
time, the only solution to the "Jewish problem" was to establish a state for
the Jews. They emphasized that the very presence of Jews in the Diaspora
was fraught with danger and that only an independent state would be able to
protect them. The Zionists posited a direct connection between the Shoah
and the State of Israel, presented as a rebirth after mass destruction. The
manner in which the tragic event is commemorated reflects the lessons that
the Zionist movement intends be learned from it.

The Israeli government introduced *Yom ha-shoah* (Day of the Shoah) in
official commemoration of the tragedy. The better to underline the connection between these two significant events in Jewish history, it precedes by
a few days *Yom ha-atzmaut* (Independence Day). The desire of the fledging
state's leaders to temper the memory of "passive suffering" — for the Zionists an object of contempt — with the theme of resistance, which evokes the
memory of the Warsaw Ghetto revolt of 1943, explains the choice of date.
The Israeli commemoration was first called *Yom ha-shoah u gevurah* (Day
of the Shoah and of Heroism). A solemn ceremony, with full participation
of the military, is held on the eve at the *Yad va-shem*, the Shoah memorial
in Jerusalem. A siren blast at midday summons the Israeli population to
observe two minutes of silence, and throughout the day citizens can tune
into special radio and television programs and attend public lectures. The

principal message of the commemoration is straightforward: there will never be another Shoah because our state will protect us. It also asserts that, had the State of Israel existed before World War II, the Shoah would never have taken place.

According to a manual distributed to IDF educational officers, Yom ha-shoah should strengthen the feeling of belonging to the Jewish people and loyalty to the state among new recruits:

> The Zionist solution establishing the State of Israel was intended to provide an answer to the problem of the existence of the Jewish people, in view of the fact that all other solutions had failed. The Holocaust proved, in all its horror, that in the twentieth century, the survival of the Jews is not assured as long as they are not masters of their fate and as long as they do not have the power to defend their survival. (Liebman 1983, 178)

The official text goes on to add that the IDF's activities are the logical continuation of resistance to the Shoah, which should imbue Israeli soldiers with moral and spiritual power.

Use of the Shoah to foster Israeli patriotism has been unflagging since the early 1960s. After an air show in Poland and with disregard for the protests of the Auschwitz Museum, three Israeli F-15 fighter jets bearing the Star of David and piloted by descendants of Shoah survivors overflew the former Nazi extermination camp while two hundred Israeli soldiers observed the flyover from the Birkenau death camp adjacent to Auschwitz. The remarks of one of the Israeli pilots stressed confidence in the armed forces: "This is triumph for us. Sixty years ago, we had nothing. No country, no army, nothing. We now come here with our own planes to honor those who can no longer be with us" (Mala).

The official commemorations of the Shoah provide regular occasions for transmitting the same message. The chief of the Israeli General Staff proclaimed, at the foot of the monument to the resistance fighters of the Warsaw Ghetto: "If you wish to know the source from which the Israeli army draws its power and strength, go to the holy martyrs of the Holocaust and the heroes of the revolt.... The Holocaust... is the root and legitimation of our enterprise" (Liebman 1983, 184). But associating the history of the Warsaw Ghetto revolt with Zionism is not as simple as it might appear. The daughter of a Jewish fighter killed in the Warsaw uprising, asks painful questions:

> As long as hundreds of Palestinians are not being lined up and shot, but are killed by Israelis only one a day, are we Jews free from worrying about morality, justice? Has Nazism become the sole norm by which Jews judge evil, so that anything that is not its exact duplicate

is considered by us morally acceptable? Is that what the Holocaust has done to Jewish moral sensibility? (Klepfisz, 130–31)

Marek Edelman, a veteran of the revolt who has continued to reside in Poland, supports the Palestinian resistance and finds in it many similarities with his own struggle against the Nazis. "Nothing infuriates Zionists more than the arguments of anti-Zionist Jews, who have such a courageous and principled history" (Foot).

Hence the need to stress the fundamental insecurity of Jewish existence in the Diaspora. A former Israeli minister of education, himself a member of the National Religious movement, expressed the message quite clearly: "The Holocaust is not a national insanity that happened once and passed, but an ideology that has not passed from the world and even today the world may condone crimes against us" (Liebman 1983, 184).

For many Jews, the Shoah provides the ultimate justification for the State of Israel. This is particularly true for many of those who survived the Shoah and undoubtedly even more so for their descendants. It was of the highest symbolic value that the first Israeli astronaut, himself a descendant of Shoah survivors, carried with him aboard the American space shuttle a souvenir of that era: a lunar landscape drawn by a child in the Theresienstadt concentration camp. The message was to be one of rebirth, of pride in belonging to Israel, against the indignity of dying in Europe.

The state is also seen as a protection against any future threat to the Jews. This belief explains how support for Israel in the Diaspora is often seen as an insurance policy. But among Orthodox rabbis, even those who share to a certain extent the philosophy of the National Religious camp, doubts persist. For example, Rabbi Sober remains sceptical about Israel's capacity to come to the aid of American Jews in any meaningful way if ever the American government were to persecute them. He finds the idea ridiculous, and citing the Talmud, concludes: "Your guarantor needs a guarantor! It is like taking out a life-insurance policy with a company that is guaranteed to go bankrupt on your death" (Sober, 49).

Zionist educators have used a wide range of methods to reinforce the conviction, both among Israelis and among the younger Jews of the Diaspora, that the very existence of the State of Israel constitutes reparation for the Shoah. What is surely the most effective official commemoration is the March of the Living, inaugurated in 1988. Young Diaspora Jews travel to the historic sites of the Shoah in Poland, such as Auschwitz, and then continue on to Israel where they join in Independence Day festivities. The message is a powerful one: after death, life; after the dark barracks of Auschwitz, the sun drenched streets of Israel's towns and cities, festooned with blue and white flags to celebrate independence. The second Intifada disrupted the March of the Living, forcing the Zionist organizers to bring their charges only to Poland, not to Israel. The culminating part of the trip was cancelled, as the parents saw the State of Israel as unsafe and forbade their children to travel there.

In addition to providing Israel with a highly persuasive *raison d'être*, the Shoah has proved a powerful means of leveraging aid. As an Israeli parliamentarian commented:

> Even the best friends of the Jewish people refrained from offering significant saving help of any kind to European Jewry and turned their back on the chimneys of the death camps... therefore all the free world, especially in these days, is required to show its repentance... by providing diplomatic-defensive-economic aid to Israel. (Liebman 1983, 184)

The quotation, taken not from a polemical work like *The Holocaust Industry* (Finkelstein) but from a political analysis by National Religious academics, indicates that ideological and political use of the Shoah has become a matter of habit and routine and that it includes manipulation of collective guilt feelings.

The State of Israel has used the Shoah in many ways. For decades, Israeli diplomacy has invoked it to mute criticism and to generate sympathy for the state, which it presents as the collective heir of the six million victims. However, this function has begun to lose its effectiveness. The generation that experienced the war is no longer in power in Europe; some are beginning to assert that the State of Israel has overused this powerful argument. The Israeli novelist Amos Oz has spoken out against Israeli haughtiness:

> Our sufferings have granted us immunity papers, as it were, a moral *carte blanche*. After what all those dirty goyim [non-Jews] have done to us, none of them is entitled to preach morality to us. We, on the other hand, have *carte blanche*, because we were victims and have suffered so much. Once a victim, always a victim, and victimhood entitles its owners to a moral exemption. (Oz, 40)

There are fears that abuse of the memory of the Shoah may breed behavior that will antagonize even Israel's allies: "the centrality of the Holocaust myth, and the core values of Jewish history and Jewish peoplehood, is relevant to understanding why Israel is apparently prepared to behave in a manner that not only many of its friends but even some of its own citizens consider irrational" (Liebman 1983, 237). By way of example, critics cite a letter sent by Prime Minister Menahem Begin to President Ronald Reagan during Israel's invasion of Lebanon in 1982. Begin told the American president that he felt like someone who had led "a courageous army to Berlin to eliminate Hitler in a bunker" (Liebman 1983, 237–38). For Zionist extremists, Palestinians are "new Nazis" (Ellis, 33).

The controversy surrounding plans to evacuate Gaza and other territories conquered in 1967 included frequent references to the Shoah. Opponents of the evacuation approved by the government of Israel referred to it as "deportation," as the first attempt since World War II to create *judenrein* space. The 1967 borders became "Auschwitz borders" in the discourse of some nationalists who reject the very idea of withdrawal from any of the occupied territories. Some of Israel's nationalist media compared Israeli soldiers sent to evacuate the Gaza settlers to the SS. Others suggested that the withdrawal from Gaza would usher a new Shoah, this time in the Land of Israel. A settlers' radio station compared Sharon to Stalin, referred to the General Securities Services (*Shin Bet*) as *Yevsektzia*, while graffiti over a major highway in Israel proclaimed "Sharon=Hitler" (*Arutz 7*, August 1, 2005). One may recall that prior to the assassination of Prime Minister Rabin, he had been portrayed in an SS uniform in leaflets published by opponents of the Oslo accords. While the symbolism of the Shoah has been mobilized mostly by the militant nationalists, their opponents have accused them of spreading fascism. No less a figure than Yeshayahu Leibowitz referred to settler vigilantes as "judeo-Nazis."

While apprehension about possible misuses of the memory of the Shoah has begun to surface even among convinced Zionists, Judaic critics of Zionism claim that the official commemoration of the Shoah, and particularly of the Warsaw Ghetto uprising, has created a misleading image of events and convey a morality at odds with Judaism. They reject the glorification of force inherent in the commemorative ceremonies, with its undue emphasis on resistance, which, in the final analysis, was rare indeed. The same sources condemn the Warsaw Ghetto insurgents: "It is clear as day that people who believe in the Lord and live according to His will do not do anything to hasten their deaths by even one moment, and certainly not something that will hasten the deaths of tens of thousands of their brethren" (Warsaw, 6).

Even some Haredim traditionally associated with Aguda have come in for criticism for claiming that pious Jews took part in the Warsaw uprising. "Why should we feel bad that the secular parties, when lifting the banner of the un-Jewish heroism of their comrades, fail to mention that religious Jews participated in this?" (Warsaw, 6). The critique itself embodies a categorical rejection of romantic heroism in Jewish tradition, which is used to justify anti-Zionist non-participation in the official commemoration of the Shoah.

In Western culture, to die fighting is seen as an act of heroism. While some deem it heroic to have brought about the obliteration of the Warsaw Ghetto by an uprising that stood not a chance against the Nazi war machine, others view it as a crime. Here, as with so many of the issues raised by the confrontation between Zionism and Judaism, there seems to be no intermediate position, no possible compromise. As we saw in Chapter 4, a gulf separates the two: the Zionists proclaim the values of bravery and heroism, while the Haredi rabbis, if they recognize such values at all, do not in the least share them. The cultural worlds of these two groups of Jews barely overlap. As we have seen, after the Shoah, the use of force became an article of faith for a large number of Jews. To cast doubts upon the legitimacy and the efficacy of force is, in Zionist circles, to face accusations of treason. When the modern Jewish sensibility meets that of the traditionalists who see the hand of God in all that happens to them, including the Shoah, the encounter provokes a certain malaise among modern Jews.

A touching collection of Hasidic stories told by survivors provides many examples of this unshakable faith in God and in His providence. One short story deals with Jewish women being led to slaughter by the SS in a ghetto. These same women requested and obtained permission to immerse themselves before death in the *mikve*, the bath used for ritual purification. To the German commanding officer who asked one of them for the reasons for this strange request from this "filthy race, the source of all disease and vermin in Europe," the Jewess answered: "God has brought our pure souls into this world in the pure homes of our parents, and we wish to return them in purity to our Father in Heaven" (Eliach, 160–61).

It was this same trust in God that gave a Hasidic rabbi the courage to request the commander of the Bergen-Belsen camp to provide him with flour and with an oven to prepare matzoh for Passover. And as he recited and discussed the Haggadah at the Passover meal, he assured the Hasidim that the Shoah was "the beginning of our Redemption." As they returned to their barracks, the Hasidim were "sure that the sounds of the Messiah's footsteps were echoing in the sounds of their own steps on the blood-soaked earth of Bergen-Belsen" (Eliach, 19).

It is noteworthy that the author, in her preface, feels obliged to reassure the reader that "This collection of Hasidic tales is not... a negation of the value of armed resistance and the physical struggle for one's life or death with honor" (Eliach, xxxii). However, none of the stories in the collection mention resistance; they bear witness only to an interpretation by the Shoah victims that is rarely heard in commemorative ceremonies. The caveat shows how difficult it is for a modern Jew — probably affected by Zionist sensibility — to receive another way of interpreting the tragedy, an interpretation that affirms Jewish tradition and derives from it a spiritual meaning.

It is hardly surprising that those Jews who cannot identify with Zionism commemorate and interpret the Shoah so differently than the Zionists. A common thread runs through the belief shared by all traditionalists: the Shoah, brought upon us by our sins, is a call for repentance. As we have seen, some religious thinkers hold Zionism responsible for the Shoah, identifying as decisive factors the challenge to the nations it represented and the rejection of the Torah that they accuse it of having promoted and encouraged. In their view, the Torah had foreshadowed both the Shoah and the State of Israel more than three thousand years ago.

While the warnings formulated in the Torah dealt principally with idol worship, those "foreign cults" that seduced the children of Israel, one admonition alone, argue certain modern-day commentators, focuses upon atheism and secularization, concepts specific to the twentieth century:

> They incensed Me with no-gods, vexed Me with their futilities; I'll incense them with a no-folk, vex them with a nation of fools. For a fire has flared in My wrath and burned to the bottom of Sheol, has consumed the earth and its increase, eaten down to the base of the hills. I will sweep misfortunes on them, use My arrows on them: Wasting famine, ravaging plague, deadly pestilence, and fanged beasts will I let loose against them, with venomous creepers in dust. The sword shall deal death without, as shall the terror within, to youth and maiden alike, the suckling as well as the aged. (Deuteronomy 32:21–25)

The image is not that of God who has "hidden His face," nor of an "eclipse of God," but rather of his active manifestation in history.

Rabbi Moshe Dov Beck welcomed me to his modest home in Monsey, in New York State. Wearing a striped caftan, identical to those worn in Meah Shearim, the rabbi related a parable to illustrate the traditionalist interpretation. In order that I could understand it, he made an exception to his avoidance of speaking Hebrew as vernacular and related the story in *loshen ha-kodesh*, Rabbinic Hebrew, spoken with an Ashkenazi inflection:

> A king had a son who had fallen mortally ill. No doctor in the world could cure him, and the child was quickly approaching death. Suddenly, a man appeared who promised to cure the lad, on condition that he would be allowed to operate without anaesthetic. The father hesitated but, considering the seriousness of his son's condition, gave his permission. He stood outside the operating room, behind a glass door through which he could watch the operation unseen by his son. The operation began, and the son began to cry out so wrenchingly that his father's heart was torn. With each cry, the father shuddered, but after a short moment, he smiled with comfort: his son was being cured. But the son, wracked with pain, unable to understand what was happening to him, called out to his father, who did not respond. His fear was that his father had abandoned him, but in reality the father had simply hidden his face.
>
> The Shoah was indeed the cause of the most grievous suffering, but God never abandoned us, nor did he even hide his face. The disease that afflicted us is called secularization. Today, more young people study the Torah than before the Second World War.

The cure has thus taken effect. But some have ill understood it. For them, there is no longer a father, there never has been, God forefend. They insist in seeing nothing in the Shoah but the weakness of the Jewish people, its lack of an army, of a state. Like a dog that bites the stick with which it has been struck, the Zionists are incapable of seeing the hand of God behind the Shoah. And, it goes without saying, they have drawn from it false and dangerous lessons. (Beck 2002)

This powerful parable interprets the Shoah as part of a succession of tragedies that Jewish tradition has placed within the moral framework of reward and punishment, of merit and transgression, of humility and arrogance toward God. The Shoah thus becomes another in a succession of tragedies, which include the biblical stories of the Golden Calf, the revolt of Korah against Moses and Aaron and the destruction of the two Temples. There is thus no need to commemorate the Shoah any differently than all the other tragedies oft attributed to the date of 9 Av of the Hebrew calendar. For Rabbi Teitelbaum, and for several other Haredi thinkers, the Shoah and the State of Israel can by no means be seen as antithetical events — as destruction and reconstruction — but rather as an ongoing process: the final eruption of the forces of evil as a prelude to redemption. The conviction that the State of Israel may be just another link in the chain of destruction and violence inaugurated by the Shoah is a frequent motif in Haredi anti-Zionist thought. The same motif, though formulated differently, is likewise present in the anti-Zionist literature produced by the Reform Jews.

Israel received substantial reparations from Germany and, later, from other countries found guilty of having helped facilitate the Shoah or profited from it. Much of the world sees the State of Israel as the legitimate heir to the millions of exterminated Jews. However, many critics, both from among the Haredim and the Reform Jews, claim that the state has profited illegitimately from German reparations, as the victims had never designated the State of Israel as their successor. Judaic critics also object to the campaigns that demand reparations from the Swiss banks and other third parties. The aggressiveness of the Jewish attorneys who lead these campaigns worries the Haredim, who reject pride and pugnacity and fear that a massive affirmation of "Jewish interests" might touch off a backlash against the Jews.

As the twenty-first century opens, numerous observers claim that anti-Semitism has once again become emboldened. The Zionists tend to define as anti-Semitism any critique of Zionism and any attempt to question the legitimacy of the State of Israel. They thus bear out those first critics of Zionism who warned, as early as the late nineteenth century, that the establishment of a Jewish state would by no means eliminate anti-Semitism, but would in fact place the Jews in greater peril by intensifying and focusing hatred of the Jews. Jewish tradition considers the concentration of Jews in any one place as hazardous. Many contemporary commentators appear to lend weight to the most serious warnings, for the State of Israel has become "the Jew among nations" and a dangerous country for a Jew. In an era of increased mobility and communication, the conflict engendered by the founding of the State of Israel now projects an increasingly greater threat of violence upon the Jewish communities of the Diaspora.

The apocalyptic prophecies invoked by Zionism's early detractors appear today far better grounded in fact and thus far more threatening than when formulated in an atmosphere of enthusiasm for the youthful and promising Zionist movement. Israel's assertive policies and their defense in the name of all Jews by the Zionist organizations may thus be seen as an extraordinary source of danger. But the critics of Zionism are likewise aware that any difficulties encountered as a result of this fallout by Diaspora Jews can only strengthen Zionist convictions.

The anti-Zionists insist that they broadcast their message to the mass media to prevent incipient tragedy. They refuse to accept the call for "Jewish unity," which they consider to be not only Zionist but anti-Semitic for it postulates the existence of common Jewish political interests, which in turn would place the well-being and the security of Diaspora Jews at risk. Given the absence of any reliable democratic mechanism, the leaders of a large number of Jewish organizations in the Diaspora tend to promote "Jewish unity" more assiduously than in Israel, where the extreme diversity of the political spectrum exposes the demagogical nature of the slogan.

On his visit to Germany in 1935, the American Rabbi Morris Lazaron was deeply touched by the presentation, by a Jewish troupe, of an opera based on the Book of Esther and performed during the festival of Purim in Berlin, in front of an audience that included Heinrich Himmler. The rabbi expressed admiration for the bravery of the Jews who demonstrated, in the face of their persecutors, their firm faith in ultimate salvation. It should be remembered that in the history of Purim, court intrigues and repentance were finally responsible for blocking plans for an imminent Shoah.

In the twentieth century, the outcome was different. From this perspective, Rabbi Teitelbaum views the founding of Israel as a violation of universal order and thus warranting punishment:

> It is clear beyond all shadow of a doubt that the buildings put up by the heretics and apostates in our Holy Land will all be burned to the ground by the Messiah, leaving not a trace behind, and in their place the Lord, may He be blessed, will raise up for us other buildings sanctified by supernatural holiness; and then "… the nations that are left around you shall know that I the Lord have rebuilt the ravaged places and replanted the desolate land," [Ezekiel 36:36] and they will not be as they were [before]. (Teitelbaum 1998, 133)

In this apocalyptic vision, total, absolute and sudden destruction awaits the State of Israel. Nonetheless, the way in which the anti-Zionists envisage the disappearance of the Zionist State underlines their acute concern for the safeguarding of human life. In their appeals for the abolition of the State of Israel, many pious anti-Zionists express the wish that punishment come directly from God rather than through the intermediary of the nations, which might cause greater harm to the Jewish people. They also pray for God's mercy. This destruction, explicit in the rabbinical critique of Zionism, defies imagination, even against the background of the Shoah. One scholar quotes a classical commentary: upon the arrival of the Messiah, only seven thousand Jews are to be found in the Land of Israel (Azulai, 22). Assuredly, the prophecy of destruction, like that of Jonas, may well turn out to be just a warning: in the Judaic system, sincere repentance can obviate the threat of divine punishment. Few things are more foreign to Jewish tradition than fatalism.

Chapter 7

Prophecies of Destruction and Strategies for Survival

Out of depths I call You, O Lord. O Lord, listen to my cry; let Your ears be attentive to my plea for mercy. If You keep account of sins, O Lord, Lord, who will survive? (Psalms 130:1–3)

The State of Israel is in peril. The sense of apprehension, often expressed by the most ardent Zionists, reveals a paradox: Israel, often presented as a safe haven, even as the ultimate refuge, has become one of the most precarious places of all for Jews. Growing numbers of Israelis have begun to feel caught in a "bloody trap." Their feelings would appear to bear out some of the most serious predictions of the country's anti-Zionist critics. Until the outbreak of the Intifada, it could be argued that a strong majority of Jews in both Israel and the Diaspora had grown accustomed to the existence of the state. The state had, in turn, acquired all the appurtenances of a natural reality — and for some perhaps even of an eternal reality. At the close of the twentieth century, the Knesset was to proclaim "united Jerusalem the eternal capital of Israel." Ever since, a sense of the state's fragility has begun to creep through Israeli society. Though he commands the region's most powerful armed forces, Ariel Sharon has claimed that the State of Israel is facing, in the Palestinian insurrection, a danger as great as it faced upon its founding in 1948. Yet it is not clear that the state is facing any such danger. While the Israel Defense Forces appear quite capable of protecting the state, it is the citizens of Israel and the Jews of the Diaspora who have begun to feel vulnerable. Some insist that the interests of the State of Israel and those of the Jews of the Diaspora do not coincide; still others assert that, in spite of its democratic structures, Israel's policies often work against the interests and welfare of its own citizens.

Some have cast Palestinians, Arabs and Muslims in the devil's role. Others point an accusing finger at the Jewish settlers in the West Bank and at the hardliners in general. But in a broader sense, doubts are now being heard about the survival of the State of Israel in its current form in the Middle East, in the heart of what many Israelis complain is a "dangerous neighborhood." Even in the eyes of some of its supporters and citizens, the State of Israel has become the last of the colonial powers, whose founding coincided with the flood tide of decolonization throughout the world.

Israeli society, which for many years stood firm against enemy encirclement, is having much less success with the Arab population under its control. Greater numbers of Israeli Jews are now said to favor the deportation of the Palestinians to the neighboring Arab countries and the outright annexation of the West Bank. Such a perspective is repugnant to many Jews, both in Israel and elsewhere in the world. Some of them have concluded that to maintain the State of Israel in its present form demands measures that are no longer acceptable to traditional Jewish morality. These Jews, many of whom are veterans of several Israeli wars, today feel a sense of dread. They have become hostages to a situation they can no longer control. They seek a peaceful outcome, one that would reflect their sense of honesty. Their growing sense of despair has made them, perhaps for the first time, receptive to the anti-Zionist arguments that have been put forward for more than a century. These arguments emphasize the dangers that Zionism and the State of Israel represent for Jews. But what exactly can anti-Zionist thinkers in all their diversity hope to offer in the historical context of the early twenty-first century?

A festive prayer recited by practicing Jews brings Israel's place in Jewish continuity into clearer focus. On the occasion of the Festivals of Pilgrimage — Passover, Pentecost and Tabernacles, which used to be celebrated in Jerusalem at the time of the Temple — Israelis and Jews of the Diaspora proclaim:

> Because of our sins we have been exiled from our land and sent far from our soil. We cannot perform our obligations in the House of Your choice, in the great and holy House upon which Your Name was proclaimed, because of the hand that was dispatched against Your Sanctuary. May it be Your will, Lord, our God and God of our forefathers, O merciful King, that You once more be compassionate upon us and upon Your Sanctuary in Your abundant mercy, and rebuild it soon and magnify its glory. Our Father, our King, reveal the glory of Your Kingship upon us, speedily; appear and be uplifted over us before the eyes of all the living. Draw our scattered ones near, from among the nations, and bring in our dispersions from the ends of the earth. Bring us to Zion, Your City, in glad song, and to Jerusalem, home of Your Sanctuary, in eternal joy. (*Complete ArtScroll Siddur*, 679)

In Jewish tradition, history has an end-point: the advent of the Messiah. But as we have seen in Chapter 3, this same tradition forbids any calculation or estimation of the time of his arrival; it discourages all attempts to hasten his arrival and even to pray excessively for his advent. While nearly half the world's Jews are currently living in the Land of Israel, no correction has been made to the prayer books. Messianic expectations thus remain intact, unaffected by the physical concentration of millions of Jews. Though all practicing Jews recite this prayer, they encompass two extremes: those who share the joyous conviction that the establishment of the State of Israel is a miracle that prefigures the imminent arrival of ultimate redemption, and those who share a haunting premonition that the Zionist revolt will one day bring about a dreadful punishment. Opinions are particularly polarized concerning the place and the role of the State of Israel in history.

The State of Israel in Jewish Continuity

The claim to the miraculous nature of salvation that is the hallmark of the anti-Zionist sources is a classical concept. The critics of Zionism are not alone in affirming this belief: the National Religious share the same view, except that for them the Zionist enterprise is, in and of itself, an expression of divine will, "the finger of God," which had made itself manifest during the exodus from Egypt. The difference between the two extremes does not lie in a disagreement about the total destruction that must precede redemption, but in their definition of what the destruction entails.

While the National Religious believe that destruction came to an end in 1945, making the Shoah the point of departure for redemption, the theoreticians of rabbinical anti-Zionism insist that both the Shoah and the very existence of the State of Israel are part of the same process of destruction. In their view, all the accomplishments of the Zionist enterprise will be eradicated before the arrival of the Messiah, who will find the Holy Land in a state of total devastation. From this perspective, categorically rejected by Zionist messianism, the State of Israel can be nothing but an obstacle on the path to redemption. By this same logic, to concentrate millions of Jews in such a dangerous place is suicidal folly.

Principled opposition to the existence of the State of Israel is what sets the several religious anti-Zionist schools of thought apart. The territory held by Israel — before or after 1967 — is not at all the issue. However, as a means to alleviate the Palestinians' suffering and to lessen the ensuing anti-Jewish sentiment, some anti-Zionists would welcome some sort of a two-state solution in the interim. The issue is the simple fact of becoming a nation in the political sense and of imposing Jewish sovereignty in the Land of Israel. A Reform rabbi would couch his opposition in a manner similar to that of a Hasidic rabbi, since their respective readings of the Torah, however divergent, would bring them to reject the transformation of the Jews into a national entity in the European sense of the term. A classical commentary stipulates that the Temple may descend from heaven at any time, other opinions hold that the entire city of Jerusalem must descend from heaven; it cannot be the fruit of human endeavor.

Far from strengthening consensus, the economic and military success of the Zionist enterprise has led to polarization among Jewish thinkers. Rather than calming passions, the existence of a prosperous, modern state has sharpened old theological and political controversies. The National Religious see, in the state's industrial, agricultural and military achievements, a portent of the advent of the Messiah, while the critics, and most vocally the anti-Zionist Haredim, condemn "the Zionist revolt" with redoubled virulence.

The contrast between the states of destruction and miraculous redemption, which permeates the Torah and its rabbinical commentaries, is inescapable in Jewish thought. Echoes can be found, for example, in the Passover Haggadah: "Not by the hand of an angel... not by the hand of a messenger, but the Holy One Blessed Be Himself in His own Glory, says the Lord" (*Shalom Hartman Institute*, 92). The emphasis is placed on the exclusive role of God in redemption. This notion of contrast is frequently re-stated in Haredi anti-Zionist thought: "Before the coming of the Messiah, the profane state will vanish and no other path will be available," writes Rabbi Teitelbaum. He is simply reformulating the underlying theological principle: "The son of David will come only after the disappearance of the unworthy Kingdom of Israel" (Teitelbaum 1985, 8). In other words, the State of Israel constitutes an obstacle on the road to redemption, which can only be achieved by a "quantum leap."

Rabbi Teitelbaum stresses that just prior to the flight from Egypt, Pharaoh's advisors had come to the conclusion that the children of Israel had begun an irremediable decline. Naturally enough, such a vision runs counter to the feeling that until recently prevailed in Israeli society, particularly among the National Religious, for whom redemption is a gradual process initiated when the Jews settled in the Land of Israel. In other words, for those who look to the Torah as the supreme reference, the debate has revolved around the nature of redemption itself: is it an event brought about unexpectedly, directly by divine agency, or is it a gradual process that can be triggered by human action and, to use a common Israeli expression, by "facts on the ground"?

Judaic critics of Zionism have begun to take the measure of militant messianism, as espoused by the National Religious. This brand of messianism, in its appeal to force, raises theoretical questions that have taken on a sudden relevance when placed against the turbulent history of Israel. Gershom Scholem, the author of a study of the false messiah Sabbatai Tzevi, expressed concerns about the power of messianic motivation: "Can Jewish history manage to re-enter concrete reality without being destroyed by the messianic claim which [re-entry is bound to] bring up from its depths?" (Ravitzky 1996, 3).

The sacralization of the State of Israel, quite common among the National Religious (albeit weakened prior to the evacuation from Gaza), has come in for particularly virulent criticism. Where the National Religious doctrine draws its inspiration from the mystical thought of Rabbi Kook, seen as "radical and revolutionary" even by Zionist historians (Avineri 1981, 188), it is precisely on the issue of messianism, the very idea that most

National Religious leaders hold dearest, that the anti-Zionists base their strongest rejection of Zionism and of the State of Israel, which for them has been "conceived in sin." We already know that for many Jews critical of Zionism the problem is not simply that the state is illegitimate and that it may be placing millions of Jews, both in Israel and throughout the world, in jeopardy — but that it has also become an obstacle on the path to the final redemption of humanity. To combat Zionism thus has come to mean tearing the veil of mystery from the messianism of the state.

For all their differences, the last Lubavitch Rebbe and Rabbi Schach, the leader of the "Lithuanian" Haredim, agreed on the place of Israel in Jewish continuity. For Rabbi Schach, before the arrival of the Messiah, the Jewish people remain in exile wherever they may find themselves, including in Israel proper. In the view of his contemporary, Rabbi Menahem Mendel Schneerson, who over time had become more open to the nationalists, "the aliya of numerous Jews to the Holy Land does not constitute a gathering of the exiled" as it is presented in the prophetic scriptures (Ravitzky 1996, 147). For him, the State of Israel has complicated redemption and sowed confusion among the Jews: "The false redemption does not allow the true redemption to be revealed, for those who think that they are already living in the redemption do not perform the [religious] actions required for the going forth from exile and the revealing of the true redemption; they cause the prolongation of the Exile, the exile of the individual, the exile of the community, the exile of all Israel, and the exile of the Shekhinah [divine presence]" (Ravitzky 1996, 147).

Their version of messianism notwithstanding, the National Religious doctrines have come under attack on another level altogether. Rabbis Kook, Reines and their disciples in the National Religious movement expected Zionist settlement to bring the secular pioneers closer to the Torah. Their expectations have proven illusory. On the contrary, as we have seen in Chapter 2, the new Israeli identity has grown more distant from Jewish tradition. What has proven to be a false prophecy, even in the eyes of the adherents of the National Religious doctrine, has strengthened the hand of those who reject Zionism, which remains, in their eyes, "a heretical enterprise and a threat to Jewish continuity" (Beck 2002). Many secular and even National Religious Jews see Israel as a civic religion, as a pillar of their identity. But for other religious Jews — and above all the Haredim — it has become an indigestible concoction of symbols and practices borrowed from Judaism, which deprive it of its central core: subordination to God. The use of religious symbols by the state cannot be interpreted as a return to traditional religion, they warn (Liebman 1983, 226). And even if it were such a return, assert the most intransigent of the Haredi anti-Zionists, the proportion of pious Jews to be found among the overall population of the state would not influence their categorical rejection of the "Zionist entity." Every vestige of the state must disappear before the Messiah may arrive, they insist.

The civic religion of Israel remains a fragile construction. The Haredim have never accepted it, reasoning that it had been introduced into the world to replace Judaism. And, for a growing number of secularists, this same civic religion is a throwback to ideologies of "blood and earth," blended with selective interpretations of Jewish tradition. Large numbers of non-practicing Jews have come to discover the pacifism and political realism of "dissident" personalities like Jeremiah and Yohanan Ben Zakkai. Their discovery has made them more sensitive to Jewish tradition and then to an awareness of the classic anti-Zionist message, which rejects the civic religion of Israel:

> Only blind dogmatism could present Israel as something positive for the Jewish people. Established as a so-called refuge, it has, unfailingly, over the past five decades, been the most dangerous place on the face of the earth for a Jew. It has been the cause of tens of thousands of Jewish deaths, of families torn apart; it has left in its wake a trail of mourning widows, orphans and friends.... And let us not forget that to this account of the physical suffering of the Jews, must be added those of the Palestinian people, a nation condemned to indigence, persecution, to life without shelter, to overwhelming despair, and all too often to premature death. (Weiss, Interview)

In the mouth of a Haredi anti-Zionist activist, such arguments add a humanitarian and moral imperative to warnings of a metaphysical nature: "It must be understood that to defy the divine decree [with regard to exile] is pre-destined to bloody failure. It must be understood that one cannot build up the hopes of one people by destroying those of another people" (Weiss, *Rescuing*).[1]

Indeed, by invoking the Shoah or the deep-seated insecurity of the Israeli population, the State of Israel has often avoided moral scrutiny. It is hardly surprising, for "whereas Judaism places man's obligations to God at the center of its value system, inferring his obligations to the community from his relationship to God, the new civil religion places the individual's obligations to the nation at its center" (Liebman 1983, 229). This is the reason why, say some Israeli political scientists, the civic religion provides no answers to questions of ultimate meaning, while at the same time it obliges its practitioners to accept the ultimate sacrifice. Civic space in Israel has become associated above all with "death for the fatherland," as another Israeli political analyst puts it (Ezrahi, 47).

Mussolini famously defined "the people" as a group of individuals who wage war together. Though this definition is in fact the operative one in Israel, the overwhelming majority of Israelis would label national identity defined in these terms as fascist. Moreover, a significant minority of Jews residing in Israel — the Haredim — do not participate in military activity and certainly do not consider the IDF as a national value.

Those who profess the Israeli civic religion sing the praises of the heroic, virile qualities of the early Zionist era and glorify the clean break with the traditional Jewish attributes they describe as "exilic." But on the other side are legions of Haredim who actively deplore that force has become the most persuasive argument in the life of the country. They denounce Israeli politicians who claim to be acting in the name of the Jewish people and yet show no concern for the impact that the actions of the Israeli armed forces might have on the image of Jews around the world. In fact, a growing number of people have come to associate Jews and Judaism with the tanks and the machine guns that they see every night on their television screens. The pugnacity displayed both by so many Israeli politicians and by their apologists in the Diaspora has confounded both Jews and non-Jews, who no longer know what Judaism means. Hence the constant reiteration, by the Judaic adversaries of Zionism, that "the Jewish people were not created to oppress another people. They were intended to be moral paragons. The desire for the land at any cost to anyone is a contradiction with our moral national mission" (Weiss, *Rescuing*).

In placing before the eyes of the world the fundamental distinctions between nationalism and obedience to the Torah, both Haredi and Reform critics have put their finger on the momentous break that has taken place: on the one hand, the traditional Jewish approach that favors compromise, and on the other, the new value system that is satisfied only with victory. While they may accept the Zionist argument that Israel now faces a new strain of anti-Semitism, they affirm that the anti-Semitism created by Zionism may be worse than the previous strain. Rabbi Weberman of Williamsburg has declared: "by their insolent behavior, and by their warlike acts, the Zionists have confirmed the worst of the anti-Semitic clichés." For him, "hatred of Jews roused by the Zionists and their state is crueler, and more overt, than the hatred that sustained the Nazis, may their memory be expunged" (Weberman).

Public Debate and Its Limits

The Judaic critics of Zionism have attempted to expand the public debate on the role of the State of Israel in Jewish continuity. They believe that the early years of the twenty-first century are crucial for the Jewish people. A debate exploring Jewish tradition may well be more fruitful than the temptation to close ranks behind inflexible ideological positions. Through the centuries, the Jews have been accused of being too cerebral, too intellectual. Have secularization, the Shoah and the Zionist enterprise made them too impassioned, too visceral to undertake such a debate? Is it truly taboo to question the State of Israel? In the Diaspora, the current consensus makes scrutiny of the Zionist question suspect: it has almost become "an unthinkable object" (Rose, 12). While occasional criticism of Israeli policies may be tolerated, all Judaic critiques of Zionism are de-legitimized, all doubt as to the Jewish authenticity of the State of Israel brushed aside. Mention that there exist religious Jews who are not Zionists, that Jews have other options than the State of Israel, and the reaction will be categorical:

> Arguing with anti-Zionists is not just pointless. It is demeaning. The intellectual battle to be fought today is not with the anti-Zionists, those who maintain that the Jewish state should never have existed, but with the post-Zionists, those who maintain that the Jewish national idea has outlived its usefulness, that it is obsolete, an impediment now both to individual self-expression and to entry into the post-sovereign world of the coming century. (Krauthammer, 16–17)

Many Diaspora Jews feel that their main role as Jews is to defend the State of Israel ("my country right or wrong"), and they can tolerate no dissent. The emotions are so strong that a prominent Canadian rabbi qualified as "the greatest enemy of the Jewish people" a modern religious Jew who had publicly questioned whether Israel by its policies endangered the Jewish Diaspora. Had the same author published an atheistic critique of Judaism, the condemnation would have been nowhere as harsh. A Haredi rabbi remarked wryly that nowadays one can tolerate criticism of one's religion but not of one's idolatry, suggesting that the State of Israel has replaced God in the value system of many Jews, including some rabbis. Indeed, if for many National Religious Jews, "religious faith sanctifies the socio-political structure, transferring it to the realm of the absolute and thereby bestowing upon it a transcendent validity" (Ravitzky 1996, 83), no criticism or even doubt would be allowed. The state becomes divine, and all of its actions, including military ones, become hallowed. All distinctions between the spiritual and the military become blurred, and as Ravitzky put it, "the Army of Israel, which is the army of the Lord, is called out of Zion to establish a *pax judaica* in the Middle East and ultimately in the world as a whole, in preparation for the fulfilment of the vision of the End of Days" (Ravitzky 1996, 84). While only a minority of Jewish Zionists would accept this vision, it appeals to millions of Christian Zionists, who are quite active in suppressing criticism of the State of Israel, let alone questioning its Zionist character.

Modern religious Jews who dare question Zionism face particular challenges. Unlike Satmar Hasidim, who are part of a closely knit supportive community, and secular Jews, who do not belong to any religious community, these Jews are part of the more diffuse National Religious movement in Israel and the Modern Orthodoxy elsewhere in the world. Some of these critics, and even their relatives, are insulted and shunned by their friends, denounced as "traitors" and thrown out of the synagogues they have attended for years. Since pious Jews must take part in collective prayers three times a day, some have found refuge in Haredi synagogues. One of these critics finds that this fallout has a silver lining:

> To be a Jew is to be grateful. The Hebrew word *yehudi* for Jew is of the same root as the word *toda*, gratitude. I am grateful to those who tried to offend me for offering me instead an opportunity to practice something that we all recite at the end of our prayers three times a day: "To those who curse me, let my soul be silent." (*Complete ArtScroll Siddur*, 119)

Ignored by Zionist intellectuals in the public forum, the anti-Zionist Haredim are also described by many Jews as "traitors to the Jewish people." Despite the traditional Jewish penchant for debate and discussion, neither the mainstream organizations nor intellectuals in the academic world have been prepared to take up the challenge that anti-Zionist positions represent for the apparent pro-Israel consensus. The reluctance to engage in debate may have several reasons.

First, neither official Israeli representatives nor their agents and allies are able to question the existence of the state that they represent and defend. Instances of such behavior are extremely rare in the political history of humanity. Critics of Zionism often point to the former USSR. Under no immediate outside threat, the very politicians who had assumed the country's leadership formally dissolved it; a nuclear superpower simply ceased to exist; its non-violent collapse entailed no serious repercussions for its security. For the anti-Zionists, the peaceful disintegration of the Soviet Union has become a heavenly portent that should reassure the Jews of the need to bring the current structure of the State of Israel to an end. But in the short term it seems no more realistic to expect an Israeli Gorbachev than it would have been to imagine, when Gorbachev assumed power, that within a few years he would preside over the abolition of the USSR.

Second, the public, Jewish and non-Jewish alike, is largely unaware of what the Orthodox critics of Zionism are saying. The anti-Zionist argument is often expressed in language filled with Talmudic quotations and Judaic references little known outside the circles of Torah scholars. Of late, some anti-Zionist Haredim have made efforts to adopt a more modern, more accessible language. Articles discussing Judaic anti-Zionism have been published in political studies journals (Weiss, *Judaism*). Though media based in Zionist-controlled Jewish communities have stifled anti-Zionist speech, the Western media are beginning to discover Judaic anti-Zionism (Klaushofer; Gruda).

In their efforts to reach a wider public, the critics of Zionism have learned to use modern media and, despite their limited resources, have organized protest campaigns, including televized opportunities to denounce the very existence of Israel. Several Haredi anti-Zionists, following in the footsteps of the Israeli left, have intensified their contacts with Palestinians, Arabs and Muslims. The various anti-Zionist groups have learned to spread their message with surprising efficiency. Ironically, though barred from most Jewish media, Hasidic representatives have contrived to break into the general media through interviews or by purchasing advertisements in the leading newspapers of various countries.

The discourse of the Judaic critics of Zionism is also present on the Internet. Aside from several highly specialized sites,[2] echoes can be found on the sites of several international left-wing movements and on Arab and Christian sites. In this sense, the Judaic adversaries of Zionism are visible. But in spite of its media successes, the anti-Zionist argument focused on the Torah is not regularly discussed either in Israel or in the Diaspora. The fear felt by many Jews over the future of the State of Israel has done little to facilitate such discussion.

The idea that Zionism itself represents a revolution in Jewish history, a discontinuity in Jewish collective awareness and an open challenge to Judaism has found little echo in the Diaspora. The Jewish workers' movements, which had earlier identified themselves with the radical aspects of Zionism, are today nothing but anaemic shadows of their former selves. Revolution, as a concept, is hardly fashionable among the Jews of the Diaspora. According to the dominant defensive logic, anything that might weaken the Zionist consensus, especially if the threat comes from Jews, must be shunned. During the celebrations of the fiftieth anniversary of the State of Israel, several Jewish institutions in the United States exerted pressure to cancel lectures by Israeli historians who had been invited to speak in such prestigious venues as the Smithsonian Institution (Brownfeld 1999, 84–85, 89).

Some years previously, when Leibowitz responded to an invitation from an American Jewish community to present a lecture entitled, "We Are One," and suggested rephrasing the title in the interrogative, "Are We One?" the invitation was withdrawn. Sensitivity to any criticism of Israel, no matter its origin — especially if it is of Israeli origin — can be easily explained: loyalty to Israel has long replaced Judaism as the foundation of Jewish identity.

Many Jews see themselves as the ultimate defenders of Israel and reject outright any consideration that might undermine that defense. Some go so far as to consider criticism of political Zionism as an argument promoting a second Shoah. In response to the suggestion that the land between the Jordan and the Mediterranean be transformed into a liberal state of all its citizens, an apologist for Israel wrote: "Behind the one-state solution lurks something truly monstrous: If Israel as a Jewish state is the centre of the Jewish people, the legatee of Holocaust, then what we are facing here is not only the liquidation of a state but, functionally, the destruction of a people" (Krantz). Quite a few people, among whom are intellectuals unfamiliar with

Judaism but also learned rabbis, display surprisingly similar reactions. They seem convinced that the future of the Jews depends entirely on the State of Israel and its strength. For some, even the future of Judaism is by now inextricably linked with the success of the Zionist enterprise. What all of them have in common is a deeply felt indignation and dread that questioning Zionism might somehow harm the State of Israel, which they see as their last and brittle refuge. Even Israel's preponderant military might does nothing to dispel their sense of fragility. A Jewish woman in Lausanne, one of the most tranquil places in the world, who attended a launching of the French-language edition of this book, objected vigorously to its very topic. She told me how fearful she was for her future and that only Israel made her feel secure, protecting her from another Shoah.

This same conviction provides the emotional support for several violent nationalist movements, such as the Jewish Defense League and its Israeli branch operation, Kach, which have not only spread terror among Arabs, but also threatened Jews whose positions seem to them to cast umbrage upon the State of Israel and, in their eyes, upon the entire Jewish people. In this spirit, Kach has compiled and posted on the Internet (Kach) a list of 7,000 persons described as "self-hating Israel threatening Jews." The list seems thorough and includes most of the living protagonists of this book, among the Haredim, Reform rabbis and left-wing activists, but also such personalities as Henry Kissinger and Woody Allen. Quite a few are Israelis. Concerned about this "threat from within," the compilers of the list invite readers to submit the names of such Jews who "are not even worthy of the name Jew." They also assure the volunteers that they will remain anonymous.

Concern for Israel is not limited to the personal fate of its Jewish inhabitants. Several intellectuals have pointed out that Israel as a political entity has taken precedence over the well-being of Jews themselves. According to Avineri, even to consider evacuating Israeli Jews from the Middle East "would be tantamount to another holocaust, because the very existence of Israel as a state is of normative significance and meaning to Diaspora Jewry. … Israel is conceived not only as an aggregate of its population, but its very existence has immanent value and normative standing" (Avineri 1981, 221). When support for Israel has come to represent the core of the new Jewish identity, even the slightest doubt about Israel has indeed become impossible.

It is not at all clear whether Judaic critics of Zionism enjoy a better reception in the Diaspora or in Israel. On the one hand, debate, even on sensitive and controversial subjects, is more open in Israel. On the other hand, a portion of Diaspora Jews, sensitized to the threatening fallout of the Middle East conflict, feel that Israeli policy is holding them hostage. Some critics believe that the demographic growth of the Haredi communities and Israel's chronic difficulties in ensuring the security of its population indicate that expressing doubts about the legitimacy the State of Israel in the name of the Torah may well, over time, find a place in Jewish public debate. The opponents of Zionism remain optimistic:

> Today, more than ever before, the total failure of the Zionist mania is obvious. Peace plans have failed. The "greatest" of right wing-ers, Ariel Sharon, has shown himself utterly incapable of solving anything. Daily the death toll mounts. All alternatives within the Zionist assumptions have been tried. People are willing to step be-yond the old clichés and entertain new — really old and traditional — solutions. The cost of failing to rethink Zionism mounts every day. (Central Rabbinical Council)

In the eyes of its opponents, Zionism has substituted Torah values for political support for Israel. They see this process as the main danger of the Zionist enterprise but also as its crucial weakness. In their view, the State of Israel represents the greatest risk for the people of Israel: it had become an insatiable monster, devouring the Jews.

We have seen that from the very beginning of Zionism, most rabbis had feared that the Torah would not only be discarded, but that Zionism would legitimize the secularization of the Jews begun a few decades before the rise of the Jewish national movement.

In terms of the Ten Commandments, religious Zionism offers Jews a possibility of worshipping "other gods" while also reassuring them that they remain faithful to the Torah. A number of Judaic thinkers see a parallel with the Biblical episode of the Golden Calf: the children of Israel justified their worship of the newly cast idol by claiming that it was "the god that brought us up out of Egypt."

The sharp accusations voiced by the Haredim, including the Satmar Rebbe, often seem implausible, exaggerated, cut from the whole cloth and expressed in outbursts of powerless rage against a victorious movement. Zionism has successfully established the State of Israel, created a formi-dable military power and a dynamic economy, and concentrated millions of Jews on its territory. But over time Israeli experts, most with Zionist credentials, have confirmed many of these accusations: the kidnapping of Yemeni children, the indifference of the Zionist leadership toward the victims of the Shoah, the anti-Semitic provocations carried out by Zionist agents in Morocco and elsewhere, the measures put in place by the Zionists to separate the immigrants, and particularly the youth, from the heritage of the Torah. What were once suspicions are now historically established facts.

It may well be that when one of the "fanatics in black frock coats" speaks, he is simply not heard. Saint-Exupéry wryly illustrates this phenomenon of selecting hearing:

This asteroid had been sighted only once by telescope, in 1909 by a Turkish astronomer, who had then made a formal demonstration of his discovery at an International Astronomical Congress. But no one had believed him on account of the way he was dressed. Grown-ups are like that.

Fortunately for the reputation of Asteroid B-612, a Turkish dictator ordered his people, on pain of death, to wear European clothes. The astronomer repeated his demonstration in 1920, wearing a very elegant suit. And this time everyone believed him. (Saint-Exupéry, 26–27)

Judaic anti-Zionists (often in the unsolicited company of the New Historians) continue to face ostracism and accusations of "washing our dirty linen in public." Convinced in Judaism's universal character, many of the anti-Zionist critics who address non-Jews respond to two overriding concerns, one doctrinal, the other practical. They wish to show the world that not all Jews are Zionists, that they do not all identify with the State of Israel or with its actions in the name of the Jews. In this sense, they feel that they are helping to save the honor of Judaism in the eyes of the nations, an undertaking known in tradition as *kiddush ha-shem*, sanctification of the name of God.

One such attempt, addressed to the general public, was an advertisement published in the *New York Times* a few days after the election of Ariel Sharon as Prime Minister of Israel:

In the aftermath of the elections in the State of Israel it has become a commonplace that religious Jews and their parties support a candidate who was in favor of slowing down or stopping the peace process. The impression has been created that ultra-Orthodox Jewry, in accordance with traditional Torah belief, are the staunchest supporters of maintaining Israel sovereignty over "territories" and the Temple Mount in Jerusalem.

In fact, nothing could be further from the truth.

Two thousand years ago, at the time of the Temple's destruction, the Jewish people were forbidden by the Creator (Kesubos [*BT* Ketubot] 111a) to exercise sovereignty over the Holy Land prior to the Messianic era. They were further forbidden to wage any form of war against other nations during their exile. Rather, the paradigm of Jewish existence in the Diaspora is to behave in a civil, honest and grateful manner towards their hosts throughout the world.

For over two thousand years the Jewish people accepted their exile as a Divine decree. Jews never attempted a rebellion against their host nations or other peoples. There were no plans or efforts ever made to wrest the Holy Land from its rulers or inhabitants at any point in the long history of Jewish exile. The sole means employed by Jewry to end their exile, throughout the ages were prayer, penance and good deeds.

In similar fashion, during the waning days of the second Temple, Rabbi Yohanan ben Zakkai defiled the Jewish zealots of his time and initiated surrender talks with the Romans.

This uniformity of belief and practice remained intact until about hundred years ago and the advent of Zionism. Zionists, representing a tiny movement, sought the metaphysically impossible. Their stated goal was to reverse the Divine decree of exile.

Zionism, by its very nature, rejects the concept of a divinely imposed exile. In addition, it has been consistently indifferent to the sufferings and dangers to which it and its embodiment, the State of Israel, have inflicted upon Jew and Gentile. Zionism represents a total and radical break with the beliefs and practices of the Jewish people throughout history....

Recently, much militant rhetoric has been heard from those who describe themselves "religious Zionist." Sadly their stance is in violation of the millennial beliefs of Torah sages and masses of Jewry.

The goal of Torah Jewry is to live in quite piety and dwell peacefully with all nations and peoples. Those following this Divine agenda are not linked to any wars that are falsely depicted as Jewish wars but are, in reality, Zionist wars. (*New York Times* 2001)

The advertisement brought a rarely seen critique of Zionism to a broader readership. The administrators of anti-Zionist websites have likewise noted that public interest, reflected in the number of hits registered, has been on the upswing since the beginning of the Intifada in 2000 (Weiss, Interview; Katz).

The anti-Zionists are sometimes denounced for maligning Israel. Their critics invoke the episode of the spies sent out to report on the Land of Israel, whose sin of "evil report" condemned the entire people to wander for forty years in the desert (Numbers 14:33). One of the Satmar leaders, a disciple of Rabbi Teitelbaum, based the legitimacy of the anti-Zionist advertisements published by his group in major North American newspapers on the *Mishne Torah*, the code drawn up by Maimonides that obliges all Jews to publicly denounce those who present a distorted image of Judaism (Maimonides). He went on to explain that the Zionists have used the Torah to justify their claims to the Land of Israel; the most militant settlers pretend to be religious Jews; Zionism has become all but synonymous with Judaism; the State of Israel has become a part of a messianic revivalist movement recognized by many Christians. All Jews, continued the rabbi, must dissociate themselves publicly from the Zionist movement and its precepts. As we have seen elsewhere in this book, even Hafetz Haim, a recognized expert on the Jewish law against improper speech, was wont to speak against Zionism in rather harsh terms. These anti-Zionist critics are seeking to undermine the popular belief that Israel is the logical culmination of Jewish history. The widespread circulation of rabbinical writings that undermine the legitimacy of the Zionist movement and the idea of a Jewish State has been deliberately calculated to loosen the automatic support many religious Jews of the Diaspora have come to give to the State of Israel.

While the Zionists can easily discredit left-wing Jews as "non-Jewish," "self-hating" or even "anti-Semitic," they cannot credibly cast doubts on the Haredim, whose practice of Judaism is consistent, rigorous and has continued uninterrupted for centuries. While some Zionists try to disgrace secular dissidents like Noam Chomsky or Ilan Pappe, and even accuse them of anti-Semitism, it would not be convincing to describe the Lubavitch or the Satmar Rebbe, Rabbi Wasserman or Hakham Alfandari as anti-Semitic. Their Judaic authority tends to embarrass those who assert that "certain forms of Judaism and Jewish life are deemed 'authentic' — those that identify with the U.S. and Israel without criticism or maps — while those Jews who resist serving the state and power are 'inauthentic'" (Ellis, 70).

It should be remembered that Jacob De Haan, the first victim of Zionist political assassination, was a socialite who represented the traditional Jewish communities in Palestine to the British and international authorities. The choice of victim may seem an illogical one at first glance: in Palestine, in the 1920s, thousands of socialist and Communist Jews were opposed to the idea of a Jewish State. But the choice made perfect sense: if the Zionists were to assume the mantle of vanguard of the Jewish people, they could not afford to ignore those Jews who were at the same time "more Jewish"; their opposition was likely to appear more authentic and give rise to serious doubts. A National Religious rabbi would later admit that:

> in all honesty, I have no certain answers. As a theologian, I am acutely aware that it is impossible to limit God's freedom of action. He may indeed, for some inscrutable reason of his own, have decided to let us down, so to speak, as He did during the Holocaust. In 1948, there was a great religious thinker, Rabbi Teitelbaum of Satmar, who warned the Jewish leadership that based on his understanding of God's Will, establishing the State of Israel would be a costly mistake in the long run. His words were overwhelmingly rejected by a Jewish community mesmerized by waving flags and marching armies and blooming deserts, but he may yet prove to have been a true prophet, in the tradition of Jeremiah and the other unpopular prophets of doom. We cannot know for sure. (Sober, 105)

Promise or Menace?

The history of the last years of the Romanov dynasty may ultimately have a greater impact on the history of Israel than on that of Russia. The Jews of the Russian Empire faced rapid modernization, which, unlike the same process in other countries of Europe, limited possibilities for social promotion to a predominantly literate population that felt frustrated in its ambitions. The radicalizing impact was substantial: a significant part of Russian Jewry had adopted a new, secular national identity and along with it, the premise of political violence. The history of the Jews in tsarist Russia remains an exceptional one. Few Jews elsewhere had espoused the use of force against their non-Jewish neighbors. Today, political lessons drawn from the events leading to the 1905 revolution in Russia continue to have an impact on contemporary Israel, whose political structure embodies some of the concepts and realities of Eastern Europe. The weight of history is heavy indeed:

> Today Jewry lives a bifurcated life. As a result of emancipation in the Diaspora and national sovereignty in Israel Jews have fully re-entered the mainstream of history, and yet their perception of how they got there and where they are is most often more mythical than real. Myth and memory condition action. There are myths that are life-sustaining and deserve to be reinterpreted for our age. There are some that lead astray and must be redefined. Others are dangerous and must be exposed. (Yerushalmi, 99–100)

This is exactly what the New Historians have been doing for the last decade: shedding new light on the founding myths of the State of Israel. Their work has had a stronger impact in Israel than in the Diaspora, where myths have been easier to sustain and where reality checks are a less pressing concern. Against a backdrop of tens of thousands of victims, the anti-Zionist argument, though a minority position, has become increasingly persuasive in Israel. Secular intellectuals have also wondered aloud if the State of Israel is not rushing headlong toward collective suicide. Indicative of this mindset is a sarcastic article comparing Sharon with Caesar, published in the Israeli daily *Haaretz* during the second Intifada:

> We start to wonder whether, for the sake of your goals, you have made a strategic decision to move the battlefield not into enemy territory, as is normally done, but into a completely different dimension of reality — into the realm of utter absurdity, into the realm of utter self-obliteration, in which we will get nothing and neither will they. A big fat zero…. One way or another, when we finally discover what those motives and reasons are, which are currently beyond us, we will understand why we have had to spend decades living in a world parallel to the one we were meant to live in, and why we

agreed to live our one and only life in a kind of latent death. Until then, we will continue to support you with all our heart. We, who are about to die — in the dozens, the hundreds and the thousands — salute thee. Hail, Caesar! (Grossman)

Despite growing opposition the Zionist position remains firm. It does not appear as an issue in the regional security negotiations that have been held in Israel and elsewhere since 1948 (Berger 1989, 1–32). The Zionist state structures are not negotiable. It goes without saying, however, that the anti-Zionists do not feel themselves constrained by this apparent consensus. While they attach no particular value to the maintenance of the State of Israel, the anti-Zionists who act in the name of the Torah have put forward strategies of reconciliation, ranging from the recognition and the correction of the injustices committed against the Palestinians, to the search for stability and even for friendship in the Holy Land. Though they are neither unified nor do they speak with one voice, the Judaic opponents of Zionism call upon the Jews to resume the historical role that they believe the Torah has bestowed upon them and to break the vicious circle of violence that they, as religious thinkers, attribute to Zionism. A document, in question-and-answer form, provides an insight into anti-Zionist thinking on the issue:

A.   Today, Zionism stands revealed before the Jewish people and, indeed, all mankind, as a failed enterprise. Zionism's founders (all Jews who had rejected their ancestral faith) claimed that it was going to solve the problem of Jewish exile and suffering. It would offer a safe haven for all of world Jewry. Over half a century later, it has proven itself incapable of the far less grandiose task of so much as protecting the Jews already living in the Holy Land.
Q.   But the state has survived, hasn't it?
A.   It is farcical to call a government that has subjected its citizens to five wars and endless suffering a desirable "survival." How much blood must be shed till Jewry shakes off the shackles of world Zionism's domination and begins to rethink this ideology's root assumptions? (Central Rabbinical Council)

This assessment of Zionist efforts to build and maintain a state closely resembles that of Rabbi Blau's widow, in the late 1970s:

To what end have all these transgressions of the Torah benefited the leaders of the Israeli State? They promised non-religious Jews a state that would be like all the world's other states. But in this small state, military service lasts longer, taxes are more onerous, wars more frequent, and physical and moral poverty are more acute than in any other Western country.... Ah, but the Jews must be saved in the State of Israel, they said, the very state that would bring to an end the misfortunes of the sons of Jacob! What are we to expect after the next war, which threatens not only this state, but the entire world? (Blau, R., 279–80)

Anti-Zionist literature regularly evokes the apocalyptic danger that the State of Israel represents for the whole world. The emergence of suicide bombing in the Middle East and around the world lends additional weight to premonitions of doom voiced by some Haredi rabbis. They are convinced that the creation of Israel, which they see as an arrogant revolt against God, may well touch off a catastrophe of worldwide proportions. This vision is already reflected in European perceptions; an opinion poll carried out in 2003 showed that Israel was seen as a more serious threat to world peace than Iran and the United States (Beaumont).

Anti-Zionist rabbis, of both Haredi and Reform persuasions, fear that when the atmosphere of political correctness that today stifles criticism of Zionism one day vanishes, the world's Jews will face the wrath of people in the West. When they realize that their support for Israel has done harm to their own national interests, the reaction may well be fierce. Once guilt over the Shoah has been neutralized by critical assessment of the activities of the IDF, the rabbis warn, the anger of the nations roused by the violence emanating from Israel may well be directed at all Jews, who could otherwise live in peace in their countries. Jews may be accused of working to further the interests of Israel, often to the detriment of the countries of which they are citizens. A recent indictment of American Jewish lobbyists for passing classified information to Israel (Abramson), as well as the case of Pollard, an Israeli spy who had channelled American military secrets to Israel, strengthens this premonition.

Among the rabbinical opponents of Zionism, warnings had been heard about the second Iraq war, which observers like the American populist conservative Pat Buchanan attributed to a joint initiative of Israeli strategists and their Zionist allies in Washington. Should the American intervention in Iraq end in debacle, Jews may well be accused of having led American forces into an adventure that was not only foreign, but also inimical, to the interests of the United States.

Pursuing this same logic, Israel can be held responsible for having exacerbated hatred of the United States and its allies among the world's Muslims, a hatred that is at the root of the current terrorist wave in Western countries. "I consider knee-jerk support of Israel as the primary cause of the unprecedented terrorist attacks on America," wrote a former American diplomat in a Reform Jewish periodical (Heichler, 5–6).

Some voices, most coming from Haredi anti-Zionist circles, have adopted an apocalyptic tone. They advance arguments that resemble those of classical anti-Semitism. Not only do they posit a link between the suicide attacks in the West and the Israel-Palestine crisis; they see in those attacks the beginning of divine punishment for Israel's transgressions. According to Rabbi Weberman, one of Zionism's most articulate foes, the State of Israel stands condemned as a violator of the global order, and all attempts to oppose God's will can only lead to an equally global disaster (Weberman). In other words, Zionism "proclaims that it would, if need be, defy the will of the world, be not just forceful but omnipotent" (Rose, 118).

Thus defined, Zionism can be seen as a universal evil, transcending the bounds of Jewish history. In this sense, the anti-Zionist declaration issued several decades earlier at Meah Shearim now assumes prophetic proportions: "The independence of the Zionists was the last straw and it broke the back of the Middle East peace and that of the entire world as well" (Meah, 9, 15). The universal dimension the anti-Zionist rabbis attribute to punishment for the sin of Zionism fully conforms to their vision of Judaism as a religion of global scope.

Dedicated Zionists consider a liberal, prosperous Diaspora as one of the major obstacles to the expansion of a Jewish national consciousness. They remain sceptical of the trust in equality and tolerance shown by more than the one half of the world's Jews, who prefer to reside in the Diaspora rather than settle in Israel. For the founders of Zionism, "acceptance of the liberal concept of society would mean the end of the Jewish people as an autonomous unit" (Sternhell, 55).

Negation of the Diaspora has a lengthy history in both Zionist theory and practice. Many rabbis are aware that the relative ease with which the Diaspora can be mobilized to justify Israeli political and military action reflects this very negation. They emphasize that even though it appears innocent, the automatic identification of the State of Israel with Jews and Judaism is dangerous, in that it suggests that ethnic sovereignty can better protect modern peoples than a pluralistic, liberal society.

The unconditional support for Israel among many Jewish community leaders has had the effect of obscuring, in public perception, important distinctions between Zionism and Judaism, between Jews and Israelis. Resisting this confusion, the Haredi and Reform Jewish critics of Zionism — in totally uncoordinated fashion — have denounced the subordination of the interests of the Jews of the Diaspora to those of the State of Israel. Indeed, as some observers have noted, the defenders of Israel in the Diaspora go well beyond the official positions of the Israeli leadership, to become "more Catholic than the Pope." They quote the case of two well-known American Jewish lawyers, Nathan Lewin, president of the International Association of Jewish Lawyers and Judges, and Alan Dershowitz, professor of law at Harvard University, who have proposed that the families of suicide commandos be executed, justifying the measure as both ethical and in conformity with Jewish Law. A representative of the Israeli Embassy immediately deplored the opinion of these fervent supporters of Israel, as did many leaders of American Reform Judaism (Eden). More recently, several Zionist leaders in North America accused Sharon of treason for evacuating settlers from Gaza. Withdrawal from Gaza resulted in overt disaffection of prominent religious Zionists from the State of Israel, one of them even calling the Satmar Rebbe's anti-Zionist stance "visionary" (Halevy).

The legitimacy of those who usually "represent the Jewish community" is increasingly being questioned. Do they represent their local co-religionists, or do they act as automatic advocates for the State of Israel? The slogan, "We are one!" has proven effective for the promotion and the defense of Zionism. Anti-Zionists point out that it has proven equally effective in promoting anti-Semitism, fuelled by the conflict between the State of Israel and the Palestinians. A journalist for the Israeli daily *Haaretz* has boldly addressed the issue: "Whether this is apathetic ignorance, lack of solidarity, or a cynical world view that regards any increase in immigrant applications as the sole goal to be pursued, Israel, which regards itself as guardian of the world's Jews, may discover it is the source of their troubles" (Marmari).

Some critics have pointed at a vicious circle. The unconditional defense of Israel by Jewish leaders has intensified anti-Semitism, which in turn, reinforces Zionism and makes the State of Israel indispensable as an insurance policy. The policy is a suicidal one for the future of the Diaspora, assert numerous Haredi and Reform rabbis in New York as well as in Jerusalem. Unknowingly, they are echoing left-wing Israeli intellectuals who have identified precisely the same trends, while recalling the eternal moral message of the Torah:

> [Israel's] actions create repulsion and opposition throughout the world. These reinforce anti-Semitism. Faced with this danger, Jewish organizations are pushed into defending Israel and giving it unqualified support. This support enables the anti-Semites to attack not only the government of Israel, but the local Jews, too. And so on.... If I were asked for advice, I would counsel the Jewish communities throughout the world as follows: break out of the vicious circle. Disarm the anti-Semites. Break the habit of automatic identification with everything our governments do. Let your conscience speak out. Return to the traditional Jewish values of "Justice, justice shall you pursue" (Deuteronomy 16:20) and "Seek peace and pursue it" (Psalms 34:15). Identify yourselves with the Other Israel, which is struggling to uphold these values at home. All over the world, new Jewish groups that follow this way are multiplying. They break yet another myth: the duty of Jews everywhere to subordinate themselves to the edicts of our government. (Avnery)

The Haredi critics of Zionism trace a direct link between the rise of anti-Jewish incidents in the Diaspora and the policies of the Israeli government. "The intensification of local anti-Semitism is a big lie," states a Haredi activist, who accuses Israel of provoking incidents so that it can exploit the consequences to convince Jews to immigrate to Israel (Filop). In his view, this vicious circle only confirms his conviction that the State of Israel represents the greatest danger for Jews, both in Israel and in the Diaspora. In earlier years, the Jews would never have "put all their eggs in one basket"; they would never have closed off — in full awareness of the danger — all possible escape routes. The allusion is to the zealots, who blocked all the exits from the city in order to mobilize the population for the defense of Jerusalem against the Romans.

Religious anti-Zionists seem to advance arguments that mesh with the usual liberal concerns:

> Political Zionism teaches Dual Loyalty and, in this dual loyalty, when the occasion arises, greater loyalty to the State of Israel than to the country of one's birth or adoption. Political Zionism is thus not only not consistent with good citizenship, but has in it most fertile seeds for proliferation of anti-Semitism.... From the very beginning, it has been the policy to deliberately incite hatred of the Jew and, then, in feigned horror, point to it to justify a Jewish state — Machiavellianism raised to the ninth degree. (Rabinowitch, 10)

We have seen that many opponents of Zionism accuse the Zionists themselves of reviving anti-Semitism and even of provoking the Shoah. These accusations are by no means limited to theological considerations, but extend to political and cultural realities as well. Anti-Semites of many stripes contend that some of the charges contained in the infamous anti-Semitic forgery, *The Protocols of the Elders of Zion*, written as the Zionist movement was expanding, appear today to be coming true. The *Protocols* depict the Jews as seeking to promote specific political interests that are foreign, and often antagonistic, to the interests of the countries of which they are citizens. The "Elders of Zion," a world Jewish cabal, whose tentacles extended to every country in the world, is behind the conspiracy. At the beginning of the twentieth century, the accusation had all the appearances of a work of fiction. The Jews were loyal citizens of the countries in which they lived; they participated in all sectors of society, including the armed forces. A century later, and a half century after the Shoah, world-wide Jewish organizations have flourished; they are present in most industrialized countries and in many professional fields: politics, law, journalism and academic life, to name but a few. The principle of the centrality of the State of Israel adopted by these organizations, whether *de facto* or *de jure*, has linked their policies to Israeli interests. Élie Barnavi, historian and former Israeli ambassador to

Paris, refers unequivocally to "a Diaspora transformed into an Israeli vassal" (Barnavi, 228).

The example of the Hillel Society is an instructive case in point. The organization was created to provide religious and cultural services to Jewish students: a welcoming environment, kosher cafeterias and the like. As Zionism became part of contemporary Jewish culture, Hillel began to organize lectures on Israeli life, courses in Modern Hebrew and evenings of Israeli folk dancing. As the Intifada touched off an upsurge of interest in Israel, Hillel emerged as the most vocal advocate of Israeli policy on university campuses. Hundreds of Hillel-trained students have attended seminars in propaganda techniques in Israel in order to be able, on returning to their homelands, to defend the interests of the State of Israel more effectively.

In the highly charged context of the hostilities that have wracked the Land of Israel, Hillel's public image has become mainly associated with pro-Israeli activities. This creates the atmosphere of hostility toward Jewish students. Neither the organization's kosher cafeterias nor Talmud courses have been targets of such hostility. But Jewish students have begun to feel besieged, and many of them have expressed greater solidarity with militant Zionism, identifying the hostility they experience as anti-Semitism. The recently established Canadian Council for Israel and Jewish Advocacy affirms in its very name the identity of interests of the State of Israel and the Jews of Canada. Its statement of purpose mentions in one breath "promoting Israel and fighting anti-Semitism" (Canadian).

To label as anti-Semitism all anti-Zionist activity is an effective method for cementing the identification of Jews with Zionism. In the words of Rabbi Goldberg of London, the Jews may well be in the process of committing a serious anachronism:

> To equate a modern Islamic political response to the State of Israel with Christian theological animadversions against the Jewish people, [as some do], is dangerously ahistorical.... We Jews do ourselves a disservice if we cry "anti-Semite!" with the same stridency at a liberal commentator who criticizes the Israeli army's disproportionate response to terrorist outrages, and at a National Front lout who asserts that the *Protocols of the Elders of Zion* is a genuine document. (Goldberg)

This approach has expanded to legal action. Accusations of anti-Semitism have been upheld by French courts against the prominent Jewish intellectual Edgar Morin, who criticized Israel's policies in a newspaper article. The Israeli film maker Eyal Sivan has also been accused of anti-Semitism for producing a documentary about the Israel/Palestinian conflict. As if in answer to the question he put in the title of his book, "May Israel be criticized?" the respected political scientist Pascal Boniface has also been accused of anti-Semitism. Even such a Zionist as Charles Enderlin, who made his aliya from France decades ago, has been branded anti-Semite for a newscast about the Intifada for French television.

In the frustration felt by many Zionists in the Diaspora at the beginning of the twenty-first century, expressions of solidarity with Israel can at times slip over into the rejection and condemnation of their own country. And though it is often put in more cautious language, the same emotional reaction is expressed by many of the leaders of Jewish organizations that claim to represent the Jews of the Diaspora. These leaders, distinguished citizens of their respective countries, are not at all reluctant to present an Israeli diplomat as "our consul" or "our ambassador." The distance traveled since the days following the declaration of the State of Israel is great indeed. Russian-born Moshe Sharet (b. Shertok, 1894–1965), on being sworn in as Israel's first foreign minister, proposed that the country not adopt as its national flag the emblem that had been used by the Zionist movement since its founding congress in Basel. While he sought to consolidate support in the Diaspora for the new state, he also wished to avoid any accusation of dual loyalty against Jews who might display the flag in their own countries (Mishory). As the twenty-first century dawns, for many Diaspora Jews, the problem remains acute:

> I fear that blind Jewish support of Israel will sooner or later give rise to suspicions of divided loyalty. It may seem absurd (for now), but as a retired US Foreign Service officer, I have nightmarish visions of Jewish Americans being excluded from the Foreign Service and other sensitive government agencies because of doubts about the reliability of their support of American policy in the Middle East. And may Heaven preserve us from another Jonathan Pollard! (Heichler, 5–6)

The transformation of Pollard into a martyr and of his defense into a Jewish community cause has been a matter of deep concern among American Jews and their friends. "Perhaps the saddest — and most dangerous — aspect of the Pollard case is that demands for his release are an enormous gift to anti-Semites.... I beg you: Stop for a moment. Ask yourself how your defense of Pollard looks to your fellow countrymen" (Peters, 2). It is not because they seek employment with the state department that Haredim of New York can be seen carrying picket signs reading *Americans — Not Israelis!* at their public demonstrations in the United States. An Israeli commentator familiar with the Diaspora and its key issues reminds us:

> Do not forget that the State of Israel does not raise the same issues as Switzerland. It is quite possible to remain a good American while keeping one's allegiance to Switzerland. The conflicts fomented by

Israel throughout the world have made loyalty to Israel much more dangerous. One must choose, but I fear that, at some point, non-Jews will make the choice. We Jews would then stand in danger of losing all that the emancipation has given us. Zionism has set us back by two centuries. (Anonymous)

Several Jewish authors have expressed public regret that loyalty to Israel has replaced allegiance to Judaism. A veteran of Jewish organizations who has taken a critical distance from his institutional past and from "Jewish community McCarthyism" has stated that for many Jewish organizations, "if you do not support the government of Israel, then your Jewishness, and not your political judgement, will be called into question" (Siegman). An American Jewish author has expressed apprehension that if the Zionist establishment successfully imposes its will and "excommunicates" any Jew who does not support Sharon, then, she argues, "If that is so — if, after all these millennia, the Conference of Presidents really gets away with instituting a kind of Jewish excommunication over its rapturous rallying behind Sharon — then Zionism will forever distort, and even threaten to destroy, the creativity, the diversity, the genius of American Jewishness. Zionism, *khas v'kholile* [God forbid], will turn out to be the greatest peril Jewish America has ever faced" (Solomon, 650).

Signs of awareness of the danger Zionism represents for Jewish continuity are becoming visible: "The twenty-first century reality is that Judaism will only survive in America as an attractive ethical and moral force, not as an unyielding foreign policy voice on behalf of Israel" (Black, 5–14). The Tikkun Community, a movement founded by Rabbi Michael Lerner around the periodical *Tikkun*, has echoed these very concerns and spoken out against the effort to reduce Jewish life in the United States to support for the State of Israel.[3]

Some Judaic critics of Zionism fear what they see as an inevitable backlash against the Jews. Though they are addressing a non-Jewish public, they feel themselves equally obliged "to encourage Jews the world over to sever their links to it, to proclaim before mankind that Judaism cannot be represented by heretics and to seek good relations with all individuals and nations" (Central Rabbinical Council). Anti-Zionist activists affirm that they are acting to preserve and protect the long-term interests of the Jews. Like the Zionists, their religious opponents see themselves as a vanguard, as those who form a bond between the past and the future of the Jewish people.

More than a few Haredi adversaries of Zionism consider the veneration of the State of Israel to be a form of idolatry. Jewish law, they argue, strictly prohibits obtaining any benefit from idolatry; the Messiah must burn all constructions "built by the heretics and apostates in the Land of Israel" and cause to be constructed other edifices conceived in holiness. Indeed, Jewish law is quite categorical with regard to idolatry and the objects associated with it. A Jew must thus destroy a golden idol rather than transform it for any other use, even to feed the poor. These anti-Zionists do not seek to transform the Zionist state into a messianic state. For most religious anti-Zionists the Zionist state must disappear, as long as it happens peacefully, with no blood shed. They remain confident that God will find a way to do so since political arrangements are of no interest to these religious thinkers.

Other Haredi anti-Zionists go beyond analysis and condemnation. Because of their firm opposition to any form of Jewish sovereignty in the Land of Israel, they propose that the State of Israel be replaced by a liberal secular state that would treat all its citizens on the basis of equality. Any regime — or foreign power — would be for them an improvement:

> Jews live in peace and security throughout the world under non-Jewish governments and the same situation could very well exist here. It might also be feasible to make some sort of "united states" with the Arab states in our region…. We have lived at peace with the Arabs for centuries and had no reason to assume trouble with them if not for Zionist agitators. I myself lived together with the Arabs in Jerusalem for two decades before the Balfour Declaration and I assure you that they are no different from any other Gentiles with whom Jews live in peace throughout the world. (Hirsch, M. 1974, 6)

The anti-Zionist group Lev Tahor, made up primarily of secular Israelis who have become Haredim, shares this vision of the political future of the Holy Land. In addition to an anthology entitled *Derekh Hatzala* (*The Path of Salvation*), the Lev Tahor activists, now established in Canada, the United States and Israel, publish pamphlets in English, Hebrew and Arabic, in which they explain their outlook. On the practical level, in addition to the transfer of sovereignty to the Palestinians, these Orthodox Jews accept the idea of a secular, democratic state. This had been the original demand of the PLO, and remains on the agenda of certain Palestinian resistance organizations to this day. Lev Tahor encourages Israelis to emigrate, as Israel has now become too dangerous a place in which to live.

Even though increasing numbers of Jews have begun to question the wisdom of setting up a Jewish State in 1948, they now feel obliged to support that state. It was established fifty years ago, they reason, and now is home to five million Jews. At odds with them, the most radical opponents of Zionism consider the state to be an incorrigible aberration of history. The only possible outcome would be to relinquish the sovereignty acquired against the will of the original inhabitants, Jews and Arabs alike, and therefore against divine will. Carried to its extreme, this logic would force withdrawal from all specifically Jewish political activity.

We have seen that, for many Haredi foes of Zionism, the existence of the state itself is blasphemous. Yet principled opposition to the State of Israel has not extinguished the strong sense of solidarity that forms an integral part of Jewish tradition and experience. The opponents of Zionism pray for the safety of the Jews, all the while condemning the state structures they hold responsible for fomenting conflict in the first place. This attitude may seem both paradoxical and utopian at first, but it meshes fully with the conceptual framework within which the adversaries of Zionism operate: the State of Israel constitutes, in their eyes, the greatest threat to the Jewish people; it must therefore be abolished.

Certain opponents of Zionism have already begun to prepare for a "post-Israel" dispensation, which explains their ongoing contacts with the Palestinians. More often than not, these contacts are more symbol than substance, such as the nomination of Rabbi Moshe Hirsch of Meah Shearim as Minister for Jewish Affairs of the Palestinian Authority. Still, an official letter written under the letterhead of the Palestinian Authority and signed by Arafat would indicate that the work of the anti-Zionists is bearing fruit. After thanking the Haredim for demonstrating against the State of Israel and exhibiting their compassion for the sufferings of the Palestinian people during the Intifada, he concludes:

> These expressions are priceless examples of the long-standing and abiding relationship between Jews and Arabs reaching back hundreds of years, and enable the entire world to see the stark contrast between the eternal and beautiful values of Judaism and those embodied in aggressive Zionism. These demonstrations and expressions are of critical importance in enabling the Palestinian people and Arabs worldwide to see this crucial difference so that everybody understands that the actions of the Israeli state do not reflect anything rooted in the traditions, beliefs and laws of Judaism. This is vital in emphasizing that there is no conflict between Jew and Arab. (Arafat)

Their overtures to the Arabs and their continuing insistence on compromise and negotiation have won for the anti-Zionist Haredim the scorn of the Zionists, who feel nothing but disdain for "this tradition of the weak" and insist on the values of courage and pride. But for the critics of Zionism from among both the Haredim and Reform Jewry, such values are not only in direct contradiction with traditional Jewish sensibility, but represent a veritable danger for the Jewish people as well.

They remind us that the Jews constitute a truly minuscule group when measured against the whole of humanity. It would be imprudent to seek confrontation and rely on force. For the anti-Zionists, it is time to abandon the illusions of grandeur and omnipotence and rediscover the gold thread that has guided generations of Jews. This gold thread, according to Rabbi

John Rayner of London, is woven through the entire continuum of the Jewish spiritual heritage. It can be simply summed up in the Midrash *Avot of Rabbi Nathan*: "Who is the greatest hero? The one who turns an enemy into a friend" (Rayner). Rabbi Rayner inveighs against the spirit of retaliation, a fundamental element in Israeli political culture, an attitude that has affected Jewish life in the Diaspora as well, and reminds us: "A gentle response allays wrath; a harsh word provokes anger.... Do not say, 'I will do to him what he did to me'" (Proverbs 15:1, 24:29). In Rayner's view, only this gold thread can bring peace to the Holy Land.

The anti-Zionists believe that the Zionist structure of the state has perpetuated the conflict. An eventual deportation of the Palestinians, an option increasingly discussed in Israel, would only, in their opinion, aggravate the violence in the long term. On this point, once again, there is a convergence of views between the Zionists, who favor an even more strong-arm approach, and the Judaic anti-Zionists, who would have the state dismantled before it is too late. Both groups are convinced that the region will never accept the presence of a Zionist state in its midst. They even agree on the threat of collective massacre hanging over the Jews in the Land of Israel. But if, for the Zionists, only the state can forestall such tragedy, for their adversaries, the state itself will be its sole, unique cause.

For decades, the Soviet Union inspired Communists the world over. Today, as we have seen, its collapse has fired the imagination of many Judaic opponents of Zionism, who see in it a precursor of the peaceful disappearance of the State of Israel. In like manner, argue some of them, the State of Israel, as a Zionist State, might well simply vanish from the face of the earth, creating no victims. The two states are ideological in nature, both created by a "triumph of the will" and thus by the use of force. Rabbi Wasserman, even before World War II, had noted the similarity, when he compared the inevitable fate of National-Socialism with that awaiting Zionism: an ignoble fall (Wasserman, 1976).

By accepting the idea that the structures of Zionism could simply be dismantled, Rabbi Sober emphasized its psychological aspect — and expressed guarded optimism about its practicality:

> A solution is not impossible; it is not even particularly costly. But it will never be achieved unless we can allow ourselves to forget for a moment our cherished beliefs for which we have sacrificed so many lives, and look instead at the actual realities of the situation. We must stop treating Israel as a romantic dream and learn to see her as a heterogeneous country in which two fiercely proud ethnic populations of similar size are struggling for control.... We, the people who gave the world the words of the prophets, must find the humility to admit that we were wrong, and the courage to do that which is right. (Sober, 26)

All discussion of the occupation simply conceals another reality, he concludes. Israel has, in fact, become a binational state that denies political rights to one of the two nations. This idea has continued to gain ground, both in Israel and in the Diaspora, in the beginning of the twenty-first century. The debate about evacuation from Gaza further revived it. Commenting on a Haredi politician's moderating reminder that "the State of Israel is not a value," a prominent Israeli journalist finds that this is "a variation on the theme of establishing a binational regime in the Land of Israel, an idea that fires the imagination and refuses to disappear from public discourse" (Segev 2005, 6). Indeed, the same issue of the *Haaretz* is indicative of the current debate about the Zionist state: "Jewish democratic Israel is facing a double threat: as a Jewish state — from those who favor 'a State of all its citizens'; as a democratic State — from those who favor a State of the Faithful [a pun on the name of *Gush Emunim*]. It is hard to decide which threat is more serious" (Tal). A letter printed in the same issue of the newspaper predicts that "Israelis and Palestinians will face two alternatives: a war of mutual extermination or the creation of one democratic state with equal rights for all." As if suggesting that the existence of the Zionist state is irrelevant to the future of the Jews, another article in the same issue of Israel's elite newspaper writes about "the unprecedented success" of American Haredim in ensuring Judaism's future at the world's largest yeshiva in Lakewood, NJ (Odenheimer). The Association for One Democratic State for Palestine/Israel has a website that contains an updated bibliography of articles developing this political option, and a recent book develops the idea of "the one-state solution" in significant detail (Tilley). Several religious authors advocating the one-state option affirm that the negation of fundamental rights cannot be the will of God.

The intensification of interest in human rights is part and parcel of the "westernization" of the Israeli intellectual world. The reality of the conflict with the Palestinians and its challenge to maintaining a heroic posture are gradually making the idea of a liberal, egalitarian state more acceptable. A Neturei Karta declaration (April 14, 2002) reveals the emergence of a common denominator from among the once disparate opinions of both anti-Zionist and post-Zionist intellectuals: "After fifty-three years of suffering and death for both Palestinian and Jew, it is high time to acknowledge that the Zionist experiment was a tragic error. The sooner it is put to rest, the better it will be for all mankind."

All these Jewish groups seek a peaceful dissolution of the State of Israel, while upholding the right of Jews to inhabit the Holy Land with the consent of their neighbors. These same groups would no doubt agree that the Zionist state structures undercut all efforts for peace between Israel and the Palestinians. For them, these efforts are simply sterile:

All of them share one fatal assumption. They find it axiomatic that the State of Israel should exist. And, in contrast to the plain evidence of the past half-century of Jewish history they see its existence as a positive development for the Jewish people.... We will demand and with God's help live to see the peaceful dismantling of the state. We will return the land to those who dwelt upon it for centuries, the Palestinian people. Under their sovereignty, we will work towards a just solution to any Jewish-Palestinian problems created by the brief period of Zionist ascendancy.... This then is the image we offer as an alternative to the current horror — of a Jewish people free of the need to kill and be killed, free to pursue their Divine task of Torah practice and free to live in peace and respect with all men. (Weiss 2001)

The account of Judaic opposition to Zionism cannot properly be termed a history, for the theological arguments used by Zionism's detractors have remained all but unchanged since their first polemical use at the end of the nineteenth century. Even though Jewish life has undergone great transformations and suffered great tragedies in the course of the twentieth century, the anti-Zionists have integrated these events into their traditional framework, which has remained largely intact.

It is true that they single out for sharp criticism different aspects of the State of Israel. For some of them, it is the new Jewish identity, freed of the "yoke of heaven"; for others, it is the strong-arm nature of the Zionist enterprise; for still others, it is the obstacle to the advent of the Messiah that the State of Israel constitutes.

Zionism has never been monolithic, and anti-Zionism has, by and large, reflected this complexity. But the multiplicity of approaches to be found within Judaic anti-Zionism has not been reflected by an evolution of its underlying principles. Jewish law, the Halakhah, evolves while preserving its unity within the limits of a given tradition. However, interpretations of a moral, political or philosophical nature, given the absence of any attempt to make them uniform, have changed little over time and have remained diverse, even divergent. Judaism accepts a great diversity of theological interpretations. The ad hoc compromises made by the anti-Zionist and non-Zionist Jews with the existence of the State of Israel have had scant impact on their theological relation to these historical phenomena. This trait can be found among a wide gamut of Jews who draw their inspiration from the values of the Torah, which they consider eternal and which they are not prepared to compromise.

Notes

1. Probably unbeknownst to him, the rabbi's remarks reflect a statement by Friedrich Engels, who held that a people cannot be free if it deprives another people of its liberty. This sentence was published on the front page of the daily

Rude Pravo, published in Prague on the day of the Soviet invasion, August 20, 1968.

2.   See, for example "Neturei Karta, Jews United Against Zionism" <www.nkusa. org>; "Jews Against Zionism" <www.jewsagainstZionism.com>.

3.   *Tikkun* <www.tikkun.org>.

Epilogue

> But he who listens to me will dwell in safety, untroubled by the terror of misfortune... (Proverbs 1:33)

On the very day that I was completing the French original of this book, a bride-to-be and her father, both observant Jews, were chatting in a quiet coffeehouse on the eve of the wedding. Suddenly, an explosion shattered their plans and dreams. In a fraction of a second, a Palestinian suicide bomber had claimed fifteen lives. The following day, those who had been preparing to attend the wedding found themselves instead accompanying the bodies of father and daughter to the cemetery. A passage from the prophet Amos rang out among the crowd that had gathered to honor the deceased: "And in that day — declares my Lord God — I will make the sun set at noon, I will darken the earth on a sunny day. I will turn your festivals into mourning and all your songs into dirges" (Amos 8:9–10). But unlike so many other funeral services for the victims of acts of terror, not a word of hatred or anger against Arabs could be heard. Instead, the spirit of meditation and introspection that mark the days preceding the Jewish New Year pervaded the throng of mourners.

Religious Jews, including the Haredim, have been dying just like everyone else in the wave of violence that is currently sweeping the Holy Land. A full busload was blown up as it returned from the Wailing Wall, claiming more than twenty victims. Many Israelis were struck by the dignity and the humility with which the Haredim reacted to the tragedy. Instead of cries of hatred and revenge, the Haredim meditated aloud upon what had been their sin. In the wake of the terrorist bombings, the walls of Meah Shearim were plastered with calls to abandon the pretension of Zionist control over the Holy Land, which has transformed it into "a bloody trap from which there is no escape."

The Judaic opposition to Zionism has shown remarkable perseverance: the near-universal perception of Israel's successes, its military victories and its vigorous economic growth have not only not silenced the critics, but made them more categorical than ever before. While in daily life, many non-Zionists have accommodated themselves to the established authorities, without, however, pronouncing the words "State of Israel," refusal to grant Judaic legitimacy to the state remains firm. These Jews are convinced that the Zionist attempt to "solve the Jewish problem," just like so many other attempts of a political nature, has hardly been a success.

At the same time, the balance of forces among the Jews has shifted dramatically in favor of the Zionists. At the beginning of the twentieth century, the voices of the anti-Zionists sounded loud and clear. A century later, the Zionists dominate Jewish community media, and some of them have become opinion-makers in the general media. In this context, the perseverance of the anti-Zionists can only be explained by the strength of their belief and their devotion to their cause.

The relationship between religion and politics, which forms the core of this study, varies widely among different anti-Zionist circles. Some, like the Satmar, are totally uninterested in political solutions; others, like the American Council for Judaism and the Hasidic group Lev Tahor, have developed political positions and formed ties with certain Arab opponents of Zionism. A faction of Neturei Karta has focused on the humanitarian dimension of the Palestinians' predicament. Judaic anti-Zionists hold seats in the Knesset and participate in the political life of Israel, without granting legitimacy to the Zionist structure of the state. All insist on the primacy of the Torah and its values. The demonization of Zionism, which reached a peak between the two world wars, has receded, even though its theological bases remain intact. For a large number of Judaic anti-Zionists, they have lost neither their value nor their pertinence. Rabbi Weberman's far-reaching accusations against Zionism draw clearly on the tradition of demonization.

The Judaic opposition to Zionism may seem negligible. In terms of sheer numbers, it remains modest, with most Jews remaining unaware of the Judaic concerns that motivate it. But it is not merely the longevity of the opposition that makes it significant. "The whole history of the Jews suggests that rigorous minorities tend to become triumphant majorities," writes the author of a popular history of the Jews, in describing the opposition to Zionism (Johnson, 549). It can thus be useful to understand its origins and intentions. After all, it is today's secularized majority of the Jewish people that would seem marginal in the context of more than three thousand years of Jewish history.

We have seen how Rabbi Simon Schwab stressed the traditional concern about the surviving "Remnant of Israel" loyal to God and His Torah, even if "only tenth will remain" (Schwab, 7). Indeed, the concept of remnant is central in the history of Judaism and can be found both in Judaic liturgy and in the appellations of many synagogues. The often-voiced concern with statistics — the rate of intermarriage and percentages of observant Jews — is quite recent and rather foreign to Jewish tradition. However, this statistical concern with "human material" is perfectly natural in the context of the Zionist enterprise and the State of Israel.

The Judaic adversaries of Zionism can thus be seen as the standard-bearers of continuity, subsisting like glowing embers in many Jewish communities today. At the same time, the pro-Israel activities of the Jewish establishment in the United States have become farther and farther estranged from the growing tendency to the "disisraelization" of the American Jews, who continue to view themselves as a religious minority rather than as a nation apart (Seliktar).

The anti-Zionist rabbis remain optimistic: "The stone that the builders rejected has become the chief cornerstone" (Psalms 118:22). Minorities, in fact, have always played a decisive role in Jewish history. Leibowitz evaluates their role in these terms:

> There can be no doubt that in Biblical times, or even during the era of the Second Temple, there had occurred a mass deviation from the Judaic norms of the Torah. But the decisive factor was that history had vomited those deviations from within the Jewish people. Throughout most of the Biblical epoch, the majority of the people adored Baal, Astarte and the Golden Calf of Jeroboam, son of Nabat. But they had no historical impact on the Jewish people. Those who did not adore Baal were to endure. We can draw the same conclusion about the Hellenizers of the Second Temple era. (Leibowitz, 159)

A story attributed to Rabbi Ebyeschütz provides an excellent illustration of how vital are minorities faithful to Torah Judaism. A Christian scholar, having noted that in Jewish tradition "the majority must decide" (Exodus 23:2), asked the rabbi why the Jews refuse to join the majority of nations that do not follow Judaism. The rabbi answered:

> We are bound to go according to the majority only where there is a doubt, where the truth is not known. But where there is no doubt, when we are quite sure where the truth lies, majority opinion has no influence. We are convinced of the righteousness of our holy Torah, we have no doubt of it, so that the great majority which is against us has no influence upon us; and cannot take us out of our way.

Rabbi Wasserman, who reports the story, sets it in the context of an attack against the Zionists and the secularists, whom he believed had already formed a majority on the eve of World War II (Wasserman 1976, 43).

Indeed, Jews have never been numerous compared to most other religious groups. Several verses of the Torah speak of God's love for His people, whom He loves for its obedience to the Torah and not for its numerical strength or its physical power. Minority dissent is an honorable tradition within Judaism. Joshua and Caleb, who were but two in number, had to confront ten others sent to spy out the Land of Israel; Jeremiah was imprisoned for his defeatist dissidence in time of war; Yohanan Ben Zakkai broke from the patriotic majority in besieged Jerusalem; Rabbi Jacob Sasportas (1610–1698) defied the majority whipped to a frenzy by the messianism of Sabbatai Tzevi; and the list could go on. The rabbinical critics of Zionism often cite the familiar adage: "A tiny light can disperse great darkness."

Their relationship with the State of Israel and with Zionism is a prism through which we can examine the ideals of behavior and self-image to which Jews aspire. The lines along which the new polarization has taken shape do not correspond to any of the habitual divisions: Ashkenazim — Sephardim, observant — non-observant, Orthodox — non-Orthodox, Hasidim — Mitnagdim. Each of these categories include Jews for whom national pride, even a certain degree of arrogance, is a positive value and who give their enthusiastic support to the state that incarnates what they identify as a life force, as a triumph of the will. As it has been shown that there is no radical break between secular and religious Zionism (Rose, 34), there may be no chasm either between secular and religious anti-Zionism. But each of these same categories includes Jews who believe that the idea of a Jewish state, and above all the human and moral price that it demands, negates all that Judaism teaches, particularly the core values of modesty, compassion and charity. For them, Jewish unity must be centered on the Torah, rather than on the Israeli flag. By its behavior, and for some even by its very existence, the State of Israel causes prejudice to the universal message of Judaism.

This is why many Jewish organizations that oppose Zionism or Israel's aggressive behavior are explicit about their concern for Judaism's moral values. For example, a prominent American Jewish group is called Not in My Name, emphasizing the moral responsibility of being a Jew. Another group, this one in Jerusalem, which documents Israel's abuses of power against Palestinians, is called B'tselem, i.e., "in the image," a reminder that all humans deserve equal treatment since all are created "in the image of God."

"Jews are being split less in terms of their experience of Israel and America than in relation to conscience and what Jews are willing to do and what they will refuse in terms of Jewish history and memory. Instead of splitting apart around issues of geography and culture, a civil war of conscience has begun" (Ellis, 47). This polarization may divide Jews as irremediably as did the advent of Christianity, which, let us remember, originated in the beliefs of a small group of Jews. Christianity emerged from a Greek reading of the Torah and, over time, split off from Judaism, which remained in a minority position. Zionism reflects a nationalist, romantic reading of the Torah and, like Christianity before it, has been able to impose its vision upon the majority. Those who reject this nationalist vision in the name of Jewish tradition may well be in the minority, but they are hardly marginal.

It remains to be seen whether the fracture between those who hold fast to Jewish nationalism and those who abhor it may one day be mended. Or, like Christianity before it, Zionism may develop into an independent focus of identity. Will the myth of Antaeus, which Ariel Sharon invokes in his memoirs, become dominant? Will it replace, in the hearts and minds of Jews, the Biblical paradigm of the conditional, fragile relationship with the Land of Israel?

It seems likely that the Judaic opposition to Zionism will persist as long as does the Zionist enterprise in the Holy Land. Even if many Haredim today have come to share the Zionist worldview — usually without admitting it — that identification is emotive and circumstantial: it lacks a theological basis. For them, most of the anti-Zionist ideas as presented in this book remain valid. In the Haredi context, it would be difficult to reject, or even to attenuate, the authority of a Hafetz Haim or a Brisker Rov, of a Satmar Rebbe or a Lubavitch Rebbe.

Nor have the anti-Zionist arguments of the Reform Jews lost any of their pertinence. For the historian Thomas Kolsky, many of their predictions have proven accurate:

> Israel did not become a truly normal state. Nor did it become a light unto the nations. Ironically, created presumably to free Jews from anti-Semitism and ghetto-like existence as well as to provide them with abiding peace, Israel became, in effect, a garrison state, a nation resembling a large territorial ghetto besieged by hostile neighbors. The ominous predictions... are still haunting the Zionists. (Brownfeld 1997)

It is true that the rejection of Zionism by the Haredim can also be explained by their somewhat selective rejection of modernity. But the opposition formulated by the thoroughly modern Reform Jews, the somewhat Westernized German Orthodox and even some left-wing religious Zionists points to a common core of Judaic opposition to Zionism, particularly in its affirmation of the values, practices and beliefs that together constitute the Jewish fact. It is essentially an opposition to the objectifying definition (national, racial, etc.) of the Jew, which, let us note in passing, had been used to lay the very foundations of anti-Semitism, including the Shoah.

By invoking the prophetic message of justice and peace that they find in the Torah, the Judaic anti-Zionists are asserting that nothing contrary to the Torah can ever endure. This is why the debate about Zionism and the state to which it has given birth has become categorical: while quite a few Zionists see in it the culmination of Jewish history, some of their detractors view it as a diabolical contraption. The Israeli historian, Boaz Evron brings a sense of proportion and sheds a more gentle light on the question that has captured our attention:

> The State of Israel, and all the states of the world, appear and disappear. The State of Israel, clearly, will disappear in one hundred, three-hundred, five-hundred years. But I suppose that the Jewish people will exist as long as the Jewish religion exists, perhaps for thousands more years. The existence of this state is of no importance for that of the Jewish people.... Jews throughout the world can live quite well without it. (Leibowitz, 154)

The rise of Jewish nationalism in Europe came relatively late. We have seen that Zionism and the State of Israel have profoundly altered the self-image of many Jews, as well as the image they project to the world. In this sense, the break has been much more thorough than in any other group whose elites — in their hopes of preserving the people — have aspired or acceded to independence. But the Jewish paradox remains instructive: the attempt to preserve the people has changed that very people so much as to make it almost unrecognizable. The philosopher Martin Buber (1878–1965) was not alone when he expressed fears that the nation could only become normal at the cost of perverting itself (Rose, 76). The fate of the Western modernizing project that is Zionism remains, in a region of traditional cultures, uncertain. The eventual end of the monopoly that Russian and other East-European settlers and their progeny have enjoyed at the helm of the Zionist state may open new opportunities. A few political leaders of Arab origin are overtly disappointed with Zionist modernization and tend to relate to Palestinian Arabs as partners rather than adversaries. The ascendancy of these new leaders may bring about significant change in the Holy Land.

Today, the 9th of Av (*Tishah be-Av*), I am completing the English version of this book, originally written and published in French. This most important day of mourning in the Jewish calendar commemorates the destruction of the two Jerusalem Temples and many other calamities. However, the Jews are expected to lament not the act of destruction but the underlying causes of that destruction. The traditional focus is not on the past but on the present: "We must use our mourning as a way of initiating an examination of our present-day feelings, thoughts and deeds. What have we done to eliminate the attitudes and practices that thousands of years ago sent our ancestors into exile — not once, but twice?" (*Chumash*, 1195). Defiance of the zealots in Jerusalem 1937 years ago is still fresh in Jewish collective memory. Today, the National Religious activists who have created a powerful amalgam of Judaism and nationalism are compared to the zealots, whom Zionist educators used to present as intrepid defenders of national independence against the Romans. No longer. Today, the attitude of the zealots is seen as too dangerous to emulate. Echoing the traditionalists, the secularist *Haaretz* sternly warns that "Tishah be-Av this year is a day of deep spiritual reckoning" and calls on its readers to resist those contemporary zealots who want "to bring down the house" (Beware). For some, this day means the loss of national independence. For others, it tolls the bell for the destruction that false messiahs have inflicted on the Jewish people over the ages. Those who see in Zionism just another false messianic movement not only mourn the past but also dread the future. But all pious Jews — whether Zionists, non-Zionists or anti-Zionists — believe that one day, when the Redemption comes, *Tishah be-Av* will turn into a day of celebration and joy.

There are also Jews who feel "innocent in both suffering and empowerment" (Ellis, 9) and blame others for what happens to them. For them, today's mourning and fasting make little sense. Self-righteousness and righteousness are known to be mutually exclusive. Pious Jews, who hope to turn Tishah be-Av into a day of joy, begin by admitting their own sins. They assume responsibility for what has happened to the Jews, trying to learn lessons for the future.

It is in this spirit that I have introduced into the English edition a few changes that reflect questions and insights addressed to me during book tours and lectures in Belgium, Canada, France, Germany, Italy, Mexico, Morocco and Switzerland. Many readers feel that this book vindicates Judaism, too often confused with Jewish nationalism. Several book reviews, including two written in Arabic, affirm that this work should help reduce anti-Jewish sentiment produced by the conflict in the Middle East. A Judaic scholar even called me from Israel to say that the book "sanctifies God's name."

On the other hand, there are those who feel offended by the very topic of this work, which, according to them, would be better kept under wraps. "You must not provide ammunition to the enemy; wash our dirty laundry in public." I believe that those who hide their past and avoid debate about the present only threaten their own future. A reviewer of the French edition of this work expects that it "will force many Jews to come to terms with the contradiction between the religion they profess to believe in and the ideology that has in fact taken hold of them" (Benazon, 137). The Torah speaks to the Jews as if they were a pilot population, whose example should instruct, inspire and influence all humanity. It stands to reason that the controversy fuelled by Zionism and its sequels will surely bring forth lessons for Jew and Gentile alike.

Afterword

Professor Yakov Rabkin's book, originally published in French as Au nom de la Torah: une histoire de l'opposition juive au sionisme, has now, fortunately, become available in English. A most timely and seminal work, this monograph challenges manifold assumptions and givens concerning the relationship of Judaism and the Zionist movement. This, as the paths and interests of Torah-true Jewry and the secular state of Israel increasingly diverge. Not for Professor Rabkin's thoughtful pen the Jewish establishment's many mantras and shibboleths, which too long have clichéd discussions of Zionism and Israel in the Jewish community. This book is required reading for every serious student of Jewish history as well as concerned layman.

Rabbi Daniel Greer
Dean, Yeshiva of New Haven
New Haven, Connecticut

Acknowledgements

I wish to thank Rabbi Baruch Horovitz, Dean of the Jerusalem Academy of Jewish Studies, for introducing me to the traditional environment for Torah study in Jerusalem. There, as a visiting scholar, I was able to delve into rabbinical thought on several issues, including the use of force. With his customary tact, Rabbi Horovitz made me aware of a variety of challenges raised by Zionism and the State of Israel.

The students and faculty of the Bet Morasha Institute for Jewish Studies in Jerusalem made it possible for me to study anti-Zionist thought in a deeply Zionist atmosphere. Several of its members were actively living their ideology in the West Bank settlements. They encouraged me to write an article on opposition to Zionism, later published in Hebrew in a special issue of their periodical *Aqdamot*, devoted to the fiftieth anniversary of the State of Israel (Rabkin).

My friends Professor Yohanan Silman and his wife Yehudit generously shared with me, in Jerusalem and elsewhere, hours of lively discussion on the State of Israel, Zionism and Israeli society. Rabbi Moshe Hirsch, whom I first interviewed in my home in 1981, startled me with anti-Zionist remarks that hardly seemed understandable at the time. In Hebron, Hagi Ben-Artzi spoke passionately of his right to live anywhere in the Land of Israel. Haim Giat introduced me to the Jews of Yemen, who revealed to me their distinctive Judaic heritage, their devout rationality, and told me, with graceful understatement, of their tribulations upon the arrival in the State of Israel. My Sephardic friends, including Edward Cohen and the late Shlomo Elbaz, helped me to appreciate the ideals of harmony and serenity to which many Sephardim continue to aspire.

My friends and acquaintances in Israel share a trait that I admire and respect: the ability to discuss often contradictory viewpoints calmly and without personal animosity. This same trait might well inspire those who claim to defend Israel from beyond its borders.

I appreciate the patience and the generosity of many rabbis and scholars, in Israel, Canada and the United States, with whom I was able to converse in the course of my work and who generously answered my questions and clarified the meaning of Judaic texts. Not all of them chose to be identified — a choice I fully respect.

Journalists, who interviewed me on issues related to the subject of this book, helped me to appreciate their perceptions of Judaism and Zionism and to gain a clearer grasp of the nature of public interest in the subject.

My daughter Miriam gave me her generous and industrious support during the research and the writing phases of this book. My children Meir, Guéula and Hinda also contributed, in a voluntary capacity, to my work.

All members of my family bore with good grace the numerous and often lengthy discussions touching on the subject matter of this book that I led with many guests at our Sabbath dinner table. Their devotion and kindness are dear to me, as are their different opinions on this subject.

Several units of the University of Montreal facilitated the final phase of my work: Faculty of Arts and Sciences, Department of History, Centre for German and European Studies, Centre for the Study of Religions, and Group of Research on International Security (GERSI) offered research assistance to defray several project-related expenses. I would also like to thank the universities of Passau, Constance, Cracow, Jerusalem and Tel Aviv for their technical assistance crucial to completing my work.

Finally, I wish to acknowledge the contribution of those who read preliminary drafts of this book, and suggested corrections and changes: Rabbi Eliahu Abitbol in Strasbourg, Rabbi Moshe Gérard Ackermann in Jerusalem, S.M. Borreman in Antwerp, Rabbi Eliezer Frankforter, Elizabeth Filion and Haim Nataf in Montreal, Dr. Charles Rhéaume in Ottawa, Estela Sasson in Montreal, Dr. Frederic Seager in Annecy, Rabbi Mayer Schiller in Spring Valley, NY, and Professor Charles Sutto, in Montreal. Of course, I remain solely responsible for the book's content.

References

JPS Hebrew-English Tanakh, 2nd Edition, Jewish Publication Society, Philadelphia, 1999, has been used for most biblical quotes.

Aberbach, David, *Revolutionary Hebrew, Empire and Crisis: Four Peaks in Hebrew Literature and Jewish Survival*, New York, New York University Press, 1998.

Abitbol, Michel, *Les deux terres promises: Les juifs de France et le sionisme*, Paris, Olivier Orban, 1989.

Abitbol, Michel, "Introduction," in Florence Heymann and Michel Abitbol, eds., *L'historiographie israélienne aujourd'hui*, Paris, CNRS éditions, 1998.

Abramson, Larry, "AIPAC Workers Indicted," <http://www.npr.org/templates/story/story.php?storyId=4785888> (accessed Aug. 2005).

Almog, Shmuel, Reinharz, Jehuda, and Shapira, Anita, eds., *Zionism and Religion*, Hanover, NH, Brandeis University Press of New England, 1998.

Angerer, Jo, *Chemische Waffen in Deutschland: Missbrauch einer Wissenschaft*, Darmstadt, Luchterhand, 1985.

"Arab American Institute and Americans for Peace Now Release," *Joint Survey of Arab American and Jewish American Opinion*, November 21, 2002.

Arafat, Yasser, *Official letter to Rabbi Moshe Hirsch*, Ramallah, April 23, 2002.

Arendt, Hannah, "To Save the Jewish Homeland" (published May 1948), in *Jew as Pariah*, New York, Grove Press, 1978.

Arutz 7: <http://www.israelnationalnews.com/> (accessed Aug. 2005).

Associaton for One Democratic State for Palestine/Israel <www.one-democratic-state.org> (accessed Aug. 2005).

Avineri, Shlomo, *The Making of Modern Zionism: The Intellectual Origins of the Jewish State*, New York, Basic Books, 1981.

Avineri, Shlomo, "Zionism and the Jewish Religious Tradition" in Almog, *op cit.*

Avnery, Uri, "Manufacturing Anti-Semites," <http://www.gush-shalom.org/archives/article213.html> (accessed September 28, 2002).

Azulai, Avraham, *Hesed Le-avraham*, Lemberg, n.p., 1863.

BT stands for the traditional edition of *Babylonian Talmud*.

Babylonian Talmud: Talmud Bavli, Kesubos [Ketubot], Brooklyn, NY, Mesorah Publications, 2000 (bilingual edition).

Barnavi, Élie, "Sionismes," in Élie Barnavi and Saul Friedlander, *Les Juifs et le XXe siècle*. Paris, Calmann-Lévy, 2000.

Bartal, Israel, "Responses to Modernity," in Almog, *op. cit.*

Beaumont, Peter, "Israel outraged as EU poll names it a threat to peace," *Guardian*, November 2, 2003.

Becher, Yosef, "From Herzl to Jabotinsky to Begin: The Road to Churban," *Jewish Guardian*, no. 12 (July 1977), p. 3–4.

Becher, Yosef, "The Torah and Political Zionism," in *Judaism or Zionism: What Difference for the Middle East?* London, Zed Books, 1986.

Beck, Moshe Dov, *Kuntras Hasbarah*, Jerusalem (no publisher), 1968 (on the consequences of the Six Day War).

Beck, Moshe Dov, *Biur al ha-atzmaut*, Jerusalem (no publisher), 1970 (on the concept of the Jewish state).

Beck, Moshe Dov, *Kumi tzei mi-tokh ha-haapekha*, Monsey (no publisher), 1998 (a warning to those who live under Israeli sovereignty).

Beck, Moshe Dov, *Brit Yitshak*, Monsey (no publisher), 2000, 2 vols. (on Hasidic reactions to Zionism).

Beck, Moshe Dov, Interview, Monsey, NY, November 11, 2002.

Bell, Y.E., "The Traditional Corner," *The Jewish Press* (New York), October 18, 2002.

Ben Hayim, Avichai, "La vision politique de rav Schach," *Yediot Aharonot*, available at <http://www.magic.fr/kountras/k87b.htm> (accessed Aug. 2005).

Ben-Yehuda, Hemda, *Eliezer Ben-Yehuda: Hayaw u-mif'alo*, Jerusalem, Mossad Bialik, 1990.

Benazon, Michael, "Where have all the rabbis gone?" *Inroads*, Summer/Fall 2005.

Benvenisti, Meron, "Loving the Homeland," *Haaretz*, October 11, 2002.

Berger, Elmer, *Judaism or Jewish nationalism: The Alternative to Zionism*, New York, Brookman Association, 1957.

Berger, Elmer, *Memoirs of an Anti-Zionist Jew*, Beirut, Institute of Palestinian Studies, 1978.

Berger, Elmer, "Zionist Ideology: Obstacle to Peace!" in Teckner, 1989.

Berlin, Naphtali Zvi Yehuda, *Ha-emek davar*, Jerusalem, Yeshivat Volozhin, 1999. (Commentary on the verse Genesis 33:4).

Bettelheim, Bruno, *The Children of the Dream*, New York, Macmillan, 1969.

"Beware the Zealots," *Haaretz*, August 14, 2005.

Black, Edwin, *The Transfer Agreement: The Dramatic Story of a Pact between the Third Reich and Jewish Palestine*, New York, Macmillan, 1984.

Blank, David Eugene, "The New York Times' Strange Attack on Classical Reform Judaism," *Issues of the American Council for Judaism* (Washington), Fall 2002.

Blau, Amram, "A Call from Jerusalem," *[Jewish] Guardian*, no. 1 (April 1974).

Blau, Ruth, *Les gardiens de la cité: histoire d'une guerre sainte*, Paris, Flammarion, 1978.

Blau, Yitzchak, "Ploughshares into Swords: Contemporary Religious Zionists and Moral Constraints," *Tradition*, vol. 34, no. 4, 2000.

Breuer, Mordechai, *Modernity within Tradition: The Social History of Orthodox Jewry in Imperial Germany*, New York, Columbia University Press, 1992.

Brownfeld, Allan C., "Religion and Nationalism: A Dangerous Mix throughout History," *Issues of the American Council for Judaism*, Autumn 2002.

Brownfeld, Allan C., "Zionism at 100: Remembering Its Often Prophetic Jewish Critics," *Issues*, American Council for Judaism, Summer 1997.

Brownfeld, Allan C., "Growing Intolerance Threatens the Humane Jewish Tradition," *Washington Report on Middle Eastern Affairs*, 1999.

Brownfeld, Allan C., "The Growing Contradiction between Jewish Values and the Use of Israeli Power," *The Washington Report on Middle East Affairs*, May 2002.

B'tselem <www.btselem.org> (accessed August 2005).

Burg, Avraham, "The End of an Era," *Haaretz*, August 5, 2005.

Canadian Council for Israel and Jewish Advocacy: <http://www.cija.ca/eng/index.cfm> (accessed Aug. 2005).

Central Rabbinical Council, *To Those Who May Wonder Why We Are Here Today*, February 7, 2002.

The Chumash, Brooklyn, NY, Mesorah Publications, 1993.

Cohen, Asher, *Israel and the Politics of Jewish Identity: The Secular-Religious Impasse*, Baltimore, MD, Johns Hopkins University Press, 2000.

Cohen, Richard, "It isn't anti-Semitic to criticize Israel," *International Herald Tribune*, May 6, 2002.

The Complete ArtScroll Siddur, Nusach Ashkenaz, Brooklyn, NY, Mesorah Publications, 2002.

Cypel, Sylvain, "Les tribulations des chrétiens américains en Israël," *Le Monde*, December 16, 2002.

Danziger, Hillel, *Guardian of Jerusalem*, Brooklyn, NY, Mesorah, 1983.

Dayan, Arieh, "A Haredi Home in Likud," *Haaretz*, November 21, 2002.

Deutsche Welle,"Berlin to Limit Immigration of Russian Jews," <http://www.dw-world.de/dw/article/0,1564,1432444,00.html> (accessed Aug. 2005).

Domb, Israel, *Transformation: The Case of the Neturei Karta*, Brooklyn, NY, Hachomo, 1989.

Eden, Ami, "Top Lawyer Urges Death for Families of Bombers," *Forward*, June 7, 2002.

Edgbaston, Rev. Charles, Letter to the author, January 6, 2003.

Efron, Noah, "Trembling with Fear: How Secular Israelis See the Ultra-Orthodox, and Why," *Tikkun*, vol. 6, no. 5, 1991.

Efron, Noah, *Real Jews: Secular versus Ultra-Orthodox and the Struggle for Jewish Identity in Israel*, New York, Basic Books, 2003.

Elazar, Daniel J., ed., *Morality and Power: Contemporary Jewish Views*, Lanham, MD, Jerusalem Centre for Public Affairs, 1990.

Eliach, Yaffa, *Hasidic Tales of the Holocaust*, New York, Vintage Books, 1982.

Ellis, Marc H, *Out of the Ashes: The Search for Jewish Identity in the Twenty-first Century*, London, Pluto Press, 2002.

Exhibition, "The History of Soviet Jews in the documents of the Central Committee of the CPSU" Summer 1994, Krymskii Val, Moscow.

Ebyeschütz, Jonathan, *Ahavat Yonathan*, Warsaw, Lebensohn, 1871, commentary on Deuteronomy, chap. 4–7 ("Vaethanan").

Ezrahi, Aaron, *Rubber Bullets: Power and Conscience in Modern Israel*, Berkeley, CA, University of California Press, 1998.

Feinstein, Moshe, *Igguerot Moshe*, Brooklyn, NY, Moriah Offset Company, 1959, section *Orah Haim, siman* (no.) 46.

Feuchtwanger, Lion, *Raquel, the Jewess of Toledo (Spanische Ballade)*, New York, Messner, 1956.

Filop, Menashe, Interview, November 11, 2002, Williamsburg, NY.

Finkelstein, Norman G., *The Holocaust Industry*, London, Verso, 2001.

Fishman, Hertzel, "Moral Behavior under Conditions of Warfare," *Avar ve-atid*, vol. 1, no. 1, 1994.

Foot, Paul, "Palestine's Partisans," *Guardian*, August 21, 2002.

Frankel, Jonathan, "Empire tsariste et l'Union soviétique" in Barnavi, *op. cit.*

Furman, Dmitrii, "Nas ob'ediniaet zhestokost'" *Moskovskie novosti* (Moscow), November 20, 2002.

Geffen, Yehonatan, "Trading Anna Karenina for Golda Meir," *Lilith*, vol. 27, no. 1, 2002.

Gilbert, Martin, *The Atlas of Jewish History*, New York, William Morrow and Company, 1992.

Gitelman, Zvi Y., *Jewish Nationality and Soviet Politics: The Jewish Sections of the CPSU*.

1917–1930, Princeton, NJ, Princeton University Press, 1972.

Gitelman, Zvi, and Ken Goldstein, "The Russian Revolution in Israeli Politics," in Asher Arian and Michal Shamir, eds., *The Elections in Israel 1999*, Albany, SUNY Press, 2002, pp. 141–69.

Glucksmann, André, *Dostoïevski à Manhattan*, Paris, Laffont, 2002.

Goldberg, Rabbi David, "Let Us Have a Sense of Proportion," *Guardian* [Manchester), January 31, 2002.

Goldwurm, Hersch, *A History of the Jewish People, Second Temple Era, Art Scroll History Series*, Brooklyn, NY, Mesorah Publications with Hillel Press, Jérusalem, 1994.

Gonen, Jay Y., *A Psychohistory of Zionism*, New York, Mason Charter, 1975.

Goran, Morris Herbert, *The Story of Fritz Haber*, Norman, OK, Oklahoma University Press, 1967.

Gordis, Robert, "Politics and the Ethics of Judaism," in Elazar, *op. cit.*

Greenstein, Howard R., *Turning Point: Zionism and Reform Judaism*, Chico, CA, Scholars Press, 1981.

Grodzinsky, Yosef, *In the Shadow of the Holocaust: The Struggle between Jews and Zionists in the Aftermath of World War II*, Monroe, ME, Common Courage Press, 2004.

Grossman, David, "Hail Cæsar," *Haaretz*, February 22, 2002.

Grozovsky, Reuven, *Be'ayot ha-zeman*, 2nd edition, Jerusalem, 1988.

Gruda, Agnès, "Un groupe de juifs ultrareligieux établi à Sainte-Agathe souhaite l'abolition d'Israël," *La Presse* (Montreal), May 26, 2002.

Gurfinkiel, Michel, *Le roman d'Odessa*, Paris, Éditions du Rocher, 2005.

Haberer, Eric, *Jews and Revolution in Nineteenth-century Russia*, Cambridge, Cambridge University Press, 1995.

Halevi, Judah, *The Kuzari. An Argument for the Faith of Israel*. New York, Shocken Books, 1964, 1.113–114.

Halevi, Yossi Klein, "Where are our children?" *Jerusalem Report*, March 21, 1996.

Halevy, S.A., "Leaving Israel because I'm Disengaged," *The Jewish Voice and Opinion* (Englewood, NJ), mid-September 2005, pp. 1-72.

Hecht, Ben, *Perfidy*, New York, Julian Messner, 1961.

Heichler, Lucian, "Israel: An Insoluble Problem," *Issues of the American Council for Judaism* (Washington), Summer 2002.

Heller, Mikhail, *Cogs in the Wheel: The Formation of Soviet Man*, translated by David Floyd, New York, Knopf, 1988.

Helmreich, William B., *The World of the Yeshiva: An Intimate Portrait of Orthodox Jewry*, New Haven, CT, Yale University Press, 1986.

Hertzberg, Arthur, *The French Enlightenment and the Jews*, New York, Columbia University Press, 1968.

Heymann, Florence, and Abitbol, Michel, eds., *L'historiographie israélienne aujourd'hui*, Paris, CNRS éditions, 1998.

Hirsch, Moshe, "Reb Amrom's Last Demonstration," *[Jewish] Guardian*, no. 2, July 1974.

Hirsch, Moshe, Interview, September 12, 2003.

Hirsch, Samson Raphael, *Horeb: A Philosophy of Jewish Laws and Observances*, translated from German by Dayan Dr. I. Grunfeld, volume II, the Soncino Press, London, 1962.

Holder, Meir, *A History of the Jewish People, From Yavne to Pumbedisa, ArtScroll History Series*, Brooklyn, NY, Mesorah Publications with Hillel Press, Jerusalem, 1995.

House of Commons Debates, Ottawa, Edmond Cloutier, 1956.

Hus, Aaron, Interview, Montreal, October 22, 2002.

JT stands for the traditional edition of the Jerusalem (or Palestinian) Talmud.

Jabotinsky, Vladimir, "O zheleznoy stene," *Razsviet* (Paris), November 4, 1923.

Jabotinsky, Vladimir, *The Story of the Jewish Legion*, New York, Bernard Ackermann, 1945.

Jabotinsky, Vladimir, *Tariag Milim: 613 (Hebrew Words). Introduction to the Spoken Hebrew in Latin Characters*, Jerusalem, Eri Jabotinsky, 1950.

Jewish Guardian, "Rav Elchonon Wasserman," no. 12, July 1977.

Jewish Guardian, "May Jews Wage War or Battles in Our Time?" vol. 2, no. 8, Spring 1984a.

Jewish Guardian, "Torah Comments During the Zionist War in Lebanon," vol. 2, no. 8, Spring 1984b.

Johnson, Paul, A *History of the Jews*, New York, Harper and Row, 1987.

Kach <http://masada2000.org/shit-list.html> (accessed Aug. 2005).

Kaganskaya, Maya, Interview: <http://www.rodina.org.il/text/text806.html> (accessed Aug. 2005).

Kapeliouk, Amnon, "Israël était-il réellement menacé d'extermination?" *Le Monde*, 3 juin 1972.

Kaplan, Yosef, *An Alternative Path to Modernity: The Sephardi Diaspora in Western Europe*, Leiden, Brill, 2000.

Karsal, Getzel, *Ha-histadrut. Arba'im Shenot Haim*, Tel Aviv, Tarbut ve Hinuch, 1960.

Kenbib, Mohammed, *Juifs et musulmans au Maroc, 1859–1948*, Rabat, Université Mohammed V, 1994.

Klaushofer, Alex, "The UnOrthodox Orthodox," *Observer* (London), July 21, 2002.

Klein, Yossi, "The Good Soldier Grozansky," *Haaretz*, February 13, 2002.

Klepfisz, Irena, *Dreams of an Insomniac*, Portland, OR, Eighth Mountain, 1990.

Klugman, Eliyahu Meir, *Rabbi Samson Raphael Hirsch: Architect of Torah Judaism for the Modern World*, (ArtScroll History Series), Brooklyn, NY, Mesorah Publications, 1996.

Kobler, Franz, *Napoleon and the Jews*, New York, Schocken Books, 1976.

Kochan, Lionel, *The Jew and His History*, New York, Schocken Books, 1977.

Kol ha-neshama, radio interviews on the 49th Israel Independence Day, May 12, 1997.

Krantz, Frederick, "One-State Would Mean the Liquidation of Israel," *The Gazette* (Montreal), November 14, 2003.

Kranzler, David, *Thy Brother's Blood: The Orthodox Jewish Response during the Holocaust*, Brooklyn, NY, Mesorah Publications, 1987.

Krauthammer, Charles, "Symposium," *The New Republic*, September 8, 1997.

Kriegel, Maurice, "Orthodoxie," in Barnavi, *op cit.*

Kuzar, Ron, *Hebrew and Zionism: A Discourse in Analytic Cultural Study*, Berlin, Mouton de Gruyter, 2001.

Landau, Shelomo Zalman, ed., *Or la-yesharim*, Warsaw, Heller, 1900.

Landry, Tristan, *La valeur de la vie humaine en Russie (1836–1936)*, Québec, Les Presses de l'Université Laval, 2000.

Laqueur, Walter, A *History of Zionism*, New York, Holt, Rinehart and Winston, 1972.

Lederhendler, Eli, *Jewish Responses to Modernity: New Voices in America and Eastern Europe*, New York, New York University Press, 1994.

Leibovici, Martine, *Hannah Arendt, une juive: Expérience, politique et histoire*, Paris, Desclée de Brouwer, 1998.

Leibowitz, Yeshayahu, *Peuple, Terre, État*, Paris, Plon, 1995.

Leitner, Abraham, Interview, Williamsburg, November 11, 2002.

Lévyne, Emmanuel, *Judaïsme contre sionisme*, Paris, Clerc, 1969.

Lewin-Epstein, Noah *et al.*, ed., *Russian Jews on Three Continents*, London, Frank Cass, 1997.

Liberal Jewish Synagogue, "A Light to the Nations?" London, September 27, 2001. <http://www.ljs.org/Religion/Sermons/Archives/YK5762-JDR.html> (accessed Aug. 2005).

Liberles, Robert, *Religious Conflict in Social Context: The Resurgence of Orthodox Judaism in Frankfurt am Main*, Westport, CT, Greenwood Press, 1985.

Liebman, Charles S., ed., *Conflict and Accomodation between Jews in Israel. Religious and Secular*, Jerusalem, Avi Chai and Keter Publishing Houses, 1990.

Liebman, Charles S., and Eliezer Don Yehiya, *Civil Religion in Israel*, Berkeley, CA, University of California Press, 1983.

Liss, Yosef, *Yosef Daath*, Bnei-Brak, (n.p.), 1999.

Lockman, Zachary, *Comrades and Enemies: Arab and Jewish Workers in Palestine, 1906–1994*, Berkeley, University of California Press, 1996.

Loew ben Betsalel, Yehuda (Maharal), *Netzah Israël*, Jerusalem, Makhon Yerushalayim, 1997, chap. 24.

Lowenstein, Steven, *Frankfort on the Hudson: The German-Jewish Community in Washington Heights, 1933–1983*, Detroit, Wayne University Press, 1989.

Luz, Ehud, *Parallels Meet: Religion and Nationalism in the Early Zionist Movement, 1882–1904*, Philadelphia PA, Jewish Publication Society, 1988.

Maimonides, Moses, *The Book of Divine Commandments*, London, Soncino Press, 1940, positive commandment 9.

Mala, Katarzyna, "Israeli Warplanes over Auschwitz," *Reuters*, September 4, 2003.

Marcus, Yoel, "Leaders who lead their people astray," *Haaretz*, August 5, 2005.

Marmari, Hanoch, "In France, Cause for Real Anxiety," *Haaretz*, May 10, 2002.

Marmorstein, Emile, "Bout of Agony," *[Jewish] Guardian*, no. 1, April 1974.

Masada website: < http://masada2000.org> (accessed August 2005).

Mavo le-kuntras "Masa Kina," Jerusalem, n.p., 2003.

McNeil, Kristine, "The War on Academic Freedom," *Nation*, November 11, 2002.

"Meah Shearim Centennial Hears Call for Jerusalem Internationalization," *[Jewish] Guardian*, no. 1, April, 1974.

Meizels, Joseph, Interview, Monsey, NY, November 10, 2002.

"Memorandum to King Hussein," *Jewish Guardian* no. 3 (November 1974).

Menahem, Nahum, *Israël: Tensions et discriminations communautaires*, Paris, L'Harmatan, 1986.

Mezvinsky, Norton, "Reform Judaism and Zionism: Early History and Change," in Teckner.

Milhamot Hashem, Monroe, NY, 1983.

Mishory, Alec, "The Flag and the Emblem," <http://www.jewishvirtuallibrary. org/jsource/History/isflag.html> (accessed Sept. 2005).

Morris, Benny, *Righteous Victims*, New York, Vintage Books, 2001.

Moshe, Avner, Interview, Montreal, November 22, 2002.

Naimi, Aharon Shalom ben-Itzhak, ed., *Ari Ala mi-Bavel*, Jerusalem, Shemesh Tsedaka, 1986.

Neturei Karta, "Jews Against Zionism," <http://www.nkusa.org/activities/recent/index. cfm> (accessed Aug. 2005).

Neturei Karta, "The Cry of the Jewish People," declaration, Washington, DC, February 7, 2002.

Neturei Karta, "Israel 'Celebrates' Fifty-four Years of Heresy and Bloodshed," Leaflet published and distributed, April 17, 2001.

Neturei Karta, "Orthodox Jews to Burn Israeli Flag in International Ceremony," declaration, February 23, 2002.

Neturei Karta, "Where are the Ultra-Orthodox? Orthodox Jews offer Alternative to Misguided Zionists," declaration, April, 14, 2002.

Neusner, Jacob, "Jew and Judaism, Ethnic and Religious: How They Mix in America," *Issues*, American Council for Judaism (Washington), Spring 2002.

New York Times, "Why are we against the Israeli Government and its Wars," February 11, 2001, p. B22 (advertisement by the Central Rabbinical Council of the USA and Canada).

New York Times, "Support the Israeli Army Reservistsw who say "No" to the Occupation," March 22, 2002, p. A23 (advertisement by the Tikkun Community)

Nicault, Catherine, *La France et le sionisme*, Paris, Calmann-Lévy, 1992.

Not In My Name <www.nimn.org> (accessed August 2005).

Odenheimer, Micha, "Only in America," *Ha'aretz Magazine*, August 5, 2005, pp. 12-14.

On the Essence of the Jewish State: A Study of Contrasting Positions of Religious Movements, Jérusalem, Mesilot, 1980.

Oz, Amos, *The Slopes of Lebanon*, San Diego, Harcourt, Brace and Jovanovich, 1989.

Oz ve-Shalom/Netivot Shalom. Movement for Judaism, Zionism and Peace,"\ see <http://www.netivot-shalom.org.il> (accessed Aug. 2005).

Patterson, Colonel Henry John, "Foreword" in Jabotinsky 1945, *op. cit.*

Peled, Rina, *Ha-adam ha-hadash shel ha maapekha ha-Tzionit (The New Man of the Zionist Revolution)*, Tel Aviv, Am Oved, 2002.

Peters, Ralph, *New York Post*, September 3, 2003, cited in "Pollard Seeks New Hearing: Jewish Groups Are Criticized for Seeking His Release," Allan C. Brownfeld, Editor, *American Council for Judaism Special Interest Report*, 32(5), 2003.

Philipof, Menashe, *Parshat ha–Kesef*, Brooklyn, NY, Nechmod, 1981.

Pirke Avot: Wisdom of the Jewish Sages, translated and commented by Rabbi Chaim Stern, Hoboken, NJ, Ktav Publishing House Inc. 1997.

Polonsky, Pinhas, Commentary on Chapter 32 of Genesis: <http://www.machanaim. org/tanach/weekly/vayishf0.htm> (accessed Aug. 2005).

Porat, Dina, "Une question d'historiographie: L'attitude de Ben-Gurion à l'égard des juifs d'Europe à l'époque du génocide," in Heymann, *op. cit.*

"Rabbis for Human Rights": <http://www.rhr.israel.net> (accessed Aug. 2005).

Rabinowitch, I.M., "Political Zionists and the State of Israel," *[Jewish] Guardian*, no. 1, April 1974.

Rabkin, Yakov M., "Ha-im medinat israel hi iyum le-emshekh ha-yehudi?" (Is the State of Israel a Danger to Jewish Continuity?) *Aqdamot* 4, 1998, pp. 71–94.

Radyshevskii, Dmitrii, "Russkie spasut Izrail," *Moskovskie novosti* (Moscow News), November 20, 2002.

Ravitzky, Aviezer, "Munkacs and Jerusalem: Ultra-Orthodox Opposition to Zionism and Agudism," in Almog, *op. cit.*

Ravitzky, Aviezer, *Messianism, Zionism, and Jewish Religious Radicalism*, Chicago, The

University of Chicago Press, 1996.

Rayner, John D., "Beyond Retaliation," *Issues of the American Council for Judaism,* Summer 2002.

Reinharz, Yehuda, "Zionism and Orthodoxy: A Marriage of Convenience" in Almog, *op cit.*

Rose, Jacqueline, *The Question of Zion,* Princeton, NJ, Princeton University Press, 2005.

Rosenberg, Aharon, ed., *Mishkenot ha-ro'yim,* New York, Nechmod, 1984–1987, 3 vols.

Rosenbloom, Noah, *Tradition in an Age of Reform: The Religious Philosophy of Samson Raphael Hirsch,* Philadelphia, Jewish Publication Society, 1976.

Rotem, Tamar, "Not just a free lunch," *Haaretz* November 18, 2005.

Rozenfeld, M., "Khanuka — evreiskaïa samooborona," cited in <http://www.judaicaru. org/luah/chanuka_istor.html> (accessed Aug. 2005).

Rubin, Israel, *Satmar: An Island in the City,* Chicago, Quadrangle Books, 1972.

Rubinstein, Amnon, *From Herzl to Rabin: The Changing Image of Zionism,* New York, Holmes and Meier, 2000.

Rumiantsev, Oleg, "Rossia i sionizm," <http://www.rodina.org.il/archiv/rl01.html> (accessed Aug. 2005).

Sachar, Howard M., *A History of Zionism,* New York, Alfred A. Knopf, 1979.

Sacks, Jonathan, <http://www.chiefrabbi.org/tt-index.html> (accessed Aug. 2005), Chapter "Beha'alotecha."

Saint-Exupéry, Antoine de, *The Little Prince,* San Diego, Harcourt, 2000.

Salmon, Yosef, "Zionism and Anti-Zionism in Traditional Judaism in Eastern Europe," in Almog, *op cit.*

Salmon, Yosef, *Religion and Zionism: First Encounters,* Jerusalem, Magnes Press, 2002.

Samuel, Maurice, *Level Sunlight,* New York, Knopf, 1953.

Schattner, Marius, *Histoire de la droite israélienne,* Paris, Éditions Complexe, 1991.

Schechtman, Joseph B., *Fighter and Prophet,* New York, Thomas Yoseloff, 1961.

Schiller, Mayer, "The New Judaism?" *Issues of the American Council for Judaism,* Summer 1998.

Schindler, Pesach, *Hasidic Responses to the Holocaust in the Light of Hasidic Thought,* Hoboken, NJ, Ktav, 1990.

Schneerson, Rabbi Shalom Baer, "Three Questions and Answers on Zionism and Zionists," *Jewish Guardian,* vol. 2, no. 8, Spring 1984.

Schonfeld, Moshe, *The Holocaust Victims Accuse: Documents and Testimony on Jewish War Criminals,* Brooklyn, NY, Neturei Karta, 1977.

Schonfeld, Moshe, *Genocide in the Holy Land,* Brooklyn, NY, NK of USA, 1980.

Schwab, Simon, *Heimkehr ins Judentums (Homecoming to Judaism),* New York, n. p., 1978 (the original German edition was published in Frankfurt, 1934).

Schwartz, Yoel, and Goldstein, Yitzchak, *Shoah: A Jewish Perspective on Tragedy in the Context of the Holocaust,* Brooklyn, NY, Mesorah, 1990.

Seforno's commentary on Genesis 33:4 (for an English version see: *Sforno,* translated by Rabbi Raphael Pelcowitz, Brooklyn, NY, Mesora, 1987, vol. 1, p. 163).

Segev, Tom, *The Seventh Million: The Israelis and the Holocaust,* New York, Hill and Wang, 1993.

Segev, Tom, *One Palestine, Complete,* NewYork, Metropolitan Books, 2000.

Segev, Tom, "On the Third Thought," *Haaretz Magazine,* August 5, 2005.

Seliktar, Ofira, *Divided We Stand*, New York, Praeger, 2002.

"Settlers Attack Reporters" *Haaretz*, October 17, 2002.

Shalev, Michael, *Labour and Political Economy in Israel*, Oxford, Oxford University Press, 1992.

Shalom Hartman Institute, *The Family Participation Haggadah: A Different Night*, Jerusalem, 1997.

Shapira, Anita, *Hand and Power: The Zionist Resort to Force*, New York, Oxford University Press. 1992.

Shapiro, Marc, *Between the Yeshiva World and Modern Orthodoxy*, Littman Library of Jewish Civilization, 1999.

Sharansky, Natan, "Temple Mount more important than peace," *The Canadian Jewish News*, October 23, 2003.

Sharon, Ariel, with David Chanoff, *Warrior: The Autobiography of Ariel Sharon*, New York, Simon and Schuster, 1989.

Shatz, Adam, *Prophets Outcast: A Century of Dissident Jewish Writing about Zionism and Israel*, New York, Nation Press, 2004.

Shemesh Marpe (Iggerot u-mikhtavim), Brooklyn, NY, Mesorah Publications, 1992.

"Shochat, Israel," *Israel and Zionism*, <http://www.jajz-ed.org.il/100/PEOPLE/BIOS/ishochat.html> (accessed Aug. 2005.).

Scholem, Gershom, "The Curious History of the Six Pointed Star: How the 'Magen David' Became the Jewish Symbol," *Commentary*, no. 8, 1949.

Shumsky, Dimitry, "Post-Zionist Orientalism? Orientalist Discourse and Islamophobia among the Russian-speaking Intelligentsia in Israel," *Social Identities*, vol. 9, no. 4, 2003.

Siegman, Henry, "Separating Spiritual and Political, He Pays a Price," *New York Times*, June 13, 2002.

Sober, Moshe, *Beyond the Jewish State*, Toronto, Summerhill Press, 1990.

Solomon, Alisa, "Intifada Dyptich," *Michigan Quarterly Review*, XLI, no. 4, 2002, pp. 634–650.

Soloveitchik, Joseph Dov, *Fate and Destiny*, Hoboken, NJ, Ktav, 2000.

Sorasky, Aharon, *Reb Elchonon*, New York, Mesora Publications, 1996.

Stampfer, Shaul, *Ha-yeshiva ha-litayit ba-me'ah ha-tesh'a-'esreh*, Jerusalem, Merkaz Zalman Shazar le-toldot Yisrael, 1995.

"Statement to UN Special Committee on Palestine," *Jewish Guardian*, no. 3, November 1974.

Steinberg, Avraham Baruch, ed., *Daat ha-rabbanim*, Warsaw, Y. Unterhendler, 1902.

Steiner, Tuvya Yoel, *Peduyot Tuvya*, Bnei-Brak (no publisher), 1996.

Steinsaltz, Adin, "Interviu," *Vremia i my*, no. 146, 2000.

Sternhell, Zeev, *The Founding Myths of Israel*, Princeton, Princeton University Press, 1998.

Stillman, Norman, *Sephardi Religious Responses to Modernity*, Luxembourg, Harwood Academic Publishers, 1995.

Sussman, Leonard R., "Judaism for All Seasons," *The Christian Century*, April 3, 1963.

Tal, Avraham, "The Faith Connection," *Haaretz*, August 5, 2005.

Teckner, Roselle, et al., eds., *Anti-Zionism, Analytical Reflections*, Brattleboro, VT, Amana Books, 1989.

Teichtal, Yissakhar Shlomo, *Restoration of Zion as a Response during the Holocaust*, Hoboken, NJ, Ktav, 1999.

Teitelbaum, Yoel, *Dibrot ha-kodesh*, Brooklyn, NY, 1983.

Teitelbaum, Yoel, *Va-Yoel Moshe*, Brooklyn, NY, Jerusalem Book Store, 1985.

Teitelbaum, Yoel, *Al ha-Geula ve al ha-Temura*, Brooklyn, NY, Jerusalem Hebrew Book Store, 1998.

Tessendorf, K.C., *Kill the Tsar: Youth and Terrorism in Old Russia*, New York, Atheneum, 1986.

Tilley, Virginia Q., *The One-State Solution: A Breakthrough Plan for Peace in the Israeli-Palestinian Deadlock*, Ann Arbor, University of Michigan Press, 2005.

Torat Rabbi Amram, Jerusalem, (n.p.), 1977.

Tremblay, Rodrigue, *Pourquoi Bush veut la guerre*, Montreal, Les Intouchables, 2003.

Vainfeld, Abraham, "Religiia I gosudarstvo Izrail': veren li raschiot?" (Religion and the State of Israel: Is this a Good Deal?) *Chornym po belomu* November 2005, pp.10–17.

Von Kressenstein, Friedrich Kress, "Im ha-Turkim el Taalat-Suez" (With the Turks toward the Suez Canal), Tel Aviv, Maarakhot (2002), cited in Dromi, Uri, "Turks and Germans in Sinai," *Haaretz*, September 27, 2002.

"Warsaw Ghetto Revolt: True or Fiction? The Torah View," *Jewish Guardian*, vol. 2, no. 8, Spring 1984.

Wasserman, Elhanan Bunim, *The Epoch of the Messiah*, Brooklyn, NY, Ohr Elchonon, 1976.

Wasserman, Elhanan Bunim, *Yalkut maamarim u-mikhtavim*, Brooklyn, NY, n.p., 1986.

Weberman, Meyer, Interview, Williamsburg, NY, November 11, 2002.

Weingott, Ephraim, *Orah le-Tzion*, Warsaw, (n.p.), 1902.

Weinman, Zvi, *Mi-Katovitz ad 5 Iyar*, Jerusalem, Vatikin, 1995.

Weinstock, Nathan, *Zionism: False Messiah*, Londres, Ink Links Ltd, 1979.

Weiss, Yisroel Dovid, "Towards a Lasting Middle East Peace," Neturei Karta Statement at the National Press Club, Washington, DC, December 11, 2001.

Weiss, Yisroel Dovid, "Judaism and Zionism. Let Us Define Our Terms," *Middle Eastern Affairs Journal*, vol. 8, nos. 1–2, 2002.

Weiss, Yisroel Dovid, "Rescuing Judaism from Zionism: A Religious Leader's View," *American Free Press*, August 2, 2002.

Weiss, Yisroel Dovid, Interview, Monsey, New York, November 12, 2002.

Weiss, Yisroel Dovid, and Katz, Moses, Interview, New York, November 2002.

Wistrich, Robert S., "Zionism and Its Religious Critics in Vienna," in Almog, *op. cit.*

Yedei Haim, Jerusalem, Yehudiof, 1988.

Yehudiof, David, *Hasabba Kadisha Baba Salé*, Netivot, Barukh Abuhatsera, vol. 2, 1987.

Yerushalmi, Yosef Hayim, *Zakhor: Jewish History and Jewish Memory*, Seattle, University of Washington Press, 1983.

Yosef, Ovadia, *Sefer Yalkut Yosef*, Jerusalem, Yeshivat Hazon Ovadia, 1990, part 2.

Zimmer, Uriel, *Torah Judaism and the State of Israel*, New York, Maurosho Publications, 1971.

"Zionist Congresses," *Encyclopaedia Judaica*, vol. 16.

Zur, Yaakov, "German Jewish Orthodoxy's Attitude toward Zionism," in Almog, *op. cit.*

Glossary

All terms, except those identified as belonging to another language, are derived from the Hebrew. The Hebrew letters "het" and "he" are transliterated as English "h."

Agudat Israel, or *Aguda* (short form): "Association of Israel," an Orthodox movement and political party founded in 1912.

aliya: "going up," meaning "immigration to Israel"; *olim*: "immigrants to Israel."

Aliyat Hanoar: "youth immigration"; Zionist organization to promote the immigration of young people whose parents would often remain in their country of origin.

be-di-avad (Aramaic): state of affairs, *a posteriori*.

Belz: city in western Ukraine, former center of a Hasidic dynasty.

Betar: acronym for *Brit Yosef Trumpeldor* (Josef Trumpeldor Alliance), militarist youth organization founded by Jabotinsky in 1923.

Bilu (pl. *Biluim*), acronym for the first four words of the verse: "O house of Jacob, come ye and let us walk in the light of the Lord" [Isaiah 2:5]: first Russian settlers' movement in Palestine, founded in 1882.

Brisker Rov (Yiddish): Rabbi of Brisk (Bresk-Litovsk), renowned innovator who introduced a new method of Talmudic studies; a follower of R. Haim Soloveitchik and R. Velvel Soloveitchik.

Bund (Yiddish), lit. "alliance": General Alliance of Jewish Workers of Russia and Poland, founded 1897.

ein berera: no way out, no choice.

Eretz Israel: Land of Israel; the term appears for the first time in Samuel I 13:9; not to be confused with the State of Israel, which has existed since 1948, or the Kingdom of Israel, founded in the tenth century before the modern era.

galut, gola: exile from the Land of Israel, a pejorative term in Israeli Hebrew.

Gamla: town in the Golan, and location of a collective Jewish suicide during the struggle against Rome in the first century. Jewish settlers established on Syrian territory occupied in 1967 have adopted the slogan: "Gamla will never fall again!" and operate a political propaganda website: <http://www.gamla.org.il/english/index.htm> (accessed August 2005).

gaon: "genius," frequently used to describe a rabbinical authority.

glasnost (Russian): "transparency," freedom of speech campaign inaugurated by Gorbachev in the late 1980s.

goyim, pl. of *goy*: "nation," "people," used today to refer to non-Jews; the Pentateuch also uses the term with reference to the children of Israel, particularly in the precept: "You shall be for me a kingdom of priests and a holy nation."

Gur: Polish city, former center of a Hasidic dynasty.

Habad, see *Lubavitch*.

hadarim, pl. of *heder*, lit., "room, hall": traditional Jewish schools.

Haggadah: corpus of Biblical and other texts relating the flight out of Egypt recited at the Passover holiday.

Hagganah, lit. "defense": military organization founded in 1920 by the Zionist Labor Movement in Palestine; integrated into the regular army of the State of Israel in 1948.

hakham, "wise man": Sephardic equivalent of "rabbi."

Hakham Bashi (Turkish): Sephardic Chief Rabbi.

Halakhah, lit. "step, progression": corpus of Jewish law based primarily on the Mishna and the Talmud.

Halukah, lit. "sharing": system for sharing gifts among the Haredi communities in the Holy Land.

Haman: Persian vizier, protagonist of the Book of Esther, who planned the total massacre of the Jews of the Empire.

Haredi, pl. *Haredim,* lit. "strictly observant": common appellation of all traditional Jewish groups; visually distinguishable by a two-color dress code: black and white; referred to in the media as "ultra-orthodox."

Hasid, pl. *Hasidim,* adj: Hasidic, followers of the mystical Jewish renewal movement begun in eighteenth-century Russia.

Haskalah, lit., "the act of making intelligent": Jewish version of the Enlightenment, which reached its high point in the nineteenth century; *maskilim*: those who follow this doctrine.

Hibbat Tzion, Hovevei Tzion, (Hebrew), lit., "love of Zion," "lover of Zion": Jewish settler movement in Palestine, founded in Russia in 1881; joined the Zionist movement after 1896.

Iyar, spring month of the Jewish calendar: the State of Israel was proclaimed on 5 Iyar.

Kaddish: praise of God recited in Aramaic during communal prayers and memorial services for the dead.

Ketuba, lit. "inscription": Jewish marriage contract.

Kippur, "expiation": tenth day of the Jewish month of Tishre, designated by the Torah as the day of expiation of sins; considered the holiest day of the Jewish calendar.

Knesset, lit., "assembly": part of the traditional expression *"bet ha-knesset"* (synagogue); used since 1948 to designate the Parliament of Israel.

Lev Tahor, "pure heart": Hasidic anti-Zionist movement founded at the end of the twentieth century mostly by Israeli nationals born into Zionist circles.

Loshen ha-kodesh, Yiddish version of the Hebrew *Leshon ha-kodesh,* "language of holiness": refers to Hebrew before its modernization and secularization in the nineteenth century.

Lubavitch: Russian city in the Smolensk region, birthplace in the eighteenth century of the Hasidic movement of the same name; also known as *Habad.*

Maskilim, see *Haskalah.*

Masada: fortress located to the west of the Dead Sea; site of a collective Jewish suicide during the Roman wars of the first century.

Midrash (adj. *midrashic*), "commentary": corpus of rabbinical commentaries written at the beginning of the common era; part of the oral Torah.

Mishna, "repetition, study" (adj., *Mishnaic*): basis of the oral Torah written by Judas the Prince in the second century; used as a basis for the Talmud, which draws from it guidance in the formulation of Jewish law and moral teaching.

Mishne Torah: title of the Jewish Code of Law drafted by Maimonides.

Mitnaged (pl. *mitnagdim*): adversary of the Hasidic movement.

mitzvah, "precept": corpus of 613 commandments that should guide a Jew's behavior, in conformity with the written and oral Torah.

Mizrahi, "oriental": allusion to the Land of Israel; also an acronym for *merkaz ruhani*, or "spiritual center"; name of the religious Zionist movement founded in 1904 by Rabbi Isaac Jacob Reines.

Moledet, "motherland": Israeli nationalist party.

moshav: cooperative agricultural settlement.

Munkacz, today Mukatchevo: Ukranian city; former center of a Hasidic dynasty.

Neturei Karta (Aramaic), "Guardians of the City": anti-Zionist movement founded in Jerusalem, 1938.

olim, see *aliya.*

Pale of Settlement: those western regions of the Russian Empire where permanent Jewish settlement was allowed; despite several minor, short-term exceptions, residence limitations remained in force until the abolition of tsarism.

peyes, Ashkenazi version of *peot*, "curls": many pious Jews interpret Leviticus 19:27 as a Biblical obligation to wear side-curls.

phylacteries (tefilin): ritual object consisting of two boxes containing the texts of the Torah, which a pious Jew attaches to his head and forearm every day except Sabbath and high holidays.

Rebbe, version of the term "rabbi": designates a Hasidic leader who exercizes both social and intellectual authority, as well as being a source of inspiration and comfort for the members of his Hasidic group.

Satmar (Sathmar, Szatmar): today a region in eastern Hungary, former center of a Hasidic dynasty.

Shas, acronym of *shomrei torah sefaradim*, "Sephardic Guardians of the Torah": allusion to one of the common designations of the Talmud; name of an Israeli Sephardic religious party.

Talmud, lit. "study": corpus of commentaries of the Mishna, which draws upon its conclusions in the formulation of Jewish law and elements of moral teaching.

teshuva, lit., "return": return to the Torah, penitence.

Torah, lit. "teaching": corpus of normative texts; includes the written Torah (Pentateuch, Prophets and Hagiographa) and the oral Torah (Mishna, Talmud, Midrash as well as commentaries and practical applications). According to tradition, Moses received both the written and oral Torah on Mount Sinai.

Vizhnitz: Ukrainian city, birthplace of the Hasidic movement of the same name.

yeshiva: Talmudic academy.

Yevsektzia (Russian), "Jewish section": Jewish section of the Bolshevik Party, responsible for the persecution of Judaism in the USSR.

yishuv, "colony, settlement": term designating Jewish settlements in the Land of Israel; the Old Yishuv consisted of the Jewish population before the arrival of the Zionists, in the 1880s.

Yom ha-atzmaut, "Independence Day": national holiday of the State of Israel.

Yom ha-shoah, "Day of the Shoah": day of Israeli state commemoration of the Shoah.

yordim, pl. of *yored*, "he who comes down": emigrant from Israel.

Biographical Notes

The capsule biographies that follow are designed to provide the reader with basic information on individuals who died during the nineteenth and twentieth centuries and whose names appear more than once in this book. This section also contains detailed material on several who share the same family name. The transliteration reflects Modern Hebrew pronunciation; the same name may be spelled differently when cited in sources from a European language that uses another transliteration system.

Alfandari, Salomon Eliezer (c. 1826-1930), prominent Sephardic scholar born in Constantinople. He played an important role as a teacher, adjudicator and as an intermediary between Jewish communities and the Ottoman authorities. He settled in Palestine as Chief Rabbi of Safed in 1904, and moved to Jerusalem in 1926. His opposition to Zionism influenced many Judaic scholars, including Rabbi Shapira of Munkacz.

Alkalai, Yehuda (1798–1878): born in Sarajevo (Ottoman, later Austro-Hungarian Empire), he pursued a rabbinical career, specializing in Hebrew grammar and Kabbalah. Took an interest in settlement in the Holy Land and settled there before his death; considered one of the precursors of Zionism.

Alterman, Nathan (1910–1970): born in Warsaw (Russian Empire), he settled in Tel Aviv at age fifteen. In the 1930s, he began to publish nationalist poetry and became a poetic spokesman of the Zionist movement. The author of several patriotic texts, he became a prominent figure in the struggle against the British authorities; advocated that Israel not return the territories occupied in 1967.

Arafat, Yasser (1929-2004), Palestinian political leader. Educated in Egypt, he became head of the Palestine Liberation Organization (PLO) in 1968. After decades in exile, he recognized the State of Israel and was allowed to move to the territories that had been under Israeli occupation since 1967. He was elected Chairman of the Palestinian Authority in 1996.

Arendt, Hannah (1906–1975): German Jewish intellectual; studied philosophy before leaving Germany for France in 1933. Settled in the United States in 1941, where she wrote her best-known works: *The Origins of Totalitarianism*, *The Human Condition* and *Eichmann in Jerusalem*.

Begin, Menahem (1913–1992): born in Brest-Litovsk (Russian Empire). A convinced Zionist from an early age, he joined Jabotinsky's Betar movement, where he played an active role in the 1930s. From 1944 to 1948 he led Irgun, the clandestine Zionist terrorist organization in Palestine; continued political activity under the State of Israel, serving as prime minister from 1977 to 1982.

Ben-Gurion, David (1886–1973): born in Plonsk (Russian Empire) to a Zionist father. As an adolescent, he participated in the Zionist movement Ezra. Founded the Histadrut, which formed the infrastructure of the state-to-be; in 1948 proclaimed the State of Israel and became its first prime minister.

Ben Yehuda, Eliezer (1858–1922): born in Lithuania (Russian Empire). Immigrated to Jerusalem, where he dedicated his life to the reconstruction and revitalization of Hebrew, transforming an ancient language into a modern idiom. His home was the first, in Ashkenazi circles, to use Hebrew in everyday life. He was bitterly opposed to traditional Judaism, and his arrival in Palestine in 1881 touched off widespread hostility among its traditionalist Jewish communities.

Berdyczewski, Micha Joseph (1865–1921): author and philosopher born in Podolya (Russian Empire). At a young age he left the Volozhin yeshiva to pursue literary studies in Switzerland and Germany and later launched a literary career in Yiddish and Hebrew. Participated in public debates over Zionism, sometimes challenging Herzl and Ahad Ha-Am.

Berger, Elmer (1908–1996): a rabbi of the classical Reform Judaism tradition, born in Cleveland. In 1942 he published an essay entitled "Why I am a Non-Zionist," which changed the direction of his career. He became vice-president of the American Council for Judaism, which promoted opposition to Zionism based on the Reform Judaic tradition. In 1969, he was instrumental in founding American Jewish Alternatives to Zionism.

Bialik, Haim Nahman (1873–1934): born in Radi (Russian Empire) into a traditional Jewish family; abandoned his yeshiva studies early to join Hovevei Tzion. Rapidly made a name for himself in Russian literary circles, later in Germany and Palestine. Zionists regard Bialik's works as classics.

Blau, Amram (1894–1974): born in Jerusalem, he opposed Zionism and went on to found the Neturei Karta movement. Refused to recognize the State of Israel. Frequently imprisoned for his vocal protests. Except for several years spent in Bnei-Brak, he lived in Jerusalem. Married a convert (see following note) after his first wife's death in 1965.

Blau, Ruth (1920–2000): born into a French Catholic family in Calais. During World War II, she took part in the Resistance, where she aided persecuted Jews. In 1951, she and her son converted to Judaism. Participated in numerous anti-Zionist activities well before becoming the second wife of Rabbi Blau of Neturei Karta.

Bloch, Joseph Samuel (1850–1923): Austrian author and rabbi; took a strong stance against the virulent anti-Semitism of the day and struggled for social acceptance for the Jews. As an Austrian patriot, he fought against Zionism and emphasized Judaism's universal character.

Brenner, Joseph Haim (1881–1921): born in the Ukraine (Russian Empire), he fled the country at the beginning of the Russo-Japanese War of 1906 to avoid military service. Arriving in Palestine in 1909 became a leading literary personality among the activists of the second aliya (1904–1914). His writings belittle Jewish tradition and Judaism in general; died in an Arab anti-Zionist riot.

Dayan, Moshe (1915–1981): born of Russian parents in the Deganya Alef kibbutz in Palestine. In the 1920s he became active in the Hagganah until 1948, then pursued a military career. Retired from the armed forces in 1958; went on to hold several key positions in the Israeli defense and diplomatic establishments until 1979.

De Haan, Jacob Israel (1881–1924): Dutch-born son of a cantor; novelist, poet and essayist. Trained as a lawyer; flirted with socialism before joining the Zionist movement; settled in Palestine where he taught in Jerusalem and wrote for the Dutch and British press. Taking a critical stance toward the movement, he joined forces with anti-Zionist rabbis and began to build a political organization. Assassinated in Jerusalem by Zionist agents.

Duschinsky, Joseph Zvi (1868-1948), Hungarian rabbi who succeeded Rabbi Sonnenfeld as head of the Eda Haredit in Jerusalem in 1933. He had been active in Agudat Israel, particularly in opposing Zionism and Zionist activities in Palestine. He also founded a yeshiva, Bet Yosef, which had hundreds of students.

Ginzberg, Asher Hirsch, pseudonym "Ahad Ha-Am" (1856–1927): born near Kiev (Russian Empire) into a Hasidic family. While involved in his commercial and administrative pursuits, he became one of the central and most influential figures of spiritual Zionism and leader of the Hibbat Tzion movement.

Gordon, Aaron David (1856–1922): born in Podolya (Russian Empire) into an observant Jewish family; became involved with the Hovevei Tzion movement and migrated to Palestine at age forty-seven. Attached semi-mystical value to agriculture and to working the land, inspiring more than a generation of Zionist farmers and workers.

Gordon, Yehuda Leib (1831–1892): born in Lithuania (Russian Empire), became one of the strongest advocates of the Haskalah, and translated the Russian and Western classics into Hebrew. Also published a number of periodicals in Hebrew and Russian written for enlightened Jews. An outspoken anti-Judaic activist, obsessed with totally eliminating Judaism from Zionist settlements in the Land of Israel.

Güdemann, Moritz (1835–1918): German-born rabbi, assumed leadership of the Vienna Jewish community in 1891. Attacked Zionism, particularly Herzl's book, *Judenstaat*, and insisted that one of the principal objectives of the Jews was to abolish all nationalism. Herzl and Max Nordau often responded to his attacks in their writings.

Herzl, Theodor (1860–1904): known as the father of Zionism. Born in Budapest and educated primarily within German culture, became a journalist in Vienna. Galvanized by the Dreyfus Affair, he published *Judenstaat* in 1896, followed by *Altneuland* in 1902. Both books sought to settle the "Jewish problem" in Europe. Organized the first Zionist congress at Basel, in 1897, signalling the birth of political Zionism.

Hirsch, Samson Raphael (1808–1888): founder of modern Orthodoxy in Germany, he split the Jewish community of Frankfurt in order to protect the interests of Orthodox Jews. Later extended the separatist approach to Europe as a whole. Integrated the general curriculum into Jewish school programs and insisted that modern Orthodox Jews learn and appreciate classical European culture. A German patriot and Judaic leader, he is best known for his six-volume Torah commentary as well as several books on Jewish philosophy.

Jabotinsky, Vladimir (1880–1940): journalist, author and Zionist leader from Odessa (Russian Empire). Deeply secularist, he admired European nationalisms, particularly the Italian variant; founded the Jewish Legion and the Betar movement. An advocate of the strong-arm approach, he commanded the Irgun Tzvai Leumi military movement. Even after his death he has remained an important source of inspiration for the Israeli right wing.

Kagan, Israel Meir, known as "Hafetz Haim" (1838–1933): born in Byelorussia (Russian Empire); one of the outstanding figures of modern-day Judaism. Best known for his *Hafetz Haim*, a work against speaking ill of others, he also wrote more than twenty books, including a primary commentary on Jewish Law, *Mishna Berura*.

Kalischer, Zvi Hirsch (1795–1874): born in Prussian-ruled Poland. As a rabbi, strongly opposed Reform Judaism. Declared in 1882 that messianic redemption would begin with a concerted effort to re-establish the Land of Israel as the national home of the Jews. Considered one of the precursors of Zionism.

Katznelson, Berl (1887–1944): born in Byelorussia (Russian Empire). Leader of the Labor Zionist movement, he became an influential figure during the second aliya (1904–1914). As a librarian, journalist and trade unionist he contributed in many ways to the rise and eventual domination of Labor Zionism in Palestine.

Karelitz, Avraham Yeshayahu, known as "Hazon Ish" (1878–1953): Polish-born Talmudic scholar and outstanding rabbinical authority. His commentary on Jewish Law, entitled *Hazon Ish*, published anonymously in Lithuania, quickly transformed him into one of contemporary Judaism's outstanding personalities. Settled in Bnei-Brak in 1933, where he wrote more than forty works of Judaic scholarship. His influence remains strong in Haredi Judaism in and outside of Israel.

Kook, Avraham Isaac (1865–1935): born in Latvia (Russian Empire), he studied in the prestigious Volozhin yeshiva before becoming a rabbi at age twenty-three. Invited to take up the position of rabbi of Jaffa, he arrived in Palestine in 1904. In 1923 he was appointed Chief Rabbi of Palestine by the British Mandate authorities. Deeply immersed in Jewish mysticism, was one of the rare rabbis of the day to encourage the Zionists. Became after his death, as interpreted by his son, an icon of the National Religious movement.

Lapidos, Alexander Moshe (1819–1906): born in Lithuania (Russian Empire), he studied under the leading rabbis of the day and became a rabbi at a young age. Supported the Hibbat Tzion movement and opposed the use of arms, proposing peaceful settlement in Palestine based on farming and the practice of Judaism. Recognized no messianic quality in the settlement movement.

Lazaron, Morris (1888–1979): born in Georgia (U.S.), he pursued his rabbinical studies within the Reform Judaism movement and held several rabbinical positions in the United States. As an opponent of political Zionism, was one of the founders of the American Council for Judaism.

Leibowitz, Yeshayahu (1903–1994): born in Riga (Russian Empire). Educated in Germany and Switzerland. Thinker and professor at the Hebrew University in Jerusalem. As an Orthodox critic of Zionism and Israeli policy he dared to express opinions and concepts often seen as controversial (i.e., the term "Judeo-Nazi"). Refused in 1992 to accept the Israel Prize, the country's highest distinction.

Margolis, Yeshayahu Asher Zelig (1893–1969): born in Poland, he arrived at a young age with his family in Palestine, where he studied under Rabbi Sonnenfeld, as well as with two influential Sephardic Kabbalists, Shelomo Eliezer Alfandari and Haim Shaul Dawik. Won a reputation for Talmudic scholarship and Kabbalah interpretation. His literary work gives a broad overview of the life and thought of Jerusalem's observant Jews. Maintained links between Judaic anti-Zionists in Palestine and their counterparts in Hungary and Slovakia.

Rabin, Itzhak (1922–1995): born in Palestine of parents from the Russian Empire, he joined the Zionist armed forces and became an officer in the newly established Israel Defense Forces (IDF), which appointed him to its high command. One year after his withdrawal from active duty he joined Israeli political life and became prime minister until his assassination by a Jewish terrorist opposed to the Oslo peace accords.

Reines, Isaac Jacob (1839–1915): born in Byelorussia (Russian Empire). As a rabbi in

Lithuania, he was one of the few religious scholars of his day to support the Zionist movement. He promoted a combination of Torah study and tilling the land, and was one of the founders of the National Religious movement Mizrahi.

Rokeah, Issachar Dov (1854–1927): born into the Hasidic dynasty of Belz. One of the principal Jewish leaders of Galicia and Hungary, he opposed the new political forms of organization of Jewish life in general and Zionism in particular.

Schach, Eliezer Menahem (1898-2001): born in Lithuania (Russian Empire). Rapidly recognized as a Talmudic genius, he completed the curricula of the greatest yeshivas of his day. During World War II he found refuge in Palestine, where, after the conflict, he commemorated the first yeshiva destroyed by the hostilities by founding Ponevezh, in Bnei-Brak. He was a member of the Council of Torah Sages, a Haredi leadership body in Israel. Toward the end of his life he won worldwide prestige as a recognized leader of the Haredim.

Schneerson, Menahem Mendel (1902–1994): for more than a quarter century the chief of the Lubavitch movement and the last to bear the title. Born in the Ukraine and established in New York since 1941, he succeeded his father-in-law as Rebbe in 1951. Acclaimed both in and outside the Hasidic movement, he exerted considerable influence in the Jewish world in the second half of the twentieth century. Under his leadership, the Lubavitch movement experienced substantial growth and became the world's best-known variant of Judaism.

Schneerson, Shalom Dov Baer (1860–1920): born in the Russian Empire, he became at a young age the Lubavitch Rebbe, succeeding Shemuel Schneerson in 1882. A dynamic personality, he founded in 1897 the Lubavitch movement's first yeshiva, Tomkhei Temimim. He founded a Jewish educational network in Georgia (Russian Empire), becoming the first Hasidic leader to spread Hasidic influence beyond the Ashkenazi world.

Scholem, Gershom (1887–1982): born into an assimilated family in Berlin, this German Jewish intellectual settled in Jerusalem in 1924; became professor at the Hebrew University; best known for his Kabbalah studies. His correspondence with Hannah Arendt contrasts his Zionist commitment with her more universalist positions.

Soloveitchik, Haim, also known as Haim Brisker (1853–1918): born in the Russian Empire, this famed Talmudic scholar, the son of Joseph Baer, developed a new method of Talmudic research that became known as "Brisker" and spread throughout the world's Jewish communities. As rabbi of Brest-Litovsk (Brisk), combined community activities with teaching and scholarly research.

Soloveitchik, Joseph Baer (1820–1892): born in Volozhin (Russian Empire). A famous Talmudic scholar, directed the prestigious Volozhin yeshiva in collaboration with Napthali Zvi Judah Berlin (the Netziv). After ten years of frequently difficult collaboration, he left Volozhin to become rabbi of Slutsk and later of Brest-Litovsk (Brisk). His devotion to Torah study, according to his contemporaries, was equalled only by his concern for the poor and downtrodden. He is often referred to as Beit Ha-Levi, for the title of his Talmudic commentary.

Soloveitchik, Isaac Zeev Ha-Levi, also known as Velvel Brisker (1886–1959): son and spiritual heir to Haim Soloveitchik, he succeeded his father as Rabbi of Bresk-Litovsk, where he taught the Talmud to a small group of students in an informal setting, emphasizing the importance of innovation. Fleeing the German occupation, he settled in Jerusalem in 1941.

Sonnenfeld, Joseph Haim (1848–1932): born in Slovakia, completed Talmudic studies at the Pressburg (Bratislava) yeshiva, then continued with Rabbi A. Shag, whom he followed to the Holy Land. As a resident of Jerusalem, he organized the community life of the Jews of Hungarian origin and opposed Zionist control. Opposed Jews participating in Jabotinsky's Jewish Legion and all forms of cooperation with the Zionists. Founded organizations independent of Zionist control, which he led until his death.

Teitelbaum, Yoel, the Satmar Rebbe (1887–1979): born in Hungary; escaped from Europe with several disciples. Settling in the United States, he rapidly rebuilt his community into an influential center of Jewish life. In 1948 he denounced the creation of the State of Israel, later publishing a major work, *Va-Yoel Moshe*, which provides a theoretical basis for Torah anti-Zionism.

Trumpeldor, Joseph (1880–1920): born in Piatigorsk (Russian Empire); lost an arm in the Russo-Japanese war. Powerfully influenced by the collectivist ideas of Leo Tolstoy; immigrated to Palestine in 1912. Deputy commander of the Jewish Legion during World War I; founded in 1918 the Zionist He-Halutz youth movement. Mortally wounded in the defense of Tel Hai, in Palestine, the dying words attributed to him—"How good it is to die for our country"—made him a hero of Zionism.

Wasserman, Elhanan (1875–1941): born in Lithuania (Russian Empire), he studied the Talmud with the masters of the day. A disciple of Hafetz Haim, he became a leading authority of Lithuanian Judaism. A Talmudic scholar and teacher, he also interpreted contemporary events, including the rise of National Socialism in Germany.

Weinberg, Jehiel Jacob (1885–1966): born in a small town in the Russian Empire, he studied in several Lithuanian yeshivas before becoming a rabbi in a small Lithuanian community. During World War I, he traveled to Berlin, then to Giessen where he completed his university studies. Became a professor and, later, rector of the Berlin rabbinical seminary founded by Rabbi Ezriel Hildesheimer. His writings on Judaism reflect a synthesis of the Lithuanian tradition and Rabbi Hirsch's German Orthodoxy.

Zeevi, Rehavam (1926–2001): born in Jerusalem of Russian parents. After a distinguished military career, became a general in the Israeli army. As a Knesset member, he proposed in 1988 the mass deportation of the Arabs. Died at the hands of Palestinian terrorists.

Index